I0448232

Index to the 1800 Massachusetts Federal Census
for the County of
Berkshire

Rebecca M. Sullivan
Deborah Lee Larsson

Index to the 1800 Massachusetts Federal Census
for the County of
Berkshire

November 2014

ISBN: 978-1503071063

All Rights Reserved
Copyright © by
Rebecca M. Sullivan
&
Deborah Lee Larsson

No part of this book may be reproduced or transmitted in any form
or by any means, electronic or mechanical, including
photocopying, recording, or by any information storage and
retrieval system, without the written permission of the author,
except where permitted by law.

Manufactured in the United States

FOREWARD:

This is the eighth volume of several containing the heads of household that were enumerated in the 1800 United States Federal Census in Massachusetts. Our eighth volume is comprised of those towns in Berkshire County. In order to make it easy for the researcher, towns are alphabetized, followed by an alphabetical index of Berkshire county.

We have made every attempt at correctly transcribing each town. However, many of these documents are torn, covered with ink, tape marks, rips and poor handwriting. Spelling errors have been left as they were originally written. Any names & enumerations illegible are denoted with an asterisk.

This book should be used as a guide and research aid. When possible the actual image should be obtained for proper verification and citation. Visit the National Archives website to find out more on how to obtain census images. www.archives.gov/research/census.

In order to get all of the information on one page to make for easy reading we had to reduce the size of the font.

Drop us a line, we'd love to hear what you're researching: rsulli1219@aol.com

Becky & Deb
November 2014

Check out our other books:

INDEX

INDEX

Berkshire County

Berkshire County Stats

Microfilm Reel Number: M32-13

Town:	Page Numbers:	Enumerated By:
Adams	133-139	Unknown
Alford	116-117	Unknown
Becket	265-269	Unknown
Bethlehem	172-173, 180-182	Unknown
Cheshire	153-158	Unknown
Clarksburg	141-142	Unknown
Dalton	191-194	Unknown
Egremont	118-120	Unknown
Great Barrington	104-110	Unknown
Hancock	158-162	Unknown
Lanesborough	146-153	Unknown
Lee	259-264	Unknown
Lenox	209-212	Unknown
Loudon	177-179	Unknown
Mount Washington	231-232	Unknown
New Ashford	162-163	Unknown
New Marlborough	232-241	Unknown
Partidgeville	185-190	Unknown
Pittsfield	194-202	Unknown
Richmond	205-209	Unknown
Sandisfield	170-177	Unknown
Savoy	139-141	Unknown
Sheffied	221-231	Unknown
Southfield	182-183	Unknown
Stockbridge	252-258	Unknown
Tyringham	110-119	Unknown

Berkshire County Stats

Microfilm Reel Number: M32-13

Town:	Page Numbers:	Enumerated By:
Washington	213-216	Unknown
West Stockbridge	246-251	Unknown
Williamstown	125-133	Unknown
Windsor	164-168	Unknown
Zoar	143	Unknown

TOWN	PG#	LN#	LAST NAME	FIRST NAME	M under 10	M 10 to 16	M 16 to 26	M 26 to 45	M 45 and over	F under 10	F 10 to 16	F 16 to 26	F 26 to 45	F 45 and over	TOTAL ALL OTHER	TOTAL SLAVES	TOTALS	DISTRICT/ TOWNSHIP	NOTES
Adams	133	1	Arnold	Comfort		2		1			1			1			5		
Adams	133	2	Cooper	Jeremiah	2	1		1	1			1					6		
Adams	133	3	Hewett	Caleb	1		1					1					3		
Adams	133	4	Hewett	Achas	1			1		2			1				5		
Adams	133	5	Bigabee	William	1		1		1	1	2		1				7		
Adams	133	6	Eddy	James	3	1		1		1	1	1	1				9		
Adams	133	7	Pierce	James	1		2		1				1	1			6		
Adams	133	8	Slocum	Benjamin	1	2		1	1	3		1		1			10		
Adams	133	9	Walker	Charles		1	1		1	1		1	1	1			7		
Adams	133	10	Fenner	Thomas		1			1			2		1			5		
Adams	133	11	Arnold	Stakely			2		1	1	1						5		
Adams	133	12	Hill	Amos	1	2			1	1		1		1			7		
Adams	133	13	Slocum	Amasa	1			1					1				3		
Adams	133	14	Hill	Levi	3		1			1	2	1	1				9		
Adams	133	15	Wilbur	Benjmain	4	1		1		1	1		1	1			10		
Adams	133	16	Martin	Benjamin	1		1	1		1	1	1		1			7		
Adams	133	17	Martin	George				1				1		1			3		
Adams	133	18	Sherman	Kelley	1		1	1		1	1	1	1				7		
Adams	133	19	Wilbur	Stephen		1	1	1			2		1				6		
Adams	133	20	Sprague	Amasa		1	1		1		1		1				5		
Adams	133	21	Shippey	Timothy				1	1	1		1		1			4		
Adams	133	22	Hopkins	Seth			1		1	1			1				4		
Adams	134	1	Carver	Peter	1			1					1				3		
Adams	134	2	Jewell	Jonathan		1	2		1		2	1		1			8		
Adams	134	3	Hill	Isaac		1		1		1	1	1	1				6		
Adams	134	4	Eddy	Elisha	1		1		1	3	1	2	1				10		
Adams	134	5	Matteson	Joshua	4		1				1		1				7		
Adams	134	6	Shippey	Henry		1	1	1	1	1			2	1			8		
Adams	134	7	Gleazon	Abner		2		1		2		1		1			7		
Adams	134	8	Darling	David Junr	3	2	1	1		3		1	2				13		
Adams	134	9	Whitman	Caleb	3			1					1				5		
Adams	134	10	Pall	James	3	2	1		1	1	1	1		1			11		
Adams	134	11	Brown	Luke	2			1		1	2		1				7		
Adams	134	12	Eddy	Eliakim	2			1		1	1		1				6		
Adams	134	13	Brown	Abraham		1	2		1		1			1			6		
Adams	134	14	Wilbur	Jeremiah		2	1	1		4	2	3	1				14		
Adams	134	15	Darling	David Junr	1	2	1		1			1		1			7		
Adams	134	16	Head	William	3			1		1							5		
Adams	134	17	Hopkins	Gid	1			1		1			1				4		
Adams	134	18	Wilbur	Gid	1	2		1		2	1		1				8		
Adams	134	19	Hathaway	Arnold	3			1		2			1				7		
Adams	134	20	Brown	Jacob	1	3		1		1	1		1				8		
Adams	134	21	Fetteplace	William	1	1		1		3	1	1	1				9		
Adams	134	22	Slye	William	2			1	1	1		1	1	1			8		
Adams	134	23	Page	William			1	1	1		1	1		1			6		
Adams	134	24	Chase	Benjamin		2	1		1	1	1		1	1			8		
Adams	134	25	Hathaway	Jonah	1	1	1		1	1	1		1				7		
Adams	134	26	Taylor	Thomas	2	2		1		1	1	1	1				9		
Adams	134	27	Cheesborough	Silvester				1		1		1		1			4		
Adams	134	28	Cheesborough	Elisha	3	1		1		1	1		1				8		
Adams	134	29	Cheesborough	Oliver	2		1	1			1		1				6		
Adams	134	30	Plorich	David Junr	2			1	1	1		1	2	1			9		
Adams	134	31	Tanner	Francis		1	1			1		1					5		
Adams	134	32	Aylsworth	Warner	3			1		2	1		1				8		
Adams	134	33	Aylsworth	Anthony				1						1			2		
Adams	134	34	Godfrey	Joseph	1		1					1					3		
Adams	134	35	Coffin	Laban	2		1	1		2		1	1				9		
Adams	134	36	White	Jason	3	1		1		1		2	1				9		
Adams	134	37	Cheesborough	Nathl	2	1		1		2		1					7		
Adams	134	38	Hathaway	Zach*		2	2	1	1	2		2		1			11		
Adams	134	39	Lapham	John		1	3	2		2		4	2				14		
Adams	134	40	Kelley	Isaac		1	1	1			1	1					7		
Adams	134	41	Farnham	Thomas				1					2				3		
Adams	135	1	Upton	John			1		1	1		1	1				5		
Adams	135	2	Whitney	Richard			1			2		1		1			5		
Adams	135	3	Mason	Barnard				1					1				2		
Adams	135	4	Gorton	John	1	1	2		1	1	2	1		1			10		
Adams	135	5	Runnells	Peter	3		2	1		1	2		1	1			11		
Adams	135	6	Tibbets	Caleb	1	1	1		1	1	2		1				8		
Adams	135	7	Smith	Stephen	1	1	1		1	1	1	2	1				9		
Adams	135	8	Peters	William	2	1	1		2	1	2	1	1	1	2		14		
Adams	135	9	Estes	Peter	1			1					2	1			7		
Adams	135	10	Dean	Asa	3		1	1				1	1				7		
Adams	135	11	Staples	Samuel				1						1			2		
Adams	135	12	Ingesham	Samuel	1			1		2			1				5		
Adams	135	13	Shreve	Caleb		1		2	1	1		1	2	1			9		
Adams	135	14	Mason	Tampson	1		2		1	2	4	1	1				12		
Adams	135	15	Cote	James	3			1		1			1				6		
Adams	135	16	Arnold	Jesse	1			1		2			1				5		

TOWN	PG#	LN#	LAST NAME	FIRST NAME	FREE WHITE MALES					FREE WHITE FEMALES					TOTAL ALL OTHER	TOTAL SLAVES	TOTALS	DISTRICT/ TOWNSHIP	NOTES
					under 10	10 to 16	16 to 26	26 to 45	45 and over	under 10	10 to 16	16 to 26	26 to 45	45 and over					
Adams	135	17	Boyd	Samuel											6		6		
Adams	135	18	Jenks	Thomas	1		2		1		2		1				7		
Adams	135	19	Jenks	Samuel	2			1		1			1				5		
Adams	135	20	Briggs	Allen	3	1	1	1		1	1	1	1				10		
Adams	135	21	Robinson	Josiah D.	1		1	1					1				4		
Adams	135	22	Comstock	Seth			1	1		1			1	1	8		13		
Adams	135	23	Browne	Ichabod	1		1		1		2	1		1			7		
Adams	135	24	Godfrey	Caleb		1			1				1	1			4		
Adams	135	25	Kingsley	Elisha	2		1	1		1		1	1	1			8		
Adams	135	26	Hoxey	Stephen	4				1	1	1		1				8		
Adams	135	27	Allen	Ebenz		1		1			1			1			4		
Adams	135	28	Arnold	Nathaniel	1	1	1	1			1			1			6		
Adams	135	29	Fisk	John	2		1	1		1		1	1				7		
Adams	135	30	Haskin	George		1	1	1		2	1	3	1				10		
Adams	135	31	Pratt	Ebenz		2		1				2		1			6		
Adams	135	32	Hanis	Benjamin			1		3			1	1				6		
Adams	135	33	Ingraham	Obadiah		1	1		1			1					4		
Adams	135	34	Mason	Jonathan	2		1	1	1	4		1	1	1			12		
Adams	135	35	Arnold	Daniel	1		1			3		1	1				7		
Adams	135	36	Anthony	David Junr	1	1		1			1	1		1			6		
Adams	135	37	Brown	William	4		1	1		2		1					9		
Adams	135	38	Booth	Peter	1			1		2	3	1	1				9		
Adams	135	39	Lord	Prudence	1								1				2		
Adams	135	40	Luther	Seth	1			1		2		1					5		
Adams	135	41	Tyler	Thomas	2			1		1			1				5		
Adams	135	42	Sayles	Oziel		1	3		1			1		1			7		
Adams	135	43	Brown	Chas			3	1		1		2	1				8		
Adams	136	1	Field	Nehemiah		1	2					1	1				6		
Adams	136	2	Alger	James	1	1		1		3			1				7		
Adams	136	3	Jenks	George	2	2		1			1		2				8		
Adams	136	4	Carpenter	Nathaniel	3	1		2		4	1	1	2				14		
Adams	136	5	Parker	Elihu	2		2	1		1	1	1					8		
Adams	136	6	Hill	James	1			1				1	1	1			5		
Adams	136	7	Brown	Eleazer	1		1		1			1		1			5		
Adams	136	8	Jenks	Edmund	3	1	1	1	1	2	1	1	2				13		
Adams	136	9	Bucklin	Jeremiah		1	3	1	1	2	1	2		1			12		
Adams	136	10	Jennings	Sylvester			1			2			1				4		
Adams	136	11	Colbourn	Eleanor				1		1				1			3		
Adams	136	12	Mason	Philip		1	2		1	3				1			8		
Adams	136	13	Miller	Samuel	1			1		1	1		1				5		
Adams	136	14	Crapo	Noah			1			1		1					3		
Adams	136	15	Arnold	Isaac		1	1	1	1	1			1				6		
Adams	136	16	White	William		1						1		1			4		
Adams	136	17	Potter	Simeon				1				1	1				3		
Adams	136	18	Bowen	David	1	1		1		1		1		1			6		
Adams	136	19	Bowen	Samuel	2			1		2		1	1				7		
Adams	136	20	Anthony	Humphrey	2		1	1		2		1	1				8		
Adams	136	21	Jenks	Stephen	3	2		1		1	1	1					10		
Adams	136	22	Staples	David	2		2		1	2		1		1			9		
Adams	136	23	Arnold	Elisha	2			1		2	2	1	1		8		17		
Adams	136	24	Southwick	Asa	2			1		1			1				5		
Adams	136	25	Shearman	Daniel	2	2	1		1			1	1	1			9		
Adams	136	26	Upton	Isaac	1					2	2			1			7		
Adams	136	27	Upton	Isaac Junr			1				1						2		
Adams	136	28	Lapham	David	2	1	1		1	1			1	1			8		
Adams	136	29	Lapham	George	4	2	1	2		2	1	2	2	2			18		
Adams	136	30	Manchester	Waterman	1		1		1			1					4		
Adams	136	31	McFarland	Daniel	3	2	1	2		3	1	2	1		1		16		
Adams	136	32	Clarke	John	1			1					1				3		
Adams	136	33	Cole	Barnet	2			1					1				4		
Adams	136	34	Walmarth	Shubael		1		1				2		2			6		
Adams	136	35	Perrey	Burden		1						1					2		
Adams	136	36	Howland	Abraham	1	1	2	2		2		2		2			13		
Adams	136	37	Lewis	Richard	2			1				1	1				5		
Adams	136	38	Smith	Benjamin	4		1	1				1	1				8		
Adams	136	39	Hodge	George	1			1		3			1				6		
Adams	136	40	Hodge	David		1	1					1	1				4		
Adams	136	41	Thompson	Joseph	2			1		1			1				5		
Adams	136	42	Nesbett	Robert	2			1		2			2				7		
Adams	136	43	Kimball	David		1	1				1	1	1				5		
Adams	136	44	Hodge	Nehemiah		1	1			3			1				5		
Adams	137	1	Smith	Laban	1		2	1		2	2		1				9		
Adams	137	2	Briggs	Benjamin	1	6	3		1		1	1		1			14		
Adams	137	3	Briggs	Elisha	2	2		1	1	3		1	1				11		
Adams	137	4	Waterman	R*d			1			2		1					4		
Adams	137	5	Braley	Caleb	3		2		1		1	1	1	1	1		11		
Adams	137	6	Nesbett	Hannah		2	1	1			1	2		1			8		
Adams	137	7	Harkness	Daniel		1	1	1		2	1	1	1				9		
Adams	137	8	Wells	Samuel		1	1	1	1	1	2	1	1	2			11		

TOWN	PG#	LN#	LAST NAME	FIRST NAME	FW Males under 10	FW Males 10 to 16	FW Males 16 to 26	FW Males 26 to 45	FW Males 45 and over	FW Females under 10	FW Females 10 to 16	FW Females 16 to 26	FW Females 26 to 45	FW Females 45 and over	TOTAL ALL OTHER	TOTAL SLAVES	TOTALS	DISTRICT/TOWNSHIP	NOTES
Adams	137	9	Wells	Peter	2		1			1		1					5		
Adams	137	10	Baker	David	1	1	1		1	1			1	1			7		
Adams	137	11	Jenks	Jacob	1		4	1		2	1	3	1				13		
Adams	137	12	Philips	Daniel		1	1		1	2				1			6		
Adams	137	13	Sheldon	Anthony	2	1		1			1	2	1				8		
Adams	137	14	Jenks	Peter	3	2			1	1		1		1			9		
Adams	137	15	Shippey	Joseph	1	1		1					1				4		
Adams	137	16	Harrington	Abraham	3	1		1			1		1				7		
Adams	137	17	Wells	Rufus	2		1	1			1						5		
Adams	137	18	Harrington	James	1				1	1	1			1			5		
Adams	137	19	Sheldon	John Junr		1				1		1					3		
Adams	137	20	Sheldon	John	2		1		1	1	2			1			8		
Adams	137	21	Frazier	John			1		1					1			3		
Adams	137	22	Hill	James		1	1		1					1			4		
Adams	137	23	Harrington	Nathaniel		1	1			1		1		1			5		
Adams	137	24	Harrington	Nicodemus	1	2	2	1				1	1				8		
Adams	137	25	Carpenter	Uriah	1			1				1	1				4		
Adams	137	26	Newell	Elisha	2			1		2			1				6		
Adams	137	27	Harrington	Daniel	1	1	3		1	1	1	1		1			10		
Adams	137	28	Estes	Samuel		1	1		1	1		1		1			6		
Adams	137	29	Estes	Israel	1			1		1			1				4		
Adams	137	30	Walling	David		1			1	1	1		1				5		
Adams	137	31	Peters	Eleazer	2				1	1	1		1				6		
Adams	137	32	Bassett	Abel				1		3	3		1				8		
Adams	137	33	Blakeley	Elizabeth	1		1					1		1			4		
Adams	137	34	Peck	Charles			1			2		1					4		
Adams	137	35	Parker	Oliver		1		1				1		1			4		
Adams	137	36	Houghton	Elisha		1		2						1			4		
Adams	137	37	Sibley	Benjm	1		2	3	1	1			1				9		
Adams	137	38	Jones	Baker	3			1		2			1				7		
Adams	137	39	Slocum	Ebenezer	3	3	1		1	2		3		1			14		
Adams	137	40	Mixton	Gideon		1				1		1	1				4		
Adams	137	41	Peters	James	3	2		1		1			1				8		
Adams	137	42	Stafford	Samuel	1		1	1		1	1	1	1				7		
Adams	138	1	Caldwell	James	2	1		1		2	1	1	1				9		
Adams	138	2	Hewet	John	1			1		1	1			1			5		
Adams	138	3	Hall	Elisha	1	1		1				1	1				5		
Adams	138	4	Ives	Amasa			1		1	2	2		1				9		
Adams	138	5	Ives	Stephen		1		1	1	1	1		1				6		
Adams	138	6	Ballou	Aaron	1		2	2	1	1	1	2	1	1			12		
Adams	138	7	Pettis	Peleg	1		1		1	1	2		1				7		
Adams	138	8	Ballou	Jonas	2		1			2			1				6		
Adams	138	9	Phillips	Rufus	1	1	1		1	1	2	1	1	1			10		
Adams	138	10	Phillips	Hannah										2			2		
Adams	138	11	Lincoln	Apollos	3	1		1					1				6		
Adams	138	12	Kimball	Noah		1		1		4	3		1				10		
Adams	138	13	Kimball	Isaac	2			2					2				6		
Adams	138	14	Kimball	Samuel	2	1		1		3	1	1	1				10		
Adams	138	15	Parsons	Charles	3	1			1		1			1			7		
Adams	138	16	Smith	Reuben	3			1					1				5		
Adams	138	17	Hodge	Otis	2			1		2	2	1					8		
Adams	138	18	Whitaker	Ezra	2			1	1		2	3		1			10		
Adams	138	19	Cook	Silas				1	1			1		1			4		
Adams	138	20	Cook	Joshua	1		2	1		2	3	1	1				11		
Adams	138	21	Luther	Eber	2			1		1	2		1		10		17		
Adams	138	22	Darby	Joseph	1	1		1		4			1				8		
Adams	138	23	Smith	Solomon				1		2			1				4		
Adams	138	24	Penniman	Christopher	2		1	1			1		1				6		
Adams	138	25	Brown	Elijah	3	2		1		1	1		1				9		
Adams	138	26	Campbell	Joseph	1				1				1				3		
Adams	138	27	Wells	Amos	1		1	1		2		1	1		1		8		
Adams	138	28	Edwards	Benjamin		3		1		1	2	2		1	1		11		
Adams	138	29	Isbell	Garner	2	1	3	2		2	1	3	1				15		
Adams	138	30	Torrey	John	1			1		1			1				4		
Adams	138	31	Carpenter	Calvin			2						1				3		
Adams	138	32	Whipple	Nathan	1			1		4	1		1				8		
Adams	138	33	Estes	David	2			1	1				1				5		
Adams	138	34	Felton	David	1			1		1			1				4		
Adams	138	35	Fenton	Asaph	3			1					1				5		
Adams	138	36	Jones	Marshal	1		2	1					2		1		7		
Adams	138	37	Coldgrove	Jeremiah		1	2	1		1	1	1	1				8		
Adams	138	38	Wing	Roger		1	1	1		1	1		1				6		
Adams	138	39	Vizee	John	1	1	2	1	1	1		1		1			9		
Adams	138	40	Knight	Richard			1		1	2		1	1				6		
Adams	138	41	Jones	Isaac	1	2	1	1	1	1	3		1	1			12		
Adams	139	1	Sawter	William	1			1		2		1					5		
Adams	139	2	Robinson	Geo.		1						1					2		
Adams	139	3	Jones	Elias	1	1	1	1	1	1	1	1		1			9		
Adams	139	4	Willey	John	3			1		3		1		1			9		

11

| TOWN | PG# | LN# | HEADS OF HOUSEHOLD | | FREE WHITE MALES | | | | | FREE WHITE FEMALES | | | | | TOTAL ALL OTHER | TOTAL SLAVES | TOTALS | DISTRICT/ TOWNSHIP | NOTES |
			LAST NAME	FIRST NAME	under 10	10 to 16	16 to 26	26 to 45	45 and over	under 10	10 to 16	16 to 26	26 to 45	45 and over					
Adams	139	5	Foster	Elnath	1		1		1	2	1	1	1		3		11		
Adams	139	6	Foster	Chillings				1		1				1			3		
Adams	139	7	Howe	Joseph	1		2			1		1					5		
Adams	139	8	Clarke	Moses	3				1		2	2		1			9		
Adams	139	9	Leeman	Andrew	1	1			1		1	1		1			6		
Adams	139	10	Staples		1	1			1	2			1				6		First name blank

TOWN	PG#	LN#	LAST NAME	FIRST NAME	FREE WHITE MALES under 10	10 to 16	16 to 26	26 to 45	45 and over	FREE WHITE FEMALES under 10	10 to 16	16 to 26	26 to 45	45 and over	TOTAL ALL OTHER	TOTAL SLAVES	TOTALS	DISTRICT/ TOWNSHIP	NOTES
Alford	116	1	Parsons	David	3			1		1			1				6		
Alford	116	2	Parsons	Joseph	3	2			1	1		1	1				9		
Alford	116	3	Kelsey	Reuben		1	1		1	2	1	3	1	1			11		
Alford	116	4	Parsons	Isaac	1			1			1		1				4		
Alford	116	5	Champeon	Lynd	3	2	1			1		1	1				9		
Alford	116	6	Hurlbut	Abijah		1	1	1	1				1				5		
Alford	116	7	Hurlbut	Isaac		1	1						1				3		
Alford	116	8	Fairchild	Moses	2		1		1	5	1	1	1				12		
Alford	116	9	Hurlbut	Hubbard		1	1	1		1			1				5		
Alford	116	10	Webster	David			1			2			1				4		
Alford	116	11	Sperrey	Enoch	2		1	1		1	2	1	1				9		
Alford	116	12	Husted	Nathl	1		1	1		1	1	1					6		
Alford	116	13	Park	Amaziah Junr				1		2			1				4		
Alford	116	14	Park	Amaziah		1		1				1		1			4		
Alford	116	15	Dollsur	John			1			1			1				3		
Alford	116	16	Hutchinson	Shubiel	2		1						1				4		
Alford	116	17	Brinsmade	Daniel	1		1						1				3		
Alford	116	18	Brinsmade	Samuel			1	1				1		1			4		
Alford	116	19	Rowse	David			1					1		1			3		
Alford	116	20	Tuttle	Isaac	1			1		2			1				5		
Alford	116	21	Miner	Rufus	2	1		1		3	1			1			9		
Alford	116	22	Tremain	Justis	3			1		2	1			1			8		
Alford	116	23	Jewell	Eliphalet		1			1				1	1			4		
Alford	116	24	Beckwith	Richard	1			1		1			1				4		
Alford	116	25	Johns	Aaron	2			1		1		1					5		
Alford	116	26	Laman	William				1						1			2		
Alford	116	27	Tyler	Solomon	1	1		1		1	1		1				6		
Alford	116	28	Laman	Jacob		1		1				1	1				4		
Alford	116	29	Brinsmade	Hubbel			1						1				2		
Alford	116	30	Lambert	Samuel	2		3		1	2	1		1				10		
Alford	116	31	Brunson	Nathan				1						1			2		
Alford	116	32	Messenger	Elisha				1		2		1		1			5		
Alford	116	33	Kellogg	Jonah	2		1			1			1				5		
Alford	116	34	Willcox	Rufus	1			1		1	2		1				6		
Alford	116	35	Kelsey	Daniel Junr		1		1					1				3		
Alford	116	36	Davis	Jabez	2			1		2			1				6		
Alford	116	37	Kelsey	Daniel			2	1		1	1		1				6		
Alford	116	38	Milk	Job			1	1						1			3		
Alford	116	39	Kelsey	Abel	1	1	3	1			1			1			8		
Alford	116	40	Gilbert	Asahel	4		1	1		2	2	1	1				12		
Alford	117	1	Gickner	Daniel				1						1			2		
Alford	117	2	Gickner	Daniel Junr	2		1						1				4		
Alford	117	3	Bloss	James	2	1		1		1			1	1			7		
Alford	117	4	Milk	Jonathan		2	3	1					1	1			8		
Alford	117	5	Ingersoll	Deodat	1	1	1	1			2	3		1			10		
Alford	117	6	Brunson	William		1	1		1	1	1		1	1			7		
Alford	117	7	Willcox	Ruben	3	1		1		1			2				8		
Alford	117	8	Willcox	Sylvanus	1			1			1	2	1				6		
Alford	117	9	Willcox	Israel			1	1		1							3		
Alford	117	10	Hurlbert	Philander	2	1		1		1			1				6		
Alford	117	11	Kellogg	Abner		1	2		1	2	1			1			8		
Alford	117	12	Hurlbert	John		1	1		1	1	2			1			7		
Alford	117	13	Darby	George Junr				1		1				1			3		
Alford	117	14	Darby	Abner	2	2		1				1					6		
Alford	117	15	Darby	George				2		1				1			4		
Alford	117	16	D*ey	Peleg				1		2	1		1				5		
Alford	117	17	Olen	Leman	1		1						1				3		
Alford	117	18	Olen	Seth		2		1			1						5		
Alford	117	19	Pickett	James		1		1					1				3		
Alford	117	20	Sprague	Benjamin	2	2	1	1	1	2		1		1			11		
Alford	117	21	Williams	Cornelius	1	2	3	1	1	3			1	1			13		
Alford	117	22	Hatch	Isaac			1	1				1	1				4		
Alford	117	23	Geed	Joseph		1							1				3		
Alford	117	24	Baker	James			1	1		1			1				4		
Alford	117	25	Baker	Calvin	1			1					1				3		
Alford	117	26	Smith	Morris	2			1		1		1					5		
Alford	117	27	Jaquins	Peter	1			1		2	1		1				6		
Alford	117	28	Merrill	Stephen		1		1		1				1			4		
Alford	117	29	Mansfield	Thomas	2			1					1				4		
Alford	117	30	Macklin	Mary	1								1				2		
Alford	117	31	Thayer	Daniel	2	1		1		2				1			7		
Alford	117	32	Palmer	Israel				1		2				1			4		
Alford	117	33	Fitch	Elijah	1	1	1	1		2	1		1				8		
Alford	117	34	Milk	Elkhanah			1						1				2		
Alford	117	35	Cabler	Hendrick	1	1	1	1	1		1			1			7		
Alford	117	36	Hamlin	Jabez		1			1		1		1	1			5		
Alford	117	37	Smith	Jabez	3		1			2	1						7		
Alford	117	38	Parsons	Amos	1			1		1							4		
Alford	117	39	Parsons	William			1					1					2		

TOWN	PG#	LN#	LAST NAME	FIRST NAME	FREE WHITE MALES					FREE WHITE FEMALES					TOTAL ALL OTHER	TOTAL SLAVES	TOTALS	DISTRICT/ TOWNSHIP	NOTES
					under 10	10 to 16	16 to 26	26 to 45	45 and over	under 10	10 to 16	16 to 26	26 to 45	45 and over					
Alford	117	40	Pope	Ebenezer		1	1				1	1					4		
Alford	117	41	Dolin	Thomas	2	1		1		2	1		1				8		
Alford	117	42	Chapman	Stephen					1					1			2		
Alford	117	43	Tremain	Nathaniel	4	2	1	1		2	1	1	1				13		
Alford	117	44	Barnum	Stephen	2	2		1		1	1		1				8		
Alford	117	45	Hill	Lemuel	1	1		1	1				1				5		
Alford	117	46	Fowler	Abiattier			1	1	1	1			1	1			6		
Alford	117	47	French	Enos				1	1			1		1			4		
Alford	117	48	Barrett	Mahitable		1								1			2		
Alford	117	49	Barrett	Eleazer		1	1		2					2			6		
Alford	117	50	Brittain	William		1			1	1				1			4		
Alford	117	51	Fin	John	1			1				1					3		
Alford	117	52	S*ipton	Jeremiah		1		1		1				2			5		
Alford	117	53	Brigham	John					1					1			2		
Alford	117	54	Parsons	Isaac		1		1		1			1				4		
Alford	117	55	Millard	Joshua Junr	1	1		1		1	1		1				6		

| | | | HEADS OF HOUSEHOLD | | FREE WHITE MALES | | | | | FREE WHITE FEMALES | | | | | | | | | |
TOWN	PG#	LN#	LAST NAME	FIRST NAME	under 10	10 to 16	16 to 26	26 to 45	45 and over	under 10	10 to 16	16 to 26	26 to 45	45 and over	TOTAL ALL OTHER	TOTAL SLAVES	TOTALS	DISTRICT/ TOWNSHIP	NOTES
Becket	265	1	Adams	Barna	2				1		1		1				5		
Becket	265	2	Adams	Ebenz		1											1		
Becket	265	3	Atwell	Joseph	2		1			1			1	1			6		
Becket	265	4	Alford	Elijah		2	1	1		2	1	1		1			9		
Becket	265	5	Adams	Elijah			1										1		
Becket	265	6	Austin	John Jr	1			1		2	1	1	1				7		
Becket	265	7	Austin	John				1									1		
Becket	265	8	Adams	Mary		1				1			1				3		
Becket	265	9	Brewster	Oliver		2		1		3	1	1	2				10		
Becket	265	10	Birchard	Nathan	1			1		3			2				7		
Becket	265	11	Barnes	Comfort	1	1	1		1	1	1		1				7		
Becket	265	12	Birchard	James & James Jr	2		1	1	1	2	1		1	1			10		
Becket	265	13	Blair	David & David Jr		2	1	1	1	1	1	2		1			10		
Becket	265	14	Blair	Thompson	1			1		3			1				6		
Becket	265	15	Bowen	Joshua	1	1			1	3	2	1	1	1			11		
Becket	265	16	Blair	Luther		1				1		1					3		
Becket	265	17	Buel	Ichabod		1		1					1				3		
Becket	265	18	Brown	Elkhanah	1	1		1		3	1		1				8		
Becket	265	19	Barnes	Moses	1			1		2			1				5		
Becket	265	20	Broga	Andrew	1			1		2	2		1				7		
Becket	265	21	Brown	David				1					1				2		
Becket	265	22	Burdell	John		1		1				1	1				4		
Becket	265	23	Chaffer	Nathan		1				1		1					3		
Becket	265	24	Conant	George		2		1		3	2		1				9		
Becket	265	25	Childs	Daniel	4			1		1			2				8		
Becket	265	26	Clarke	Joseph	3			1		1		1					6		
Becket	265	27	Cushman	Jonah				1		3	2		1				7		
Becket	265	28	Chaffer	Jonathan 2d	4		1						1				6		
Becket	265	29	Childs	Jonas				1						1			2		
Becket	265	30	Childs	Isaac	1	1	1			1		2					6		
Becket	265	31	Chaffer	Thomas		2	1				1			1			5		
Becket	265	32	Chaffer	Jonathan 2d	1		1			2	1						5		
Becket	265	33	Chaffer	Benja	3	1		1			2	1					8		
Becket	265	34	Case	Hannah Wid	1					1			1				3		
Becket	266	1	Church	Anthony	1	1		1		1	1		1				6		
Becket	266	2	Chaffee	Thomas Jr	5		1						1				7		
Becket	266	3	Crane	Abel	3	1		1		1	2		1				9		
Becket	266	4	Clarke	Keziah		1	1				1			1			4		
Becket	266	5	Clarke	Thomas	1		1			2			1				5		
Becket	266	6	Conant	Thatcher	2		1			3	1		1	1			9		
Becket	266	7	Carter	Marcus	1		1						1				3		
Becket	266	8	Cadwell	Jeremiah	1		1						1				3		
Becket	266	9	Chase	Richard			1			2	3	1		1			8		
Becket	266	10	Cogswell	Daniel				1									1		
Becket	266	11	Dewey	Abel	2	1	1		1	1		1	1				8		
Becket	266	12	Dennison	Boswell	2		1			1	1						5		
Becket	266	13	Dwolf	Horace		1											1		
Becket	266	14	Daniels	Amariah			1										1		
Becket	266	15	Eames	David				1						1			2		
Becket	266	16	Eames	Abner		1		1		1				1			4		
Becket	266	17	Eames	Joel	3		1						1				5		
Becket	266	18	Eames	Zephariah			1				1						2		
Becket	266	19	Eames	Leml	1		1			1			1				4		
Becket	266	20	Eames	Amos	2	1	1			1			1				6		
Becket	266	21	Ellis	Manoah		1	2		1	2	4			1			11		
Becket	266	22	Frarey	John	3		1			1			1				6		
Becket	266	23	Frarey	Eleazer	2	2		1		1			1				7		
Becket	266	24	Framan	Benja		1						1					2		
Becket	266	25	Farrar	Joseph				1		3	1		1				6		
Becket	266	26	Finney	Abram	2		1			1	1						5		
Becket	266	27	Finney	Sylvanus		1											1		
Becket	266	28	Frarey	Joseph		1	1						1				3		
Becket	266	29	Frarey	Joseph Jr	1		1			1			1				4		
Becket	266	30	Gibs	Saml				1						1			2		
Becket	266	31	Gibs	Saml Jr	3	1		1		1			1				7		
Becket	266	32	Gilbert	Oreemus	2		1						1				4		
Becket	266	33	Glezan	Ezekiel		1	2	1				3		1			8		
Becket	266	34	Gabriel	Thomas	1												1		
Becket	266	35	Hooker	Nathana		1											1		
Becket	266	36	Higby	Joseph		1	1	1		1	1		1				6		
Becket	266	37	Higby	Benja		1											1		
Becket	267	1	Higby	Ozias	2		1			2							5		
Becket	267	2	Harris	James & James Jr		1		1		3	2	1					8		
Becket	267	3	Harris	Daniel	2	1	2		1	1	1	1					9		
Becket	267	4	Harris	Nathan		1		1		2	1		1				6		
Becket	267	5	Henry	Robt						2	1						3		
Becket	267	6	Johnson	Runnels		2	1						1				4		
Becket	267	7	Johnson	William	2		1			1			1				5		
Becket	267	8	Jager	Elias		2	1	1					1				5		

TOWN	PG#	LN#	HEADS OF HOUSEHOLD		FREE WHITE MALES					FREE WHITE FEMALES					TOTAL ALL OTHER	TOTAL SLAVES	TOTALS	DISTRICT/ TOWNSHIP	NOTES
			LAST NAME	FIRST NAME	under 10	10 to 16	16 to 26	26 to 45	45 and over	under 10	10 to 16	16 to 26	26 to 45	45 and over					
Becket	267	9	Johnson	Jesse	1		1			1		1					4		
Becket	267	10	Johnson	Dyer	1		1			2		1					5		
Becket	267	11	Johnson	Moody	1			1		2		1	1				6		
Becket	267	12	Kingsley	Enos	3		1	1		2	1	2	1				11		
Becket	267	13	Kingsley	Martin	1	1	1	1		1	1	1	1				8		
Becket	267	14	Kingsley	Amos	3			1		2		1	1				8		
Becket	267	15	Kingsley	Nathan		1			1		1			1			4		
Becket	267	16	Kingsley	Isaiah		1	2		1	1		1		1			7		
Becket	267	17	King	Reuben			1			1		1					3		
Becket	267	18	Kendrick	Polly											3		3		
Becket	267	19	King	Solomon				1					1				2		
Becket	267	20	Kingsley	Mary		1							1	1			3		
Becket	267	21	Kingsley	Joseph			1			3			1				5		
Becket	267	22	Kellogg	Joseph			1						1				2		
Becket	267	23	Kingsley	Sarah			1						2				3		
Becket	267	24	Luer	Simeon	5		1	1		1			1				9		
Becket	267	25	Lester	Lemuel				1					1				2		
Becket	267	26	Lester	Steward			1			3		1					5		
Becket	267	27	Lester	John		1	1					1					3		
Becket	267	28	Loomis	Jonathan	1		2	1		2	2			1			9		
Becket	267	29	Lyman	Jeremiah	1			1		2			2	1			7		
Becket	267	30	Leonard	Elijah			1										1		
Becket	267	31	Mills	Ezekiel			3							1			4		
Becket	267	32	Messenger	Hiram			1	1			1	1		1			5		
Becket	267	33	Messenger	John		1		1		3		1	1				7		
Becket	267	34	Messenger	Ebenz N	3	1		1		1	2		1				9		
Becket	267	35	Merryfield	Oliver			1			1		1					3		
Becket	267	36	McCullen	David	1		1			1		1					4		
Becket	268	1	Merrifield	Richard			1			1		1					3		
Becket	268	2	Messenger	Billy	1	3	1	1		3		1	1	1			12		
Becket	268	3	Merrifield	Thomas	2	1	1		1	3		1		1			10		
Becket	268	4	Millard	Oliver	2	1		1					1				5		
Becket	268	5	Millard	Orram				1		1			1				3		
Becket	268	6	Mann	Joseph		2	1		1		1	1	1				7		
Becket	268	7	Moore	Asher		1											1		
Becket	268	8	Nichols	John		2	2		1	3			1	1			10		
Becket	268	9	Nichols	John Jr				1		1			1				3		
Becket	268	10	Nichols	Stephen	1			1		2			1				5		
Becket	268	11	Nichols	Rachel	2								1				3		
Becket	268	12	Nesbitt	Robert	2	1			1	3	2		1				10		
Becket	268	13	Ormsby	Eliajah	2	1	1		1	1			1	1			8		
Becket	268	14	Perkins	Ephraim		2	3		1			1	1	1			9		
Becket	268	15	Pratt	Jacob	1	2	1		1	1		2		1			9		
Becket	268	16	Putnam	David			1			3			1				5		
Becket	268	17	Putnam	Nathan			1	1		2	1	1	1				7		
Becket	268	18	Putnam	Joel			1			1			1				3		
Becket	268	19	Phelps	Jared	2	2		1	1	2	1		1	1			11		
Becket	268	20	Patterson	Eb	2			1		1	3		1				8		
Becket	268	21	Pinney	Silas			1										1		
Becket	268	22	Pinney	Aaron			1							1			2		
Becket	268	23	Pinney	Benja			1			1							2		
Becket	268	24	Rudd	Elisha & Jesse				1	1	4		1	1	1			9		
Becket	268	25	Rudd	James	2	2	1		1	1	1			1			9		
Becket	268	26	Rhodes	Cynthia						2			1				3		
Becket	268	27	Snow	Sylvanus					1			1		1			3		
Becket	268	28	Segar	Charles	3			1		1		1					6		
Becket	268	29	Snow	Oliver	1		2		1	2	1	3	1				11		
Becket	268	30	Snow	Oliver Jr			1						1				2		
Becket	268	31	Smith	James	4			1		4			1				10		
Becket	268	32	Snow	Timothy		2			1				1	1			5		
Becket	268	33	Snow	Levi	1			1		1	2		1				6		
Becket	268	34	Snow	James		2	3		1		2	1		1			10		
Becket	268	35	Scott	John	2	1		1		1			1				6		
Becket	268	36	Snow	Asa	2	2			1	1		1	1				8		
Becket	268	37	Snow	Nathan	1	1		1		1	2		1				7		
Becket	268	38	Stricton	Alpheus				1		2		1	1				5		
Becket	269	1	Wadsworth	Stephen		1	1		1		1		1	1			6		
Becket	269	2	Wadsworth	Jabez	1	2		1				1		1			6		
Becket	269	3	Wadsworth	Seth	4		1	1		1			2	1			10		
Becket	269	4	White	Vasal	3			1		2			1	4			11		
Becket	269	5	Walker	Ebenezer	2			1		2	2		1				8		
Becket	269	6	Walker	Amasa	2			1		3				1			7		
Becket	269	7	Walker	James	1	1		1		3	1		1				8		
Becket	269	8	Slaughter	Patrick	2		1		1	1	2			1			8		
Becket	269	9	Seely	John	2	1		1		2	1	1		1			9		
Becket	269	10	Stevens	Thomas	1	1			1	1			1				5		
Becket	269	11	Snow	Amaziah	4			1		1			1				7		
Becket	269	12	Stewart	George					1	3	2	3		2			11		
Becket	269	13	Shaw	Duncan	4			1					1				6		

TOWN	PG#	LN#	LAST NAME	FIRST NAME	FREE WHITE MALES					FREE WHITE FEMALES					TOTAL ALL OTHER	TOTAL SLAVES	TOTALS	DISTRICT/ TOWNSHIP	NOTES
					under 10	10 to 16	16 to 26	26 to 45	45 and over	under 10	10 to 16	16 to 26	26 to 45	45 and over					
Becket	269	14	Simpson	Jonathan				1						1			2		
Becket	269	15	Snow	Eli			1			2				1			4		
Becket	269	16	Snow	Edmund			1					1					2		
Becket	269	17	Titus	David	1		1					1		1			4		
Becket	269	18	Tobey	Martha											3		3		
Becket	269	19	Victs	Henry				1						1			2		
Becket	269	20	Victs	Henry Junr				1		2		1	1				5		
Becket	269	21	Walden	Eben				1						1			2		
Becket	269	22	Wadsworth	Jonathan		1	1	1					1				4		
Becket	269	23	Wadsworth	Benja		1		1			1	1		1			5		
Becket	269	24	Wadsworth	Benja Jr	2		1					1					4		

TOWN	PG#	LN#	LAST NAME	FIRST NAME	FREE WHITE MALES					FREE WHITE FEMALES					TOTAL ALL OTHER	TOTAL SLAVES	TOTALS	DISTRICT/ TOWNSHIP	NOTES
					under 10	10 to 16	16 to 26	26 to 45	45 and over	under 10	10 to 16	16 to 26	26 to 45	45 and over					
Bethlehem	172	1	Chamberlain	Samuel	1			1		3	1		1				7		
Bethlehem	172	2	Rice	Chester	1			1		1			1				4		
Bethlehem	172	3	Rice	Watson	1		1			1		1					4		
Bethlehem	172	4	Rice	Elizabeth Wid		1				3	1		1				6		
Bethlehem	172	5	House	Benijah		1			1	1				2			5		
Bethlehem	172	6	Barker	Eleazer	2		2	1		2	1	1	1				10		
Bethlehem	172	7	Baker	Eliphalet	1		2	1		3			1				8		
Bethlehem	172	8	Fuller	Judah	3	1		1	1	1	1		1				9		
Bethlehem	172	9	Fuller	Lot	1	1	1		1	2		2		1			9		
Bethlehem	172	10	Benton	Abraham		1	2	2	1			2		1			9		
Bethlehem	172	11	Manley	George & David	2	2		1	1				1	1			8		
Bethlehem	172	12	Allen	John H.	1	1		1		2	1		1				7		
Bethlehem	172	13	Warner	Consider	2	1		1		2	1		1	1			9		
Bethlehem	172	14	Allen	Elijah	2	1		1		2			1				7		
Bethlehem	172	15	Abba	Thomas	2	2		1		2	1		1				9		
Bethlehem	173	1	Stafford	David	1		1			1			1				4		
Bethlehem	173	2	Morley	Derick		1	1	1		2	1		1				7		
Bethlehem	173	3	Jones	Joseph				1		1		1		1			4		
Bethlehem	173	4	Morley	Israel				1									1		
Bethlehem	173	5	Heath	Samuel		1	2		1	1				1			6		
Bethlehem	173	6	Heath	Roswell	1			1		2		1					5		
Bethlehem	173	7	Kilborn	Robbins	3			1		2			1				7		
Bethlehem	173	8	Comstock	Jeremiah	1			1		3			1				6		
Bethlehem	173	9	Miller	Seth				1		3			1				5		
Bethlehem	173	10	Hubbard	Nathaniel		1		1					1	1			4		
Bethlehem	173	11	Chappel	Samuel	2		2		1	1	2		1				9		
Bethlehem	173	12	Chappel	Edgecomb			1					1					2		
Bethlehem	173	13	Miller	Abner		1	1		1	1	2		1				7		
Bethlehem	173	14	Jones	John	1	2		1		3			1		1		9		
Bethlehem	173	15	Dodge	Francis		2		1					1				4		
Bethlehem	173	16	Pease	Elam	1		1			3			1				6		
Bethlehem	173	17	Rice	Jerusha								1					1		
Bethlehem	173	18	Holman	Thomas Junr	1	1			2	3		1	1	1			10		
Bethlehem	173	19	Manley	John	1	2		1	1	2			1				8		
Bethlehem	173	20	Cook	Eunice								1					1		
Bethlehem	173	21	Bozworth	Jabez		1	1	1				1	1	1			6		
Bethlehem	173	22	Smith	Elisha	1	1	2	1		2		1		1			9		
Bethlehem	173	23	Logan	William			1			1		1					3		
Bethlehem	180	1	Sumner	Hezekiah Senr				1					1				2		
Bethlehem	180	2	Sumner	Clemmons		1		1		1			1				4		
Bethlehem	180	3	Sumner	Hezekiah Jr	1	1	2	1		1	1	1	1				9		
Bethlehem	180	4	Granger	Thadeus	3	1		1					1				6		
Bethlehem	180	5	Beard	Kindol	2			1		1			1				5		
Bethlehem	180	6	Beard	Moses	3	2		1		1	1	2	1				11		
Bethlehem	180	7	Beard	Asa	3		2	1		2	1		1				10		
Bethlehem	180	8	Beard	Aaron					1					1			2		
Bethlehem	180	9	Adams	Asahel	2	1	1	1		1		1	1				8		
Bethlehem	180	10	Adams	Ebenezer	1	1				1		1					4		
Bethlehem	180	11	Phelps	Nathan	2			1		2	1		1				7		
Bethlehem	180	12	Elmer	Solomon				1		2			1				4		
Bethlehem	180	13	Corfin	Solomon				1		1			1				3		
Bethlehem	180	14	Shaw	Joshua	2			1		2			1				6		
Bethlehem	180	15	Cowl	Timothy	1	1		1		1			1				5		
Bethlehem	180	16	Jackson	Jacob	2			1		2	2		1				8		
Bethlehem	180	17	Smith	Daniel	1	1	1		1	1	1	1		1			8		
Bethlehem	180	18	Smith	Lucias	2			1		1		1					5		
Bethlehem	180	19	Heath	Stephen	2			1		2	3		1				9		
Bethlehem	180	20	Kingsley	Seth		2			1	3	1		1				8		
Bethlehem	181	1	Hunter	Isaac	1			1					1	1			4		
Bethlehem	181	2	Hunter	John				1		3	1		1				6		
Bethlehem	181	3	Snow	Solomon	2			1				1					4		
Bethlehem	181	4	Knight	Lydia Wid									1				1		
Bethlehem	181	5	Anabel	Ebenezer	2			1		2			1				6		
Bethlehem	181	6	Smith	Justus	3			1					1				5		
Bethlehem	181	7	Mills	Ezekiel A	1		1	1		1			1				5		
Bethlehem	181	8	Merrit	John	1			1		2	1		1				6		
Bethlehem	181	9	Wood	Hiram	4	2		1					1				8		
Bethlehem	181	10	Pearl	Richard		1	3	1					1	1			7		
Bethlehem	181	11	Ward	Seth	2			1		2			1				6		
Bethlehem	181	12	Webster	Simeon	1			1		3	1		1				7		
Bethlehem	181	13	Underwood	Samuel	2			1				1					4		
Bethlehem	181	14	Manley	Shubael	1			1		2			1				5		
Bethlehem	181	15	Kimbal	Edmond			1										1		
Bethlehem	181	16	Smith	Elijah		2	1		1		1	1	1				7		
Bethlehem	181	17	Sheperd	Nathaniel	2			1					1				4		
Bethlehem	181	18	Manley	Daniel		1		1		2	3		1				8		
Bethlehem	181	19	Bozworth	Osborn	1	1		1		1			1				5		
Bethlehem	181	20	Bozworth	Ichabod	3			1		1			1				6		
Bethlehem	181	21	Webster	David	1			1		1			1				4		

TOWN	PG#	LN#	LAST NAME	FIRST NAME	FREE WHITE MALES					FREE WHITE FEMALES					TOTAL ALL OTHER	TOTAL SLAVES	TOTALS	DISTRICT/ TOWNSHIP	NOTES
					under 10	10 to 16	16 to 26	26 to 45	45 and over	under 10	10 to 16	16 to 26	26 to 45	45 and over					
Bethlehem	181	22	Adams	Amos	3			1		3			1				8		
Bethlehem	181	23	Adams	Samuel Jun		1		1				1	1	1			5		
Bethlehem	181	24	Jones	Milles	2	1		1		2			1				7		
Bethlehem	181	25	Smith	Samuel	2			1		1			1				5		
Bethlehem	181	26	Spear	John	3			1				1	1				6		
Bethlehem	181	27	Brakenridge	James	2	2		1		1		1	1				8		
Bethlehem	181	28	Kyes	Ephraim	1			1		1			1				4		
Bethlehem	181	29	Sumner	Daniel	1	1	2	1		1	2	1	1				10		
Bethlehem	181	30	Manley	Martin	2			1		2			1				6		
Bethlehem	181	31	Slocum	Edward	5				1		1		1				8		
Bethlehem	181	32	Gallop	Samuel					1			1		1			3		
Bethlehem	181	33	Jones	Adonijah	2	1	1			1		2	1		1		9		
Bethlehem	181	34	Webb	Benoni	1		1						1				3		
Bethlehem	181	35	Kingsbery	Joseph	2			1		2	1		1				7		
Bethlehem	181	36	Deming	Jonathan	1		1			1		1					4		
Bethlehem	181	37	Kingsbery	Jabez	2			1					1				4		
Bethlehem	181	38	Adams	William Son	1		1		1				1				4		
Bethlehem	181	39	Couch	William	5			1			1		1				8		
Bethlehem	181	40	Boardman	Edward	2		1						1				4		
Bethlehem	181	41	Morley	Abner	2		1	1		2			1	1			8		
Bethlehem	181	42	Alden	Israel	3			1					1				5		
Bethlehem	181	43	Smith	Joel	2			1		3			1				7		
Bethlehem	181	44	Webb	Reuben	1			1					1				3		
Bethlehem	182	1	Webb	Samuel	1			1					1				3		
Bethlehem	182	2	Sperry	Elijah	2	1		1				2	1				7		
Bethlehem	182	3	Webb	Jonah				1		1		1					3		
Bethlehem	182	4	Fowler	Daniel	5			1	1			2	1	1	2		13		
Bethlehem	182	5	Rice	Francis			1						1				2		
Bethlehem	182	6	Webb	Daniel		1		1		1			1	1			5		
Bethlehem	182	7	Baldwin	Benjamin		1		1		5	1		1				9		
Bethlehem	182	8	Rockwell	Ephraim	1	2	1		1	2			1		1		9		
Bethlehem	182	9	Spring	Amos	2		2		1	1	2	1		1			10		
Bethlehem	182	10	Judd	Oliver		2	1	1				1	1	1			7		
Bethlehem	182	11	Curtis	Sarah									1				1		
Bethlehem	182	12	Owles	Sarah	1	1						1	1				4		
Bethlehem	182	13	Alden	Timothy	2		1	1		3			1				8		
Bethlehem	182	14	Judd	Timothy Son			1	1						1			3		
Bethlehem	182	15	Webster	John	1			1		4			1				7		
Bethlehem	182	16	Benton	Elijah	1			1		1		1					4		
Bethlehem	182	17	Cruttendon	Wm S	1	1			1	4			1				8		
Bethlehem	182	18	Ward	Thomas		1	1		1			1	1	1			6		
Bethlehem	182	19	Jones	Sarah Daughter								1	1				2		
Bethlehem	182	20	Ward	Elisha	1		1						1				3		
Bethlehem	182	21	Black	Isaac	2	2		1		1	1		1				8		

TOWN	PG#	LN#	HEADS OF HOUSEHOLD		FREE WHITE MALES					FREE WHITE FEMALES					TOTAL ALL OTHER	TOTAL SLAVES	TOTALS	DISTRICT/ TOWNSHIP	NOTES
			LAST NAME	FIRST NAME	under 10	10 to 16	16 to 26	26 to 45	45 and over	under 10	10 to 16	16 to 26	26 to 45	45 and over					
Cheshire	153	1	Whipple	Stephen	1	1	1		1					1			5		
Cheshire	153	2	Hix	Thomas		1	1			1		1					4		
Cheshire	153	3	Wood	Simeon				1		1			3				5		
Cheshire	153	4	Whipple	Samuel	1			2		2			1				6		
Cheshire	153	5	Mason	Brooks		1	1		1		1			1			5		
Cheshire	153	6	Bliss	Samuel	2			1		2			1				6		
Cheshire	153	7	Horton	Isaac	3	1			1	3		2	1				11		
Cheshire	153	8	Bliss	Timothy	2			1		2			1				6		
Cheshire	153	9	Hix	Eliphalet	1	3	1	1		4	1		1				12		
Cheshire	153	10	Broadway	Jeremiah	2		1			1		1					5		
Cheshire	153	11	Wood	Edward		2	3		1	1		2		1			10		
Cheshire	153	12	Coomer	Daniel	1	1	3		1		1	2		2			11		
Cheshire	153	13	Clark	Hannah	1						1		1				3		
Cheshire	153	14	Durfy	Robert				1					1				2		
Cheshire	153	15	Burton	Amos		1		1		1		1		1			5		
Cheshire	153	16	Mason	Nathan	1		1	1		3	4		1				11		
Cheshire	153	17	Lane	William		1	1		1	1	1		1				6		
Cheshire	153	18	Durphy	David	2			1		2			1				6		
Cheshire	153	19	Frink	Minor	1			1		2			1				5		
Cheshire	153	20	Hix	Amos		1		1					1				3		
Cheshire	154	1	Westcott	Stephen		1		1		3	1		1				7		
Cheshire	154	2	Westcott	Reuben	2			1		1		1	1				6		
Cheshire	154	3	Angel	James	1	1			1	1			1				5		
Cheshire	154	4	Slade	William				1		2		2	1				6		
Cheshire	154	5	Bliss	Nathaniel	1	3	1		1	1		1	1				9		
Cheshire	154	6	Mason	Nathan				1						1			2		
Cheshire	154	7	Mason	Daniel	2	1		1		2		1	1				8		
Cheshire	154	8	Barker	James			2		1			1	1				5		
Cheshire	154	9	Carpenter	Rufus				1		3	2		1		1		8		
Cheshire	154	10	Barker	Newell	1		1	1		3	1		1				8		
Cheshire	154	11	Tracy	Solomon	1			1			1	1	1				5		
Cheshire	154	12	Clark	Benjamin		1	1		1		2	1		1			7		
Cheshire	154	13	Hilliard	Henry		2	2		1	1		2		1			9		
Cheshire	154	14	Lyon	Ruth				1						1			2		
Cheshire	154	15	Mason	William	1			1				1					3		
Cheshire	154	16	McCluth	Solomon	3			1		3	1		1				9		
Cheshire	154	17	Baker	Oney				1		1			1				3		
Cheshire	154	18	Fisk	Caleb	2			1		1			1				5		
Cheshire	154	19	Lyons	John		1		1		1	2		1				6		
Cheshire	154	20	Hall	Calvin		1	1			3		1			1		7		
Cheshire	154	21	Mason	David	1	1	1	1		5			1				10		
Cheshire	154	22	Mason	Rufus	1			1		1	1		1				5		
Cheshire	154	23	Green	Eli			1					1	2				4		
Cheshire	154	24	Brown	Daniel		1	1	3	2	3		1	2	2			15		
Cheshire	154	25	Bucklin	John				1						1			2		
Cheshire	154	26	Bryant	David		1				1		1					3		
Cheshire	154	27	Claflin	George		1				1		1					3		
Cheshire	154	28	Wescott	Moses	2		1	1		1	1		1				7		
Cheshire	154	29	Wells	Thomas	1			1		2			1				5		
Cheshire	154	30	Barker	Ezra	2	1	1	1	1		2		1	1			10		
Cheshire	154	31	Grosvenor	Caleb	1		2		1	1		2		1			8		
Cheshire	154	32	Price	William	1			1		2	2		1				7		
Cheshire	154	33	Green	Oliver			1	1		1		1					4		
Cheshire	154	34	Burton	William	2	1		1		1	1	1					7		
Cheshire	154	35	Potter	Asahel	1	1		2		2		2					8		
Cheshire	154	36	Pratt	Jonathan		1	1	1		1			1				5		
Cheshire	154	37	Green	Peleg	2	1	1	1		2		2	1				10		
Cheshire	154	38	Nap	Jonathan	1		2	1		3		1	1	1			10		
Cheshire	154	39	Paine	William	1		2	1		1		2	1				8		
Cheshire	154	40	Brown	Elisha		1	1	1	1	1	1	2		1			9		
Cheshire	155	1	Brown	Benjamin	1	2		2		3	1	1					10		
Cheshire	155	2	Brown	William	2	1	1	1	1	2	2		1				11		
Cheshire	155	3	Dow	Benjamin	1	1		1		1	2		1				7		
Cheshire	155	4	Whitaker	William	2		1		1		1	1		1			7		
Cheshire	155	5	Stafford	Richard	1	2		1	1	1		1	1				8		
Cheshire	155	6	Bennett	John	2	1	1	1		1	1	1	1	1	1		11		
Cheshire	155	7	Brown	Ezech	1		1	1		2	2		1				8		
Cheshire	155	8	Edmonds	Edward	2	2	2		1	2	2	1		1			13		
Cheshire	155	9	Staples	Jacob	1		1					2					4		
Cheshire	155	10	Mason	Dexter	2	1	1	1				1	1				7		
Cheshire	155	11	Brown	Dexter		1	2			4	1		1				9		
Cheshire	155	12	Brown	Joseph				1						1			2		
Cheshire	155	13	Burlingame	Charles	2	1		1			1	1		1			7		
Cheshire	155	14	Claflin	Allen			1			1	2		1				5		
Cheshire	155	15	Burlingame	Jeremiah	4		1			2	1		1				9		
Cheshire	155	16	Briggs	Harmon	1		1		1			1	1				5		
Cheshire	155	17	Bowen	Nathan		2	2	1		1	1	1	1	1			10		
Cheshire	155	18	Bowen	Hezekiah		1	1		1		2	1		1			7		
Cheshire	155	19	Smith	Daniel	3	1	1	1				1					7		

20

TOWN	PG#	LN#	LAST NAME	FIRST NAME	FREE WHITE MALES					FREE WHITE FEMALES					TOTAL ALL OTHER	TOTAL SLAVES	TOTALS	DISTRICT/ TOWNSHIP	NOTES
					under 10	10 to 16	16 to 26	26 to 45	45 and over	under 10	10 to 16	16 to 26	26 to 45	45 and over					
Cheshire	155	20	Bliss	Benjamin	2		1	1		3		1	1				9		
Cheshire	155	21	Burton	Elijah	2	2			1		1	1	1		1		9		
Cheshire	155	22	Wyman	Frederick	1			1				1					3		
Cheshire	155	23	Bowen	Aaron	1			1		2		1	1				6		
Cheshire	155	24	Read	Benjamin	1			2			1	3		1			8		
Cheshire	155	25	Dean	Joseph	2	1		1		1	3	1	1				10		
Cheshire	155	26	Burlingame	Elisha	1	1		1		2	2	1		1			9		
Cheshire	155	27	Farnsworth	John	1			1		3			1				6		
Cheshire	155	28	Wells	Charles	2	1		1		1		1	1				7		
Cheshire	155	29	Wells	John	1	1	1	1	1	2		4	1	1			13		
Cheshire	155	30	Lipit	John				1			2		1				4		
Cheshire	155	31	Horsford	Eri			1	1		2			2				6		
Cheshire	155	32	Mason	Samuel		1	1			1		1					4		
Cheshire	155	33	Webster	Adonijah											6		6		
Cheshire	155	34	Vickery	William				1		3			1				5		
Cheshire	155	35	Daniels	Moses				1		3		1					5		
Cheshire	155	36	Brown	Allen	2	1		1	1	1			2				8		
Cheshire	155	37	Cushington	David	2	1	1	1		1			1				7		
Cheshire	155	38	Worden	Peter				1			1			1			3		
Cheshire	155	39	Worden	Peter Jun	2	2	1	1	1	1		2	1	1			12		
Cheshire	155	40	Scott	Silvanus	1	2			1		1	3		1			9		
Cheshire	155	41	Arnold	Joseph	3		1	1		2		1	1				9		
Cheshire	155	42	Manchester	Isaac	1		1	3		3	1		2				11		
Cheshire	156	1	Burton	Anthony			1				1	1					3		
Cheshire	156	2	Farnum	Jonathan	2			1		3	1		1				8		
Cheshire	156	3	Remington	John	2	1		1		1	1		1				7		
Cheshire	156	4	Mason	Timothy				1						1			2		
Cheshire	156	5	Hall	Nicholas	1		1	1		1	1						5		
Cheshire	156	6	Brayton	Isaac	2	1	1	1		1		2	1				9		
Cheshire	156	7	Reed	Daniel	1	1	1		1	1			1				6		
Cheshire	156	8	Green	Henry	2			1		1		1	1				6		
Cheshire	156	9	Howe	Isaac G.	1	2	1				1		1				7		
Cheshire	156	10	Brayton	Stephen		1			1			1		1			4		
Cheshire	156	11	Brayton	Arnold			1			2		1					4		
Cheshire	156	12	Brayton	Stephen Jun	1			1					1				3		
Cheshire	156	13	Waterman	John	3	1	2		2	2	2	1			1		14		
Cheshire	156	14	Bucklin	Darius	1		2	1					2				6		
Cheshire	156	15	Jenks	George	1			1		3			1				6		
Cheshire	156	16	Brown	Nicholas	1	1	2	1		2	1	1	1		1		11		
Cheshire	156	17	Leland	John	1		1		1	3	3		1				10		
Cheshire	156	18	Jenks	Jesse	2	1	2	1		3		1	1				11		
Cheshire	156	19	Jacob	Moses	1	1		1		2		1	1				7		
Cheshire	156	20	Fisk	Ephraim		1	3		1	2	1		1				9		
Cheshire	156	21	Wells	Elisha	1		1	1		4	1	1	1				10		
Cheshire	156	22	Brown	John	2	1		1		1		1	1				7		
Cheshire	156	23	Arnold	Smith	1			1		3		1					6		
Cheshire	156	24	Aldridge	Samuel		2	1		1	1	3	2	1				11		
Cheshire	156	25	Wilson	Thomas	2			1				1					4		
Cheshire	156	26	Fuller	Aaron	1			1		2			1				5		
Cheshire	156	27	Rush	Samuel	1				1	1	1			1			5		
Cheshire	156	28	Franklin	Oliver					1					1			2		
Cheshire	156	29	Cornwall	Joseph		1	1						1				3		
Cheshire	156	30	Carpenter	Stephen	1		2		1	1				1			6		
Cheshire	156	31	Thrasher	Charles					1					1			2		
Cheshire	156	32	Sheldon	John					1			1	1				3		
Cheshire	156	33	Bradford	Elisha	3	3			1	1		3	1				12		
Cheshire	156	34	Cole	Israel			2		1			1	1				5		
Cheshire	156	35	Ferrington	Ephraim	2		1	1					1				5		
Cheshire	156	36	Cole	Israel 2d		1	1	1		2		2					7		
Cheshire	156	37	Martin	Ebenezer		2	1		1	2		1	2				9		
Cheshire	156	38	Richardson	Jonathan	1		2		1		1			2			7		
Cheshire	156	39	Hathaway	William	1			1		1		1					4		
Cheshire	156	40	King	Medad		1		1	1	1		1		2			7		
Cheshire	156	41	King	Noble	1			1		1		1	1				5		
Cheshire	157	1	King	Curtis				1		1			1				3		
Cheshire	157	2	Green	Eli		1	1					1					3		
Cheshire	157	3	Dean	Eliphalet			1			1		1					3		
Cheshire	157	4	Mason	Silas			1					1					2		
Cheshire	157	5	Mason	Alexander			1				1		1	1			4		
Cheshire	157	6	Richmond	Selah	1					1		1	1				4		
Cheshire	157	7	Mason	Barnard			1	1				1		1			4		
Cheshire	157	8	Mason	Jesse		1	1			1	1	1		1			6		
Cheshire	157	9	Mason	Reuben	1			1		2		1					5		
Cheshire	157	10	Brown	Levi	1	1		1			1		1				5		
Cheshire	157	11	Brown	Caleb	1	2	1		1	3		1	1				10		
Cheshire	157	12	Mason	Levi		2	2	1		4	1	1		1			12		
Cheshire	157	13	Corwall	William	1	1	1	1		2	1	2	1				10		
Cheshire	157	14	Jones	Daniel	1	1			1	2	2		1				8		
Cheshire	157	15	Shelly	John				1		1		1					3		

TOWN	PG#	LN#	LAST NAME	FIRST NAME	FREE WHITE MALES					FREE WHITE FEMALES					TOTAL ALL OTHER	TOTAL SLAVES	TOTALS	DISTRICT/ TOWNSHIP	NOTES
					under 10	10 to 16	16 to 26	26 to 45	45 and over	under 10	10 to 16	16 to 26	26 to 45	45 and over					
Cheshire	157	16	Chace	John		1		1	1	1			1	1			6		
Cheshire	157	17	Simmons	Aaron	1			1	1	1		1		1			6		
Cheshire	157	18	Pratt	Paul		1		1		1	1		1				5		
Cheshire	157	19	Phillips	Abizer	1		1		1			1		1			5		
Cheshire	157	20	Hathaway	Maletiah			1	1		1			1				4		
Cheshire	157	21	Mason	Joshua	1		2				1						4		
Cheshire	157	22	Walker	Hezekiah	1		1			1		1					4		
Cheshire	157	23	McGloth	Laurence				1					1	1			3		
Cheshire	157	24	Williams	Nathaniel	2			1		1			1				5		
Cheshire	157	25	McGloth	Lewis	2			1		2	1		1				7		
Cheshire	157	26	Miranville	Robert	2			1					1				4		
Cheshire	157	27	Mason	Nathan			1		1	1	1		1				5		
Cheshire	157	28	Mason	Nathan J			1			1		1					3		
Cheshire	157	29	Swift	Silas				1		2	3		1				7		
Cheshire	157	30	Mason	Hezekiah	1	2	3		1	2	1	2		1			13		
Cheshire	157	31	Root	Selah	2		1			1		1					5		
Cheshire	157	32	Buck	Asahel	2	3		1		1		1	1				9		
Cheshire	157	33	Fish	William		1	1		1		1	1		1			6		
Cheshire	157	34	Fish	Jonathan		1	1	1		4	1		1	1			10		
Cheshire	157	35	Williams	Isaac	1			1		1		1					4		
Cheshire	157	36	Fish	Isaac				1		1			1	1			4		
Cheshire	157	37	Bowen	Joseph	5	1		1		1		1	1				10		
Cheshire	157	38	Rounds	Jabez	2			1		3			1				7		
Cheshire	157	39	Chace	Nehemiah			1		1	1		1		1			5		
Cheshire	157	40	Horton	Moses			1		1	1		1		1			5		
Cheshire	157	41	Westcott	Dickins	2		1	1		1			1	1			7		
Cheshire	157	42	Walker	Hezekiah	1		1			1		1					4		
Cheshire	157	43	McGloth	Laurence				1					1	1			3		
Cheshire	157	44	Williams	Nathaniel	2			1		1			1				5		
Cheshire	157	45	McGloth	Lewis	2			1		2	1		1				7		
Cheshire	157	46	Miranville	Robert	2			1					1				4		
Cheshire	157	47	Mason	Nathan			1		1	1	1		1				5		
Cheshire	157	48	Mason	Nathan J			1			1		1					3		
Cheshire	157	49	Swift	Silas				1		2	3		1				7		
Cheshire	157	50	Mason	Hezekiah	1	2	3		1	2	1	2		1			13		
Cheshire	157	51	Root	Selah	2		1			1		1					5		
Cheshire	157	52	Busk	Asahel	2	3		1		1		1	1				9		
Cheshire	157	53	Fisk	William		1	1		1		1	1		1			6		
Cheshire	157	54	Fisk	Jonathan		1	1	1		4	1		1	1			10		
Cheshire	157	55	Williams	Isaac	1			1		1		1					4		
Cheshire	157	56	Fisk	Isaac				1		1			1	1			4		
Cheshire	157	57	Bowen	Joseph	5	1		1		1		1	1				10		
Cheshire	157	58	Rounds	Jabez	2			1		3			1				7		
Cheshire	157	59	Chace	Nehemiah	3			1		2			1				7		
Cheshire	157	60	Horton	Moses			1		1	1		1		1			5		
Cheshire	157	61	Westcott	Dukins	2		1	1		1			1	1			7		
Cheshire	158	1	Sullivan	Daniel	3			1		2			1				7		
Cheshire	158	2	Philips	Abiner 2d	1		1					1					3		
Cheshire	158	3	Simmons	Thomas Jr	2			1				1					4		
Cheshire	158	4	Simmons	Thomas	1	1	1		1	1	2	1		1			9		
Cheshire	158	5	Barden	Isaac			1		1			1		1			4		
Cheshire	158	6	Barden	Isaac Jun	3			1				1					5		
Cheshire	158	7	Fetterman	Charles	1			1	1	2		1	1	1			8		
Cheshire	158	8	Jones	Seth		1	4	1	1	3		3		1			14		
Cheshire	158	9	Jones	Isaac	1			1		2		1					5		
Cheshire	158	10	Bliss	Elkanah			1			1		1					3		
Cheshire	158	11	Wood	Nathan	1		2	1	1	4	3		2				14		
Cheshire	158	12	Lyman	Moses		1		1	1				1				4		
Cheshire	158	13	Bourn	Francis		1		1		2	2	1	1				8		
Cheshire	158	14	Wood	Daniel	2	2	1		1		2	4		1			13		
Cheshire	158	15	Ingals	Stephen	1		1					1					3		
Cheshire	158	16	Warren	Jonas	4	2		1		1	1		1				10		
Cheshire	158	17	Northrup	Stephen	1	1	1		1		3			1			8		

TOWN	PG#	LN#	LAST NAME	FIRST NAME	FREE WHITE MALES					FREE WHITE FEMALES					TOTAL ALL OTHER	TOTAL SLAVES	TOTALS	DISTRICT/ TOWNSHIP	NOTES
					under 10	10 to 16	16 to 26	26 to 45	45 and over	under 10	10 to 16	16 to 26	26 to 45	45 and over					
Clarkesburg	141	1	Herrenden	Isaiah			1	1	1			2		1			6		
Clarkesburg	141	2	Harris	Robert	2			1				1					4		
Clarkesburg	141	3	Herrenden	Seth	2			1					1				4		
Clarkesburg	141	4	Shipley	Silas	2		1	1		3	3		1				11		
Clarkesburg	141	5	Herrenden	Daniel				1		1			1				3		
Clarkesburg	141	6	Cook	Abraham	1			1		1			1				4		
Clarkesburg	141	7	Potter	Abel				1					1				3		
Clarkesburg	141	8	Clarke	Stephen			1		1	1	1			1			5		
Clarkesburg	141	9	Robbins	Peter	3	1		1					1				6		
Clarkesburg	141	10	Clarke	Nicolas	1	2	3	2	1		1	1		2			13		
Clarkesburg	141	11	Ketchum	Epenetus			1	2	1					2			6		
Clarkesburg	141	12	Ketchum	Eleazer	4			1		1		1					7		
Clarkesburg	141	13	Ketchum	David	3			1		1			1				6		
Clarkesburg	141	14	Buerall	Isaac				1		3			1				5		
Clarkesburg	141	15	Sumner	Abner	1			1		1	1		1				5		
Clarkesburg	141	16	Ketchum	Samuel			1		1			1		1			4		
Clarkesburg	141	17	Brown	Jesse Jrn		1		1	1	2		1		1			7		
Clarkesburg	141	18	Horich	Daniel	1	1	2	1		2	3		1				11		
Clarkesburg	142	1	Ross	John	1			1		1		1					4		
Clarkesburg	142	2	Cook	Martin	1		1			1		1					4		
Clarkesburg	142	3	Dillingham	George			1					1					2		
Clarkesburg	142	4	Sheldon	Nathan	1		1					1					3		
Clarkesburg	142	5	Pratt	Joel & Ebenezer			2										2		
Clarkesburg	142	6	Camp	Jonah	1		1					1					3		
Clarkesburg	142	7	Stroud	John	2		1			1		1					5		
Clarkesburg	142	8	Stroud	William	1		1			1		1					4		
Clarkesburg	142	9	Lessure	Isaiah	1		1	2	1	1				2			8		
Clarkesburg	142	10	Grover	Jona	3			1		1	2		1				8		
Clarkesburg	142	11	Wilcox	James	1	1			1	1	1	1	1	1			8		
Clarkesburg	142	12	Brayton	David	2	1		1		2	2		1				9		
Clarkesburg	142	13	Estes	Elijah	2			1		1			1				5		
Clarkesburg	142	14	Harington	Jefferson		1		1					1				3		
Clarkesburg	142	15	Estes	John				1	1					1			3		
Clarkesburg	142	16	Estes	John Jr	3	2		1		1	1	1	1				10		
Clarkesburg	142	17	Estes	Samuel	1			1		2		1	1				6		

23

TOWN	PG#	LN#	LAST NAME	FIRST NAME	FREE WHITE MALES					FREE WHITE FEMALES					TOTAL ALL OTHER	TOTAL SLAVES	TOTALS	DISTRICT/ TOWNSHIP	NOTES
					under 10	10 to 16	16 to 26	26 to 45	45 and over	under 10	10 to 16	16 to 26	26 to 45	45 and over					
Dalton	191	1	Barden	James		1	3		1	1	1	2		1			10		
Dalton	191	2	Bartlett	Nicholas					1		1			1			3		
Dalton	191	3	Bartlett	Stephen	1			1		1		1	1				5		
Dalton	191	4	Bassett	Nathan	3	1		1				1	1				7		
Dalton	191	5	Baxter	Wm				1						1			2		
Dalton	191	6	Baxter	Wm Junr	4	2		1					1				8		
Dalton	191	7	Beslow	Job	2	1		1		3	1		1				9		
Dalton	191	8	Bicknell	Otis	1			1		2			1				5		
Dalton	191	9	Bow	Jacob	3	1		1				1	1				7		
Dalton	191	10	Bill	Rhoda	1					1			1				3		
Dalton	191	11	Bordman	Danl				1						1			2		
Dalton	191	12	Bordman	Danl Jr	1	1		1		3		1					7		
Dalton	191	13	Bridges	Edmund		1		1		1			1				4		
Dalton	191	14	Butts	Josiah	1			1		2	1		1				6		
Dalton	191	15	Buchard	Matthew	1	1	1		1	1	1	1		1			8		
Dalton	191	16	Beckwith	Jonah	2	2		1		2			1				8		
Dalton	191	17	Cady	Rufus	2	1	1	1	1	2	2			1			11		
Dalton	191	18	Carrier	Elisha	1			1		1			1				4		
Dalton	191	19	Cady	Wm. Waterman	1			1		1			1				4		
Dalton	191	20	Cady	Chester	2			1					1				4		
Dalton	191	21	Chamberlin	Joseph					1				2	1			4		
Dalton	191	22	Chamberlin	Eliph			2		1			1	1	1			6		
Dalton	191	23	Chamberlin	Benja		2			1	1	1	1		1			7		
Dalton	191	24	Chamberlin	Martin	2	1	1	1		1	1	1	1				9		
Dalton	191	25	Chamberlin	Jacob	3		1	1		1				1			7		
Dalton	191	26	Chamberlin	John Jr			1	3	1								5		
Dalton	191	27	Chamberlin	Elisha	1			1		3			1				6		
Dalton	191	28	Clark	Solomon	3	1		1		1	1		1				8		
Dalton	191	29	Clark	John Cook	3			1			1		2				7		
Dalton	191	30	Clark	Ephraim	3	1		1		1				1			7		
Dalton	191	31	Couch	John	1	2		1		3	1		1				9		
Dalton	191	32	Cleveland	Henry		2			1				3	1			7		
Dalton	191	33	Cleveland	Sarah	2		1			2	1	1					7		
Dalton	191	34	Cleveland	Jedediah	3	1		1		1	2	2	1				11		
Dalton	191	35	Cleveland	Aaron	3	1				2			1				7		
Dalton	191	36	Cleveland	Asahel			1				1						2		
Dalton	191	37	Cole	Justin		2		1		4	1		1	2			11		
Dalton	191	38	Curtis	Elijah				1			2		1				4		
Dalton	191	39	Curtis	Elijah Jr	1		1	1		2	2		1				8		
Dalton	191	40	Curtis	John	1			1		2		1					5		
Dalton	191	41	Curtis	Ebenezer	1	1		1		2		1					6		
Dalton	191	42	Curtis	Epaphras	2						1		1				4		
Dalton	191	43	Curtis	Alford	2			1					1				4		
Dalton	191	44	Convers	Edward	2	1			1	1			1	1			7		
Dalton	192	1	Day	Daniel	3	1			1	2			3	1			11		
Dalton	192	2	Day	Charles	1	1	1		1	2	4	1		1			12		
Dalton	192	3	Day	Amasa	1	2	1	1	1	1	1		1				10		
Dalton	192	4	Durkee	Henry	2			1						1			4		
Dalton	192	5	Ensign	William	2	2	2		1			1		1			9		
Dalton	192	6	Farnam	Isaiah	1			1		1			1				4		
Dalton	192	7	Finney	Benja	1			1		3			1				6		
Dalton	192	8	Foot	Daniel	1	1	1		1	1	1		1				7		
Dalton	192	9	Fox	Abiah			1			1				1			3		
Dalton	192	10	Follett	Roger	2	1		1		1			1				6		
Dalton	192	11	Frost	Amasa	1			1		2			1				5		
Dalton	192	12	Frost	Nehemiah	2	1		1		2	1		1				8		
Dalton	192	13	Gallup	Benja			1		1	1		2		1			6		
Dalton	192	14	Gallup	Urrial	1			1		1			1				4		
Dalton	192	15	Gallup	Olive			2			2		1	1	1			7		
Dalton	192	16	Goodrich	Sela	1			1		3			1				6		
Dalton	192	17	Hale	William	2		1		2	1	2	1	1				10		
Dalton	192	18	Hill	Nathl	3		2							1			6		
Dalton	192	19	Hovey	Luke	1		1		2	1			1	1			7		
Dalton	192	20	Hovey	Jonathan	2	1	1	1		3			1				9		
Dalton	192	21	Hall	Nathan				1		2		1					4		
Dalton	192	22	Henry	Malcom	1			1	1			1		1			5		
Dalton	192	23	Hovey	John	1	1		1		2	1		1				7		
Dalton	192	24	Hinsdale	Theodore		3	2	1	1		1	1		1	1		11		
Dalton	192	25	Hulbert	John	2		1			1		1					5		
Dalton	192	26	Hulbert	Thaddeus				1		1				1			3		
Dalton	192	27	Hubbard	Enoch	3		1	1		1			1	1			7		
Dalton	192	28	Jones	Elkanah		1		1		1			1				4		
Dalton	192	29	Jones	Benajah				1	1					1			3		
Dalton	192	30	Jones	Eli	2			1		1		1					5		
Dalton	192	31	Isaacs	Chloe						1	1	1					3		
Dalton	192	32	Johnson	John											7		7		
Dalton	192	33	Kellogg	Nathl	1	1			1	1	1			2			7		
Dalton	192	34	Kellogg	Nathl Jr	1			1					1				3		
Dalton	192	35	Kittridge	Abel	1	1		1		1			2				6		

24

TOWN	PG#	LN#	LAST NAME	FIRST NAME	under 10	10 to 16	16 to 26	26 to 45	45 and over	under 10	10 to 16	16 to 26	26 to 45	45 and over	TOTAL ALL OTHER	TOTAL SLAVES	TOTALS	DISTRICT/ TOWNSHIP	NOTES
Dalton	192	36	Lawrence	Joseph		2			1	1		1		1			6		
Dalton	192	37	Lawrence	Thomas			2	1	1			1		1			6		
Dalton	192	38	Lawrence	Daniel	2		1			1		1					5		
Dalton	192	39	Lawrence	Jona	2		1						1				4		
Dalton	192	40	Lawrence	Josiah				1					1				2		
Dalton	192	41	Lovernan	George		1				1		1					3		
Dalton	192	42	Maynard	Ezra	1			1				1					3		
Dalton	193	1	Marsh	Henry	3	1	1	1		1	1	2	1	1			12		
Dalton	193	2	Merriman	Daniel		1			1			1		1			4		
Dalton	193	3	Merriman	Jesse	3	1		1		1			1				7		
Dalton	193	4	Merriman	Nathl	1			1		1	1	1					5		
Dalton	193	5	Merriman	Daniel Jr	1		1	2					1				5		
Dalton	193	6	Newell	Ephraim	1	2			1		1			1			6		
Dalton	193	7	Nichols	Lemuel		1	1	1		2	1		1				7		
Dalton	193	8	Noble	Royal			1			3		1					5		
Dalton	193	9	Nichols	Amos	2	1		1		2			1				7		
Dalton	193	10	Parks	Abijah		1	1	1	1		1	1		1			7		
Dalton	193	11	Partridge	John		2		1		1	2	1		1			8		
Dalton	193	12	Pease	William		1						1					2		
Dalton	193	13	Peck	Benjamin	1	2				2			1				6		
Dalton	193	14	Pitts	Samuel	1					1	1		1				4		
Dalton	193	15	Peck	Israel	1	2			1	4	1		1				10		
Dalton	193	16	Porter	Abraham	2	1	2		1		1	2		1			10		
Dalton	193	17	Putnam	John		1		1		3			1				6		
Dalton	193	18	Pike	Barnabas	2	1		1		1	1	1		1			8		
Dalton	193	19	Powers	William	3			1		2			1				7		
Dalton	193	20	Roberts	Aaron	1			1		1			1				4		
Dalton	193	21	Roberts	Edward		1			1	2	2	1	1				8		
Dalton	193	22	Roberts	Edward Jr		1	1					1					3		
Dalton	193	23	Rogers	William	1	1		1		1			1				5		
Dalton	193	24	Smith	George H	4			1		3		1					9		
Dalton	193	25	Smith	Amos		3		1		1		1	1				7		
Dalton	193	26	Smith	Abner	1			1		1		1					4		
Dalton	193	27	Smith	Joshua	1		1	1		1		2					6		
Dalton	193	28	Southworth	Thomas		1	1			1		1					4		
Dalton	193	29	Spafard	Amos	1		1	1		3			1				7		
Dalton	193	30	Sprague	Calvin				1						1			2		
Dalton	193	31	Tracy	Sarah			1			2			1				4		
Dalton	193	32	Tufts	Peter		1	1	1		1		1					5		
Dalton	193	33	Talcott	Joseph		1	2		1	2			1				7		
Dalton	193	34	Walds	Galvin	2		1	1	1	4	2		1		1		13		
Dalton	193	35	Walker	Walter	2	2		1		1			1				7		
Dalton	193	36	Warner	Nathan	3	2			1		1	1	1	1			10		
Dalton	193	37	Waterman	Glading	2	2	1	1		2	1	1	2	1			13		
Dalton	193	38	Webb	Zebulon			1			1			1				3		
Dalton	193	39	Waldron	Taber	3	1			1	1		1					7		
Dalton	193	40	Wakefield	Nathn		1			1	1	1		1				5		
Dalton	193	41	Webb	Naphtali		1			1	1	1	1	1				6		
Dalton	193	42	Webb	Lebbeus	2			1		1			1				5		
Dalton	193	43	Wiley	John				1						1			2		
Dalton	193	44	Wiley	Samuel	3			1		1	1		1				7		
Dalton	194	1	Wing	James	2	1		1		2	1		1				8		
Dalton	194	2	Williams	William		1	2		1	1	1	1	1				9		
Dalton	194	3	Wood	Joseph				2		1			2		2		7		
Dalton	194	4	Wood	Joseph Junr	2			1	1	1			1				6		
Dalton	194	5	Wentworth	Daniel	2	1	1	1		2	1	1	1				10		
Dalton	194	6	Whipple	Samuel	3			1		2		1					7		
Dalton	194	7	Wright	Samuel	2		1	1		1			1	1			7		

TOWN	PG#	LN#	HEADS OF HOUSEHOLD LAST NAME	FIRST NAME	FREE WHITE MALES under 10	10 to 16	16 to 26	26 to 45	45 and over	FREE WHITE FEMALES under 10	10 to 16	16 to 26	26 to 45	45 and over	TOTAL ALL OTHER	TOTAL SLAVES	TOTALS	DISTRICT/ TOWNSHIP	NOTES
Egremont	118	1	Smith	Ebenezer	1			1		1		1					4		
Egremont	118	2	Nash	Jonathan	2			1		2		1					6		
Egremont	118	3	Benedict	Peter	1			1		1		1					4		
Egremont	118	4	Millard	Peter	1			1		1			1				4		
Egremont	118	5	Olds	Seth	1		1					1					3		
Egremont	118	6	Bassett	Justus	1			1		2		1					5		
Egremont	118	7	Olds	Isaac	1			1		1		1					4		
Egremont	118	8	Blakesley	Jared	6	3		1				1		1			12		
Egremont	118	9	Hatch	Ebenezer	1			1		2	1		1				6		
Egremont	118	10	Daley	Absalom		1		1		1		2					5		
Egremont	118	11	Haws	Benjamin	1	2		1		2	1	1	1				9		
Egremont	118	12	Hurlbut	Samuel	1	3	1	1		2	1		1				10		
Egremont	118	13	Geed	Isaac	1				1					1			3		
Egremont	118	14	Webb	Josiah	1			1		2			1				5		
Egremont	118	15	Allen	Elijah	1	1			1	2	4		1				10		
Egremont	118	16	Goulbourn	William				1				1	1				3		
Egremont	118	17	Andrus	Appleton	2	1		1		2		1	1				8		
Egremont	118	18	Winchel	Andrew				1		2			1				4		
Egremont	118	19	Rase	Darius	1	1		1		1		1					5		
Egremont	118	20	Winchel	Ephraim Jr			2	1			1		1	1			6		
Egremont	118	21	Winchel	Absalom	2			1		2		1					6		
Egremont	118	22	Loomis	Daniel			1		1	1	1			1			5		
Egremont	118	23	Millard	Josiah			1					1					2		
Egremont	118	24	Done	Jane		2	1				1		1				5		
Egremont	118	25	Rase	Isaac	1	2			1	2	2	1		1			10		
Egremont	119	1	Loomis	Josiah		1			2					2			5		
Egremont	119	2	Daly	Mary				2				1	1				4		
Egremont	119	3	Kaline	Jacob		1		1					1				3		
Egremont	119	4	Finney	Joseph				1		2	1		1				5		
Egremont	119	5	Moore	Henry	1		1						1	1			4		
Egremont	119	6	Rorepaugh	Thomas	2	1		1	1	1	1			1			8		
Egremont	119	7	Coe	Jesse	2			1		1			2				6		
Egremont	119	8	Rase	Abraham	2		2		1	1							6		
Egremont	119	9	Crippen	Reuben	2	1		1		1			1				6		
Egremont	119	10	Fellows	Samuel			2	3				1					6		
Egremont	119	11	Bacon	Samuel		1	2	2		2	1		1				9		
Egremont	119	12	Bacon	Andrew	3		1	1		2	1		1				9		
Egremont	119	13	Fuller	John		1	2	2	1	2	1		1				10		
Egremont	119	14	Jewit	Joseph	1	1		1		3			1		1		8		
Egremont	119	15	Karner	Jacob		1		1		1			1	1			5		
Egremont	119	16	Karner	Stephen		1							1				2		
Egremont	119	17	Days	Samuel	3	1	1	1		1	1	1					9		
Egremont	119	18	Holmes	Alpheus		1		1									2		
Egremont	119	19	Ransford	Solomon	1			1					1				3		
Egremont	119	20	Alcott	Jared	1		1	1		2	2		1				8		
Egremont	119	21	Wood	Jeptha	1			1		3	1		1				7		
Egremont	119	22	Karner	Felix	2			1		3			1				7		
Egremont	119	23	Randolph	Benjamin			2		1			1		1			5		
Egremont	119	24	Ingraham	Benjamin	1		2		1			1		1			6		
Egremont	119	25	Willard	Elijah		2	2		1		2	2					9		
Egremont	120	1	Phillips	Lacheus	1			1		1		1					4		
Egremont	120	2	Rase	Phillip	2	2	2		1	1	1			1			10		
Egremont	120	3	Hollenbeck	Domick	1				1			1		1			4		
Egremont	120	4	Olds	Ebenezer			1	1				1	1	1			5		
Egremont	120	5	Toms	Robert	3		1	1		3		1	1				10		
Egremont	120	6	Holmes	William		1				1		1					3		
Egremont	120	7	Hollenbeck	Darius		1				1		1					3		
Egremont	120	8	Daley	Ammon	1			1		1		1					4		
Egremont	120	9	Preston	Ira	2			1		3			1				7		
Egremont	120	10	Crippin	David	3		1	1					1	1			7		
Egremont	120	11	Brunson	John	2	1		1		3			1				8		
Egremont	120	12	Benjamin	Joseph	3	1	2			1		1	1				9		
Egremont	120	13	Westover	Jonah	2			1	1	1	1	1		2			10		
Egremont	120	14	Bunts	Ephraim Jr	3	1		1		1	1		1				8		
Egremont	120	15	Heare	Nicholas	2			1		1		2	1				7		
Egremont	120	16	Heare	Francis	1	1	2		1	1		2	1				9		
Egremont	120	17	Fullar	Seneca	1		2		1	1		1	1				7		
Egremont	120	18	Gerralds	Hyder			1		1			1	2	1			6		
Egremont	120	19	Curtis	Joseph	1	1	3	1		1		1	1				9		
Egremont	120	20	Austin	Judah	1	1			1	1		1	1				6		
Egremont	120	21	Austin	Amasa		1							1				2		
Egremont	120	22	Hubbard	Booker	2			1	1	1		1	1	1			7		
Egremont	120	23	Laman	Clement		2	1	1	1	1		1		1			8		
Egremont	120	24	Winchel	Martin	2			1		3	2		1				9		
Egremont	120	25	Rynders	Evert	1	3			1		1		1				7		
Egremont	120	26	Root	James					1					1			2		
Egremont	120	27	Pierce	Amasa			1					1					2		
Egremont	120	28	Crippin	Nathaniel			1			1		1					3		
Egremont	120	29	Loomis	Andrew	4	1	2	1				1	1				10		

| TOWN | PG# | LN# | HEADS OF HOUSEHOLD | | FREE WHITE MALES | | | | | FREE WHITE FEMALES | | | | | TOTAL ALL OTHER | TOTAL SLAVES | TOTALS | DISTRICT/ TOWNSHIP | NOTES |
			LAST NAME	FIRST NAME	under 10	10 to 16	16 to 26	26 to 45	45 and over	under 10	10 to 16	16 to 26	26 to 45	45 and over					
Egremont	120	30	Allen	Luke	1	1	1	1		3	2	3	1				13		
Egremont	120	31	Winchel	Amos	3			1		1	1		2	1			9		
Egremont	120	32	King	Elijah	2		2	1		3	2	1	1	1			13		
Egremont	120	33	Lightbody	John	3	1			1	1	1		1				8		
Egremont	120	34	Daley	William	2	1		1		1	1		1				7		
Egremont	120	35	Webb	John	2		1	1		1	2	1	1				9		
Egremont	120	36	Joiner	Octavus	2		1	1	1	4	2		1	1			13		
Egremont	120	37	Scribner	Nathan	1	1	1		1	2	1		1	1			9		
Egremont	120	38	Webb	James	2		1			2			1				6		
Egremont	120	39	Baldwin	James	4	1	2	1					1				10		
Egremont	120	40	Baldwin	Joseph					1				1	1			3		
Egremont	120	41	Perry	John		1	1	2	1		1			2			8		
Egremont	120	42	Webb	Thomas				1	1			2	1	1			6		
Egremont	120	43	Gray	Jaduthan	2	2	1		1	2	1		1				10		

TOWN	PG#	LN#	LAST NAME	FIRST NAME	FREE WHITE MALES					FREE WHITE FEMALES					TOTAL ALL OTHER	TOTAL SLAVES	TOTALS	DISTRICT/ TOWNSHIP	NOTES
					under 10	10 to 16	16 to 26	26 to 45	45 and over	under 10	10 to 16	16 to 26	26 to 45	45 and over					
Great Barrington	104	1	Pynchon	Walter	1	1	1										3		
Great Barrington	104	2	Hopkins	Moses	1	2	2		1	1	2		1				10		
Great Barrington	104	3	Pynchon	Theophilus	1			1					1				3		
Great Barrington	104	4	Jones	Solomon	3			1		3	2	1					10		
Great Barrington	104	5	Whiting	Abrah A.	1		1	1		2			1				6		
Great Barrington	104	6	Whiting	William		1	1	1			1		1				5		
Great Barrington	104	7	Whiting	Samuel			1	2				2		2			7		
Great Barrington	104	8	Baker	Thomas	2	1	1		1	1	1	1		1			9		
Great Barrington	104	9	Whiting	John			1					3		1			5		
Great Barrington	104	10	Kellogg	Ezra			1		1	3	3	2	1		1		12		
Great Barrington	104	11	Riley	Samuel	1		1			1	1	1					6		
Great Barrington	104	12	Walling	Margaret	2						1	2					5		
Great Barrington	104	13	Whiting	Mason				1				2					3		
Great Barrington	104	14	Ives	Thomas	1	1	2		1	5	1	1	2				14		
Great Barrington	104	15	Van Deusen	Isaac Jr	1	2	1		1	1		1	1				8		
Great Barrington	104	16	Foster	Melaneton	2			1		1		1					5		
Great Barrington	104	17	Ornsby	Levi	3			1					1				5		
Great Barrington	104	18	Preston	Isaac	2			1				1	1				5		
Great Barrington	104	19	Cooper	Simeon	1	1	1	2		3	1	1	2				12		
Great Barrington	104	20	Walker	Jacob											2		2		
Great Barrington	104	21	Stewart	John	3			1				1					5		
Great Barrington	104	22	Phelps	Aaron	2			1				1					4		
Great Barrington	104	23	Wainwright	David	1	1	1	1	1	3	2	2	1	1			14		
Great Barrington	104	24	June	Benjamin	1	1		1		1	1		1				6		
Great Barrington	104	25	Burgharot	John 3d	2	1	1		2		1		1	1			9		
Great Barrington	105	1	Church	Joseph		1		1			1		1				4		
Great Barrington	105	2	Tucker	Silas			1			2		1	1				5		
Great Barrington	105	3	Ransom	Elias	1	1	1	1		1	1		1				7		
Great Barrington	105	4	Wheeler	Truman	1		2		1	1	2	1					8		
Great Barrington	105	5	Lee	Solomon N	2		2	1			1	1					7		
Great Barrington	105	6	Sage	Elisha	3		3		1	2	1	1		1			12		
Great Barrington	105	7	Lee	Henry	2			1		1	1		1				5		
Great Barrington	105	8	Gibron	John		1		2	2	1		3		1			10		
Great Barrington	105	9	Hopkins	Ichabod		2			1	1		1					5		
Great Barrington	105	10	Tucker	John	2			1		1		1	1				6		
Great Barrington	105	11	Sacklin	James											2		2		
Great Barrington	105	12	Freeman	Ceasar											6		6		
Great Barrington	105	13	Coy	Eddy	1	2		1		4		1					9		
Great Barrington	105	14	Ives	Samuel	2			1		1			1				5		
Great Barrington	105	15	Lantman	James											4		4		
Great Barrington	105	16	Lester	Silas	2			1		2			1				6		
Great Barrington	105	17	Grant	Sylvester	2			1		2			1				6		
Great Barrington	105	18	King	Lucius	1	2			1	1	2		1				8		
Great Barrington	105	19	Spencer	Eliphalet	1	2	1	1		1	1	1		1			9		
Great Barrington	105	20	Gilbert	Ebenezer				1					1				2		
Great Barrington	105	21	Grant	Hezekiah	1			1		1	1	1					5		
Great Barrington	105	22	Olds	Aaron	2	1		1		2	1		1				8		
Great Barrington	105	23	Woodworth	Dudley	1		3	1				1	1				7		
Great Barrington	105	24	Chappell	Dan	2	2	1	1		1		1	2				10		
Great Barrington	105	25	Mansfield	Abijah	1			1									2		
Great Barrington	105	26	Mansfield	Daniel			1	1					1				3		
Great Barrington	105	27	Sibley	Stephen	4	1	1	1		1		1		1			10		
Great Barrington	105	28	Hopkins	Samuel	1	1		1		1			1				5		
Great Barrington	105	29	Sanford	David	3	2	1	1		1		1	1				10		
Great Barrington	105	30	Porter	Joshua	1	2		1			2	1	1				8		
Great Barrington	105	31	Dewey	Hugo	4	1		1	1	1	1	2	1				12		
Great Barrington	105	32	Dewey	Justin	3	3	1		1	1							10		
Great Barrington	105	33	Hitchcock	David	1			1					1				3		
Great Barrington	105	34	Johnson	Jacob		1							2				3		
Great Barrington	105	35	Kilborn	Robert	2		1	1		1			1				6		
Great Barrington	105	36	Hull	Cornelius					1		1	1	2				5		
Great Barrington	105	37	Woodworth	Stephen	2					1		1	2				6		
Great Barrington	105	38	Kilborn	Charles		1		1					1				3		
Great Barrington	105	39	Turner	Elijah	3	1		1		2			1				8		
Great Barrington	105	40	Hogets	Emanuel				1					1				2		
Great Barrington	105	41	Pixley	Hall Junr				1		2		1					4		
Great Barrington	105	42	Pixley	Hall	1	1	1		1		2	1					7		
Great Barrington	105	43	Cleaveland	Lemuel	1			1		1		3	1				7		
Great Barrington	105	44	Burghardt	John 2d		1	1	1					1	2			6		
Great Barrington	105	45	Worthy	Benjamin	1	1		1		1			1				5		
Great Barrington	105	46	Conner	John				1					1				2		
Great Barrington	105	47	Nash	Abigail			1	1		2	1	1	2				8		
Great Barrington	106	1	Ingersoll	Horton			1			1		1					2		
Great Barrington	106	2	Rogers	Benjamin		1	2						1				4		
Great Barrington	106	3	Stanly	George	1			2	1	1		3	1				9		
Great Barrington	106	4	King	William				1						2			3		
Great Barrington	106	5	Haight	Elijah	2		3			2		1					8		
Great Barrington	106	6	Pixley	William				1		2			1				4		
Great Barrington	106	7	Pixley	Silas			1			1	1	1					4		

TOWN	PG#	LN#	LAST NAME	FIRST NAME	FREE WHITE MALES					FREE WHITE FEMALES					TOTAL ALL OTHER	TOTAL SLAVES	TOTALS	DISTRICT/ TOWNSHIP	NOTES
					under 10	10 to 16	16 to 26	26 to 45	45 and over	under 10	10 to 16	16 to 26	26 to 45	45 and over					
Great Barrington	106	8	Pixley	Alexander	1			1		2		1					5		
Great Barrington	106	9	Pixley	Daniel			1			1		1					3		
Great Barrington	106	10	Root	James	1	1			1	1		1		1			6		
Great Barrington	106	11	King	Reuben	1		1						1				3		
Great Barrington	106	12	Farnum	John	2		2	1		2	1		1				9		
Great Barrington	106	13	Pixley	Olive									1				1		
Great Barrington	106	14	Remele	William		1	1		1			3		1			7		
Great Barrington	106	15	Phelps	Josiah				1					1				2		
Great Barrington	106	16	Burghardt	Andrew	1	1		1			1		1	1			6		
Great Barrington	106	17	Burghardt	John				1					2		1		4		
Great Barrington	106	18	Van Deusen	Isaac	1			1	2	2		2			3		11		
Great Barrington	106	19	Van Deusen	John			1	1	1			1					4		
Great Barrington	106	20	Dewey	Roswell				1		1		1					3		
Great Barrington	106	21	Van Deusen	Abram			2		1	2			1	1			7		
Great Barrington	106	22	Van Deusen	Conrad		1	2	2	1		1	2		1			10		
Great Barrington	106	23	Pixley	Jonathan	2		2		1	2	1		1		1		10		
Great Barrington	106	24	Bates	Martin		2	1		1	2		3	1	1			11		
Great Barrington	106	25	Mires	John				1					1		7		9		
Great Barrington	106	26	Robinson	James											2		2		
Great Barrington	106	27	Van Deusen	Jacob		1			1	2		1		1	2		8		
Great Barrington	106	28	Van Deusen	Abrahm 2d	1			2		1			1				5		
Great Barrington	106	29	Seely	Abrm	1	2		1		2			1				7		
Great Barrington	106	30	Seely	Isaac	2	1	1		1	2	1		1				9		
Great Barrington	106	31	Arnold	John	1	1		1		2	1	2	1				9		
Great Barrington	106	32	Arnold	Timothy	2			1		1			1				5		
Great Barrington	106	33	Arnold	Jacob			3		1	2	1		1				8		
Great Barrington	106	34	Turner	Jabez	2	2	2	1		1		1					9		
Great Barrington	106	35	Bradley	Dimon	1	2		1	1	4		2		1			12		
Great Barrington	106	36	Day	William			1		1		1	1		1			5		
Great Barrington	106	37	Hart	Martin	1			1		3	1	1	1				8		
Great Barrington	106	38	Fleming	William	2	1		1		2	2		1				9		
Great Barrington	106	39	Tyler	Amasa	1			1	1	1			1				5		
Great Barrington	106	40	Ford	Jonathan	1	1	2	1	1		1			1			8		
Great Barrington	106	41	Willard	Daniel		1			1				1				3		
Great Barrington	106	42	Crain	William		2		1		1	2	2		1			9		
Great Barrington	106	43	Seely	John		3		1		1		2		1			8		
Great Barrington	106	44	Wilty	John				1									1		
Great Barrington	106	45	Younglove	Daniel	1	1		1		2			1				6		
Great Barrington	107	1	Younglove	John	2			1				3		1			7		
Great Barrington	107	2	Hulbert	Russell	3		2		1	2		1	1	1			11		
Great Barrington	107	3	Trowbridge	Tabitha										1			1		
Great Barrington	107	4	Butler	Martin			1			2		2					5		
Great Barrington	107	5	Baker	Nathan		1	4		1	1		1		1			9		
Great Barrington	107	6	Tuttle	Simon				1					1				2		
Great Barrington	107	7	Sprague	Barnabas	2	2		1		2		1	1				9		
Great Barrington	107	8	Morse	Seth		2	1	1		2		2	1				9		
Great Barrington	107	9	Douglas	Thos James		1	1		1	4	2	1	1	1			12		
Great Barrington	107	10	Mansfield	Lydia			1							1			2		
Great Barrington	107	11	Hendrick	Daniel	2			1		3	1		1				8		
Great Barrington	107	12	Cady	Reuben	1	1		1		1	1		1				6		
Great Barrington	107	13	Houk	John	4	2		1			2		1				10		
Great Barrington	107	14	Houk	Martin	2	2		1		2			1				8		
Great Barrington	107	15	Wier	Francis	1	5	3		1	2	2		1				15		
Great Barrington	107	16	Murry	Conn	3			1		1	2		1				8		
Great Barrington	107	17	Bostwick	Adolphus	1			1		2			1				5		
Great Barrington	107	18	Dewey	Josiah	2	2		1			1	1	1				8		
Great Barrington	107	19	Burghardt	Lambert	1	2			1	2			1	1			8		
Great Barrington	107	20	Willson	Solomon	1		1			1			1				4		
Great Barrington	107	21	Matthews	Justice				1					1				2		
Great Barrington	107	22	Cherrytree	Reuben	3	1		1		2			1				8		
Great Barrington	107	23	Parmele	Joel		1			1			1	1				4		
Great Barrington	107	24	Bevins	James			1			1		1					3		
Great Barrington	107	25	Scripture	Simeon			1			1		1					4		
Great Barrington	107	26	Winchester	Stephen			1			1		1					3		
Great Barrington	107	27	Watson	Robert	2			2		1		1	1				7		
Great Barrington	107	28	Nie	Davis	1			1					1				3		
Great Barrington	107	29	Olmstead	Nehemiah			1				2		1				4		
Great Barrington	107	30	O'Brian	John			1	1				3		1			6		
Great Barrington	107	31	Beebee	Joseph		1	1		1		1			1			5		
Great Barrington	107	32	Orcott	Peter	1	1		1		2	1	1	2				9		
Great Barrington	107	33	Olmstead	Nathl	2			1	1		1		1				6		
Great Barrington	107	34	Hatch	Benjamin	3	1		1		1		2		1			10		
Great Barrington	107	35	Gray	Hezekiah				1						1			2		
Great Barrington	107	36	Palmer	Annie		1		1					1				3		
Great Barrington	107	37	Fairchild	Zacharia	2	1	1		1	2	3		1				11		
Great Barrington	107	38	Parsons	Oliver		1						1					2		
Great Barrington	107	39	Cherrytree	John	1			1		3			1				6		
Great Barrington	107	40	Knapp	Daniel	2	1		1		3	1	1	1				10		
Great Barrington	107	41	Van Deusen	John Jr	1	1		1		1			1				5		

TOWN	PG#	LN#	HEADS OF HOUSEHOLD — LAST NAME	FIRST NAME	FREE WHITE MALES under 10	10 to 16	16 to 26	26 to 45	45 and over	FREE WHITE FEMALES under 10	10 to 16	16 to 26	26 to 45	45 and over	TOTAL ALL OTHER	TOTAL SLAVES	TOTALS	DISTRICT/TOWNSHIP	NOTES
Great Barrington	107	42	Spencer	John		1		1					1				3		
Great Barrington	107	43	Comstock	Thomas	3			1		1	1		1				7		
Great Barrington	107	44	Robbinson	Andrew		1	1		1		1			1			5		
Great Barrington	107	45	Potter	Job	1	2	2		1	1	1	5	1				14		
Great Barrington	107	46	Burghardt	Hendrick			3	1	2		2	1	1	1			11		
Great Barrington	107	47	Kline	Conrad				1				2					3		
Great Barrington	107	48	Cook	Jesse					1				1				2		
Great Barrington	108	1	Cook	Serad	3	2		1		1	2	1	1				11		
Great Barrington	108	2	Root	Joshua	3			1		2			1				7		
Great Barrington	108	3	Davis	William	2	3	1		1	2	1	2	1	1			14		
Great Barrington	108	4	Hurd	Josiah		1			1	2	1			1			6		
Great Barrington	108	5	Nokes	Isaac	1		1		1	2		1		1			7		
Great Barrington	108	6	Conner	Daniel	1				1	3			1	1			7		
Great Barrington	108	7	Burghardt	Jack											11		11		
Great Barrington	108	8	Younglove	Oliver	1			1					2	1			5		
Great Barrington	108	9	Younglove	Jonathan	1			1					1				3		
Great Barrington	108	10	Buttolph	Roger		1			1				1				3		
Great Barrington	108	11	Hopkins	Daniel	2			1			2		1				6		
Great Barrington	108	12	Root	John		1		1	1			1	1				5		
Great Barrington	108	13	Huggins	John				1				1	1				3		
Great Barrington	108	14	Noble	David			1	2					1				4		
Great Barrington	108	15	Eddy	Briant	1	1		1		1	1		1				6		
Great Barrington	108	16	Robberts	John			1		1		2						4		
Great Barrington	108	17	Fullar	Joel	2	2	1	1					1				7		
Great Barrington	108	18	Dunham	Benajah					2	1				2			5		
Great Barrington	108	19	Chamberlain	Joel	2	1		1		1	2		1				8		
Great Barrington	108	20	Murray	Jack													4		
Great Barrington	108	21	Ross	James													4		
Great Barrington	108	22	Budd	John		1		1	2	1		2	1				8		
Great Barrington	108	23	Chapman	Barnabas			1		1		1		1	2			6		
Great Barrington	108	24	Wheeler	Payton R.	1			1				2					4		
Great Barrington	108	25	Louis	Ebenz	1	1			1	1	2		1				7		
Great Barrington	108	26	Root	David	1			1	1	2	1		1				7		
Great Barrington	108	27	Wadsworth	Reuben	2			1		1	1		1				6		
Great Barrington	108	28	Root	Israel			1		1				1				3		
Great Barrington	108	29	Knight	Samuel		1			1	1			1				4		
Great Barrington	108	30	Notewire	George	2	2			1	3			1				9		
Great Barrington	108	31	Douglas	Samuel	1			1					1				3		
Great Barrington	108	32	Kellogg	John		1	3		1			1		1			7		
Great Barrington	108	33	Church	Samuel	2	2	1	1		2		1	1				10		
Great Barrington	108	34	Powell	Elizabeth			1			2	2	1		1			7		
Great Barrington	108	35	Hurlbat	William		1			1	1		1		1			5		
Great Barrington	108	36	Beach	Josiah	1			1		1		1					4		
Great Barrington	108	37	Gibson	John 2d	2		1				1	2		1			7		
Great Barrington	108	38	Laird	Joseph	2	2	2	1		1	2		1				11		
Great Barrington	108	39	Judd	Elnathan	1			1		1	1		1				5		
Great Barrington	108	40	Ray	William	2	1	2		1	2	1	1	1	1			12		
Great Barrington	108	41	Wickwire	Jonas	1	1			1		2	1		1			7		
Great Barrington	108	42	North	Seth			1		1				1				3		
Great Barrington	108	43	Ray	James	1	2	1	1	1	1	4			1			12		
Great Barrington	108	44	Smith	Samuel		1	1		1			1		1			5		
Great Barrington	108	45	Smith	Jesse		2			1	4	1		1				9		
Great Barrington	108	46	Atwood	Phineas	3			1		2			1				7		
Great Barrington	108	47	Atwood	Hezekiah				1						1			2		
Great Barrington	108	48	Martin	Jesse				1									1		
Great Barrington	108	49	King	Asahel	2			1					1				4		
Great Barrington	109	1	Nichols	John					1		1		1	1			4		
Great Barrington	109	2	Billings	Samuel					1			1					2		
Great Barrington	109	3	Bliss	William	2	1			1	1	1	1		1			8		
Great Barrington	109	4	Deming	Justus	1	1		1		2			1				6		
Great Barrington	109	5	Umphrey	Hugh	1	1	3		1		2			1			9		
Great Barrington	109	6	Holdridge	Israel	3			1		1			1				6		
Great Barrington	109	7	Chapman	Ezra	1		2		1		2	3		1			10		
Great Barrington	109	8	Cheney	William	1						1		1				3		
Great Barrington	109	9	Van Deusen	Mathew			1						1				2		
Great Barrington	109	10	Avery	Miles		3		1		1	1		1				7		
Great Barrington	109	11	Fargo	Nehemiah	2	1	1	1		1	1		1				8		
Great Barrington	109	12	Dresser	David	1	1	1	1		1	1			1			7		
Great Barrington	109	13	Graham	Aaron	1			1	1	1			1	1			6		
Great Barrington	109	14	Chapman	Jebediah	2			1		1			1				5		
Great Barrington	109	15	Comstock	Lancaster					1					1			2		
Great Barrington	109	16	Comstock	Perrygrine	2	2	1		1	1	1	1	1				10		
Great Barrington	109	17	Comstock	Ebenz		1			1	4	1		1				8		
Great Barrington	109	18	Bolles	Hezekiah	1			1		2			1				5		
Great Barrington	109	19	Harris	Elijah	2		2		1	2	2	2		1			12		
Great Barrington	109	20	Harris	Elisha		1							1				2		
Great Barrington	109	21	Bradley	Josiah	2	1	1		1	2	2	1	1				11		
Great Barrington	109	22	Dobill	John	1	2			1	3		3	1				11		
Great Barrington	109	23	Andrews	Elisha		1	2		1			3		1			8		

TOWN	PG#	LN#	LAST NAME	FIRST NAME	FWM under 10	FWM 10 to 16	FWM 16 to 26	FWM 26 to 45	FWM 45 and over	FWF under 10	FWF 10 to 16	FWF 16 to 26	FWF 26 to 45	FWF 45 and over	TOTAL ALL OTHER	TOTAL SLAVES	TOTALS	DISTRICT/ TOWNSHIP	NOTES
Great Barrington	109	24	Bailey	Oliver			1		1	1	2		1				6		
Great Barrington	109	25	Bailey	Scoville			1			1			1				3		
Great Barrington	109	26	Porter	Nathaniel		1		1						2			4		
Great Barrington	109	27	Dickinson	Lodowick	1			1	1	2			1				6		
Great Barrington	109	28	Deming	Elijah				1					1				2		
Great Barrington	109	29	Patterson	David			1			1			1				3		
Great Barrington	109	30	Palmer	Nathan			1		1	1				1			4		
Great Barrington	109	31	Blackney	Eldad	1			1		1			1				4		
Great Barrington	109	32	Wheeler	Joshua	1				1	1				1			4		
Great Barrington	109	33	Orcutt	Moses	1				1		1			1			4		
Great Barrington	109	34	Denton	William	1		1		1	1	3			1			8		
Great Barrington	109	35	Denton	William Jr			1			2			1				4		
Great Barrington	109	36	Stimson	Anthony			2		1				3	1			7		
Great Barrington	109	37	Smith	Amos		1			1					1			3		
Great Barrington	109	38	Remele	Jacob	3		2		1	1	2	1		1			11		
Great Barrington	109	39	Prichard	Benjamin	2	2			1	3	1		1				10		
Great Barrington	109	40	Hubbard	Hezekiah	2	1		1		2			1				7		
Great Barrington	109	41	Heath	George	1			1		2	2	1		1			8		
Great Barrington	109	42	Phillips	Seth	1		1	1				1	1				5		
Great Barrington	109	43	Clark	Rodman	2	2	1			1			1				7		
Great Barrington	109	44	Tooley	Isaac				1			2		2				5		
Great Barrington	109	45	Kilborn	Elijah			1			2			1				4		
Great Barrington	109	46	Ross	William	3	1		1					1				6		
Great Barrington	109	47	Rhodes	John	1	1	1		1	1	2			2			9		
Great Barrington	109	48	Chadwick	Caleb	3	1			1	1				1			7		
Great Barrington	110	1	Tucker	Newman	2			1		1			1				5		
Great Barrington	110	2	Taylor	Elisha	2	1	2	1		3			1				10		
Great Barrington	110	3	Webster	John	1			1		2	2		1				7		
Great Barrington	110	4	Ross	Thomas			1	1						1			3		
Great Barrington	110	5	Collins	Jacob			1			1		1					3		
Great Barrington	110	6	Leaming	Jeremiah	2			1		3			1				7		
Great Barrington	110	7	Kilborn	Richard			1		1	1			1	1			5		
Great Barrington	110	8	Rice	Manly		1					1	1	4	1			8		
Great Barrington	110	9	Barrey	Jonathan				1					1				2		
Great Barrington	110	10	Rathbun	Nathanl				1					1	1			3		
Great Barrington	110	11	Manning	William			3	1		1			1				6		
Great Barrington	110	12	Rathbun	Samuel	1	2	1		1				3	1			9		
Great Barrington	110	13	Hall	Abel	1	2		1		2	1	1		1			9		
Great Barrington	110	14	Davis	Samuel	3	2		1		2			1				9		
Great Barrington	110	15	Joy	Ceasar											5		5		

TOWN	PG#	LN#	LAST NAME	FIRST NAME	FREE WHITE MALES					FREE WHITE FEMALES					TOTAL ALL OTHER	TOTAL SLAVES	TOTALS	DISTRICT/ TOWNSHIP	NOTES
					under 10	10 to 16	16 to 26	26 to 45	45 and over	under 10	10 to 16	16 to 26	26 to 45	45 and over					
Hancock	158	1	Goodrich	Daniel			2	5	7			3	7	6			30		
Hancock	158	2	Cogswell	Daniel			9	1				3	7				20		
Hancock	158	3	Slosson	Eliphalet			2	8				2	8				20		
Hancock	158	4	Talcott	John		1	1	3	4	1	1	2	4	4			21		
Hancock	158	5	Dewey	David		1	1		1	1		1		1			6		
Hancock	158	6	Stanton	Augustus			1		1	2	2		1				9		
Hancock	158	7	Mills	Daniel	1			1		1			1				4		
Hancock	158	8	Penfield	Isaac				1				1		1			3		
Hancock	158	9	Thompson	Lodowick	2			1					1				4		
Hancock	158	10	Stanton	Oliver				1		4		1					6		
Hancock	158	11	Goodrich	Timothy	2			1		2			1				6		
Hancock	158	12	Goodrich	Seth				1			1	1					3		
Hancock	158	13	Talcott	Israel			2	1	4			4		4			15		
Hancock	158	14	Shapley	David		1	1	1	1				1	1			6		
Hancock	158	15	Cummins	Nathan			1		1			1		1			4		
Hancock	158	16	Spires	John			3	4	5			4	3	14			33		
Hancock	158	17	Stovers	Amos			3	7	1			6	12	4			33		
Hancock	158	18	Smith	Joseph			3	1	4			5	2	8			23		
Hancock	158	19	Hall	Noah				2					4	4			10		
Hancock	158	20	Beldin	Daniel	1		1		1				1	1			5		
Hancock	159	1	Burdick	Wait			1						1	1			3		
Hancock	159	2	Burdick	Asa		1		1		3		1	1				7		
Hancock	159	3	Adams	Jacob	1			1		1			1				4		
Hancock	159	4	Stevens	Eliphalet			1	1				2		1			5		
Hancock	159	5	Stevens	Jeremiah	2			1		3			1				7		
Hancock	159	6	Chapman	Amasa	4	2	1		2	2	4	2		2			19		
Hancock	159	7	Lilly	Benjamin	2			1		1			1				5		
Hancock	159	8	Broad	Amos	1	1		1		1	2		1				7		
Hancock	159	9	Wood	Elisha	1			1		1			1				4		
Hancock	159	10	Cain	William O.	2			1		1			1				5		
Hancock	159	11	Fitch	Prentice	2	2		1		2	2		1				10		
Hancock	159	12	Smith	John	3			1		1	1		1				7		
Hancock	159	13	Lawrence	Aaron	3		2	1				1	1				8		
Hancock	159	14	Osborn	Hezekiah			1	1						1			3		
Hancock	159	15	Daniels	Reuben			1			3			1				5		
Hancock	159	16	Osborn	James	1	1	1	1		4	1	1	1				11		
Hancock	159	17	Hamton	Henry	1		1	1					1	1			5		
Hancock	159	18	Blading	Ephraim	2	1		1						1			5		
Hancock	159	19	Swift	Nathan		2		1					1	1			5		
Hancock	159	20	Martin	Simeon	2	1	1		1	3			2	1			11		
Hancock	159	21	Martin	Gideon	1	1			1		1	2	1				7		
Hancock	159	22	Gracher	Peter	1		1	1		2		1	1	1			9		
Hancock	159	23	Berry	William		2	1		1	2	1	2		1			10		
Hancock	159	24	Goodrich	John				2				3		1			6		
Hancock	159	25	Goodrich	Elijah		2			2	2	2		1	1			10		
Hancock	159	26	Goodrich	Uriah	2			1		2			1				6		
Hancock	159	27	Goodrich	Justus	2			1				1	1				5		
Hancock	159	28	Goodrich	Daniel	3			1		1			1				6		
Hancock	159	29	Barber	James	1		1						1				3		
Hancock	159	30	Burdick	Hasard	3			1		1	1		1				7		
Hancock	159	31	Goodrich	Solomon	1		1	1		2		1	1				7		
Hancock	159	32	Green	Archibald	2			1		2			1				6		
Hancock	159	33	Curtis	Jonah		1		1			1		1				4		
Hancock	159	34	Wiley	Robert	1	2	1		1	2	1			1			9		
Hancock	159	35	Pierce	Ephraim	1			1		1			1				4		
Hancock	159	36	Gardner	Caleb		1	2		1	1	1	2		1			9		
Hancock	159	37	Gardner	John	1		1						1				3		
Hancock	159	38	Cranstone	John	1	2		1		1	1	1					8		
Hancock	159	39	Vaughn	David	1				2		1			1			5		
Hancock	159	40	Vaughn	David Jun	2	1		1		2	2		1				9		
Hancock	160	1	Harris	George	2			1		1			1				6		
Hancock	160	2	Southworth	George	2		1	1		3		1	1				9		
Hancock	160	3	Hadrdel	Joseph			3		1	2		3	2	1			12		
Hancock	160	4	Vaughn	Jabez	2			1		3	1		1				8		
Hancock	160	5	Starkwather	Lemuel			2						1				3		
Hancock	160	6	Hall	George	3	1	2		1	2	1			1			11		
Hancock	160	7	Corey	Reuben			2		1		1			1			5		
Hancock	160	8	Tubs	Seth				1						1			2		
Hancock	160	9	Alger	Elijah	1			1		3	1		1				7		
Hancock	160	10	Corey	Benjamin	1			1		1			1				4		
Hancock	160	11	Palmer	Asahel	1	1	3		1	2	1		1				10		
Hancock	160	12	Hadrdel	Elijah	1			1		2			1				5		
Hancock	160	13	Potter	William				1		5			1				7		
Hancock	160	14	Pierce	Caleb	4	2		1		2	1		1				11		
Hancock	160	15	Jones	Benjamin	4	1		1			1		1				8		
Hancock	160	16	Grippin	Silas	2			1		1			1				5		
Hancock	160	17	Sherman	Edmond	1			1		2	3	1	1				9		
Hancock	160	18	Hadrdel	Isaac	3			1					1				5		
Hancock	160	19	Capron	Danfield	1	1			1	1			1				5		

TOWN	PG#	LN#	LAST NAME	FIRST NAME	FREE WHITE MALES					FREE WHITE FEMALES					TOTAL ALL OTHER	TOTAL SLAVES	TOTALS	DISTRICT/ TOWNSHIP	NOTES
					under 10	10 to 16	16 to 26	26 to 45	45 and over	under 10	10 to 16	16 to 26	26 to 45	45 and over					
Hancock	160	20	Niles	John		1		1		3	1		1				7		
Hancock	160	21	Briggs	Carey		2		1		1	2	1	1		1		9		
Hancock	160	22	Green	Benjamin	1			1		1			1	1			5		
Hancock	160	23	Austin	Elizabeth						3	1		1				5		
Hancock	160	24	Ford	Simeon	3	1		1			2		1				8		
Hancock	160	25	Rogers	Clark				1			1		1				3		
Hancock	160	26	Garr	Robert	2	1	1	1	1	2	1		1	1	1		12		
Hancock	160	27	Foster	Joshua	1	1	1	1	1	3			1				9		
Hancock	160	28	Garr	Caleb	2	2		1			1		1				7		
Hancock	160	29	Rogers	Gideon	3			1		1			1	1			7		
Hancock	160	30	Hazard	Rodman	2	1	1			2		1					7		
Hancock	160	31	Hazard	Henry				1			1		1				3		
Hancock	160	32	Clark	Caleb	3	1		1		1	1		1				8		
Hancock	160	33	Pierce	Ebenezer				1					1				2		
Hancock	160	34	Pierce	Sanford	1			1		1			1				4		
Hancock	160	35	Hall	Benjamin	1	1		1		2			1				6		
Hancock	160	36	Foster	John			3	1			1		1				6		
Hancock	160	37	Cunningham	John	1	1		1		3	1		1				8		
Hancock	160	38	Smith	Daniel	3			1		2	1		1				8		
Hancock	160	39	Jones	Amos	3			1					1				5		
Hancock	160	40	Bills	Jabez	2	1			1	1	1		1				7		
Hancock	161	1	Nichols	Jonathan	2			1		2	1		1				7		
Hancock	161	2	Corey	Abel	2			1		2			1				6		
Hancock	161	3	Howard	Jesse	3	1		1		1	2		1				9		
Hancock	161	4	Hand	Edmond	1			1				1					3		
Hancock	161	5	Ely	Reuben		1	2		1		1			1			6		
Hancock	161	6	Cogswell	Solomon	1		1		1		1			1			5		
Hancock	161	7	Eldridge	Rebecca	3	1		1		1	2	1	1				10		
Hancock	161	8	Dawley	Job		1	1		1		1	1	1	1			7		
Hancock	161	9	Eldridge	Thomas	1		2		1			1		1			6		
Hancock	161	10	Sweet	Jeremiah		2	1		1	1	2			1			8		
Hancock	161	11	Sweet	John				1		3			1				5		
Hancock	161	12	Perry	Josiah		1		1		2		1					5		
Hancock	161	13	King	Ward	1			1		1			1				4		
Hancock	161	14	Stafford	Thomas	1	2		1		4	2		1				11		
Hancock	161	15	Ely	John		1	4		1	1	1	2		1			10		
Hancock	161	16	Washburn	Samuel	2	2	2	1		1	1		1				10		
Hancock	161	17	King	Reuben	2	1		1		2	1		1				8		
Hancock	161	18	Gardner	Sylvester			2	1			1	2	1				7		
Hancock	161	19	Gardner	Willet	1		1				1	1					4		
Hancock	161	20	Kibbe	Samuel						4	1		1				6		
Hancock	161	21	Howe	Jonathan		1	1	1				1	1				5		
Hancock	161	22	Corey	Caleb			1			2		1					4		
Hancock	161	23	Corey	John	1			1		1			1				4		
Hancock	161	24	Fowler	Caleb	3	1		1		1	1		1				8		
Hancock	161	25	Morey	Gideon	1			1		4	3	1	1				11		
Hancock	161	26	Adams	Shubel	2			1		2		1					6		
Hancock	161	27	Smith	William	1	1	1		1	1	1	2		1			9		
Hancock	161	28	Jones	Daniel	1				1	2			1	1			6		
Hancock	161	29	Smith	Shubel	2	2	2	1		1	1	1	1				11		
Hancock	161	30	Straight	William	2		1		1	3		2		1			10		
Hancock	161	31	Brown	Elijah		1				2		1					4		
Hancock	161	32	Rounds	Joseph	2			1		1	2		1				7		
Hancock	161	33	Brown	Nathan			1			3			1				7		
Hancock	161	34	Strander	Abraham O		2		1		3	1		1				8		
Hancock	161	35		Cato (negro)									1		1		2		
Hancock	161	36	Glother	Asa	1		1	1			1		1				5		
Hancock	161	37	Stiles	John	1	1		1				1					4		
Hancock	161	38	Eldridge	Griffin	2			1		2			1				6		
Hancock	161	39	Remmington	Allen	2	1		1	1	3	2	1	1	1			13		
Hancock	161	40	Boss	John	2	1	1	1		1		1	1				8		
Hancock	162	1	Gardner	Nathaniel		1	1				1	1		1			6		
Hancock	162	2	Gardner	Robert	2	1	1	1		2	1		1	1			10		
Hancock	162	3	Hall	John				1					1				2		
Hancock	162	4	Green	Russel	3	2		1			1		1				8		
Hancock	162	5	Hadsdel	Nathan	1			1		3	1		1				7		
Hancock	162	6	Townier	Nathan	3	2		1		1	1		1	1			10		
Hancock	162	7	Townier	Martin	2	1	2	1		3	2	1	1				13		
Hancock	162	8	Gardner	Daniel				2		2	1		1				6		
Hancock	162	9	Townier	Martin Jun	1		1	1				1		1			5		
Hancock	162	10	Barber	Silas	2			1		2			1				6		
Hancock	162	11	Cowan	Isaac	1			1		3	2		1				8		
Hancock	162	12	Ellis	Gideon	1	1		1		1	1		1				6		
Hancock	162	13	Wheaton	Lucus	1			1		1			1				4		
Hancock	162	14	Kelley	Benjamin		1	1	1				1		1			5		
Hancock	162	15	Reynolds	James		1	2	1		1	1			2			8		
Hancock	162	16	Whitman	John				1									1		
Hancock	162	17	Olden	Gideon	1		3			1		1					6		
Hancock	162	18	Sweet	George	2	2			1	1			1				7		

TOWN	PG#	LN#	LAST NAME	FIRST NAME	M under 10	M 10 to 16	M 16 to 26	M 26 to 45	M 45 and over	F under 10	F 10 to 16	F 16 to 26	F 26 to 45	F 45 and over	TOTAL ALL OTHER	TOTAL SLAVES	TOTALS	DISTRICT/ TOWNSHIP	NOTES
Lanesborough	146	1	Allen	John	1		1						1				3		
Lanesborough	146	2	Allen	Peleg	1	1			1			2		1			6		
Lanesborough	146	3	Bagg	Aaron	2		1		1		2	2	1				9		
Lanesborough	146	4	Bacon	Samuel	1	1	1	1		4	1	1	1				11		
Lanesborough	146	5	Burhance	Henry	1			1					1				3		
Lanesborough	146	6	Billings	Daniel	1		2		1	1	3	2	1	1			12		
Lanesborough	146	7	Bradley	Uri	1	1	2	1					3		1		10		
Lanesborough	146	8	Bradley	Joel		1		2	1	1		1	1	1			8		
Lanesborough	146	9	Babbit	Samuel	1	2		1		1	1						7		
Lanesborough	146	10	Barnes	Joseph	3			1	1				1	1			7		
Lanesborough	146	11	Barnes	Joseph Jr		2	2		1		1			1	3		10		
Lanesborough	146	12	Bradley	Ephraim	1		1		1	1		1	1				6		
Lanesborough	146	13	Barker	Silas		1	1	3				1	1				7		
Lanesborough	146	14	Buck	Ebenezer	3	1			1	1	2		1				9		
Lanesborough	146	15	Bagg	Joseph			1		1			2		1			5		
Lanesborough	146	16	Bagg	Abner	1		1			1		1					4		
Lanesborough	146	17	Bagg	Silas	1			1		1		1					4		
Lanesborough	147	1	Bliss	Ebenezer			1					1	1				3		
Lanesborough	147	2	Bradley	Asahel	1	2		1		1		1	2				8		
Lanesborough	147	3	Bliss	Levi				1					1				2		
Lanesborough	147	4	Butler	Silas	1			1		1		1					4		
Lanesborough	147	5	Burgin	Benjamin		1		1					1				3		
Lanesborough	147	6	Brundige	Nathan		1				1		1					3		
Lanesborough	147	7	Babbit	David	2	1		1		1		1	1				7		
Lanesborough	147	8	Bradley	Joel 2d		1		1			1		1	1			5		
Lanesborough	147	9	Brundige	Nathan	1			1					1				3		
Lanesborough	147	10	Baker	Samuel		2		1		4	1	1	1				10		
Lanesborough	147	11	Burhance	Henry				1					1				2		
Lanesborough	147	12	Bingham	Eliphalet	2			1		1			1	1			6		
Lanesborough	147	13	Babbit	John			1	1				1	1				4		
Lanesborough	147	14	Baker	Bethiel	1	1	1	1	1			1		1			7		
Lanesborough	147	15	Baker	Francis	1	1		1				1		1			6		
Lanesborough	147	16	Baker	Benejab	2		1		1		2	2					9		
Lanesborough	147	17	Bull	Nehemiah		2			1					2			5		
Lanesborough	147	18	Clark	Hezekiah	3	1		1		2	2		1				10		
Lanesborough	147	19	Clark	Levi	1	2	4		1	2	1	2		1			14		
Lanesborough	147	20	Collins	Daniel	2			1		1	1		1				6		
Lanesborough	147	21	Church	Samuel W.	1		1			1			1				4		
Lanesborough	147	22	Carter	Peter B.	2	2	1		1	2	1	2		2			13		
Lanesborough	147	23	Curtis	Peter	1		1					1					3		
Lanesborough	148	1	Smith	Jonathan		2		1		1			1				5		
Lanesborough	148	2	Smith	Asahel	1	1	2	1		2		1	2				10		
Lanesborough	148	3	Wright	Josiah			1	1		1	1	1					5		
Lanesborough	148	4	Hubbell	Wolcott	2	1	2	1	1	2	1	2	2				14		
Lanesborough	148	5	Whitney	Timothy	3			1		1			1	1			7		
Lanesborough	148	6	Wells	Melankton W.	2		1	1		1			1	1			7		
Lanesborough	148	7	Wells	John			1					1					2		
Lanesborough	148	8	Weed	Jonathan	3	1		1		1	1		1				9		
Lanesborough	148	9	Talmage	Joseph	4	1	1		1	2		1		1			11		
Lanesborough	148	10	Hirch	Asher	2	3		1				1		1			8		
Lanesborough	148	11	Hall	Lyman	1	1	2	1		2	1		1				9		
Lanesborough	148	12	Johnson	George		2		1		1	1	1	1				7		
Lanesborough	148	13	Smith	George		1			1	2	1		1				6		
Lanesborough	148	14	Tiffany	Eleazer		1		1					1	1			4		
Lanesborough	148	15	Strong	Solomon			2					1					3		
Lanesborough	148	16	Wheeler	David				1				1		1			3		
Lanesborough	148	17	Wheeler	Samuel			1	1				1		1			4		
Lanesborough	148	18	Smith	Jacob			1	1	1				1				4		
Lanesborough	148	19	Sunderland	James	1			1		1		1					4		
Lanesborough	148	20	Rockwell	Josiah	3	1	1	1		2			1				9		
Lanesborough	148	21	Wheeler	Jonathan		2	1		1	1			1				6		
Lanesborough	148	22	Wheeler	William	1			1				1					4		
Lanesborough	148	23	More	Ishmael											5		5		
Lanesborough	148	24	Warren	Levi	5			1		1	1		1				9		
Lanesborough	148	25	Seymour	Levi			1			1		1					3		
Lanesborough	148	26	Redeway	Martha	1	1							2				4		
Lanesborough	148	27	Powell	Miles	2	1	1			1	1	1		1			9		
Lanesborough	148	28	Lamphier	Phinehas	1	2		1			2		1				7		
Lanesborough	148	29	Wildman	Nirum	1			1		1		1					4		
Lanesborough	148	30	Soot	Amos			1			1		1					3		
Lanesborough	148	31	Hall	Ambrose	1	2	3	1	1			2		2	1		13		
Lanesborough	148	32	Hatcher	Gamaliel	1			1		1		1	1				5		
Lanesborough	148	33	Hubbel	Calvin	1	4	4	2		2	1	1	1				16		
Lanesborough	148	34	Farnum	Joseph		1			1				1	1			4		
Lanesborough	148	35	Farnum	Joseph Jun		1						1					2		
Lanesborough	148	36	Williams	Eunice	3	1				2			1				7		
Lanesborough	148	37	Williams	Hoddan	1		1	1		1	1		1		1		7		
Lanesborough	149	1	Chilson	Louise			1		1			1	2	1			6		
Lanesborough	149	2	Wheeler	Gideon	1		1		1	1	2			1	1		8		

TOWN	PG#	LN#	LAST NAME	FIRST NAME	FREE WHITE MALES under 10	10 to 16	16 to 26	26 to 45	45 and over	FREE WHITE FEMALES under 10	10 to 16	16 to 26	26 to 45	45 and over	TOTAL ALL OTHER	TOTAL SLAVES	TOTALS	DISTRICT/TOWNSHIP	NOTES
Lanesborough	149	3	Nichols	David	1	1		1		2			1				6		
Lanesborough	149	4	Joseph	Cud (Negro)											4		4		
Lanesborough	149	5	Malby	Frederick			1			1		2			2		6		
Lanesborough	149	6	Thatcher	Gamaliel	1			1		1	1	1					5		
Lanesborough	149	7	Farnam	Benjamin		1		1		1		1		1			5		
Lanesborough	149	8	Foot	Joseph			1	1		1		1					4		
Lanesborough	149	9	Tuttle	Sarah	2					1			1				3		
Lanesborough	149	10	Youngs	John				1					1				2		
Lanesborough	149	11	Williams	Jedediah		1	1	1		1		1					5		
Lanesborough	149	12	Wilcox	Stephen		1		1		1		1					4		
Lanesborough	149	13	Hall	Ezra	2		1	1		1			1				6		
Lanesborough	149	14	Star	Samuel	1		1	1		1			1				5		
Lanesborough	149	15	Gregory	Elnathan	2	1	3	1		1	1	1	1				11		
Lanesborough	149	16	Rice	Adonijah		1	2		1		2	3	1				10		
Lanesborough	149	17	Rice	Asahel	2			1				1	1				5		
Lanesborough	149	18	Jarvis	Joseph	2	2	1		1	2	1		2				11		
Lanesborough	149	19	Walker	Mary								1					1		
Lanesborough	149	20	Card	William	1		1			2			1				5		
Lanesborough	149	21	Green	Jeremiah F.			2						1				3		
Lanesborough	149	22	Pettibone	Jonathan	1			1				1		1			4		
Lanesborough	149	23	Pettibone	Philo	2		1	1		3		1	1				9		
Lanesborough	149	24	Southwick	Warren			1			4			1	1			7		
Lanesborough	149	25	Pettibone	Amos	2			1		2	1		1				7		
Lanesborough	149	26	Robinson	Peter			1			1			1				3		
Lanesborough	149	27	Noble	Timothy				1	2		1	1		2			7		
Lanesborough	149	28	Wade	Silvanus	3			1		2			1				7		
Lanesborough	149	29	Turrell	Samuel			1		1	1		1		1			5		
Lanesborough	149	30	Youngs	John S.	1		1		1	1	1	1		1			6		
Lanesborough	149	31	Noble	Winthrop			1					1		1			3		
Lanesborough	149	32	Mason	Brooks	3			1		1			1				6		
Lanesborough	149	33	Northrop	Joseph	1		1		1	1	1			1			6		
Lanesborough	149	34	Powell	Mary						2			1				3		
Lanesborough	149	35	Powell	David			2	1				1	1				5		
Lanesborough	149	36	Horton	Asa	4	1		1		1			1				8		
Lanesborough	149	37	Hart	John		2		1			1	2	1				7		
Lanesborough	149	38	Stone	John				1		3			1				5		
Lanesborough	150	1	James	Jonathan					1		1	1		1			4		
Lanesborough	150	2	Farnham	John	1			1		1		1	1				5		
Lanesborough	150	3	Powell	Robert	2			1	1	2			2	1			9		
Lanesborough	150	4	Hubbel	Diah				1						1			2		
Lanesborough	150	5	Hubbel	Hicock	3	2		1		1			1				8		
Lanesborough	150	6	Wheeler	Simeon				1						1			2		
Lanesborough	150	7	Wheeler	Simeon Jr	1		1	1		2			2				7		
Lanesborough	150	8	Giffords	Rufus			1			1			1				3		
Lanesborough	150	9	Squire	Andrew	4	1		1		1	1		2				10		
Lanesborough	150	10	Squire	Bostwick	2			1				1	1				5		
Lanesborough	150	11	Durwin	Thomas		1	1		2		1	1		1			7		
Lanesborough	150	12	Day	Nehemiah	3			1		1			1				6		
Lanesborough	150	13	Day	Thomas	1	1		1					1				4		
Lanesborough	150	14	Jewitt	David		1			1		1		1				4		
Lanesborough	150	15	Darwin	Ephraim		1			1		1			1			4		
Lanesborough	150	16	Mead	Zadock	1		1					1					3		
Lanesborough	150	17	Thompson	Thomas	1				1	3	2		1				8		
Lanesborough	150	18	Powell	Thomas	2			1		1			1				5		
Lanesborough	150	19	Stoddard	Nathan	3			1		1			1				6		
Lanesborough	150	20	Powell	Ephraim	1			3	1			3					8		
Lanesborough	150	21	Guiteau	Francis	1	1	2		1			2	1				8		
Lanesborough	150	22	Turrell	Trueman		3	1	1		2		1	1				9		
Lanesborough	150	23	Stephens	Samuel	2	2	1		1			2		1			9		
Lanesborough	150	24	Godwin	Moses			1		1					1			3		
Lanesborough	150	25	Warren	Samuel		1		1		1				1			4		
Lanesborough	150	26	Warren	Seth				1		1		1		1			4		
Lanesborough	150	27	Warren	Daniel				1		1		1	1				4		
Lanesborough	150	28	Turrell	John		2	1	1		1	1		2				8		
Lanesborough	150	29	Pettibone	Elisha			1			3		1	1				6		
Lanesborough	150	30	Pettibone	Roger	3	2		1		1	1	1	1				10		
Lanesborough	150	31	Redeway	Joel	1		1	1		2	3	1		1			10		
Lanesborough	150	32	Umberfield	Samuel			1			1		1					3		
Lanesborough	150	33	Fuller	Zadock	3			1	1				1	1			8		
Lanesborough	150	34	Camp	Daniel											3		3		
Lanesborough	150	35	Webster	Clark	2		1						1				4		
Lanesborough	150	36	Goodwich	Ashbel		1	2	1		2	1	2	1				10		
Lanesborough	151	1	Pratt	John		2	2	1				2	1				8		
Lanesborough	151	2	Dunton	Nathaniel	2			1		2				1			6		
Lanesborough	151	3	Turner	Peregreen	4	1		1				1	1				8		
Lanesborough	151	4	Powell	Solomon	1			1		2		1	1				6		
Lanesborough	151	5	Platt	Abiel		2	1	1				2		1			7		
Lanesborough	151	6	Powell	Samuel	1	1		1		1			1				5		
Lanesborough	151	7	Powell	William	2			1		1			2				6		

TOWN	PG#	LN#	LAST NAME	FIRST NAME	FREE WHITE MALES under 10	10 to 16	16 to 26	26 to 45	45 and over	FREE WHITE FEMALES under 10	10 to 16	16 to 26	26 to 45	45 and over	TOTAL ALL OTHER	TOTAL SLAVES	TOTALS	DISTRICT/ TOWNSHIP	NOTES
Lanesborough	151	8	Lockwood	Jeremiah	3	1		1		1			1				7		
Lanesborough	151	9	Short	Daniel	1			1		3			1				6		
Lanesborough	151	10	Umphry	Chauncy	1		1			1		1					4		
Lanesborough	151	11	Clark	Jahleel	1	1	1	1	1		1	1	1	1			9		
Lanesborough	151	12	Woodson	John	2			1		2			1				6		
Lanesborough	151	13	Green	Nathan	1			1		1	1	1					5		
Lanesborough	151	14	Wilson	Abner	1	2	1		1	1	1		1				8		
Lanesborough	151	15	Loomis	Elijah	1			1		3		1					6		
Lanesborough	151	16	Lincoln	Jonathan	2		1	1		1		1					6		
Lanesborough	151	17	Talcott	Nehemiah			2	1		3		1	1				8		
Lanesborough	151	18	Hall	John	1	2	1	1					1	1			7		
Lanesborough	151	19	Osborn	John	2	1		1		1	2		1				8		
Lanesborough	151	20	Goodrich	Thomas	1	2	1		1	2		1		1			9		
Lanesborough	151	21	Goodrich	James					1		1			1			3		
Lanesborough	151	22	Reed	Thomas	2	1		1		2			1				7		
Lanesborough	151	23	Sprague	Peter	2			1		3	1		1				8		
Lanesborough	151	24	Lyon	Seth	1			1		2			1				5		
Lanesborough	151	25	Sherman	Job	3	1		1		4			1				10		
Lanesborough	151	26	Sherman	Timothy	2	2		1			2	1	1				9		
Lanesborough	151	27	Sherman	Joel				1					1				2		
Lanesborough	151	28	Hitchcock	Jesse	2	1		1		1	2		1				8		
Lanesborough	151	29	Wilson	Josiah	1		1		1	1			1				5		
Lanesborough	151	30	Perkins	John	4			1					1				6		
Lanesborough	151	31	Lyon	Thomas	1	1	1		1	1	1	1		1			8		
Lanesborough	151	32	Garlick	Seth				1			1			1			3		
Lanesborough	151	33	Corhal	Thomas				1						1			2		
Lanesborough	151	34	Garlick	Seth Jun			1			2		1					4		
Lanesborough	151	35	Hoyt	David H.			1			3			1				5		
Lanesborough	151	36	Hollister	George				1					1				2		
Lanesborough	151	37	Covell	William	1			1		2			1				5		
Lanesborough	151	38	Phelps	Elijah	2			1		4	1		1				9		
Lanesborough	151	39	Mead	Stephen	3		1	1		1	3		1	1			11		
Lanesborough	152	1	Jecocks	Samuel	1	1		1			1		1				5		
Lanesborough	152	2	Wood	Titus	4	1	1	1			3	1	1				12		
Lanesborough	152	3	Garlick	Henry	2			1	2	2			1	1			9		
Lanesborough	152	4	Sherlock	Ichabod			2			1	2			1			6		
Lanesborough	152	5	Lasell	Joshua	1		1	1	1	1		1		1			7		
Lanesborough	152	6	Hungerford	Thomas	1	2			1				1				8		
Lanesborough	152	7	Terrey	Hiram	2			1		4	2		1				10		
Lanesborough	152	8	Potter	Peleg	1	1	1		1		2	2		1			9		
Lanesborough	152	9	Potter	Jesse			1					1					2		
Lanesborough	152	10	Rice	Jehiel	1	2	1	1		2			1				8		
Lanesborough	152	11	Smith	John	1			1		1			1				4		
Lanesborough	152	12	Collins	William	1			1		1			1				4		
Lanesborough	152	13	Newell	Ebenezer	1			2	1		1	1		1			7		
Lanesborough	152	14	Smith	Isaac			1		1				1	1			4		
Lanesborough	152	15	Stearns	Ebenezer	2	1		1		3	2	1		1			12		
Lanesborough	152	16	Squire	Andrew	1		1	1	1	1		1	1				8		
Lanesborough	152	17	Squire	Amos	1			1		2			1				5		
Lanesborough	152	18	Tillotson	Bejamin	1	1		1		1			1	1			6		
Lanesborough	152	19	Norton	Charles		1	2		1		2	1		1			8		
Lanesborough	152	20	Casey	Edward	2		1		1	2	1		1				8		
Lanesborough	152	21	Smith	Isaac		1		1		1			1				4		
Lanesborough	152	22	Durwin	Ephraim Jr		1	1	1			1		1				5		
Lanesborough	152	23	Perkins	Joseph	3	1		1		2			1				8		
Lanesborough	152	24	Walker	Elias	1	1			1	1	2	2		1			9		
Lanesborough	152	25	Hoyt	Jonathan L.	1		2	1			2	1	1				8		
Lanesborough	152	26	Newton	Gershom				1		5			1		1		8		
Lanesborough	152	27	Simonds	James	2			1		2			1				6		
Lanesborough	152	28	Newton	Philo	4	1		1					1		2		9		
Lanesborough	152	29	Skeels	David	1				1	2			1				5		
Lanesborough	152	30	Merrils	Asa	2			1					1	1			5		
Lanesborough	152	31	Fisk	Charles	2	1		1		2			1				7		
Lanesborough	152	32	Powell	John	3	2	1		1	2	1		1	1			12		
Lanesborough	152	33	Durwin	Hannah	1	1	1			3	1		1				8		
Lanesborough	152	34	Durwin	Russel	3	2		1		3			1				10		
Lanesborough	152	35	Wright	Eli				1			1	1		1			4		
Lanesborough	152	36	Stodard	Lemuel	2			1		1			1				5		
Lanesborough	153	1	Rublee	William	3		1	1		1		1	1				8		
Lanesborough	153	2	Stearns	Isaac		1		1				1	1				4		
Lanesborough	153	3	Prince	Phebe											5		5		
Lanesborough	153	4	Carven	James		2	1					1		1			6		

TOWN	PG#	LN#	LAST NAME	FIRST NAME	FREE WHITE MALES					FREE WHITE FEMALES					TOTAL ALL OTHER	TOTAL SLAVES	TOTALS	DISTRICT/ TOWNSHIP	NOTES
					under 10	10 to 16	16 to 26	26 to 45	45 and over	under 10	10 to 16	16 to 26	26 to 45	45 and over					
Lee	259	1	Austin	James	1			1			1		1				4		
Lee	259	2	Bassett	Cornelius Jr	2	1			1		2		1				7		
Lee	259	3	Baikus	Seth	3	2	2		1		2		1				11		
Lee	259	4	Baikus	Nathan			1										1		
Lee	259	5	Ball	Nathan			1	1		2		1					5		
Lee	259	6	Bailey	Thomas	3			1		1		1					6		
Lee	259	7	Bassett	Isaac				1		1		1	1	1			5		
Lee	259	8	Bassett	Cornelius		2	1		1	3			1				8		
Lee	259	9	Barlow	Lemuel	3	1		1		1			1				7		
Lee	259	10	Barlow	Seth			1		1	1				1			4		
Lee	259	11	Bassett	Nathan	2	1		1		1	1	2	1				9		
Lee	259	12	Barlow	Peleg			1			1			1		1		4		
Lee	259	13	Burden	Lot		1		1		3			1				6		
Lee	259	14	Burden	Seth	2			1		1			1				5		
Lee	259	15	Baker	David	3	1		1		2	1	1					9		
Lee	259	16	Bassett	Anne	1	1		1			1						4		
Lee	259	17	Bennett	George		1			1	2			1				5		
Lee	259	18	Blackman	Jonathan					1				1	1			3		
Lee	259	19	Ball	John		2	2			1	2		1				8		
Lee	259	20	Bradley	Stephen	2			1		1			1				5		
Lee	259	21	Baikus	Ichabod	2	2			1	1			1				7		
Lee	259	22	Barlow	Reuben	1			1		1			1				4		
Lee	259	23	Bradley	Eli	2	1	2	1		1	3		1				11		
Lee	259	24	Baikus	Lydia								2	1	1			4		
Lee	259	25	Bradley	Jared	2		1	1		1	2	1	1				9		
Lee	259	26	Bradley	Joseph	1		1	1		3			1				7		
Lee	259	27	Bradley	Jesse & Jesse Jr		1		1	1	4	1		1	1			10		
Lee	259	28	Baikus	Wally	1			1		2		1					5		
Lee	259	29	Bassett	Nathan	1		1		1	1	2	2	1	1			10		
Lee	259	30	Burden	Noah		1			1					2			4		
Lee	259	31	Baikus	Marcy										1			1		
Lee	259	32	Crocker	Jedediah		2	1	1		3	1		1				9		
Lee	260	1	Chadwick	Abiatha	2	1			1	3	1	1	1				10		
Lee	260	2	Couch	Samuel		1		1		2			1				5		
Lee	260	3	Couch	Stephen	1		1	1		2	2		1				8		
Lee	260	4	Couch	John Jr	1	1	1		1	2	1	1	1				9		
Lee	260	5	Crocker	Josiah	3			1				1	1	1			7		
Lee	260	6	Chase	Levi		1	1		1	2			1				6		
Lee	260	7	Crosby	John Jr	1		2	1		1		1					6		
Lee	260	8	Crosby	Abijah	2			1				1					4		
Lee	260	9	Crosby	John		1		1	1		1		1				5		
Lee	260	10	Chanter	George		1	1		1				1				4		
Lee	260	11	Chanter	William	1		1		1				1				4		
Lee	260	12	Clarke	Jesse	3	1		1		2	2	1	1				11		
Lee	260	13	Church	Anna						1	1		1				3		
Lee	260	14	Church	Levi		1	1					1					3		
Lee	260	15	Childs	Job	2			1	1			1		1			6		
Lee	260	16	Childs	William		1											1		
Lee	260	17	Crocker	Joseph	3		1		1	2	3		1				11		
Lee	260	18	Chadwick	Sama		2	1							2			5		
Lee	260	19	Clarke	Jabez	4	2	3	1		1	1	2	1				15		
Lee	260	20	Clarke	Jonathan	2	3		1		2			1				9		
Lee	260	21	Chadwick	Archelaus	2	2		1		1	1			1			8		
Lee	260	22	Culver	Simon	2			1		3			1				7		
Lee	260	23	Crocker	Elisha	2	2			1	2		3	1				11		
Lee	260	24	Chadwick	Thomas			1					1					2		
Lee	260	25	Dimmick	Sylvanus					1	1		1					3		
Lee	260	26	Davies	Samuel	3	1	1		1	1	1	1	1				10		
Lee	260	27	Davies	Nathan	2	1		1		2	1	2	1				10		
Lee	260	28	Davies	Isaac				1						2			3		
Lee	260	29	Davies	Calvin	1			1				1					3		
Lee	260	30	Dickinson	Elizar			1	1	1		1	2	1				7		
Lee	260	31	Dodge	Elisha		1											1		
Lee	260	32	Dillingham	Nathan	4		1	1		1	2	1	1				11		
Lee	260	33	Davies	Hope				1					1				2		
Lee	260	34	Dexter	Stephen	1		1	1		2		1					6		
Lee	260	35	Ewer	Paul	3	1			1	1	1		1				8		
Lee	260	36	Ellis	John	1			1		2			1				5		
Lee	261	1	Foot	Asahel	2	1		1	1	2			2	1			10		
Lee	261	2	Foot	David		2		1		2	1		1				7		
Lee	261	3	Foot	Fenner	3		2	1		2	1	1	1				11		
Lee	261	4	Foot	Jonathan Jr		2	1			1	1		1				7		
Lee	261	5	Foot	Alvin	1		1					1					3		
Lee	261	6	Freeman	Elisha	1	1	1		1	1	2		1				8		
Lee	261	7	Freeman	William	2		1			2			1				6		
Lee	261	8	Freeman	John		1	2		1		3		1				8		
Lee	261	9	Foot	Elisha	1		1			1	1	2					6		
Lee	261	10	Foot	William		1		1		2		1					5		
Lee	261	11	Finney	Calvin			1										1		

TOWN	PG#	LN#	LAST NAME	FIRST NAME	FREE WHITE MALES under 10	10 to 16	16 to 26	26 to 45	45 and over	FREE WHITE FEMALES under 10	10 to 16	16 to 26	26 to 45	45 and over	TOTAL ALL OTHER	TOTAL SLAVES	TOTALS	DISTRICT/ TOWNSHIP	NOTES
Lee	261	12	Fuller	Jethro	2	1		1		1			1				6		
Lee	261	13	Fordick	Ezeka				1					1				2		
Lee	261	14	Gifford	Sylvanus				1					1				2		
Lee	261	15	Gifford	Jesse	1	2		1		1	2	3	1				11		
Lee	261	16	Gifford	Cornell				1					1				2		
Lee	261	17	Gifford	John	1	1	1	1		1	1	1	1				8		
Lee	261	18	Gifford	James	2			1		1			1				5		
Lee	261	19	Green	John	4			1		1			1				7		
Lee	261	20	Grant	Elisha	1	1	1		1		1	1		1			7		
Lee	261	21	Gardner	Lodwick			1			1		1					3		
Lee	261	22	Gardner	John		1						1					2		
Lee	261	23	Garfield	Enoch		2	1		1	1	1			1			7		
Lee	261	24	Griffin	Samuel	1			1		1		1					4		
Lee	261	25	Gardner	William		1						1					2		
Lee	261	26	Gardner	Varnum	1			1		2		1					5		
Lee	261	27	Hurlburt	William		1	1					1					3		
Lee	261	28	Hyde	Alvan	3		1	1		1		1	1				8		
Lee	261	29	Hall	Moses	4			1		2	1		1				10		
Lee	261	30	Hall	David		1											1		
Lee	261	31	Heath	Abraham	1			1		2			1				5		
Lee	261	32	Heath	John	1	1		1		3	1		2				9		
Lee	261	33	Howk	Isaac	3	1		1		1	1		1		1		9		
Lee	261	34	Hamblin	Job		1		1						1			3		
Lee	261	35	Hamblin	Cornelius	2			1					1				4		
Lee	261	36	Hamblin	David		1		1		2		1		1			6		
Lee	261	37	Hatch	Wait				1						1			2		
Lee	262	1	Handy	Joseph & Seth			1	1						1			3		
Lee	262	2	Hall	John				1									1		
Lee	262	3	Hinkley	Heman	2	2	1	1	1	1		1	1	1			11		
Lee	262	4	Hinkley	Joseph			1			2	1						4		
Lee	262	5	Hinkley	Edmund			1			1				1			3		
Lee	262	6	Hatch	Jonah				1						1			2		
Lee	262	7	Hulett	Samuel	1	1		1		2			1				6		
Lee	262	8	Hulett	John	3			1		1	1	1	1	1			9		
Lee	262	9	Hulett	Asa	3			1		1			1				6		
Lee	262	10	Hulett	Sylvanus	1	1		1		3	1		1				8		
Lee	262	11	Hurlburt	Christopher		1	1	1		1	1						6		
Lee	262	12	Hurlburt	Nathanl	2	1		1				2	1	1			8		
Lee	262	13	Hurlburt	Royal	1			1				1					3		
Lee	262	14	Hinkley	Benja	1	1		1			1	1					5		
Lee	262	15	Humphrey	Elias	1		1			1	1	1					5		
Lee	262	16	Howland	Nathanll		1						2		1			5		
Lee	262	17	Ingersoll	William			1							1			2		
Lee	262	18	Ingersoll	William Jr	3	2		1		1	1	1	1				10		
Lee	262	19	Ingersoll	David	2	1	1	1		4	1	1	1	1			13		
Lee	262	20	Ingersoll	Elijah	5		1	1			2	2	1				12		
Lee	262	21	Ingersoll	Calvin	4			1		1	1	1					9		
Lee	262	22	Ingersoll	Jared	3	2		1		2	2		1				11		
Lee	262	23	Ingersoll	Moses	1		1		1	1			1				5		
Lee	262	24	Jenkins	Ebenezer		1		1						1			3		
Lee	262	25	Jenkins	Ebenz Junr	4			1		1		1					7		
Lee	262	26	Jones	Samuel	1			1		3			1				6		
Lee	262	27	Keep	John	3	2		1			1		1				8		
Lee	262	28	Langdon	John	1	1		1			1			2			6		
Lee	262	29	Langdon	Christopher	1					1			1				3		
Lee	262	30	Leonard	Samll		1											1		
Lee	262	31	Maltby	Zacherus	1		1	1		1		1	1				6		
Lee	262	32	Monson	Freeman		4	1	1		4			1				11		
Lee	262	33	Morey	Edy	2			1		1			1				5		
Lee	262	34	Marsh	Reuben	3			1		1			1				6		
Lee	262	35	Merrill	Abijah	1	2		1				2		1			7		
Lee	262	36	Nye	Lewis Jun		1		1				1		1			4		
Lee	262	37	Nye	Seth	1		1	1		1	1	1					7		
Lee	262	38	Nye	John	1	2		2		2		1	1	1			10		
Lee	263	1	Nash	James		1											1		
Lee	263	2	Orton	Roger	4	1	1	1		1	2		1				11		
Lee	263	3	Parker			3	1	1		2			1				8		First name blank
Lee	263	4	Perry	Abraham	2	1		1		1	1		1				7		
Lee	263	5	Parker	George	1	1		1		2	1	1		1			8		
Lee	263	6	Porter	Samuel		1		1		1	2	2		1			8		
Lee	263	7	Porter	Ebenezer			1										1		
Lee	263	8	Porter	David			2	1			2		1				6		
Lee	263	9	Perrin	Edward	2	1		1		2	2		1				9		
Lee	263	10	Pearce	Isaac		1											1		
Lee	263	11	Perry	William		1		1				3	1	1			7		
Lee	263	12	Prout	William		1		1						1			3		
Lee	263	13	Powers	John				1						1			2		
Lee	263	14	Polly	Eleazer			1						1				2		
Lee	263	15	Penayer	James	1		1	1				1		1			5		
Lee	263	16	Putnam	Rebekah	1					1			1				3		

TOWN	PG#	LN#	HEADS OF HOUSEHOLD LAST NAME	FIRST NAME	FREE WHITE MALES under 10	10 to 16	16 to 26	26 to 45	45 and over	FREE WHITE FEMALES under 10	10 to 16	16 to 26	26 to 45	45 and over	TOTAL ALL OTHER	TOTAL SLAVES	TOTALS	DISTRICT/ TOWNSHIP	NOTES
Lee	263	17	Peet	Elijah	2	1		1		1		1	1				7		
Lee	263	18	Perritt	Mary						1	1		1				3		
Lee	263	19	Robinson	Levi		1		1		3	1	1	1				8		
Lee	263	20	Roberts	Amos	2	1		1		1		1	1				7		
Lee	263	21	Remel	John			1			2			1				4		
Lee	263	22	Rathburn	John			1					1					2		
Lee	263	23	Ramsdale	John	1	1	1		1		1	1		1			7		
Lee	263	24	Stevens	Benja	2			1		1	3		1				8		
Lee	263	25	Stevens	Daniel		1	2		1					1			5		
Lee	263	26	Stevens	James	3		1	1			1		1				7		
Lee	263	27	Stevens	John	2	1	1		1	1	1	2	1				10		
Lee	263	28	Squire	Ebenz		1		2			1		1				5		
Lee	263	29	Sturges	William	1		1	1		2		1		1			7		
Lee	263	30	Stanton	Rufus	2		1		1	1		1		1			7		
Lee	263	31	Sheldon	Ephraim		1			1	1	1	1		1			6		
Lee	263	32	Stone	Squier	4		1	1		1	1		1				9		
Lee	263	33	Santer	Danl											2		2		
Lee	264	1	Smith	Benja		1	1		1	1	1			1			7		
Lee	264	2	Sargeant	Erastus			1										1		
Lee	264	3	Seymour	John	2	1		1		1			1				6		
Lee	264	4	Thayer	Nathan	2			1					1				4		
Lee	264	5	Tyler	Ruth					1					2			3		
Lee	264	6	Tobey	Nathanl			1	1		1	1	1		1			6		
Lee	264	7	Tobey	Stephen		2	1	1		2	1						7		
Lee	264	8	Tuttle	James	1			1		1	1			1			5		
Lee	264	9	Thatcher	John	2		1	1		2			1				7		
Lee	264	10	Taylor	William			1					1					2		
Lee	264	11	Thomas	Elijah	1	1	1	1		1	1		1				7		
Lee	264	12	Thatcher	Rowland			2	1	1			2	1	1			8		
Lee	264	13	Tilley	Samll			1						1				2		
Lee	264	14	Duzen	Matthew	1		1		1	1	2			1			7		
Lee	264	15	Vallett	Jeremiah					1					1			2		
Lee	264	16	Wormer	Jeremiah		2			1			1		1			5		
Lee	264	17	Williams	Ephraim			1						1				2		
Lee	264	18	Winegar	Samll	1		1			1			1				4		
Lee	264	19	Woodruff	James	1				1	2			1				5		
Lee	264	20	West	Elijah	2	1	3		1	2	1		1				11		
Lee	264	21	Whitney	William		1	1		1	2	1	2	1	3			12		
Lee	264	22	Warner	Aaron	1	1	1			1			1				6		
Lee	264	23	Willcox	Peter		1		1				2		1			5		
Lee	264	24	Willcox	Daniel	1			1		1			1				4		
Lee	264	25	Winegar	Elizabeth			3				1	1	1	1			7		
Lee	264	26	Wansey	Henry	2	2	1	1		3	1	1	1				12		
Lee	264	27	Willoughby	Josiah				1		3			1				5		
Lee	264	28	West	Ebenz	3	1	2	1		1	2		1				11		
Lee	264	29	West	Oliver		1	3		1				1	1			7		
Lee	264	30	Winegar	Jacob	1			1		1			1				4		
Lee	264	31	Whiten	Joseph	1		1	1		3	1		1				8		
Lee	264	32	Whiton	James			1										1		
Lee	264	33	Wedger	Abel	2			1					1				4		
Lee	264	34	West	Levi	1			1		2		1	1				6		
Lee	264	35	Willcox	Edward	3	1		1		1	1		1				8		
Lee	264	36	Yale	Josiah	1	2			1	2		3	1				10		
Lee	264	37	Yale	John			1										1		

TOWN	PG#	LN#	LAST NAME	FIRST NAME	FREE WHITE MALES					FREE WHITE FEMALES					TOTAL ALL OTHER	TOTAL SLAVES	TOTALS	DISTRICT/ TOWNSHIP	NOTES
					under 10	10 to 16	16 to 26	26 to 45	45 and over	under 10	10 to 16	16 to 26	26 to 45	45 and over					
Lenox	209	1	Abbot	Seth	2			1		1			1				5		
Lenox	209	2	Beldin	Oliver Jun	1	1	1	1	2	1			2				9		
Lenox	209	3	Bateman	Luther	1	1			1	1	2	2		1			9		
Lenox	209	4	Billins	N*1	1	1	1	1		1	1		1				7		
Lenox	209	5	Barrot	Nathan	2		2		1					1			6		
Lenox	209	6	Beldin	Oliver	1		1		1			1		1			5		
Lenox	209	7	Brown	Thomas	2	1		1		2		1	1				8		
Lenox	209	8	Butler	Jethro	2		3		1	2	2		1				11		
Lenox	209	9	Brewer	Eliab	4			1					1				6		
Lenox	209	10	Bozworth	David	1	1	2		2	1		2		2			11		
Lenox	209	11	Benton	Amos			1	1				1					3		
Lenox	209	12	Blossom	Enos	1	2	2		1	3			1				10		
Lenox	209	13	Bangs	Abner	3	2		1		1	1		1				9		
Lenox	209	14	Bangs	Elisha				1					1				2		
Lenox	209	15	Butler	Matthew		1	1	1		1	2	2	1				9		
Lenox	209	16	Booth	Lemuel				1		1	2		1				5		
Lenox	209	17	Carrol	James	1			1	1	3		1	2				9		
Lenox	209	18	Collins	Lemuel		1	1		1		1	3		1			8		
Lenox	209	19	Carpenter	Joshua	2			1		3			1				7		
Lenox	209	20	Chapman	Jesse	3	1	1	1	1	1			1				9		
Lenox	209	21	Dunbar	David	3		1	1		2	1	1	1				10		
Lenox	209	22	Dunbar	Samuel				1			1		1				3		
Lenox	209	23	Dunbar	Daniel			1		1		1	1					4		
Lenox	209	24	Drury	Paul	1	1	1	1	1	2	2	1	1	1			12		
Lenox	209	25	Drury	Paul Junr	1	1		1		1	1		1				6		
Lenox	209	26	Dunham	Joseph	2	2	1	1		1	1		1				9		
Lenox	209	27	Egleston	Azariah	1		1	1		3			2		2		10		
Lenox	209	28	Foster	Jedidiah	1	1	2	1				2	1				8		
Lenox	209	29	Foster	Jonathan			1	1			1		1	1	1		5		
Lenox	210	1	Hadley	Samuel		2		2	2	1	3		1				11		
Lenox	210	2	Ford	Ichabod	1		1		1			1		1			5		
Lenox	210	3	Goodwin	Joseph	3		1	1		2	3	1	1				12		
Lenox	210	4	Gates	Elijah	1		2		1	2	2	2		1			11		
Lenox	210	5	Gates	Thomas		1			1			1		1			4		
Lenox	210	6	Gregory	John	2		1	2		1		1	1				8		
Lenox	210	7	Glezen	Amasa	1		1	1		1	1		1				6		
Lenox	210	8	Goodspead	William		1	1		1			1		1			5		
Lenox	210	9	Hunt	John	2	2	1	1		1			1				8		
Lenox	210	10	Hayward	Moses			1	1			1		1				4		
Lenox	210	11	Hubbard	Zadoch P.	1			1		3			1				6		
Lenox	210	12	Hamlin	Ichabod	2	1			1		1	2		1			8		
Lenox	210	13	Hollister	Gurdin	2			1		2			1				6		
Lenox	210	14	Hamlin	Nathaniel		1	1		1			1		1			5		
Lenox	210	15	Hinsdale	Jonathan			1	1					1				3		
Lenox	210	16	Hill	Ashbel	1		1	1		2			1				6		
Lenox	210	17	Hyde	Andrew				1				1	1				3		
Lenox	210	18	Hunt	Benjamin	1		1	1		3			1	1			8		
Lenox	210	19	Hyde	Andrew Junr	1		2	1		3			1				8		
Lenox	210	20	Hyde	Caleb			2	1		1			1		1		6		
Lenox	210	21	Hubbard	Zadoch			3		1	1	1	3		1			10		
Lenox	210	22	Judd	Uriah	1	2		1		1			1				6		
Lenox	210	23	Judd	Seymour	1			1					1				3		
Lenox	210	24	Jubell	Nathan	2	1		1	1	2	1		1				9		
Lenox	210	25	Judd	Samuel		1	1		1		1	2		1			7		
Lenox	210	26	Judd	Keziah		1					1	3		1			6		
Lenox	210	27	Landers	Asael	2	1		1		2		1	1				8		
Lenox	210	28	Landers	Thomas				1					1				2		
Lenox	210	29	Loomis	Andrew	1	1		1	1		1			1			6		
Lenox	210	30	Lewis	Eldad	3		2		1	1		1	1				9		
Lenox	210	31	Malloon	Charles		1	1		1		1	2	1	1			8		
Lenox	210	32	Martindale	Edward	1	1	2		1	1	1	1	1	1			10		
Lenox	210	33	Metcalf	Alton	1			1		2			1				5		
Lenox	210	34	Morrel	John	4	1	1		1	1			1	1			10		
Lenox	210	35	Murwin	Moses				1		2	1	1		1			6		
Lenox	210	36	Northrup	Elijah	1	1			1			1		1			5		
Lenox	210	37	Newell	Josiah			2		1		1			1			5		
Lenox	210	38	Osborn	Josiah	1		4		1		1			1			8		
Lenox	210	39	Peck	Elisha	1	2		1		1		1	1				8		
Lenox	210	40	Parker	Titus Jun	1			1			1		1				4		
Lenox	210	41	Parker	Marcy	2					1			1				4		
Lenox	211	1	Parker	Titus	1			1				1	1				4		
Lenox	211	2	Percival	Elisha	1		1		1		1	2	1	1			8		
Lenox	211	3	Quincy	Samuel	2			1		1			1				5		
Lenox	211	4	Randel	Jesse	1			2		2			1				6		
Lenox	211	5	Rash	Jacob	3	1			1	1	1		1	1			9		
Lenox	211	6	Root	Reuben	1	2	2		1			1		1			8		
Lenox	211	7	Sears	David		1	1		1				1				4		
Lenox	211	8	Sears	Philip	1	1		1		1			1				5		
Lenox	211	9	Shepard	Samuel	1	1		1		1	1		1				6		

TOWN	PG#	LN#	LAST NAME	FIRST NAME	FREE WHITE MALES					FREE WHITE FEMALES					TOTAL ALL OTHER	TOTAL SLAVES	TOTALS	DISTRICT/ TOWNSHIP	NOTES
					under 10	10 to 16	16 to 26	26 to 45	45 and over	under 10	10 to 16	16 to 26	26 to 45	45 and over					
Lenox	211	10	Sears	Calvin				1		1		1	1				4		
Lenox	211	11	Sedgwick	Asher		1		1		2	2		1	1			8		
Lenox	211	12	Steel	Thomas		1	1		1			1		2	1		7		
Lenox	211	13	Steel	Thomas Jun	2		1	1			1		1				6		
Lenox	211	14	Standly	Amos		1	1		1		1			1			5		
Lenox	211	15	Stone	Enos		1	2		1	1		1		1			7		
Lenox	211	16	Stearns	Daniel	3			1		2	2		1				9		
Lenox	211	17	Sears	Isaac	1			1		1							3		
Lenox	211	18	Thompson	Thaddeus	1	2	2		1	1		1	1				9		
Lenox	211	19	Taylor	Jonathan	2	2			1	2	1	2	1				11		
Lenox	211	20	Malloon	John	3			1		1	1	1	1				8		
Lenox	211	21	Tyler	John	2	1		1		3			1				8		
Lenox	211	22	Wright	Samuel	2	1	2		1	3	1		1	1			12		
Lenox	211	23	Washburn	Jacob	2	3		1		3			1				10		
Lenox	211	24	West	Daniel	3	1			1	1	1			1			8		
Lenox	211	25	Whelply	William		1	1		1		1	1	1				6		
Lenox	211	26	Weller	Paul	1			1		3			1				6		
Lenox	211	27	Way	Timothy	1		2		1	1	2	3		1			11		
Lenox	211	28	Willard	John	1		1	1		2	1		1				7		
Lenox	211	29	Whitlock	John			1	1					1				3		
Lenox	211	30	Willard	Ebenezer	3	1			1		1	1	1				8		
Lenox	211	31	Whiting	Gamaliel B.	2		1	2		1	1				1		9		
Lenox	211	32	Whiting	William	1		2		1	2	2	2	2	1			13		
Lenox	211	33	Walker	William		1	2		1		1	1	2		1		9		
Lenox	211	34	Wells	Stephen		1	2		1	1	1			1			7		
Lenox	211	35	Yale	Thomas	1	2	2	1		2	2	1	1				12		
Lenox	211	36	Yale	Justus	2	1	1		1		1	1					7		
Lenox	211	37	Gates	Luke			2	1		3		2					8		
Lenox	211	38	Parker	Jonathan				1		1	1		1				4		
Lenox	211	39	White	John			1			1	1						3		
Lenox	211	40	Sikes	Elijah			1			2		1					4		
Lenox	212	1	Ford	Ichabod Jun	2			1		2		1					6		
Lenox	212	2	Clark	Samuel			1	1		1	3	1	1				8		
Lenox	212	3	Hill	Arunah	2	1	1		1	1	2		1				9		
Lenox	212	4	Smith	Jesse	2	1		1		2	1	2	1				10		
Lenox	212	5	Wells	William				1					1				2		
Lenox	212	6	Stone	Ethan		1		1			1	2					5		
Lenox	212	7	Williams	Daniel	1			1		2			1				5		
Lenox	212	8	Blossom	Ezra	2			1		2	2	1	1				9		
Lenox	212	9	Marwin	Ebenezer				1				1		1			3		
Lenox	212	10	Smith	Heman			1	1		3			1				6		
Lenox	212	11	Walker	Edward				1			1		1	1			4		
Lenox	212	12	Warren	Stephen	2	2		1	1	1			1	1			9		
Lenox	212	13	White	Solomon	3	1	1	1					1				7		
Lenox	212	14	Wright	Gad	1		1			1			1				4		
Lenox	212	15	Smith	Zenar			2										2		
Lenox	212	16	Curtis	Justus			1			2		1					4		
Lenox	212	17	Dove	John		2			1	1		2		1			7		
Lenox	212	18	Andrews	Solmon	2	1			1		1			1			6		
Lenox	212	19	Peters	Robert											4		4		
Lenox	212	20	Way	Moses	1			1			1		1	1			5		

TOWN	PG#	LN#	HEADS OF HOUSEHOLD LAST NAME	FIRST NAME	FREE WHITE MALES under 10	10 to 16	16 to 26	26 to 45	45 and over	FREE WHITE FEMALES under 10	10 to 16	16 to 26	26 to 45	45 and over	TOTAL ALL OTHER	TOTAL SLAVES	TOTALS	DISTRICT/ TOWNSHIP	NOTES
Loudon	177	1	Hawley	Ozias	1	1		1		3	1		1				8		
Loudon	177	2	Hickland	Daniel			1			2		1					4		
Loudon	177	3	Waterhouse	Thomas	2	3		1		1	2		1				10		
Loudon	177	4	Marvin	Sylvanus	1			1		3			1				6		
Loudon	177	5	Jones	Phinehas	1	1			1	4			1				8		
Loudon	177	6	Alderman	John	1	1	2		1	2	2	1	1				11		
Loudon	177	7	Gibbins	Peter		2	2		1		1		1				7		
Loudon	177	8	Norton	Jonathan Sr	2		1	1	1	2	1	2		1			11		
Loudon	177	9	Norton	Jonathan Jr	1	2		1		3			1				8		
Loudon	177	10	Davison	Benjamin	3			1			2		1				7		
Loudon	177	11	Larkum	Paul	3	1		1		2	1		1				9		
Loudon	177	12	Larkum	Silas	2			1		1			1				5		
Loudon	177	13	Bridgen	John	1			1		3			1				6		
Loudon	177	14	Knowles	Seth	1	1		1		2			1				6		
Loudon	177	15	Cotton	William	3	1	1		1					1			7		
Loudon	177	16	Spelman	Levi	2	1		1		1			1				6		
Loudon	177	17	Butter	Isaac			1					1	1				3		
Loudon	177	18	Whitney	Timothy Esq				1						1			2		
Loudon	177	19	Whitney	Hezekiah	2		1	1		3			1				8		
Loudon	177	20	Loveland	Amos	3	2		1		2			1	1			10		
Loudon	178	1	Loveland	Isaac		1		1		1	2		1				6		
Loudon	178	2	Man	William	2	1		1		2			1				7		
Loudon	178	3	Finch	Isaac			1		1		1	1		1			5		
Loudon	178	4	Pelton	Ephraim	1			1		3			1	1			7		
Loudon	178	5	Clark	Comfort	2			1		4			1	1			9		
Loudon	178	6	Babb	John	1		1		1	1	2	1		1			8		
Loudon	178	7	Cotton	Walter			1					1	1				3		
Loudon	178	8	Case	James	2	1	1		1	2		3	1				11		
Loudon	178	9	Babb	Benjamin	2	1		1		3			1				8		
Loudon	178	10	Perry	Joseph W.	1		2					1					4		
Loudon	178	11	Clark	James	1	1		1		3	1		1				8		
Loudon	178	12	Clark	Joseph W.			1		1					1			3		
Loudon	178	13	Winter	Alpheus	1			1	1			1	1	1			6		
Loudon	178	14	Pelton	Stephen	1			1		2	1		2				7		
Loudon	178	15	Dibble	Heman	2	1		1		2			1				7		
Loudon	178	16	Coft	Eliphalet	1			1		2		1					5		
Loudon	178	17	Pelton	Samuel		1		1		2	1		1				6		
Loudon	178	18	Francis	Hosea		1		1					1				3		
Loudon	178	19	Whitney	Jonas	3			1					1				5		
Loudon	178	20	Webster	Seth				1		1		1					3		
Loudon	178	21	Miles	Elijah	2			1				1					4		
Loudon	178	22	Webster	John	2			1		1			1	1			6		
Loudon	178	23	Cook	Moses	1			1					2				4		
Loudon	178	24	Owen	Elijah Sen		1	2	1	1				1				6		
Loudon	178	25	Owen	Elihah Jun	1	1		1		1			1				5		
Loudon	178	26	Adams	Ebenezer	1			1		2			1				5		
Loudon	178	27	Scott	David	2			1		2	1		1				7		
Loudon	178	28	Owen	Erastus				1		1		1					3		
Loudon	178	29	Lloyd	David	1			1		2			1				5		
Loudon	178	30	Phelps	Isaac		1	2	1		1	1	1	1				8		
Loudon	178	31	Root	Joseph	2		4	2	1			1		1	1		12		
Loudon	178	32	Belamy	Simeon Sen			1		1		1	2					6		
Loudon	178	33	Kibbee	Daniel	1			1		3	1						6		
Loudon	178	34	Snow	Selah				1				1					2		
Loudon	178	35	Kibbee	John	2	3		1		2		2	1				11		
Loudon	178	36	Parish	Benjamin	2			1					1	1			5		
Loudon	178	37	Cook	Josiah	3	3	1		1	1			1				10		
Loudon	178	38	Hawley	Thomas	2		1	1		1	1		1				7		
Loudon	178	39	Davison	Samuel	3			1		1			1				6		
Loudon	178	40	Davison	Zepheniah	1			1					1	1			4		
Loudon	178	41	Davison	Thomas	1	2		1					1	1			6		
Loudon	179	1	Davison	John	3			1		1	1		1				7		
Loudon	179	2	Fay	John	2	1		1		1	1		1				7		
Loudon	179	3	Marcy	Smith		1			1		1	1		1	1		6		
Loudon	179	4	Marcy	Howland	2			1		2			1				6		
Loudon	179	5	Marcy	Thomas	2			1			1	1	1				6		
Loudon	179	6	Marcy	Lawton		1		1		3			1				6		
Loudon	179	7	Kibbee	William	1			1	1	1			1				5		
Loudon	179	8	Kibbee	Ebenezer	2			1					1	1			5		
Loudon	179	9	Cuff	Sampson											1		1		
Loudon	179	10	Cook	Elisha	3	2	1	1				2	1	1	1		12		
Loudon	179	11	Cook	John	1	1		1				2	1				6		
Loudon	179	12	Case	Truman				1		4	1		1				7		
Loudon	179	13	Case	Ozias	2	1	1	1		2	1			1			9		
Loudon	179	14	Woodworth	Jonathan	4			1		2			1				8		
Loudon	179	15	Barber	Benjamin		1		1		1		1	1				5		
Loudon	179	16	Case	Timothy	3	1		1		1	3	1	1				11		
Loudon	179	17	Barber	Abel	1			1		2			1				5		
Loudon	179	18	Baldwin	Samuel	1			1		4			1				7		

TOWN	PG#	LN#	LAST NAME	FIRST NAME	FREE WHITE MALES					FREE WHITE FEMALES					TOTAL ALL OTHER	TOTAL SLAVES	TOTALS	DISTRICT/ TOWNSHIP	NOTES
					under 10	10 to 16	16 to 26	26 to 45	45 and over	under 10	10 to 16	16 to 26	26 to 45	45 and over					
Loudon	179	19	Case	Farran	1			1				1					3		
Loudon	179	20	Barber	Roswell			1			2		1					4		
Loudon	179	21	Cook	Moses H.	1		1					1					3		
Loudon	179	22	Pettebone	David				1		2	2		1				6		
Loudon	179	23	Wolf	James D.	1	2		1		2			1				7		
Loudon	179	24	Lee	Samuel	2				1	1			1	1			6		
Loudon	179	25	Daily	Jeremiah	1			1		1			1				4		
Loudon	179	26	Egelston	Aaron	3	2		1		2			1				9		
Loudon	179	27	Thomas	Samuel	1	1	1		1	2	2	1		1			10		
Loudon	179	28	Wolf	Ezekiel D.	1	2		1		3	1		1				9		
Loudon	179	29	Ames	Joshua	2			1		3			1				7		
Loudon	179	30	Wolf	Matthew D					1					1			2		
Loudon	179	31	Case	Ozias Jr			1			2		1					4		
Loudon	179	32	Cook	Thomas			1			1		1					3		
Loudon	179	33	Messenger	Elijah	3	1		1		1			1				7		
Loudon	179	34	Dimick	Isaac		1	1		1		1	3		1			8		
Loudon	179	35	Warner	Daniel					1			1		1			3		
Loudon	179	36	Pierce	Adam	1	1		1		1			1				5		
Loudon	179	37	Martin	William											4		4		

TOWN	PG#	LN#	LAST NAME	FIRST NAME	FREE WHITE MALES					FREE WHITE FEMALES					TOTAL ALL OTHER	TOTAL SLAVES	TOTALS	DISTRICT/ TOWNSHIP	NOTES
					under 10	10 to 16	16 to 26	26 to 45	45 and over	under 10	10 to 16	16 to 26	26 to 45	45 and over					
Mount Washington	231	1	Tullar	John Jun	1	1		1		2		1					6		
Mount Washington	231	2	Reed	Wm		1	2		1		1			1			6		
Mount Washington	231	3	Reed	Joseph				1		2			1				4		
Mount Washington	231	4	Reed	Wm Jun	1			1					1				3		
Mount Washington	231	5	Hall	Smith	3			1		2			1				7		
Mount Washington	231	6	Patterson	Charles		1	2		1	2	2			3			11		
Mount Washington	231	7	Stevens	Ezra	1	1			1	1	2		1				7		
Mount Washington	231	8	Kline	John Jun				1		2			1				4		
Mount Washington	231	9	Ward	James	1	1	1	1		1			1				6		
Mount Washington	231	10	Groat	Philip	1			1				1					3		
Mount Washington	231	11	Dibble	John	1			1	1	2			1				6		
Mount Washington	231	12	Dibble	Daniel				1		2		1					4		
Mount Washington	231	13	Thigbee	Ruth	1								1				2		
Mount Washington	231	14	Cline	Frederick	1			1		1		1					4		
Mount Washington	231	15	Jones	Thomas	3	2	1		1			1		1			9		
Mount Washington	231	16	Covey	Luther		1				3		1					5		
Mount Washington	232	1	Woodin	John		1							1	1			3		
Mount Washington	232	2	Osbourne	Joseph			1			1		1					3		
Mount Washington	232	3	Jones	John	3		1					1					5		
Mount Washington	232	4	Mead	Jesse	3	1	2		1	1	1		1				10		
Mount Washington	232	5	Sturdevant	Cezar	1	1		1		1			1				5		
Mount Washington	232	6	Cade	Thomas				1			1		1				3		
Mount Washington	232	7	Winans	Isaac		2	2		1		1	2		1			9		
Mount Washington	232	8	Pierce	Jonathan		1			1				1				3		
Mount Washington	232	9	Dibble	Saml		1			1	2			1				5		
Mount Washington	232	10	Winchel	Ephraim					1	1	1		1				3		
Mount Washington	232	11	Patterson	Levi	1			1		2			1				5		
Mount Washington	232	12	Peek	Nathan	2	1	2		1			1		1			8		
Mount Washington	232	13	Peek	Nathan Junr		1						1					2		
Mount Washington	232	14	Coe	Amos	1	1	1			2		1					6		
Mount Washington	232	15	Knapp	David	2			1				1					4		
Mount Washington	232	16	Campbell	Robert			2	1		1		1					5		
Mount Washington	232	17	Merit	Cornbury	1	1		1		2	1	1	1				8		
Mount Washington	232	18	Osbourne	Isaac				1					1				2		
Mount Washington	232	19	Osbourne	Isaac Junr		1				1		1					3		
Mount Washington	232	20	Lee	William	1	1	1		1	2	1	2		1			10		
Mount Washington	232	21	Coan	David	1	1		1			1		1				5		
Mount Washington	232	22	Horton	Andrew			1	1					1				3		
Mount Washington	232	23	Coe	Seth			1			2		1					4		
Mount Washington	232	24	Woodin	Solomon	1	2		1		4			1	1			10		
Mount Washington	232	25	Grant	John		1			1	2	1	1	1	1			8		
Mount Washington	232	26	Berazee	Case	2	2	3		1	2	1			1			12		
Mount Washington	232	27	Berazee	Frederick	1			1		3	1		1				7		
Mount Washington	232	28	Fox	Jona	2			1		3	1		1				8		
Mount Washington	232	29	Palmer	Sarah						3				1			4		
Mount Washington	232	30	King	John		1			1		1	1		1			5		
Mount Washington	232	31	King	Fenner	4	2			1	2			1				10		
Mount Washington	232	32	Smith	Merit				1				1					2		
Mount Washington	232	33	Smith	Samuel		1			1	1			1				4		
Mount Washington	232	34	Pierce	Orange	1			1		2		1					5		
Mount Washington	232	35	Lord	Daniel	1	1			1	1	2		1				7		
Mount Washington	232	36	Stevens	Peter	3			1		1		1					6		
Mount Washington	232	37	Patterson	John				1		1	1						3		

TOWN	PG#	LN#	LAST NAME	FIRST NAME	FREE WHITE MALES					FREE WHITE FEMALES					TOTAL ALL OTHER	TOTAL SLAVES	TOTALS	DISTRICT/ TOWNSHIP	NOTES
					under 10	10 to 16	16 to 26	26 to 45	45 and over	under 10	10 to 16	16 to 26	26 to 45	45 and over					
New Ashford	162	1	Tyler	Samuel			1		1	3	3			1			9		
New Ashford	162	2	Birch	Gideon	4	1		1		1			1				8		
New Ashford	162	3	Tyler	Barchal				1			2	1	1				5		
New Ashford	162	4	Sherwood	Benjamin		1	2	1		1	3	1					9		
New Ashford	162	5	Goodale	Elijah		1		2			1	1					5		
New Ashford	162	6	Goodale	Stephen	3				1		1	1					6		
New Ashford	162	7	Spink	Shibnah	3	3	1	1		1	1	1					11		
New Ashford	162	8	Ingraham	Jonathan	2			1		5	1	1					10		
New Ashford	162	9	Newton	Jason				1			1			1			3		
New Ashford	162	10	Thompson	Joseph	2		1		1		1			1			6		
New Ashford	162	11	Ingalls	William	1		2					1					4		
New Ashford	162	12	Young	George	2			1			1		1				5		
New Ashford	162	13	Rice	William	2	1				1	1		1				7		
New Ashford	162	14	Lewis	James			1			1		1	1				4		
New Ashford	162	15	Moger	Reuben	2			1				1	1				5		
New Ashford	162	16	Mallery	Eli	2	1			1	1	1	1	1				8		
New Ashford	162	17	Bracee	Christopher	2		1	1		1	1	1	1				8		
New Ashford	162	18	Danley	Esther	1	1	1			2	1	1	1				8		
New Ashford	162	19	Lewis	Gideon			1		1	1	1			1			5		
New Ashford	163	1	Webber	Benjamin	3			2		1		1	1				8		
New Ashford	163	2	Williams	James	1			1		2			1				5		
New Ashford	163	3	Banter	Thadeus	1			1		2			1				5		
New Ashford	163	4	Kent	Nathaniel	2	1			1	2	1			1			8		
New Ashford	163	5	Gregory	Esbon	2			1		2			1				6		
New Ashford	163	6	Prouce	Samuel	1	2	1		1					2			7		
New Ashford	163	7	Dewey	Henry	1			1		1		1					4		
New Ashford	163	8	Slade	William	3		1	1		1			1				7		
New Ashford	163	9	Banter	John	2	1	2	1		3	2	1	1				13		
New Ashford	163	10	Beach	Tyler	3			1		2	2		1				9		
New Ashford	163	11	Banter	David				1					1				2		
New Ashford	163	12	Beach	Archibald	4			1		2	1		1				9		
New Ashford	163	13	Beach	Hezekiah Jr	2			1		1			1				5		
New Ashford	163	14	Beach	Hezekiah			2		1			1		1			5		
New Ashford	163	15	Campbel	William	2	1	1		1	2				1			8		
New Ashford	163	16	Bartner	Pitt*	3		1	1			3		1				9		
New Ashford	163	17	Mallery	Uriah		1	1	1		1		1	1	1			7		
New Ashford	163	18	Owens	Rhoda	2								1				3		
New Ashford	163	19	Mudge	Stephen	1			1	1	3	3		1				10		
New Ashford	163	20	Jourdan	Francis	1	2		1	1			3		1			9		
New Ashford	163	21	Cole	Jacob	1	1		1		2			2				7		
New Ashford	163	22	Babbit	Mary	2	1	3				1	2		1			10		
New Ashford	163	23	Virgison	Daniel				1		3	1	1					6		
New Ashford	163	24	Spink	Shibnah					1				1				2		
New Ashford	163	25	Cole	Ebenezer	1		2			1		1					5		
New Ashford	163	26	Fish	Matthew			1			3			1				5		
New Ashford	163	27	Stills	John		1		1			1		1				4		
New Ashford	163	28	Way	Azariah	4		1	1					2				8		
New Ashford	163	29	Clother	Jesse	1	1	1	1			1	1	1				7		
New Ashford	163	30	Hammond	Gaius	1		2		1			1		1			6		
New Ashford	163	31	Barns	Moses	1		1	1	1	1	1		1				7		
New Ashford	163	32	Grover	David S.	1			1			1		1				4		
New Ashford	163	33	Reed	Jesse	3	2		1		1	1		1	1			10		
New Ashford	163	34	Griffiths	Paul	2	1		1		1			1				6		
New Ashford	163	35	Pratt	Elias	2			1		3			1	1			8		
New Ashford	163	36	Shattuck	Timothy		1	1		1					1			4		
New Ashford	163	37	Cole	James	1	1	1	1		3	2		1				10		
New Ashford	163	38	Pomeroy	Medad	3	2		1			1		1	1			9		
New Ashford	163	39	Morell	Hugh			2		1					1			4		

TOWN	PG#	LN#	HEADS OF HOUSEHOLD		FREE WHITE MALES					FREE WHITE FEMALES					TOTAL ALL OTHER	TOTAL SLAVES	TOTALS	DISTRICT/ TOWNSHIP	NOTES
			LAST NAME	FIRST NAME	under 10	10 to 16	16 to 26	26 to 45	45 and over	under 10	10 to 16	16 to 26	26 to 45	45 and over					
New Marlborough	232	1	Spaulding	Uriah	3	1	1		1				1	1			8		
New Marlborough	232	2	Birchard	David		1		2				1	1				5		
New Marlborough	232	3	Underwood	Edmond	3			1		2		1					7		
New Marlborough	232	4	Fosket	Ebenezer	1		1	1	1	1			1	1			7		
New Marlborough	232	5	Harmon	David		1		1		2			1				5		
New Marlborough	232	6	Chapins	Jonathan	1			1		2		1					5		
New Marlborough	232	7	Harmon	Eli		1			1				1				3		
New Marlborough	232	8	Sheldon	Eben	2	1		1		1			1				6		
New Marlborough	232	9	Sprague	James	1		1	1					1				4		
New Marlborough	232	10	Fosket	Ephraim	3		1		1	3	2	1					11		
New Marlborough	232	11	Huggins	Medad		1		1		1	2		1				6		
New Marlborough	232	12	Clark	Winthrop		1						1					2		
New Marlborough	232	13	Gleason	Uriel	1		1					1					3		
New Marlborough	232	14	Cole	Asa	2	1	1	1		3	1		1	1			11		
New Marlborough	232	15	Brooks	James	2	2		1			1		1				7		
New Marlborough	232	16	Cone	Frederick	1			1		1			1				4		
New Marlborough	232	17	Freeman	Silas		2	1	1	1	1		1		2			9		
New Marlborough	232	18	Freeman	James	1		1						1				3		
New Marlborough	232	19	Supon	Jedediah	3		1			1			1				6		
New Marlborough	232	20	Freeman	Silas	3			1		1	1						6		
New Marlborough	232	21	Clark	Thomas	1	1		1					1				4		
New Marlborough	232	22	Hall	Ebenezer	1	1	1		1	2	2	1	1				10		
New Marlborough	232	23	Jackson	David			1			2		1					4		
New Marlborough	232	24	Keyes	Elias	1			1					1				3		
New Marlborough	232	25	Blackman	Titus	3			1		1	2		1				8		
New Marlborough	232	26	Spaulding	Moses				1						1			2		
New Marlborough	232	27	Thomas	William	2			1		1	1		1				6		
New Marlborough	232	28	Noble	William	2			1				1					4		
New Marlborough	232	29	Baker	Abel	1	1			1	1	1		1				6		
New Marlborough	232	30	Clark	George	2		1			1	1		1				6		
New Marlborough	232	31	Philips	Samll Jn			1			1		1					3		
New Marlborough	232	32	Hobbs	Humphry				1		1		1					3		
New Marlborough	232	33	Rogers	Jonathan	2	2		1		2		1					8		
New Marlborough	232	34	Clark	John				1									1		
New Marlborough	232	35	Brown	Rhoda	1					1			1				3		
New Marlborough	233	1	Dean	Zebediah					1				1	1			3		
New Marlborough	233	2	Chapel	Joseph		1	1						1	1			4		
New Marlborough	233	3	Chapel	Giles	1		1			1		1					4		
New Marlborough	233	4	Dickinson	Thomas	2	2		1		2	1	1	1				10		
New Marlborough	233	5	Lockwood	Gershom		1		1		1	1	1	1				6		
New Marlborough	233	6	Dodge	John		2	2		2	2		2		1			11		
New Marlborough	233	7	Howe	James		1						1					2		
New Marlborough	233	8	Huff	Josiah	1		1			1			1				4		
New Marlborough	233	9	Shaw	Ammi	2			1		3			1				7		
New Marlborough	233	10	Chapins	Phinehas	3	1		1		2	1		1				9		
New Marlborough	233	11	Carter	Lyman		1				1		1					3		
New Marlborough	233	12	Underwood	Alpheus		2		1		1		1					5		
New Marlborough	233	13	Smith	Oreon			1	1						1			3		
New Marlborough	233	14	Stevens	Richard		2	1		1	1		1					6		
New Marlborough	233	15	Tracey	David	4		1		1				1	1			8		
New Marlborough	233	16	Smith	Samll	1	1	1		1			1	1				6		
New Marlborough	233	17	Hutchinson	Paul	1		1		1	2		1	1	1			8		
New Marlborough	233	18	Spaulding	Benjamin	2	1		1		2			1	1			8		
New Marlborough	233	19	Blackman	Paul	1	1	2	1	1		1	2	1	1			11		
New Marlborough	233	20	Howe	Uriah	1			1		1			1				4		
New Marlborough	233	21	Howe	Lemll		1	1		1	1	1	1		1			7		
New Marlborough	233	22	Taylor	Micah	1	1	1		1	1	1	1		1			8		
New Marlborough	233	23	Blakely	Stephen		1				1		1					3		
New Marlborough	233	24	Hutchinson	Joel	1			1		1			1				4		
New Marlborough	233	25	Rhodes	David	1		1		1	2	1	1					7		
New Marlborough	233	26	Stevens	Ebenezer					1				1				2		
New Marlborough	233	27	Stevens	Richard Jun			1			1	1	1					4		
New Marlborough	233	28	Jackson	Azar	1		1			1			1				4		
New Marlborough	233	29	Beach	Nathll		2	1				2		1				6		
New Marlborough	233	30	Hart	Solomon	2	1	1	1		3	2		1				11		
New Marlborough	233	31	Beach	Stiles	1			1		2			1				5		
New Marlborough	233	32	Shead	Samuel	3			2		1	1		1				8		
New Marlborough	233	33	Chapins	Nathan	1	1		1	1	1	2	1	1				9		
New Marlborough	234	1	Rugg	Seth	1		1	1					1				4		
New Marlborough	234	2	Kellogg	Joel	2			1		1	1		1				6		
New Marlborough	234	3	Huggs	Daniel				1		1			1				3		
New Marlborough	234	4	Brown	Horatio			1					1	1				3		
New Marlborough	234	5	Kingman	Samll	1			1		2			1				5		
New Marlborough	234	6	Howe	Nathll					1					1			2		
New Marlborough	234	7	Hyde	John	1		3		1	2	1	1	1	2			12		
New Marlborough	234	8	Warner	Jason	3			1					1				5		
New Marlborough	234	9	Warner	Samll			1							1			2		
New Marlborough	234	10	Wheeler	Benjamin	3	3	1	1					1	1			10		
New Marlborough	234	11	Hyde	Zenas	1			1		2		1			1		6		

TOWN	PG#	LN#	LAST NAME	FIRST NAME	FWM under 10	FWM 10 to 16	FWM 16 to 26	FWM 26 to 45	FWM 45 and over	FWF under 10	FWF 10 to 16	FWF 16 to 26	FWF 26 to 45	FWF 45 and over	TOTAL ALL OTHER	TOTAL SLAVES	TOTALS	DISTRICT/ TOWNSHIP	NOTES
New Marlborough	234	12	Hyde	Mercy										1			1		
New Marlborough	234	13	Baker	Nelson		1		1		1	1	2		1			7		
New Marlborough	234	14	Hyde	Ebenezer			1			1		1	1				4		
New Marlborough	234	15	Hyde	Freeman	1			1					1				3		
New Marlborough	234	16	Adams	Davenport		1	2		1	2	2	3		2			13		
New Marlborough	234	17	Stevens	William Pitt	1	1	3	1		2	1	2	1				12		
New Marlborough	234	18	Shaw	Mylo	2	1		1	1	3			1				9		
New Marlborough	234	19	Hollister	Benjamin	2		2	1		2		1	1				9		
New Marlborough	234	20	Taylor	Daniel Esq	1	1	1		1		2			1			7		
New Marlborough	234	21	Stevens	Anna			1	1		2	2		1				7		
New Marlborough	234	22	Catlin	Elijah	3	1	1	1		1	1		1	1			10		
New Marlborough	234	23	Sheldon	Asa	2		1		2	3		1	1	1			11		
New Marlborough	234	24	Sheldon	Samuel			1	1	1	1		2	1	1			7		
New Marlborough	234	25	Sheldon	Samll			1						1				2		
New Marlborough	234	26	Catlin	Elijah	1			1		4		1	1				8		
New Marlborough	234	27	Arnold	David	1			1		1			1				4		
New Marlborough	234	28	Church	Noah			3	1			1	1	1				8		
New Marlborough	234	29	Gates	Levi	1		2	1		1		1					6		
New Marlborough	234	30	Maxon	Thompson S		1	1		1		1			1			5		
New Marlborough	234	31	Bird	Nathll		2		1		4			1				8		
New Marlborough	234	32	Powell	Stephen	1		1	1		1			1				4		
New Marlborough	234	33	Chapin	Aaron	1			1		1			1				4		
New Marlborough	235	1	Sheldon	Elijah		1	2		1			1	1	2			8		
New Marlborough	235	2	Brigham	Joel	2	1		1	1			1	1				7		
New Marlborough	235	3	Rawson	Paul										1			1		
New Marlborough	235	4	Rawson	Joel	2			1		1			1				5		
New Marlborough	235	5	Bullard	Benjamin	3			1	1	1			1				7		
New Marlborough	235	6	Buck	Ebenezer	2			1		2	1		1				7		
New Marlborough	235	7	Bullard	Eleazer		1	1		1		1	2		1			7		
New Marlborough	235	8	Jones	Thomas	2	2			1	1	1	2	1				10		
New Marlborough	235	9	Wright	Calvin	1	1		1		1			1				5		
New Marlborough	235	10	Bullard	Elijah	1			1		1			1				4		
New Marlborough	235	11	Harmon	Aran Jun			1			1							3		
New Marlborough	235	12	Harmon	Aran	1	1			1			2	1	1	1		8		
New Marlborough	235	13	Brewer	Isaac	1	1		1			1		1				5		
New Marlborough	235	14	Brewer	Joshua	1			1		1	1	1		1			6		
New Marlborough	235	15	Brewer	Joseph Jun	1	1		1		2	2		1				8		
New Marlborough	235	16	Kelcey	David	1	1		1		3			1				7		
New Marlborough	235	17	Forsyth	Abigail			1			2	1		2				6		
New Marlborough	235	18	Chapel	Amos	1			1		2	1	2		1			8		
New Marlborough	235	19	Merriam	Miriam		1	2					1	1				5		
New Marlborough	235	20	Alden	Noah	3			1		1		1					6		
New Marlborough	235	21	Hale	Nathll	3	1	1	1		1		1	1				9		
New Marlborough	235	22	Claflin	Abner		1	1	1		1		2		1			7		
New Marlborough	235	23	Smith	Jonathan		1	2	1		1			1	1			7		
New Marlborough	235	24	Smith	Stephen		1	2					1					4		
New Marlborough	235	25	Hall	Elisha	1	1	1		1	1	1		1				8		
New Marlborough	235	26	Hall	Luke	1	1						1					3		
New Marlborough	235	27	Doland	Elijah		1						1					2		
New Marlborough	235	28	Wheeler	Zenas	2	2	1	1				1	1				8		
New Marlborough	235	29	Philips	Samuel	2	1	1		1	2		1	1				9		
New Marlborough	235	30	Wilcocks	Zaccheus			1						1				2		
New Marlborough	235	31	Hyde	John 2d	1	1	1	1		1			1	2			8		
New Marlborough	236	1	Walker	David		1	1	1				1	1		1		6		
New Marlborough	236	2	Chapin	Amos	1	1	1		1	1	2	1	1				9		
New Marlborough	236	3	Chapin	Joshua				1						1			2		
New Marlborough	236	4	Slater	Samuel				1						1			2		
New Marlborough	236	5	Chapins	Peter	2	1	2	1		2		2		1			11		
New Marlborough	236	6	Alexander	William		2	1		1	1		1		1			7		
New Marlborough	236	7	Hitchcock	Abner			1		1	1				1			4		
New Marlborough	236	8	Wright	Caleb				1						1			2		
New Marlborough	236	9	Sheldon	Eleazer	3	2	1		1	2		1		2			12		
New Marlborough	236	10	Sheldon	Elisha	2	1	2				1	1					8		
New Marlborough	236	11	Clark	Phebe	1									1			2		
New Marlborough	236	12	Norton	Seth	1		1		1	2			1	1			7		
New Marlborough	236	13	Harmon	Uriah		1	1						1	1			4		
New Marlborough	236	14	Norton	David	3	2		1		1		3	1				11		
New Marlborough	236	15	Sheldon	Seth			2		1		1			1			5		
New Marlborough	236	16	Kingman	Amos		1							1				2		
New Marlborough	236	17	Taylor	John	1			1		2			1				5		
New Marlborough	236	18	Taylor	Elias	1			1					1				3		
New Marlborough	236	19	Freeman	Paul											9		9		
New Marlborough	236	20	Harmon	William		1							1				2		
New Marlborough	236	21	Harmon	Jonth				1		1			1				3		
New Marlborough	236	22	Harmon	Jonathan	1			1		1			1				4		
New Marlborough	236	23	Shepherd	Nathll			3		1	1	1	3		1			10		
New Marlborough	236	24	Harmon	Samll			1										1		
New Marlborough	236	25	Brigham	Mary	3		1			2	3	1	1				11		
New Marlborough	236	26	Harmon	Rufus	1		1	1		1		1	1				5		

TOWN	PG#	LN#	LAST NAME	FIRST NAME	FREE WHITE MALES					FREE WHITE FEMALES					TOTAL ALL OTHER	TOTAL SLAVES	TOTALS	DISTRICT/ TOWNSHIP	NOTES
					under 10	10 to 16	16 to 26	26 to 45	45 and over	under 10	10 to 16	16 to 26	26 to 45	45 and over					
New Marlborough	236	27	Harmon	Josiah	1			1		2			1				5		
New Marlborough	236	28	Harmon	Asa		1			1	1		2	1	1			7		
New Marlborough	236	29	Harmon	Elisha			1	1		2	1		1				6		
New Marlborough	236	30	Canfield	Gideon	1			1		1		1					4		
New Marlborough	236	31	Phelps	Eliphalet	3	1		1		2	1		1				9		
New Marlborough	236	32	Taylor	Eleazer		1		1				3		1			6		
New Marlborough	237	1	Harrison	Isaac	1		1			2	1		1				7		
New Marlborough	237	2	Brigham	Francis			1	1					1	1			4		
New Marlborough	237	3	Brigham	Jedediah			1			2			1				4		
New Marlborough	237	4	Brigham	John	3			1					1				5		
New Marlborough	237	5	More	William		1			1	1	1		2				6		
New Marlborough	237	6	Shepherd	Daniel		2	2	1		2		1		1			9		
New Marlborough	237	7	Shepherd	Solomon			1		1			1		1			4		
New Marlborough	237	8	Smith	Joshua	2			1				1					4		
New Marlborough	237	9	Shepherd	Thomas	2	1	3		1	1				1			9		
New Marlborough	237	10	Wilcox	Thomas	2	1	2		1	1		3	1				11		
New Marlborough	237	11	Norton	Phinehas			1	1		1	1	2	1				6		
New Marlborough	237	12	Pike	Ozias	4	1		1		1	2		1				10		
New Marlborough	237	13	Ward	Elihu	1			1		2	1		1	1			7		
New Marlborough	237	14	Benedict	William	1	1		2		1		1	2				8		
New Marlborough	237	15	Canfield	Oran		1				2		1					4		
New Marlborough	237	16	Chapin	Rachel		1					1		1				3		
New Marlborough	237	17	Taft	Lovet	3	2	1	1		2		1	1	1			12		
New Marlborough	237	18	Mason	Adam	2	2		1		2	3	1	1	1			13		
New Marlborough	237	19	Ward	Edmund	1			1		1			1				4		
New Marlborough	237	20	Hitchcock	Cornish	1	1		1		2			2				7		
New Marlborough	237	21	Smith	Elijah	1	1		1		2		2	1	1			9		
New Marlborough	237	22	Royce	John	2			1					1				4		
New Marlborough	237	23	Sharon	Salmon			1					1					2		
New Marlborough	237	24	Maxon	Thomas		1				2		1					4		
New Marlborough	237	25	Mudge	Jervis	3	2	1	1		2		1	1				11		
New Marlborough	237	26	Canfield	Gideon	2	1			1		1		1				6		
New Marlborough	237	27	Norslot	Daniel	1		1					1					3		
New Marlborough	237	28	Andrews	Philo	1			1		1		1	1				5		
New Marlborough	237	29	Woodruff	Lambert Jr	1	2	1	1		2			1				8		
New Marlborough	237	30	Shepherd	Samll			1			1	1						3		
New Marlborough	237	31	Stevens	Phebe		1	1						1				3		
New Marlborough	237	32	Ward	Jedediah		4	1		1			1	1	1			9		
New Marlborough	237	33	Norton	Samuel				1		2	1	1			1		6		
New Marlborough	238	1	Butler	Nathan	2			2	1	1	1		2				9		
New Marlborough	238	2	Baldwin	David	2	1	1		1	1		1		1			8		
New Marlborough	238	3	Ward	Obadiah Esq	2		1	1				1	1	2			9		
New Marlborough	238	4	Hitchcock	Jonathan			1			3			1				5		
New Marlborough	238	5	Harmon	Jehiel	2	1	2	1	1	1	1	1	1				11		
New Marlborough	238	6	Johnson	Samll	1			1		3	2	1	1				9		
New Marlborough	238	7	Clark	Jacob		1		1			1		1				4		
New Marlborough	238	8	Knapp	Ezra	2		2		1	2	1	1	2				11		
New Marlborough	238	9	Brown	Perez	1	1		1		3	1	2	1				10		
New Marlborough	238	10	Bristol	Chloe	2		1		1	2	2	1	1				10		
New Marlborough	238	11	Turner	Samll				1		1				1			3		
New Marlborough	238	12	Turner	Anna							1		1				2		
New Marlborough	238	13	Ward	Ralph	1	1	1			1		1					6		
New Marlborough	238	14	Brooks	Elizabeth	1					1		1					3		
New Marlborough	238	15	Pottiss	Joseph	1	1		1					1				4		
New Marlborough	238	16	Turner	Isaac	1			1		1	1						4		
New Marlborough	238	17	Harmon	Joseph	4	1		1		2		1					9		
New Marlborough	238	18	Chapman	John	3	1	2		1	2	2			1			12		
New Marlborough	238	19	Harmon	Moses		1		1					1				3		
New Marlborough	238	20	Harmon	Mark			1			3		1					5		
New Marlborough	238	21	Peck	Zebulon				1					1				2		
New Marlborough	238	22	Clark	Daniel	4	2		1			1		1	1			9		
New Marlborough	238	23	Whiting	Josian	1	1	1		1	1		1		1			7		
New Marlborough	238	24	Case	Seth		1		1				2		1			5		
New Marlborough	238	25	Dean	Walter	1	1	2		1	2		1	1				9		
New Marlborough	238	26	Ward	Calvin			1			4			1				6		
New Marlborough	238	27	Wheeler	James T	2		1	1		1	2		1	1			9		
New Marlborough	238	28	Bryan	Elizabeth		1							1				2		
New Marlborough	238	29	Smith	Obadiah	1			1		2			1				5		
New Marlborough	238	30	Beman	Reuben		1	2		1	1	1		1				7		
New Marlborough	238	31	Smith	Ebenezer		1			1	1	3		1				7		
New Marlborough	238	32	Huxley	Dan			2	1				1	1				5		
New Marlborough	238	33	Brewer	Elisha		1		2		1			1				5		
New Marlborough	239	1	Smith	Benjamin	2		1	1		2	1	1	1				10		
New Marlborough	239	2	Norton	Samuel	1	3	1		1		1	1		1			9		
New Marlborough	239	3	Pomeroy	Phinehas	1		1	1	1	2		2		1			9		
New Marlborough	239	4	Dorchester	Daniel				1					1				2		
New Marlborough	239	5	Canfield	Samuel Jun	2			1		2		1					6		
New Marlborough	239	6	Fitch	Joseph			1		1					1			3		
New Marlborough	239	7	Wilcox	Oliver	5	1		1					1				8		

TOWN	PG#	LN#	LAST NAME	FIRST NAME	FREE WHITE MALES					FREE WHITE FEMALES					TOTAL ALL OTHER	TOTAL SLAVES	TOTALS	DISTRICT/ TOWNSHIP	NOTES
					under 10	10 to 16	16 to 26	26 to 45	45 and over	under 10	10 to 16	16 to 26	26 to 45	45 and over					
New Marlborough	239	8	Shepherd	Isaac		1				1		1					3		
New Marlborough	239	9	Knapp	Mary	1		1	1			1	1		1			6		
New Marlborough	239	10	Smith	Thomas	1			1		4			1				7		
New Marlborough	239	11	Sturdevant	James	2	1	1	1					1				6		
New Marlborough	239	12	Sturdevant	Ira	2			1		1			1				5		
New Marlborough	239	13	Walter	Heman	5		1	1					1				8		
New Marlborough	239	14	Lewis	Oliver	2	1	1	1		3	3		1				12		
New Marlborough	239	15	Case	Lemuel	1	1		1				1					4		
New Marlborough	239	16	Curtiss	Nathanael		1			1					1			3		
New Marlborough	239	17	Price	Hurd	5			1					1	1			8		
New Marlborough	239	18	Sturdevant	Levi	1			1		2		1					5		
New Marlborough	239	19	Camp	John	1			1		2			1				5		
New Marlborough	239	20	Norton	James	1			1		1			2				5		
New Marlborough	239	21	Leonard	Timothy									1				1		
New Marlborough	239	22		Jacob Negro											4		4		
New Marlborough	239	23	Ford	Abel				1		1			1				3		
New Marlborough	239	24	Ford	Joel		1	3			1		1					6		
New Marlborough	239	25	Gaylord	Munson		1	1			1		1					4		
New Marlborough	239	26	Peck	Eleazer		1	2		1	1	1		1				7		
New Marlborough	239	27	Barber	Zachheus	3		1	1		2			1				8		
New Marlborough	239	28	Wilcox	Ezekiel				1					1				2		
New Marlborough	239	29	Hockley	Asahel	1	1	1	1	1	2		1	2	2			12		
New Marlborough	239	30	Babbett	Asa	1	1				1		1					5		
New Marlborough	239	31	Benedict	Francis		1				1		1					3		
New Marlborough	239	32	Fitch	Joseph Jun	1	1		1					1				4		
New Marlborough	239	33	Granger	Phinehas		1		1		2			1				5		
New Marlborough	239	34	Spaulding	Daniel	1	2	1	1		1	1	2	1				10		
New Marlborough	239	35	Seymour	Jacob	2	1	1	1			1	1					7		
New Marlborough	240	1	Canfield	Daniel	4	1		1		2			1				10		
New Marlborough	240	2	Canfield	Samuel					1	1				1			3		
New Marlborough	240	3	Conn	Robert	4				1	2	1		1				9		
New Marlborough	240	4	Brooks	Luther	1		1	1		3			1	1			8		
New Marlborough	240	5	Brooks	David			1	1		2	3		1				8		
New Marlborough	240	6	Flannards	John	1	1	1		1	4			1				9		
New Marlborough	240	7	Collar	Silas	1			1		1			1				4		
New Marlborough	240	8	Brooks	Jabez	1	1		1			2		1				6		
New Marlborough	240	9	Lewis	Ebenezer	1	1	2		1	2	2	2		1			12		
New Marlborough	240	10	Allen	Joseph	3			1		2			1				7		
New Marlborough	240	11	Lee	Abner	1			1			1		1				4		
New Marlborough	240	12	Bence	Rory		2		1		1		1					5		
New Marlborough	240	13	Collar	John	1	2	1	1		3	1	1	1				11		
New Marlborough	240	14	Norton	Isaac	3	1	1	1		1	2	1	1				11		
New Marlborough	240	15	Lane	Isaac	3	1	1	1		1	2	1	1				11		
New Marlborough	240	16	Allen	Rufus	2	2		1		2	1	1	1				10		
New Marlborough	240	17	House	Sarah	2								1	1			4		
New Marlborough	240	18	Collar	Asa	1			1		3			1				6		
New Marlborough	240	19	Kingman	Caleb	2		2	1		1	2		1	1			10		
New Marlborough	240	20	Howe	Bowers	2			1		1			1				5		
New Marlborough	240	21	Cook	Solomon	1		1	1		1	1		1				6		
New Marlborough	240	22	Cook	Levi	2		1		1	1		1		1			7		
New Marlborough	240	23	Smith	Gilbert			1			1		1					3		
New Marlborough	240	24	Foster	Ezekiel	2		2	1		1		1	2				9		
New Marlborough	240	25	Collar	Moses	2	1		1			1		1				6		
New Marlborough	240	26	Cook	Russell	2		1	1		1	1		2	1			9		
New Marlborough	240	27	Goodenough	Solomon	1	1		1		1	1		1				6		
New Marlborough	240	28	Keyes	Thaddeus	3		1	1	1	1			1	1			9		
New Marlborough	240	29	Lee	Elias	2	1			2	1	1	1	1				9		
New Marlborough	240	30	Bryan	Reuben	2			1		3			1				7		
New Marlborough	240	31	Smith	Elisha	2			1		1			1				5		
New Marlborough	240	32	Smith	Joel	2			1	1				1	1			6		
New Marlborough	240	33	Allen	Levi	1			1		2			1	1			6		
New Marlborough	240	34	Austin	Dan	2	1			1	2	2		1				9		
New Marlborough	240	35	Cook	Mary										2			2		
New Marlborough	240	36	Howe	Bates	1		1					1					3		
New Marlborough	241	1	Camp	Hannah	2							1		1	2		6		
New Marlborough	241	2	Spaulding	Aaron				1	1				1	2			5		
New Marlborough	241	3	Adams	Zebediah	3	1	2		1	1	1		1				10		

TOWN	PG#	LN#	LAST NAME	FIRST NAME	FREE WHITE MALES					FREE WHITE FEMALES					TOTAL ALL OTHER	TOTAL SLAVES	TOTALS	DISTRICT/ TOWNSHIP	NOTES
					under 10	10 to 16	16 to 26	26 to 45	45 and over	under 10	10 to 16	16 to 26	26 to 45	45 and over					
Partridgefield	185	1	Adams	John	2			1		1			1				5		
Partridgefield	185	2	Adams	Thomas	1			1		2	1		1				6		
Partridgefield	185	3	Apthorp	James	2	1		1		1	2	1	1				9		
Partridgefield	185	4	Abbey	Obadiah			1		1			1		1			4		
Partridgefield	185	5	Abbey	Roger	2			1		3			1				7		
Partridgefield	185	6	Allen	Thomas			1				1	1					3		
Partridgefield	185	7	Byxbe	Solomon	1		1					1					3		
Partridgefield	185	8	Bull	Seth			1			1			1				3		
Partridgefield	185	9	Browning	Joseph	1			1		2	1		1				6		
Partridgefield	185	10	Blackman	Abraham Jr	3			1		1			1				6		
Partridgefield	185	11	Barrett	Amos	1	2	1			3		1	1				9		
Partridgefield	185	12	Barrett	Nathan	3	1		1		2		1	1				9		
Partridgefield	185	13	Burnett	Daniel	3			1		2			1				7		
Partridgefield	185	14	Bass	Henry		1						1					2		
Partridgefield	185	15	Baleau	Elias		1	2		1	1		1		1			7		
Partridgefield	185	16	Blackman	Nathl	2			1					1				4		
Partridgefield	185	17	Blackman	Abraham		1	1		1			1		1			5		
Partridgefield	185	18	Bullard	Lemuel	1	1	1			2		1					6		
Partridgefield	185	19	Benson	Noah		1	1			1			1				4		
Partridgefield	185	20	Browning	Solomon	1			1		1		1					4		
Partridgefield	185	21	Bass	Jonathan	2			1	1	2		1		1			8		
Partridgefield	185	22	Butts	Rufus		2	1		1	3	1	1					10		
Partridgefield	185	23	Bad*	Henry	1			1		1			2	1			6		
Partridgefield	186	1	Bowen	Peter	1		1	1		1		1	1				6		
Partridgefield	186	2	Bacon	Joseph	2		1	1	1	2	1	1	1				10		
Partridgefield	186	3	Bowen	Christopher		1	2		2	1		1		2			9		
Partridgefield	186	4	Barnabe	Chandler	1	1	1	1		2	1	1	1				9		
Partridgefield	186	5	Byxbe	Aaron				2					1				3		
Partridgefield	186	6	Belcher	Andrew		1		1		1	2	1	1				7		
Partridgefield	186	7	Babcock	John		2		1		2	1	1		1			8		
Partridgefield	186	8	Burnham	Elizeer		1	1						1				3		
Partridgefield	186	9	Blackman	Eleazer						3		1					4		
Partridgefield	186	10	Browning	David		1		1					1				3		
Partridgefield	186	11	Browning	Tristram	2	1		1		2	2	1	2				11		
Partridgefield	186	12	Beaton	Jacob	3	1		1		1	1		1	1			9		
Partridgefield	186	13	Booth	Jesse	1			1				1					3		
Partridgefield	186	14	Booth	Isaiah		1						1					2		
Partridgefield	186	15	Booth	Jacob	1		1	1		1		1		1			6		
Partridgefield	186	16	Brown	Daniel	1		1			2		1					5		
Partridgefield	186	17	Belcher	Calvin		1				3		1					5		
Partridgefield	186	18	Grace	Sybil	2					2	1		1	1			7		
Partridgefield	186	19	Brown	David 2d	2	1	1	1		2	1	1					9		
Partridgefield	186	20	Colt	Richard			1			1	1	*	*	*			3		image torn
Partridgefield	186	21	Cone	Daniel	1		1	*		*	*	*	*	*			2		image torn
Partridgefield	186	22	Curtiss	Francis	1		1	1									3		
Partridgefield	186	23	Curtiss	Comfort	1		1			1	1						4		
Partridgefield	186	24	Curtiss	Amasa	2			1		1							4		
Partridgefield	186	25	Crozier	John	1	2		1		2	1		1				8		
Partridgefield	186	26	Clark	Joseph	1			1		2	1	1	1	1			8		
Partridgefield	186	27	Cad	Phineas		2	1	1		1	2		1				8		
Partridgefield	186	28	Cole	Ezra	4		1	1			3	1	1				11		
Partridgefield	186	29	Cady	Philip	1		1	1				1	1				5		
Partridgefield	186	30	Chamberlin	Asa	2		1			1	1	1					6		
Partridgefield	186	31	Cady	Eleazer	3			1		1	2		1				8		
Partridgefield	186	32	Crary	Christopher	1	1		1		3	1	1	1				9		
Partridgefield	186	33	Diball	Eritha	1		1			1		1					4		
Partridgefield	186	34	Dibol	Eli	1		1			1		1					4		
Partridgefield	186	35	Daniels	Walter	2		1			3		1					7		
Partridgefield	186	36	Dresser	Isaac	1	1		1		2	1		1				7		
Partridgefield	186	37	Davenport	Joseph		1		1		1		1	1				5		
Partridgefield	186	38	Everett	Andrew			1	2	1	1				1			6		
Partridgefield	186	39	Ferguson	James				1						1			2		
Partridgefield	186	40	Frissel	Amasa	2			1		1			1				5		
Partridgefield	186	41	Fish	Ervin		1				1		1					2		
Partridgefield	186	42	Ford	Charles	2		1			2		1					6		
Partridgefield	186	43	Frink	Israel	1		2	1		1				1			6		
Partridgefield	187	1	Frissel	William		3	1	1					1				6		
Partridgefield	187	2	Fletcher	William	1		1	1	1			1		1			6		
Partridgefield	187	3	Freeman	Ebenezer	1		1			1		1					4		
Partridgefield	187	4	Ford	Sybil						1		1					2		
Partridgefield	187	5	Frissel	William Jr	2	1		1					1				5		
Partridgefield	187	6	Forbes	Elisha		1						1					2		
Partridgefield	187	7	Goldthwait	Joseph		2		1		1		1	1				6		
Partridgefield	187	8	Gilbert	Elijah		2		1		1	2		1				7		
Partridgefield	187	9	Geer	John	2	3	1	1		2	1		1				11		
Partridgefield	187	10	Goldthwait	Daniel	1		1			1		1					4		
Partridgefield	187	11	Goodrich	Elijah	2		1			2		1					6		
Partridgefield	187	12	Gasper	Joseph	2	1	1			1		1					6		
Partridgefield	187	13	Goldthwait	Nathan	3		1					1					5		
Partridgefield	187	14	Gilbert	Elizabeth									1	1			2		

TOWN	PG#	LN#	LAST NAME	FIRST NAME	FREE WHITE MALES					FREE WHITE FEMALES					TOTAL ALL OTHER	TOTAL SLAVES	TOTALS	DISTRICT/ TOWNSHIP	NOTES
			HEADS OF HOUSEHOLD		under 10	10 to 16	16 to 26	26 to 45	45 and over	under 10	10 to 16	16 to 26	26 to 45	45 and over					
Partridgefield	187	15	Gilbert	Henry		1			1	3	2		1				8		
Partridgefield	187	16	Howard	Henry			2			1	1	1		1			6		
Partridgefield	187	17	Holbrook	Benajah			1					1					2		
Partridgefield	187	18	Hatheway	John	1			1				1					3		
Partridgefield	187	19	Hall	Parker	1	1	2		1	1	1	1					8		
Partridgefield	187	20	Hatheway	Seth		1		1		1		1					4		
Partridgefield	187	21	Hapall	Roger	1	2	1		1	3		1	1				10		
Partridgefield	187	22	Henry	John	4			1		2	1		1				9		
Partridgefield	187	23	Hascal	Jeremiah	1	4	2		1	2		1	1				12		
Partridgefield	187	24	Howard	Artemas	1			1		2			1				5		
Partridgefield	187	25	Hubbard	Ephraim		1		1		1				1			4		
Partridgefield	187	26	Hibbard	Nathan	1	1	1	1				1		1			6		
Partridgefield	187	27	Hening	Samuel				1									1		
Partridgefield	187	28	Ide	Oliver				1					1	1			3		
Partridgefield	187	29	Ide	David	3			1		1			1				6		
Partridgefield	187	30	Jackson	Joshua		1	1	1			1	1		1			6		
Partridgefield	187	31	Jones	Samuel	1					1			1				3		
Partridgefield	187	32	Goodrich	Asa		2		1		2	1		1				7		
Partridgefield	187	33	Kingsley	Jedidiah		2	1	1	1	2		1		1			9		
Partridgefield	187	34	Kingsley	Silas	1			1		2			1				5		
Partridgefield	187	35	Lealand	John		1			1	1	1		1				5		
Partridgefield	187	36	Lealand	John Jun		1						1					2		
Partridgefield	187	37	Lealand	Moses	1			1		1			1				4		
Partridgefield	187	38	Loomer	Darius	3			1					1	1			6		
Partridgefield	187	39	Lyman	Joel	3			1			1	1					6		
Partridgefield	187	40	Loveland	Levi	2			1		1	2		1				7		
Partridgefield	187	41	Loomer	Charles	3	1		1			2	1	1				9		
Partridgefield	187	42	Loomis	Eleazer		3		1		2		1	1				8		
Partridgefield	187	43	Lyman	Samuel	1			1		2	1		1				6		
Partridgefield	187	44	Lyman	Isaac	1			1		3			1				6		
Partridgefield	188	1	Loveland	Philip		1		1		4			1				7		
Partridgefield	188	2	Miner	Joshua	1		1					1					3		
Partridgefield	188	3	Miner	Christopher	2			1	1	2		1	1	1			9		
Partridgefield	188	4	Marsh	Lemuel			1	1					3	1			6		
Partridgefield	188	5	Marsh	Lemuel Jun	1		1					1					3		
Partridgefield	188	6	Marsh	Samuel			1			2	2		1				6		
Partridgefield	188	7	Malloon	Ruth		1	3			1	3			1			9		
Partridgefield	188	8	Miner	Treat	2			1		1		1					5		
Partridgefield	188	9	Messenger	Nathll	1		1					1					3		
Partridgefield	188	10	Mathews	Thomas	1			1		1			1				4		
Partridgefield	188	11	Miner	Isaac	2	1			1	2	1		1				8		
Partridgefield	188	12	Miller	David			1		1	1	1			2	1		7		
Partridgefield	188	13	Morly	David	1	1		1		2	1		1				7		
Partridgefield	188	14	Nicholson	Nathan	2			1		2			1				6		
Partridgefield	188	15	Olds	Daniel	2	2	1	1	1	1			1	1			10		
Partridgefield	188	16	Payn	Allen	2			1		1			1	1			6		
Partridgefield	188	17	Parker	Abel Junr		1	1					1					3		
Partridgefield	188	18	Poole	John	1		1	1		2	2		1				8		
Partridgefield	188	19	Parker	Abel		1			1	1	1			1			5		
Partridgefield	188	20	Pease	James		3		1		1	1	1	1				8		
Partridgefield	188	21	Perry	John		1	1	1		4	2	1	1				11		
Partridgefield	188	22	Perry	Joseph	5	1		1					1				8		
Partridgefield	188	23	Peirce	Ebenezer	2	1	1		1	1	2	1		2			11		
Partridgefield	188	24	Peirce	John	1		1			1		1					4		
Partridgefield	188	25	Peirce	Levi	1	1	3	1			1		1	1			9		
Partridgefield	188	26	Peirce	Benja		1		1				1	1				4		
Partridgefield	188	27	Phillips	Smith	1	1		1		3		1	1				8		
Partridgefield	188	28	Pomeroy	Daniel	1	1	1	1		2			1				7		
Partridgefield	188	29	Parks	Asa	2		2		1	3	1	2	1				12		
Partridgefield	188	30	Prentiss	Thomas		1		1		2		2	1				7		
Partridgefield	188	31	Payn	Ebenezer	4	3		1					1				9		
Partridgefield	188	32	Payn	Stephen		1				1		1					3		
Partridgefield	188	33	Post	Ichabod	1			1		2			1				5		
Partridgefield	188	34	Pearse	William		1	1		1	2	1	1		1			8		
Partridgefield	188	35	Peirce	George	1		1	1		1			1				5		
Partridgefield	188	36	Richards	William		2	1		1	2	1	1		2			10		
Partridgefield	188	37	Reefs	Ebenezer	3			1		1	1	1	2	1			10		
Partridgefield	188	38	Rockwell	Amasa	3	1		1				2	1				8		
Partridgefield	188	39	Robbins	Ebenezer			1			3		1					5		
Partridgefield	188	40	Rockwood	Daniel	2			1		2			1				6		
Partridgefield	188	41	Richmond	Elihu	1		1	1	1	2			1	1			8		
Partridgefield	188	42	Richmond	Abner	1			1		2		1					5		
Partridgefield	188	43	Raymond	Amos	1	1	1	1		1	2		1				8		
Partridgefield	188	44	Richmond	Zebulon	1	1	1	1		2	1	1	1				9		
Partridgefield	189	1	Sackett	Walter			2						1				3		
Partridgefield	189	2	Stebbins	Dan	1	1		1					1				4		
Partridgefield	189	3	Scovel	Jonas	1	1	1		1		1	1		2			8		
Partridgefield	189	4	Scovel	Jonas Junr	1		1										3		
Partridgefield	189	5	Starr	Richard		1	1		2	1	2	2		1			10		

TOWN	PG#	LN#	LAST NAME	FIRST NAME	FREE WHITE MALES under 10	10 to 16	16 to 26	26 to 45	45 and over	FREE WHITE FEMALES under 10	10 to 16	16 to 26	26 to 45	45 and over	TOTAL ALL OTHER	TOTAL SLAVES	TOTALS	DISTRICT/TOWNSHIP	NOTES
Partridgefield	189	6	Snow	Orin	2			1					1				4		
Partridgefield	189	7	Standish	Jonas	1				1		3			1			6		
Partridgefield	189	8	Siblee	Benja	2		1					1					4		
Partridgefield	189	9	Smith	Ebenezer				1				1		1			3		
Partridgefield	189	10	Stowell	Harvey	1		1	1				2	1	1			7		
Partridgefield	189	11	Stowell	Cyrus		1		1		1	1	2	1				7		
Partridgefield	189	12	Stearns	Elias	2	1	1		1	1	1		1				9		
Partridgefield	189	13	Smith	John	1	1		1		3		1	1	1			9		
Partridgefield	189	14	Smith	Isaac		1		1		2	1	1					6		
Partridgefield	189	15	Smith	Hugh	3	1	1	1			1		1				8		
Partridgefield	189	16	Smith	George	4	1		1		2			1				9		
Partridgefield	189	17	Stevens	Wm	2	1		1		2		1	2				9		
Partridgefield	189	18	Siblee	Elisha	1		1					1					3		
Partridgefield	189	19	Standish	Jonas Jr	1		1			1		1					4		
Partridgefield	189	20	Stearns	Asa				1		3		1					5		
Partridgefield	189	21	Thompson	Artemas				1					1	1			3		
Partridgefield	189	22	Torrey	Nathan		1	1	1				1		1			6		
Partridgefield	189	23	Tracy	Nathll		2	2		1			1		1			7		
Partridgefield	189	24	Tracy	James	1			1		2			1				5		
Partridgefield	189	25	Thompson	Daniel		1	1	1						1			4		
Partridgefield	189	26	Thompson	Peter	1		2		1			2	1	1			8		
Partridgefield	189	27	Thompson	Nathan	1	2	2		1	1	1	1	1				10		
Partridgefield	189	28	Thompson	Simeon	2		1	1		2			1				7		
Partridgefield	189	29	Thompson	William	1			1		1			1				4		
Partridgefield	189	30	Thompson	Elias 2d				1		1			1				3		
Partridgefield	189	31	Thompson	Elias			2						1				3		
Partridgefield	189	32	Thompson	Levi	1			1		2		1					5		
Partridgefield	189	33	Thompson	Amherst	1	1		1		2	1		1				7		
Partridgefield	189	34	Teethill	Nathan		1	1	1	1	3	1	1		1			10		
Partridgefield	189	35	Tinney	Oliver	2	1		1		3	1		1				9		
Partridgefield	189	36	Tinney	Isaac				1			1		1				3		
Partridgefield	189	37	Thayer	Jonathan	3	2	1		1	2	1		1				11		
Partridgefield	189	38	Thomas	Samuel	2			1		1			1				5		
Partridgefield	189	39	Wilcox	Samuel		1						2		1			4		
Partridgefield	189	40	Watkins	John		2	2		1			3		1			9		
Partridgefield	189	41	Watkins	Andrew	1			1		3			1				6		
Partridgefield	189	42	Watkins	Gilbert	2	1		1		2		1	1				8		
Partridgefield	189	43	Watkins	James			1		1		1	1		1			5		
Partridgefield	190	1	Watkins	Oliver	1						1	1					3		
Partridgefield	190	2	Watkins	Jason	3			1		3			1				8		
Partridgefield	190	3	Whitmore	John				1				1	1	1			4		
Partridgefield	190	4	Whitney	John			1		2	1				2			6		
Partridgefield	190	5	Whitney	Jabez	2	2			1	2	1	1		1			10		
Partridgefield	190	6	Witter	Ebenezer		1		1						1			3		
Partridgefield	190	7	Watkins	Zech Junr	1		1	1				2		1			6		
Partridgefield	190	8	Watkins	Samuel		1	2	1				2		1			7		
Partridgefield	190	9	Watkins	Elisha	3			1		1	1						6		
Partridgefield	190	10	Watkins	Saml Jr				1		1		1					3		
Partridgefield	190	11	Wheelock	Ralph	2	1	1	1		1	1		1				8		
Partridgefield	190	12	Witter	Joseph Junr	2	1	1	1	1	1	2		2				11		
Partridgefield	190	13	Washburn	Abraham				2		1			1				4		
Partridgefield	190	14	Witter	Sephimus	1	1		1		1		1					5		
Partridgefield	190	15	Wing	Seth			1		1		2		1	1			6		
Partridgefield	190	16	Wing	Elisha	2	1		1		2	2	1	1				10		
Partridgefield	190	17	Wheeler	Ephraim	1			1		1			1				4		
Partridgefield	190	18	Watson	John	2			1		2	1		1				7		
Partridgefield	190	19	Wood	Amariah			2		2	3				2			9		
Partridgefield	190	20	Watkins	Amasa	3			1					1				5		
Partridgefield	190	21	Whitmore	Oliver	1			1		1			1				4		
Partridgefield	190	22	Watkins	Rufus	1		1						1				3		
Partridgefield	190	23	Whiling	Charles				1			1	1	1				4		
Partridgefield	190	24	Whiling	Ebenezer				1		1			1				3		
Partridgefield	190	25	Watkins	Simpson	1	1	1	1				2					6		
Partridgefield	190	26	Yeamans	Moses	1		1						1				3		
Partridgefield	190	27	Mathews	Samuel				1				1					2		

TOWN	PG#	LN#	HEADS OF HOUSEHOLD		FREE WHITE MALES					FREE WHITE FEMALES					TOTAL ALL OTHER	TOTAL SLAVES	TOTALS	DISTRICT/TOWNSHIP	NOTES
			LAST NAME	FIRST NAME	under 10	10 to 16	16 to 26	26 to 45	45 and over	under 10	10 to 16	16 to 26	26 to 45	45 and over					
Pittsfield	194	1	Allen	Thomas	2	1			1	2	1			1			8		
Pittsfield	194	2	Allen	Thomas Jun	1		1	2							1		5		
Pittsfield	194	3	Allen	Rufus	2	1			1			2		1	1		8		
Pittsfield	194	4	Allen	Sarah									1	1			2		
Pittsfield	194	5	Allen	Horace	1		1				1	1					4		
Pittsfield	194	6	Ashley	David Junr		1	1	1		4	1	1	1				10		
Pittsfield	194	7	Brown	James	1		2	2			1	1					7		
Pittsfield	194	8	Brattle	William	1		1		1	2	1		1		1		8		
Pittsfield	194	9	Brattle	James	1	1			2	1		1	1	2			9		
Pittsfield	194	10	Barber	Matthew		1		1				2	1	1			6		
Pittsfield	194	11	Boyndon	Joshua		1	1					2	2	1			7		
Pittsfield	194	12	Blackman	Isbon											6		6		
Pittsfield	194	13	Braley	Nathl		2		1		1							4		
Pittsfield	194	14	Barton	Robert		1		1		1			1				4		
Pittsfield	194	15	Barrett	Solomon	2			1		2			1				6		
Pittsfield	194	16	Barrett	Jonathan		1		1	1			2		1			6		
Pittsfield	194	17	Babcock	James	1	1	1		1	3	1			1			9		
Pittsfield	194	18	Bailey	Joseph				1					1				2		
Pittsfield	194	19	Ball	Jonas	1			1		2			1				5		
Pittsfield	194	20	Butler	George	4	1			1			1		1			8		
Pittsfield	194	21	Brown	Thomas	3			1		1	1		1	1			8		
Pittsfield	194	22	Bush	David Junr	3	2	2		1			1	2				11		
Pittsfield	195	1	Bush	David	2		1	1	1	1			1	1			9		
Pittsfield	195	2	Barnard	Richard	3			1				1		1			6		
Pittsfield	195	3	Blackman	Dan	3	1	1	1		2	1		1				10		
Pittsfield	195	4	Bingham	Septimus	1		1	1		1				1			5		
Pittsfield	195	5	Williams	Bancroft	2	1		1		1			1				6		
Pittsfield	195	6	Blackman	Samuel	2	1		1				1		1			7		
Pittsfield	195	7	Bates	Ezekiel		2				1		1					4		
Pittsfield	195	8	Bagg	Martin Jun	1		1			1			1				4		
Pittsfield	195	9	Brooks	Reuben	3			1		1	1		1				7		
Pittsfield	195	10	Butler	Simeon			1						1				2		
Pittsfield	195	11	Baker	Aaron			1	1	1	3		1	1	2			10		
Pittsfield	195	12	Baker	Joshua	1			1		1			1				4		
Pittsfield	195	13	Bagg	Martin		1	1		1	1	1	1		1			7		
Pittsfield	195	14	Bishop	Charles	2		1	1		2			1	1			8		
Pittsfield	195	15	Burt	Oliver			1	1				1		1			4		
Pittsfield	195	16	Burt	Thomas		1	1	1		4	1		1				9		
Pittsfield	195	17	Burt	Ebenezer	1			1		3			1				6		
Pittsfield	195	18	Butler	Joseph		1	1	1	1		1	1		1			7		
Pittsfield	195	19	Butler	Josiah		1	1		1	1		1		1			6		
Pittsfield	195	20	Burdich	Francis				1		2			1				4		
Pittsfield	195	21	Bagg	Elijah	2		2	1		3			1	1			10		
Pittsfield	195	22	Bryant	John	2	1		1			1		1				6		
Pittsfield	195	23	Beckwith	Reynolds	1	2	1	1		1	1			1			8		
Pittsfield	195	24	Brown	Abraham C	1			1		2	2		1				7		
Pittsfield	195	25	Burgess	Joseph	1	1		1		1			1				5		
Pittsfield	195	26	Bacon	Asa	2	2	1		1	2		1	1				10		
Pittsfield	195	27	Baker	John				1						1			2		
Pittsfield	195	28	Brooks	Jabez	1	1	2		1	1	2			1			9		
Pittsfield	195	29	Baker	Elisha	1	1		1		2			1				6		
Pittsfield	195	30	Colt	William		1	1					1					4		
Pittsfield	195	31	Childs	Timothy	2		1	1	1	2	3		1				11		
Pittsfield	195	32	Cogswell	Benja		1	1	1		2	1	1	1				8		
Pittsfield	195	33	Chapman	Olcutt	3	1		1					1				6		
Pittsfield	195	34	Churchill	John		2			1		1	1		1			6		
Pittsfield	195	35	Churchill	John 2d	1	1		1		4	1		1				9		
Pittsfield	195	36	Crandal	Ezekiel	1	1		1		2			1				6		
Pittsfield	195	37	Colt	James D	2	2	1		1	1	2	1	1		3		14		
Pittsfield	195	38	Clark	Ichabod	1	1			1	1	3			1			8		
Pittsfield	195	39	Cadwell	Timothy	2	1		1	1			1	4	1			11		
Pittsfield	195	40	Cadwell	Abigail		1	1					1	1	1			5		
Pittsfield	195	41	Chapman	David		1			1	1		1	3	1			8		
Pittsfield	195	42	Colt	Jabez		1		1		2		1					5		
Pittsfield	196	1	Cadwell	Eliar	3		1	1		1	1		1				8		
Pittsfield	196	2	Cogswell	Rufus		1		1		1		2	1				6		
Pittsfield	196	3	Clark	Nathan		1				1			1				3		
Pittsfield	196	4	Cottin	Jonathan	1			1		1			1				4		
Pittsfield	196	5	Campbell	David	2	1	2	1		2	2		1				11		
Pittsfield	196	6	Culver	Henry	1			1		3			1				6		
Pittsfield	196	7	Crowfoot	Simeon		2		1			1			1			5		
Pittsfield	196	8	Chamberlin	John		1		2						1			4		
Pittsfield	196	9	Clark	Thomas	1	1	1		1	1	1		1				7		
Pittsfield	196	10	Colt	James D Junr	3		2	1		1		1	1		1		10		
Pittsfield	196	11	Crane	Stephen						1			1				2		
Pittsfield	196	12	Colt	John			1						1				2		
Pittsfield	196	13	Dunbar	Calvin	1	1	2	1			1	1		1			8		
Pittsfield	196	14	Dyke	Elias	2			1		1			1				5		
Pittsfield	196	15	Dickinson	Olr P.		1	1	1		2	1		2	1	1		10		

TOWN	PG#	LN#	LAST NAME	FIRST NAME	FREE WHITE MALES					FREE WHITE FEMALES					TOTAL ALL OTHER	TOTAL SLAVES	TOTALS	DISTRICT/ TOWNSHIP	NOTES
					under 10	10 to 16	16 to 26	26 to 45	45 and over	under 10	10 to 16	16 to 26	26 to 45	45 and over					
Pittsfield	196	16	Danforth	Joshua	1		1	1		3		1	2				9		
Pittsfield	196	17	Deane	Solomon		1		1			1		1				4		
Pittsfield	196	18	Davis	James				2		5			2				9		
Pittsfield	196	19	Dickinson	John			2	1	1	1		1					6		
Pittsfield	196	20	Derning	John		1	2	3	7	1		3	6	3			26		
Pittsfield	196	21	Durwin	Abner	1			1		3			1				6		
Pittsfield	196	22	Deane	Pearl			1			1		1					3		
Pittsfield	196	23	Durfey	John					1					1			2		
Pittsfield	196	24	Davis	Cyrus			2						1				3		
Pittsfield	196	25	Dighton	John B	2	3			1	2			1				9		
Pittsfield	196	26	Edgerton	Ebenezer	3		1	1		1			1				7		
Pittsfield	196	27	Ells	John	1			1		1		1					4		
Pittsfield	196	28	Eddy	Caleb			2	3					6	4			16		
Pittsfield	196	29	Ellithorp	Ichabod	1			1		1		1	1	1			6		
Pittsfield	196	30	Ensign	Jacob		2		1					1				4		
Pittsfield	196	31	Ensign	Elijah	1	3	1	1		2	1	1	1				11		
Pittsfield	196	32	Ensign	Polly	1	1				2	1	1	1				7		
Pittsfield	196	33	Ellis	John	1		2		1			1		1	1		7		
Pittsfield	196	34	Eason	Joseph	1	1			1	2		1	1				7		
Pittsfield	196	35	Fairfield	Nathll		2	3	1	1		1	1		1			10		
Pittsfield	196	36	Fairfield	Joseph	1	1			1	1			1	1			6		
Pittsfield	196	37	Fairfield	Joseph Jr	1		1	1		2	1		1				7		
Pittsfield	196	38	Fairfield	John	1			1				1			1		4		
Pittsfield	196	39	Fairfield	Enoch	3		1	1					1				6		
Pittsfield	196	40	Farr	Joseph		1		1		2			1	1			6		
Pittsfield	196	41	Fanning	Orionel	2		3	1		2			1	1			10		
Pittsfield	196	42	Fuller	Asa	3	1		1		2	1	3	1				12		
Pittsfield	196	43	Fletcher	John	2	1		1		2			1				7		
Pittsfield	196	44	Frisby	Edward	1		6			2	1		1				11		
Pittsfield	197	1	Fuller	Oliver		1				1			1				3		
Pittsfield	197	2	Ford	Rhoda									2				2		
Pittsfield	197	3	Finney	David	2		1		1				1	1			6		
Pittsfield	197	4	Fitch	Dyar	2	1	1	1		2			1				8		
Pittsfield	197	5	Francis	Luke	1			1					1				3		
Pittsfield	197	6	Francis	William	1		1	1	1	2			1	1			8		
Pittsfield	197	7	Francis	Robert	2			1	1	2	2		1				9		
Pittsfield	197	8	Fowler	Stephen		2	1		1			1		1			6		
Pittsfield	197	9	Francis	Josiah		1	1	1					1	1			5		
Pittsfield	197	10	Francis	Josiah Jun	1	1		1		1		1	1				6		
Pittsfield	197	11	Francis	John	1			1		1	2	1	1				7		
Pittsfield	197	12	Foulton	John	2			1		1			1				5		
Pittsfield	197	13	Forbes	Alexander		1	2		1	1		1		1			7		
Pittsfield	197	14	Goodrich	Moses	1	2			1	1		1	1				7		
Pittsfield	197	15	Goodrich	Jesse	2			1		2	2		1	1			9		
Pittsfield	197	16	Goodrich	Butler	4		1	1					1	1			8		
Pittsfield	197	17	Goodale	Isaac	2	2		1		2	1	1	1				10		
Pittsfield	197	18	Goodrich	Orionel	2		2	1		1			1				7		
Pittsfield	197	19	Geer	Hezekiah	3		1	1		3			1				9		
Pittsfield	197	20	Griswold	Simeon		1	1		1	3	1			1			8		
Pittsfield	197	21	Gifford	Eliab		1		1		1		2					5		
Pittsfield	197	22	Goodrich	Abigail	1	1	3			1	1	2	2				11		
Pittsfield	197	23	Griswold	Samuel	2			1					1				4		
Pittsfield	197	24	Gunn	Gideon					1			1	1				3		
Pittsfield	197	25	Gold	Thomas	1	2	3	2		3	4	2	1				18		
Pittsfield	197	26	Good	Charles	2	2	1		1		1	3		1			11		
Pittsfield	197	27	Gunn	Calvin			1			1			1				3		
Pittsfield	197	28	Hubbard	James		2			1	1		2		1			7		
Pittsfield	197	29	Hubbard	James Jr	2			1		2			1				6		
Pittsfield	197	30	Hubbard	Daniel	1		1						1				3		
Pittsfield	197	31	Hooper	Zalonanna	1		2			1			1				5		
Pittsfield	197	32	Hooper	Archelaus	1			1		3			1				6		
Pittsfield	197	33	Hanchit	Simeon		1	1		1	2	1						5		
Pittsfield	197	34	Hicock	Aaron	1			1		2		2					6		
Pittsfield	197	35	Hanmer	Alenson	2	1		1		1	1		1				7		
Pittsfield	197	36	Hayes	William	3		1			1	1						6		
Pittsfield	197	37	Hicock	John	1		2						1				4		
Pittsfield	197	38	Hutchinson	Paul				1		1		1	1	2			5		
Pittsfield	197	39	Hulbert	Timothy	1	2		1		3	1		1				9		
Pittsfield	197	40	Hicock	Ichabod		1	2	1						1			5		
Pittsfield	197	41	Hubbard	Zadoch Jr		1	1			1			1				4		
Pittsfield	197	42	Hoadley	Jacob		1		1						1			3		
Pittsfield	197	43	Hubby	Hardes		1	1						1	1			4		
Pittsfield	197	44	Hearich	Jason	4	1		1		1			1				8		
Pittsfield	198	1	Hammond	James	3			1				1	1				6		
Pittsfield	198	2	Hearich	Zebulon	1				1					1			3		
Pittsfield	198	3	Henry	William			1		1		1			1			4		
Pittsfield	198	4	Hearich	Zebulon Jr	2	1		1		1		1	1				7		
Pittsfield	198	5	Howland	Joseph	2			1				1	1				5		
Pittsfield	198	6	Hibbard	Nathan	4			1		1		1	1				8		

54

TOWN	PG#	LN#	LAST NAME	FIRST NAME	FREE WHITE MALES					FREE WHITE FEMALES					TOTAL ALL OTHER	TOTAL SLAVES	TOTALS	DISTRICT/ TOWNSHIP	NOTES
					under 10	10 to 16	16 to 26	26 to 45	45 and over	under 10	10 to 16	16 to 26	26 to 45	45 and over					
Pittsfield	198	7	Hitchcock	Eli	1	2			1	1				1			6		
Pittsfield	198	8	Hollister	William	5			1		1	1	1	1		1		11		
Pittsfield	198	9	Hulbert	John			1			2			1				4		
Pittsfield	198	10	Hall	Nathan				1				1		1			3		
Pittsfield	198	11	Jarrett	Stephen			1		1		1			1			4		
Pittsfield	198	12	Ingersoll	Jared			1		1	1	2			1			6		
Pittsfield	198	13	Johnson	Rufus		1	1	1		1			1		1		6		
Pittsfield	198	14	Johnson	Isaac			1	1			1		1	1			5		
Pittsfield	198	15	Isham	Lemuel	1	1		1				1					4		
Pittsfield	198	16	Janes	Seth	1	1	1	2			1		1				7		
Pittsfield	198	17	Jeffords	Amasa	1			1		1			1				4		
Pittsfield	198	18	Jeffords	John				1		1		2		1			5		
Pittsfield	198	19	Jarvis	John				1		1				1			3		
Pittsfield	198	20	King	Paul				1				2		1			4		
Pittsfield	198	21	Kingsley	Jona	4			1		1			1	1			8		
Pittsfield	198	22	Keeler	Elias	2		1	1	1	1		2					8		
Pittsfield	198	23	Keeler	Benjamin		1	2		1	1	1		1				7		
Pittsfield	198	24	Kennedy	Andrew		1	1				1		1				4		
Pittsfield	198	25	Kent	Benjamin	1	1		1		1			1	1			6		
Pittsfield	198	26	Knealand	John	1			1		2			1				5		
Pittsfield	198	27	Kittridge	William		1	1	4		2	2	1	2				13		
Pittsfield	198	28	Knealand	Polly									1				1		
Pittsfield	198	29	Leach	Elijah		1			1	2	1	2		1			8		
Pittsfield	198	30	Lee	Jonathan				1		1				1			3		
Pittsfield	198	31	Lawrence	Josiah	2	2		1		1	1	1	1				9		
Pittsfield	198	32	Little	Woodbridge	1	1		1			1		1	2			7		
Pittsfield	198	33	Larned	Simon	5		1		1	2	1	1					11		
Pittsfield	198	34	Lathrop	Uriah	1	2		1		4	2		1				11		
Pittsfield	198	35	Luce	Joshua	2		2	1		1	2	1	1				10		
Pittsfield	198	36	Lyman	Miles			1					1					2		
Pittsfield	198	37	Loomis	Jonathan	1	1	1		1	1	1		1				7		
Pittsfield	198	38	Longworthy	Willard	1			1				1					3		
Pittsfield	198	39	Luce	Benjamin	1	2	1	3			1	2	1				11		
Pittsfield	198	40	Luce	Hezekiah	2		1	2	1	2		1	1	1			11		
Pittsfield	198	41	Lewis	Joseph			1			1		1		1			4		
Pittsfield	198	42	Luce	David	1	1		1				2					5		
Pittsfield	199	1	Luce	Cornelius	2		1			2			1				6		
Pittsfield	199	2	Mead	Stephen				1					1				2		
Pittsfield	199	3	Moon	Seth		1	1				1		1				4		
Pittsfield	199	4	Maynard	Jotham	3		1			2		1	1				8		
Pittsfield	199	5	Montague	Seth	2	1		1			2		1				7		
Pittsfield	199	6	Mott	Lyman			1					1					2		
Pittsfield	199	7	Mead	Ephraim	2		2	1				2		1			8		
Pittsfield	199	8	Millard	Jason	3	1		1		2			1				8		
Pittsfield	199	9	Moseley	Chester	1		1			2			1	1			6		
Pittsfield	199	10	Mead	Stephen Junr	1	1		1		1			1				5		
Pittsfield	199	11	Moseley	Josiah	3	2	1	1	1			2		1			11		
Pittsfield	199	12	Millard	Matthew		2	1		1	1	1	1		2			9		
Pittsfield	199	13	Merrill	Daniel	1		1	1		3			1	1			9		
Pittsfield	199	14	Merrill	Ezekiel		1		1				1					3		
Pittsfield	199	15	Merrill	Hosea	3	2		1		2	2		1	1			12		
Pittsfield	199	16	Merry	Samuel	1			1		3			1				6		
Pittsfield	199	17	Mellen	William	1		2	1		3	1	1	1				10		
Pittsfield	199	18	Maynard	Eli	1		1			2		1					5		
Pittsfield	199	19	Miller	Timothy	2	1		1			1	1	1				7		
Pittsfield	199	20	McCoy	Paul	3	1		1		1	1		1				8		
Pittsfield	199	21	Moore	Mattew B.	1		1			1			1				4		
Pittsfield	199	22	Noble	Aaron		1	1					1					3		
Pittsfield	199	23	Newell	Aaron	2		1					1					4		
Pittsfield	199	24	Noble	David	1					3		1	1				6		
Pittsfield	199	25	Norton	Abel			1			1		1					3		
Pittsfield	199	26	Nogard	Isaac	1			1		1			1				4		
Pittsfield	199	27	Osborn	Richard				1			1	1		1			4		
Pittsfield	199	28	Osborn	John	1		1			1	1						4		
Pittsfield	199	29	Powars	Ephraim	1		1			1	1		1				5		
Pittsfield	199	30	Palmer	Lydia	1					2			1				4		
Pittsfield	199	31	Parmele	Asa						3		1	1				5		
Pittsfield	199	32	Partridge	William	1	2		1		4			1				9		
Pittsfield	199	33	Parker	Linas	4	1	1	1		2			1				10		
Pittsfield	199	34	Pomeroy	Lemuel		1	4	1				1	1		1		9		
Pittsfield	199	35	Peirce	Jonathan	2	1		1		1	1	1	1				8		
Pittsfield	199	36	Phelps	Benjamin	1	1	1	1	1	4	2		1				12		
Pittsfield	199	37	Pierson	David		1		1			1			1	1		5		
Pittsfield	199	38	Phelps	Luther			1			1		1		1			4		
Pittsfield	199	39	Plummer	Edward	1		1			1	1	1					5		
Pittsfield	199	40	Pomeroy	William	2		1					1					4		
Pittsfield	199	41	Platt	Joseph		1		1		1		1		1			5		
Pittsfield	199	42	Root	John		2		1		1	1		1				6		
Pittsfield	199	43	Rockwell	Elijah		1		1		1				1			4		

TOWN	PG#	LN#	HEADS OF HOUSEHOLD LAST NAME	FIRST NAME	FREE WHITE MALES under 10	10 to 16	16 to 26	26 to 45	45 and over	FREE WHITE FEMALES under 10	10 to 16	16 to 26	26 to 45	45 and over	TOTAL ALL OTHER	TOTAL SLAVES	TOTALS	DISTRICT/ TOWNSHIP	NOTES
Pittsfield	200	1	Root	Oliver	1	1	3		1		1	1		1			9		
Pittsfield	200	2	Robbins	Marcus			1			3			1		2		7		
Pittsfield	200	3	Robbins	Experience	1	1								1			3		
Pittsfield	200	4	Root	Azariah	3			1		1	1		1				7		
Pittsfield	200	5	Remington	John		1	1		1				1	1			5		
Pittsfield	200	6	Remington	John				1		4	1		1				7		
Pittsfield	200	7	Root	Samuel	3			1		2	1	1					8		
Pittsfield	200	8	Root	Aaron	1	1		1		1			1	1			6		
Pittsfield	200	9	Robbins	Elizabeth	2		3	1				2		2			10		
Pittsfield	200	10	Rathbun	Reuben	1			1					1				3		
Pittsfield	200	11	Rathbun	Benjamin					1	5	2		1	1			10		
Pittsfield	200	12	Rando	John G				1		4			1				6		
Pittsfield	200	13	Robbins	Silvester		1		1		4			1				7		
Pittsfield	200	14	Robbins	William		1		1					1				3		
Pittsfield	200	15	Root	Josiah				1		5	1		2				9		
Pittsfield	200	16	Robbins	Lucas	1		1					1					3		
Pittsfield	200	17	Reddington	Daniel	3					2		1	1				7		
Pittsfield	200	18	Root	William	2	1	1						1				5		
Pittsfield	200	19	Ripley	Perez		1		1		1			1				4		
Pittsfield	200	20	Root	Eli		1			1	1			1	1			5		
Pittsfield	200	21	Root	Rossel	3	2		1					1				7		
Pittsfield	200	22	Root	Daniel			2			1	1						4		
Pittsfield	200	23	Root	Abner				1			1		1		1		4		
Pittsfield	200	24	Root	Ezekiel	1	2	1	1	1			1		1	1		9		
Pittsfield	200	25	Richmond	Jemima	1					2	1		1				5		
Pittsfield	200	26	Rogers	Ezra				1					1				2		
Pittsfield	200	27	Root	Zenas	1			1					1				3		
Pittsfield	200	28	Roberts	Abner		1				1			1				3		
Pittsfield	200	29	Strong	Jonathan		1	1		1	1			1	1			6		
Pittsfield	200	30	Strong	Jonathan Jr		1							1				2		
Pittsfield	200	31	Stanford	Oliver	1				2	3	1		1				8		
Pittsfield	200	32	Smith	Betty								1	1				2		
Pittsfield	200	33	Shaw	Nathan	3		1	1		2			1				8		
Pittsfield	200	34	Smith	Samuel						1	1						2		
Pittsfield	200	35	Sprague	Samuel				1		3			1				5		
Pittsfield	200	36	Sturtevant	Friend	2			1					1				4		
Pittsfield	200	37	Strong	Ashbel		1	1	1	1	2			1	1	2		10		
Pittsfield	200	38	Stevens	Simeon		1		1						1			3		
Pittsfield	200	39	Stanton	Robert	2			1		2			1	1			7		
Pittsfield	200	40	Sackett	Solomon	1			1		1		1	2	1			7		
Pittsfield	200	41	Snow	John	3			1		1	1		1				7		
Pittsfield	200	42	Saxton	Jesse					1	2	1		1				5		
Pittsfield	200	43	Selwey	Thomas	1	1	1	1	1	3	2	1	1				12		
Pittsfield	201	1	Shepard	Jerre	2			1		2			1				6		
Pittsfield	201	2	Sackett	Richard						2		1	1				4		
Pittsfield	201	3	Shearer	Joseph		1	1			1	1		1		2		7		
Pittsfield	201	4	Smith	John		2			1	3			1				7		
Pittsfield	201	5	Stocking	Thomas	1	1	1		1	1	1		1				7		
Pittsfield	201	6	Strong	Noble	2		1						1				4		
Pittsfield	201	7	Sackett	Erastus				1	1	4	2	1	1				10		
Pittsfield	201	8	Smith	William		1				1		1					3		
Pittsfield	201	9	Stiles	Zebediah		1	1	2		1			2	1			8		
Pittsfield	201	10	Stevens	Joel		1	2		1			3		1			8		
Pittsfield	201	11	Snow	Ezra	2		2		1	1	1	1					8		
Pittsfield	201	12	Strong	King		1	1		1	2	1	5		1			12		
Pittsfield	201	13	Sackett	Daniel					1	1				1			3		
Pittsfield	201	14	Sackett	Lemuel	3	1		2		1			1	1			9		
Pittsfield	201	15	Taylor	James	3	2	1		1	1		2	1				11		
Pittsfield	201	16	Taylor	Abigail									1				1		
Pittsfield	201	17	Taylor	Thomas	1				1	2		1		1			6		
Pittsfield	201	18	Treat	Ebenezer				1		2		1					4		
Pittsfield	201	19	Tracy	Ezra			2		1	1				1			4		
Pittsfield	201	20	Tracy	Seth	2	1	1	1		1	2	1	1				10		
Pittsfield	201	21	Tracy	Elam				1					1				2		
Pittsfield	201	22	Tayler	Nathan	2	1		1					1				5		
Pittsfield	201	23	Thompson	Isaac				1		2	1	1					5		
Pittsfield	201	24	Torrey	Nathaniel	2				1	3			1				7		
Pittsfield	201	25	Torrey	David		1		1	1				1	1			5		
Pittsfield	201	26	Thompson	Samuel		1							1				2		
Pittsfield	201	27	Vanschaach	Henry	1	1			1				1		1	3		8		
Pittsfield	201	28	Whitney	Abijah				1		2			1				4		
Pittsfield	201	29	Whitney	Asa	1	1	4		1	1	2		1				11		
Pittsfield	201	30	Whitney	Joshua			2		1	1	1	1		1			7		
Pittsfield	201	31	Whitney	Joshua Jr			1			1			1				3		
Pittsfield	201	32	White	Abigail		1	3		1	1	3		1				10		
Pittsfield	201	33	Williams	Absolem		1	1		1	1	1	1	1				7		
Pittsfield	201	34	Williams	John C			1	1		1	3	1	1	1	1		9		
Pittsfield	201	35	Weston	Jonathan	3	1			1		1	2	1				9		
Pittsfield	201	36	Williams	Willm P	2			1		2	1		1				7		
Pittsfield	201	37	Ward	Isaac	2	1		1		1	1	1	1				8		

TOWN	PG#	LN#	LAST NAME	FIRST NAME	FREE WHITE MALES					FREE WHITE FEMALES					TOTAL ALL OTHER	TOTAL SLAVES	TOTALS	DISTRICT/ TOWNSHIP	NOTES
					under 10	10 to 16	16 to 26	26 to 45	45 and over	under 10	10 to 16	16 to 26	26 to 45	45 and over					
Pittsfield	201	38	Ward	Josiah	1	1	1	1		2		1	1				8		
Pittsfield	201	39	Ward	Jacob					1		1	1		1			4		
Pittsfield	201	40	Williams	Daniel			1			2			1				4		
Pittsfield	201	41	Weller	William	1			1			1		1		2		6		
Pittsfield	201	42	Whitney	Noah	2		2	4				2					10		
Pittsfield	201	43	Wetherel	Edward	2			1		2			1				6		
Pittsfield	202	1	Waldron	Michael	2			1					1				4		
Pittsfield	202	2	Wyman	S. Johnson	1	1		1		3	1		1				8		
Pittsfield	202	3	Waters	Philemon	2			1		1			1				5		
Pittsfield	202	4	Warner	Ebenezer	1	1	1	2		2		3					10		
Pittsfield	202	5	Waters	Josiah					1				1				2		
Pittsfield	202	6	West	Ichabod			1					1					2		
Pittsfield	202	7	Wright	Josiah				1			1		1	1			4		
Pittsfield	202	8	Waddams	Caleb	2			1		2	3	1		1			10		
Pittsfield	202	9	Wright	Titus			2	1						2			5		
Pittsfield	202	10	Weller	Daniel		1	2	1			1			1			6		
Pittsfield	202	11	Weller	Daniel Jr	2		1	1	2	3	1	1	1				12		
Pittsfield	202	12	Weller	Enoch	3		1	1		2			1				8		
Pittsfield	202	13	Weller	Justus	2	2			1	2	2	2	1				12		
Pittsfield	202	14	West	Samuel		1		1				2					4		
Pittsfield	202	15	West	Frederick	2		1					1					4		
Pittsfield	202	16	Ward	John	1	1	1		1	2	1	1		1			9		
Pittsfield	202	17	Williams	Oswald		1	2	1			1	2		1			8		
Pittsfield	202	18	West	Mason			1			2			1				4		
Pittsfield	202	19	Wright	Joseph															Enumeration blank
Pittsfield	202	20	Wright	Jonathan	1			1		3			1				6		Enumeration blank
Pittsfield	202	21	Wright	John															
Pittsfield	202	22	Walton	Silas	2				1	1	1		1	1			7		
Pittsfield	202	23	Dunton	David	3	1		1		1	1		1				8		
Pittsfield	202	24	a negro	Thomas											2		2		
Pittsfield	202	25	Bow	Simon											5		5		
Pittsfield	202	26	Avero	Benajah											2		2		
Pittsfield	202	27	Freeman	Pomp											3		3		
Pittsfield	202	28	Grant	Titus											5		5		
Pittsfield	202	29	a negro	Hartford											4		4		
Pittsfield	202	30	Fethergill	Joseph				1							2		3		
Pittsfield	202	31	Hazel	Bathsheba											2		2		
Pittsfield	202	32	a negro	Hagar											3		3		
Pittsfield	202	33	Erskine	Christian											3		3		
Pittsfield	202	34	Payn	Abel											4		4		
Pittsfield	202	35	Venduzer	Jacob											2		2		
Pittsfield	202	36	Wills	Sampson											9		9		

TOWN	PG#	LN#	HEADS OF HOUSEHOLD		FREE WHITE MALES					FREE WHITE FEMALES					TOTAL ALL OTHER	TOTAL SLAVES	TOTALS	DISTRICT/ TOWNSHIP	NOTES
			LAST NAME	FIRST NAME	under 10	10 to 16	16 to 26	26 to 45	45 and over	under 10	10 to 16	16 to 26	26 to 45	45 and over					
Richmond	205	1	Parker	Deborah				1		1	1		1				4		
Richmond	205	2	Scott	Nathan		1		1			2	1	2				7		
Richmond	205	3	Cook	Philip		1	2		1		1	3		1	1		10		
Richmond	205	4	Rosseter	Nathan				1				2		1			4		
Richmond	205	5	Rosseter	Abraham	1	1		1		2		1	1				7		
Richmond	205	6	Peirson	Henry	1			1		2		1			2		7		
Richmond	205	7	Rosseter	Noah	3	1		1			1		1				7		
Richmond	205	8	Rowley	Thomas	1				1				1				3		
Richmond	205	9	Hackley	Samuel					1				1		1		3		
Richmond	205	10	Hackley	Peter		1		1		2	1		1				6		
Richmond	205	11	Leadbetter	Thomas	1			1		3		1	1				7		
Richmond	205	12	Patterson	Joseph		1			1	1		2	1	1			7		
Richmond	205	13	Griffing	Russel					1	1	3	2		1			8		
Richmond	205	14	Rowley	Reuben	3			1					1				5		
Richmond	205	15	Hull	David					1				1				2		
Richmond	205	16	Lewis	Abel	1	1			1	4			1				8		
Richmond	205	17	Rowley	Richmond	3	2		1		2			1				9		
Richmond	205	18	Rowley	Erastus			2				1		1				4		
Richmond	205	19	Tracy	Erastus	3	1		1		1			1				7		
Richmond	205	20	Bishop	Leonard	2			1			1		1				5		
Richmond	205	21	Austin	Levi		2	2	1			2	1					8		
Richmond	205	22	Hough	Simon		1		1				1		1			4		
Richmond	205	23	Benton	Stephan		2	2	1				1		1			7		
Richmond	205	24	Moten	Jeremiah	1	1		1		1	1		1	1			7		
Richmond	206	1	Gates	Samuel		1	4	1			1		1	2			10		
Richmond	206	2	Strong	Asael	1	1		1	1		1		1	1			7		
Richmond	206	3	Leadbetter	Israel	1			1						2			4		
Richmond	206	4	Chittenden	William			1	1					1				3		
Richmond	206	5	Scott	Thomas			1						1	1			3		
Richmond	206	6	Sherril	Samuel	2		1		1	2	1	1	1	1			10		
Richmond	206	7	Williams	Nehemiah		1		1			1		1				4		
Richmond	206	8	Harris	William H.	1	1		1		3			1				7		
Richmond	206	9	Leadbetter	William S.			3						2				5		
Richmond	206	10	Plumb	Ebenezer		1	1			1		1					4		
Richmond	206	11	Johnson	Lemuel	1		2		1	1	2	1	1				9		
Richmond	206	12	Hillock	Robert		1		1		1			1				4		
Richmond	206	13	Stevens	Elisha	2	1	2		1		1	3		1			11		
Richmond	206	14	Gaston	John	1	2	1		1	2	1	2		1			11		
Richmond	206	15	Gates	James O.	3	1	1	1		2		1	1				10		
Richmond	206	16	Gaston	Robert	1		1		1		1	2		1			7		
Richmond	206	17	Booth	Samuel		2		1		2	1			1			7		
Richmond	206	18	Castle	Ebenezer		1		1				1	1	1			5		
Richmond	206	19	Castle	Samuel	1			1		1			1				4		
Richmond	206	20	Gaston	Alexander	1	2	1	1		3	1		1				10		
Richmond	206	21	Stevens	Parker		1			1	1	3	1	1				8		
Richmond	206	22	Gaston	Naomi		3					2	1		1			7		
Richmond	206	23	Stevens	Silas	1			1		2			1				5		
Richmond	206	24	Redfield	Edmund			1						1				2		
Richmond	206	25	Redfield	Beriah	1		1		1	2	2	3					10		
Richmond	206	26	Dryer	John	2		1		1	2	1	1	1				9		
Richmond	206	27	Gaston	William			1			1							2		
Richmond	206	28	Stevens	David		1		1			1		1				4		
Richmond	206	29	Hochkin	Joseph		1	1			1	1		1				5		
Richmond	206	30	Slosson	Daniel				1					1				2		
Richmond	206	31	Slosson	Nathaniel	3			1					1				5		
Richmond	206	32	Slosson	Joseph			1						1				2		
Richmond	206	33	Bebee	Levi		2	1	1					1				5		
Richmond	206	34	Cook	Erastus		1						1					2		
Richmond	206	35	Holcomb	Richard	3			1					1				5		
Richmond	206	36	West	Abner		1		1				3	1	1			7		
Richmond	206	37	Cook	Walter		1		1		3			1				6		
Richmond	206	38	Nickols	John				1				1	1				3		
Richmond	206	39	Andrews	Oziah			2	2	1		1	4		1			11		
Richmond	206	40	Andrews	Selah			1			1		1	1				4		
Richmond	206	41	Andrews	Leonard			1			1		1					3		
Richmond	206	42	West	Abner Junr			1					1					2		
Richmond	206	43	Barns	William		3		1			1	1		1			7		
Richmond	206	44	Johnson	Lewis		2						1	1				4		
Richmond	207	1	Bacon	John	1	1		1	1	1			2	1			8		
Richmond	207	2	Bacon	John Junr	1			1		2		1	1				6		
Richmond	207	3	Rathbon	Daniel		1	1		1	1			1				5		
Richmond	207	4	Branch	Levi			1			2	1	1					5		
Richmond	207	5	Brooks	Jabez	2	2		1		2		1	1				9		
Richmond	207	6	Redington	Nathaniel	2	1		1		2	2		1				9		
Richmond	207	7	Branch	Cyprian	1	1		1		1			1				5		
Richmond	207	8	Beacher	Thomas	1		1		1					2			5		
Richmond	207	9	Cole	Benjamin			1			1		1					3		
Richmond	207	10	Cole	Timothy	3			1		2			1				7		
Richmond	207	11	Hall	David			1		1	1			1	1			5		

TOWN	PG#	LN#	LAST NAME	FIRST NAME	under 10	10 to 16	16 to 26	26 to 45	45 and over	under 10	10 to 16	16 to 26	26 to 45	45 and over	TOTAL ALL OTHER	TOTAL SLAVES	TOTALS	DISTRICT/ TOWNSHIP	NOTES
					HEADS OF HOUSEHOLD		FREE WHITE MALES				FREE WHITE FEMALES								
Richmond	207	12	Dewey	Samuel	1		1	1			1		1				5		
Richmond	207	13	Colt	Jabez			2		1	1				1			5		
Richmond	207	14	Dudley	William		3		1				1	2				7		
Richmond	207	15	Goodrich	Benjamin			2	1		1	1		1				6		
Richmond	207	16	Bartlet	William	1	1	1	1				1	1	1			7		
Richmond	207	17	Peirson	Nathan Jnr			2						1				3		
Richmond	207	18	Joseph	Edward	1			1		1			1				4		
Richmond	207	19	Joseph	Nathaniel			1	1	2				1				5		
Richmond	207	20	Sherril	Henry	2	2	1		1	2	1		1				10		
Richmond	207	21	Peirson	Zachariah	3	1	1	1	2		1	2		1			12		
Richmond	207	22	Atkins	Seth	3			1		1			1				6		
Richmond	207	23	Wood	Comfort		1		1	1			1		1			5		
Richmond	207	24	Barns	Jeremiah	4	1	1	1		1	1	1					10		
Richmond	207	25	Rosseter	Benjamin		1	1	2		1		2					7		
Richmond	207	26	Bishop	Nathaniel	1		2		1			1	1				6		
Richmond	207	27	Chappel	James	2			1		1			1				5		
Richmond	207	28	Hand	Daniel		1		1				1	1				4		
Richmond	207	29	Taylor	Silas	1		2					1					4		
Richmond	207	30	Smith	Richard	1			1		1		1					4		
Richmond	207	31	Pixley	Moses	1		1		1	1		1		1			6		
Richmond	207	32	Nicholes	John Jun			1	1		4	3	1	1				11		
Richmond	207	33	Edwards	Daniel		1	1		1			1		1			5		
Richmond	207	34	Kidington	Jacob		2	1		1			3		1			8		
Richmond	207	35	Saxton	Michal	1			1				1					3		
Richmond	207	36	Wood	Gideon		2			1	3	1	1		1			9		
Richmond	207	37	Betts	Uriah		1	1	1		2		2					7		
Richmond	207	38	Dudley	John				2	1			1	1				5		
Richmond	207	39	Graves	Rufus		1	1		1	1	1	2					7		
Richmond	207	40	Chapin	David	1	2	2		1	1	2			1			10		
Richmond	207	41	Dudley	John Jun	2	1	2	1		1		1	1				9		
Richmond	207	42	Betts	Zebulon	2	1	1	1		3			1				9		
Richmond	207	43	Betts	Aaron	1	1	1	1		2	2	1					9		
Richmond	207	44	Dewey	Asaph	2	4		1		1		1	1				10		
Richmond	208	1	Lewis	David			1					1					2		
Richmond	208	2	Plummer	Francis	1	1	1		1			3		1	1		9		
Richmond	208	3	Burt	Henry	1	1	1		1				1				5		
Richmond	208	4	Rosseter	David		1	2		1	1			1				6		
Richmond	208	5	Harrison	Abel	1	1		1	2	1			2	1			9		
Richmond	208	6	Betts	Comstock					1				1				2		
Richmond	208	7	Cook	Isaac	1			2		2			1	1			7		
Richmond	208	8	Crocker	John	1				1			1		1			4		
Richmond	208	9	Collins	Menarah	1	1	1		1	1		1		1			7		
Richmond	208	10	Evarts	Eli				1		1		1					3		
Richmond	208	11	Meriman	Abraham	1	1	1		1			1		1			6		
Richmond	208	12	Merriman	Benja				1		1		1	2	1			6		
Richmond	208	13	Fuller	Matthias	3	1		1				2		1			8		
Richmond	208	14	Hall	John			3		1	1	1	2	1	1			10		
Richmond	208	15	Crittenden	Levi	2		2	1		2		4	1				12		
Richmond	208	16	Bishop	Richard		1		1		4	1		1				8		
Richmond	208	17	Loomis	Timothy		2	1	1		1	1	2	1				9		
Richmond	208	18	Collins	Dan		1		1		1	1	3	1	1			9		
Richmond	208	19	Andrews	Oliver		1						1					2		
Richmond	208	20	Collins	Ralph		1	1					1					3		
Richmond	208	21	Perry	David	1	2	4		1	2	1	2		1			14		
Richmond	208	22	Cogswell	Samuel	1	1			1	1		1		2			7		
Richmond	208	23	White	Reuben	3			1			1		1				6		
Richmond	208	24	Comstock	Ezekiel		1	1					1					3		
Richmond	208	25	Winston	Daniel				1		2			1				4		
Richmond	208	26	Peirson	Nathan		2	4	1	2	2	1	2	2				16		
Richmond	208	27	Scott	Abijah			2						1				3		
Richmond	208	28	Flowers	John	3			1		1			1				6		
Richmond	208	29	Griffing	Timothy	2	1	1	1				1	1				7		
Richmond	208	30	Chittendin	Calvin	2			1		1			1				5		
Richmond	208	31	Carpenter	Simeon			1		1			1		1			4		
Richmond	208	32	Raymond	Joseph		1		1	1	1	1		1				6		
Richmond	208	33	Williams	David				1			1		1	1			4		
Richmond	208	34	Williams	John	4			1	1			2	1		1		10		
Richmond	208	35	Brown	Tristram	1			1		1			1	1			5		
Richmond	208	36	Dorchester	Stephen		1		1					1				3		
Richmond	208	37	Babcock	William	2		1		1	3	1	1		1			10		
Richmond	208	38	Raymond	Paul	1	1			1			3		1			7		
Richmond	208	39	Blackman	James	1				1	2	1		1				6		
Richmond	208	40	Robinson	Edward	5	2			1	1	1		3				13		
Richmond	208	41	Ford	Absalom			1			3	1	2	1				8		
Richmond	208	42	Lyman	Noah Jun	1			1				1	1				4		
Richmond	208	43	Lyman	Noah					1					1			2		
Richmond	208	44	Hedges	Jonathan	1	1			1	2		1	1				7		
Richmond	208	45	Redington	Eliphalet	2		1		1	1		3		1			9		
Richmond	209	1	Delano	Amos	2			1		2	1	3					11		

TOWN	PG#	LN#	HEADS OF HOUSEHOLD		FREE WHITE MALES					FREE WHITE FEMALES					TOTAL ALL OTHER	TOTAL SLAVES	TOTALS	DISTRICT/ TOWNSHIP	NOTES
			LAST NAME	FIRST NAME	under 10	10 to 16	16 to 26	26 to 45	45 and over	under 10	10 to 16	16 to 26	26 to 45	45 and over					
Richmond	209	2	Tracey	Simeon	2			1	1	2		1	1	1			9		
Richmond	209	3	Hochkin	Ebenezer	2		1	1		1			1				6		
Richmond	209	4	Griffey	Jasper	1	2		1		1	1		1				7		
Richmond	209	5	Ford	James		1		1	1	3		3		1			10		
Richmond	209	6	Branch	Wine		1	2		1	1	1	1		1			8		
Richmond	209	7	Scott	Samuel	1	1			1	2		1	1				7		

TOWN	PG#	LN#	LAST NAME	FIRST NAME	FREE WHITE MALES under 10	10 to 16	16 to 26	26 to 45	45 and over	FREE WHITE FEMALES under 10	10 to 16	16 to 26	26 to 45	45 and over	TOTAL ALL OTHER	TOTAL SLAVES	TOTALS	DISTRICT/ TOWNSHIP	NOTES
Sandisfield	170	1	Knowles	Paul	2	3		1	1	3			1				11		
Sandisfield	170	2	Tilden	Thomas		1	1		1	1		1		1			6		
Sandisfield	170	3	Holbert	Eliphalet	2	1			1	3	1		1				9		
Sandisfield	170	4	Jones	Benoni	4			1		1			1				7		
Sandisfield	170	5	Jones	Israel	2				2	1	3	1		2			11		
Sandisfield	170	6	Judd	Orange	3	1		1		1	2		1				9		
Sandisfield	170	7	Havens	Nathan	1			1		2	2	2					8		
Sandisfield	170	8	Cruttenden	Ichabod Sen	2		3		1	1	1	2		1			11		
Sandisfield	170	9	Nelson	James	1			1	1	1		1	1	1			7		
Sandisfield	170	10	McCartey	John	1			1		4			1				7		
Sandisfield	170	11	Wilcox	Joel			4		1	2	2			1			10		
Sandisfield	170	12	Snow	Reliance								1					1		
Sandisfield	170	13	Walker	Isaac	2	1		1		3	1		1	1			10		
Sandisfield	170	14	Baker	Daniel				1		1	1		1	1			5		
Sandisfield	170	15	Wilson	Justin	2			1		4		1	1				9		
Sandisfield	170	16	Smith	Jabez		1	1				1	1		1			5		
Sandisfield	170	17	Hide	Agur				1									1		
Sandisfield	170	18	Parsons	Enos				1									1		
Sandisfield	170	19	Denning	Benjamin	4	1		1		2			1	1			10		
Sandisfield	171	1	Smith	Elizabeth									1				1		
Sandisfield	171	2	Holcomb	Oliver	1			1		4		1					7		
Sandisfield	171	3	Holcomb	Noadiah			1					1					2		
Sandisfield	171	4	Williams	Oliver	1	1		1		1	1		1				6		
Sandisfield	171	5	Ward	John	1			1		1		1		1			5		
Sandisfield	171	6	Clark	Benjamin				1		1	1	2	1	1			7		
Sandisfield	171	7	Clark	James	1	1		1		1		1					5		
Sandisfield	171	8	Lucas	William	2			1		1		1	1				6		
Sandisfield	171	9	Woodruff	Roswell	1		1	1		1		1					5		
Sandisfield	171	10	Woodruff	Isaiah	2			1				1					4		
Sandisfield	171	11	Ward	Daniel				1			3		1		1		6		
Sandisfield	171	12	Pickett	John	2		1	2		2	2		1				10		
Sandisfield	171	13	Downs	Abraham	1		2	1		1	1		1	1			8		
Sandisfield	171	14	Dunham	Joseph			1	1				2		2			6		
Sandisfield	171	15	Underwood	Simon	1	2		1		3		1	3				11		
Sandisfield	171	16	Dening	Ozias	2	1		1		2	1		1				8		
Sandisfield	171	17	Shelpon	Ceaser											2		2		
Sandisfield	171	18	Marvin	Nathan	3		1		1	3		1	1				10		
Sandisfield	171	19	Hawley	Elijah				1						1			2		
Sandisfield	171	20	Heath	Jacob	4			1					1				6		
Sandisfield	172	1	Hayes	Elisha		1			1	2				1			5		
Sandisfield	172	2	Hawley	John Sen				1			1	1	1				4		
Sandisfield	172	3	Hawley	John Jr	1			1		4	1		1				8		
Sandisfield	172	4	Adams	Richard		1			1			2		1			5		
Sandisfield	172	5	Rew	Eliathath		1			1					1			3		
Sandisfield	172	6	Sedgwick	Chancey	1			1		1		1					4		
Sandisfield	172	7	Morey	Stephen		1		1		3	1	1					7		
Sandisfield	172	8	Hulet	Obadiah			1										1		
Sandisfield	172	9	Kingsbery	Lemuel				1		1	1		1				4		
Sandisfield	172	10	Spring	Henry Junr		1		1	1	5	1		1	1			11		
Sandisfield	172	11	Stickland	Peter			2		1					1			4		
Sandisfield	172	12	Barker	Jairus		2		1		3		1	1				8		
Sandisfield	172	13	Barker	Nathan	2								1				4		
Sandisfield	172	14	Smith	Lot		1	2	1		1		1	1				7		
Sandisfield	172	15	Soper	Hezekiah	2			1		2			1				6		
Sandisfield	172	16	Soper	Levi			2	1						1			4		
Sandisfield	172	17	Adams	James			2	1				1		1			5		
Sandisfield	172	18	Clark	Samuel			1										1		
Sandisfield	173	1	Parsons	Eli	1	1	1	1		2	1	1	1				9		
Sandisfield	173	2	Hubbard	Theophhilas			1			1	1		1				4		
Sandisfield	173	3	Morse	Asahel	3			1					1				5		
Sandisfield	173	4	Hubbard	John & Son		1		1	1	3	1	2	1	1			11		
Sandisfield	173	5	Hubbard	John Jr				1		1			1				3		
Sandisfield	173	6	Deland	Obadiah		2	1			1	1	1		1			8		
Sandisfield	173	7	Deland	John	2			1		1			1				5		
Sandisfield	173	8	Wentworth	Joseph	1	2			2		2	1		1			9		
Sandisfield	173	9	Hubbard	Jadimer	3		1		1	1	2	1	1	1			11		
Sandisfield	173	10	Hartwell	Jesse	3			1		2			1				7		
Sandisfield	173	11	Fargo	Ezekiel	2			1			3	2		2			10		
Sandisfield	173	12	Claffen	Robert	3			1		1		1					6		
Sandisfield	173	13	David	Nathaniel B. & Son	1		2		1		1	1		1			7		
Sandisfield	173	14	Fargo	Jabez	1	1		1		2			1				6		
Sandisfield	173	15	Fargo	Moses Jr	3			1		1	1		1				7		
Sandisfield	173	16	Fargo	Moses Sen				1						1			2		
Sandisfield	173	17	Fargo	Samuel	1			1		2		1					5		
Sandisfield	173	18	Heath	Aaron	2	1	1		1	3	2	1	1	1			13		
Sandisfield	173	19	Heath	Levi	1		2		1	1	1		1	1			8		
Sandisfield	173	20	Sage	Abel	3	1	1	1	1	1		1	1				10		
Sandisfield	173	21	Belding	James		1	2		1	2	2	2		2			12		
Sandisfield	173	22	Belding	David			1			2		1					4		

TOWN	PG#	LN#	LAST NAME	FIRST NAME	FWM under 10	FWM 10 to 16	FWM 16 to 26	FWM 26 to 45	FWM 45 and over	FWF under 10	FWF 10 to 16	FWF 16 to 26	FWF 26 to 45	FWF 45 and over	TOTAL ALL OTHER	TOTAL SLAVES	TOTALS	DISTRICT/ TOWNSHIP	NOTES
Sandisfield	173	23	Belding	Daniel	1			1					1				3		
Sandisfield	173	24	Smith	Levi 1st	4			1			1		1	1			8		
Sandisfield	173	25	Warner	Timothy	2			1		2			1				6		
Sandisfield	173	26	Pease	Elisha	1		1						1				3		
Sandisfield	173	27	Wolcott	William			1	1					1				3		
Sandisfield	173	28	Wolcott	Samuel Jun				1				1	1	1			4		
Sandisfield	173	29	Wolcott	Abiather			1			2			1				4		
Sandisfield	173	30	Knowles	Willard Jr	2		1			1			1				5		
Sandisfield	173	31	Bozworth	Constant		1		1				1		1			4		
Sandisfield	173	32	Servent	James				1		1	1			1			4		
Sandisfield	173	33	Baxter	John				1						1			2		
Sandisfield	173	34	Beach	Orra	1		1						1				3		
Sandisfield	173	35	Parsons	Benjamin	2	1	1		1	1		1	1	1			9		
Sandisfield	173	36	Parsons	Elihu	1		1						1				3		
Sandisfield	173	37	Holt	Ebenezer		1	1	1					1	1			5		
Sandisfield	173	38	Smith	Perigran	2			1		4	3		1				11		
Sandisfield	174	1	Pease	Henry	3			1		2			1				7		
Sandisfield	174	2	Smith	Jonathan 2nd	1	1		1		4	1		1				9		
Sandisfield	174	3	Solomon	Jacob & Elmer			1	1					1				3		
Sandisfield	174	4	Elmer	Joel		2		1			1	1	1				6		
Sandisfield	174	5	Lewis	Joseph	1	2	1		1	2				1			8		
Sandisfield	174	6	Claffen	Joshua	1			1		3			1				6		
Sandisfield	174	7	Deming	David	1			1			1			1			4		
Sandisfield	174	8	Sears	Paul Sen & Son			1		1			2	1				5		
Sandisfield	174	9	Sears	Paul Jr	1			1		2			1				5		
Sandisfield	174	10	Sherman	James	3			1		2			1				7		
Sandisfield	174	11	Granger	Thadeus	1			1		2			1				5		
Sandisfield	174	12	Smith	Levi 2nd	1			1		3		1	1	1			8		
Sandisfield	174	13	Pratt	Barnabas & Son			1	1				1		1			4		
Sandisfield	174	14	Pratt	Aaron	1			1		4			1				7		
Sandisfield	174	15	Brown	Sanford	2		1	1		1	1	1	1				8		
Sandisfield	174	16	Graham	James				1		3	1		1				6		
Sandisfield	174	17	Nickerson	Jesse			1			1			1				3		
Sandisfield	174	18	Denslow	Joseph Jr			1						1				2		
Sandisfield	174	19	Denslow	Joseph Sen				1				1		1			3		
Sandisfield	174	20	Denslow	Bartemas		1											1		
Sandisfield	174	21	Deming	Solomon	2			1		2	1		1				7		
Sandisfield	174	22	Smith	Benjamin	2	1			1	1	1		1	1			8		
Sandisfield	174	23	Hanley	Flavel	3	1		1		2			1				8		
Sandisfield	174	24	Sage	Samuel Jr	3	1		1		2	1		1				9		
Sandisfield	174	25	Sage	Samuel Sen				1						1			2		
Sandisfield	174	26	Hanley	William Jr	3		2	1		1	2	2	1				12		
Sandisfield	174	27	Hills	Drake Esq	4	1	1	1		1	2	3	1				14		
Sandisfield	174	28	French	Joseph	1	1		1		1	1	1		1			8		
Sandisfield	174	29	Parsons	Ashbel			1			3			1				5		
Sandisfield	174	30	Snow	Sparrow	1	1	1		1	2	1	1		1			9		
Sandisfield	174	31	Snow	James		1			1	1	1	3		1			8		
Sandisfield	174	32	Moar	John	1	1		1		4				1			8		
Sandisfield	174	33	Smith	Eleazer & Benjm	1		1	1		1		1	1	1			7		
Sandisfield	174	34	Smith	Elizabeth & Persla										2			2		
Sandisfield	174	35	Smith	Amasa	2	2	1		1	1	1	1		1			10		
Sandisfield	174	36	Spelman	Nathan Sen		1		1		1		2		1			6		
Sandisfield	174	37	Spelman	Nathan Jr			1			2			1				4		
Sandisfield	174	38	Arnold	Jonathan	2		1		1	2	1	2		1			10		
Sandisfield	174	39	Wilcox	George	2	1		1		1			1				6		
Sandisfield	174	40	Crane	Elijah & Son	1		4		1	5	1	1	2	1			16		
Sandisfield	174	41	Williams	Louis Wido			4			1			1	1			7		
Sandisfield	175	1	Deming	John			1		1			2		1			5		
Sandisfield	175	2	Crane	David									1				1		
Sandisfield	175	3	Hubbard	Seth & Son	2		2		1	4	3	4	1				17		
Sandisfield	175	4	Pease	Henry C.			1		1			1	2	1			6		
Sandisfield	175	5	Cornish	John & Son			1		1	1	1	2					6		
Sandisfield	175	6	Hurd	Jabez	2			1		3			1				7		
Sandisfield	175	7	Wolcott	Joseph & Son		1	1	1		1	1	1		1			8		
Sandisfield	175	8	Granger	William	1	1		1		3			1				7		
Sandisfield	175	9	Storrs	Eleazer Rev.		1	1	1					1	2			6		
Sandisfield	175	10	Smith	Reuben 2nd	1			1		3			1				6		
Sandisfield	175	11	Underwood	Roswell		1							1	1			3		
Sandisfield	175	12	Hull	Eliakim & Arnold	1	1		2		2		1	1				8		
Sandisfield	175	13	Bozworth	John	2	1	1		1	2			3	1			11		
Sandisfield	175	14	Roberts	William & Son	2		1	1	1	1			1	1			8		
Sandisfield	175	15	Parsons	John Jr	3	1		1		1				1			7		
Sandisfield	175	16	Canfield	John Jr	2			1					1				4		
Sandisfield	175	17	Canfield	John Esq	2		2		1	3	2	3		1			14		
Sandisfield	175	18	Wilcox	Abel Sen		1			1	1		1	1	1			6		
Sandisfield	175	19	Wilcox	Abel Jr	1			1		2			1				5		
Sandisfield	175	20	Holden	Samuel	1	2			1	2	2		1				9		
Sandisfield	175	21	Roberts	Joseph	2			1		1			1				5		
Sandisfield	175	22	Parsons	John Sen		1	1		1			1	1				6		

TOWN	PG#	LN#	HEADS OF HOUSEHOLD LAST NAME	FIRST NAME	FREE WHITE MALES under 10	10 to 16	16 to 26	26 to 45	45 and over	FREE WHITE FEMALES under 10	10 to 16	16 to 26	26 to 45	45 and over	TOTAL ALL OTHER	TOTAL SLAVES	TOTALS	DISTRICT/ TOWNSHIP	NOTES
Sandisfield	175	23	Wright	Noah			1		1	1		1	1				5		
Sandisfield	175	24	Parsons	Timothy	3	1		1		1			1				7		
Sandisfield	175	25	Wright	Charles		2		1		1	1	1					7		
Sandisfield	175	26	Smith	Uriel	1		1		1			1		1			5		
Sandisfield	175	27	Smith	Lemuel	1	1	1		1	1		1	1	2			9		
Sandisfield	175	28	Kibbe	Ebenezer	1	1			1			1	2	1			7		
Sandisfield	175	29	Couch	Samuel	3	1			2		1	1	1	2			11		
Sandisfield	175	30	Cone	Joseph	1			1		4			1				7		
Sandisfield	175	31	Cone	Cornelius & Son			1		1			2	2	1			7		
Sandisfield	175	32	Smith	Asahel			1										1		
Sandisfield	175	33	Knowles	Willard Sen				1						2			3		
Sandisfield	175	34	Kneeland	Dudley	1			1		1			1				4		
Sandisfield	175	35	Snow	Freeman	1	1	1		1	1		2		1			8		
Sandisfield	175	36	Goodrich	Michael	1	1	1		1		2	1		1			8		
Sandisfield	175	37	Webster	Jacob	4	1			1		1			1			8		
Sandisfield	175	38	Paine	Nathan			1										1		
Sandisfield	176	1	Shelby	Ephraim	2		3		2	1	1			1			10		
Sandisfield	176	2	Webster	Abner	1		2	1					1				5		
Sandisfield	176	3	Stevens	John		1		1					1				3		
Sandisfield	176	4	Herrick	Daniel	3			1		1	1	1	1				8		
Sandisfield	176	5	Webster	Ebenezer	1			1					1				3		
Sandisfield	176	6	Shepard	Jonathan	3	1		1			1		1				7		
Sandisfield	176	7	Emms	Joshua		1	1	1					1	1			5		
Sandisfield	176	8	Hall	Amos	3	1		1		2			1				8		
Sandisfield	176	9	Kellogg	Asahel	1		1	1		1	1		1				6		
Sandisfield	176	10	Sage	Stephen	2	1	3		1	2	2			1			12		
Sandisfield	176	11	Smith	Solomon & Son	1	1			1	2	2			1			8		
Sandisfield	176	12	Paine	Joseph			2	1		1		1	1	1			7		
Sandisfield	176	13	Smith	Solomon Jr	1		1						1				3		
Sandisfield	176	14	Sage	Jedediah	2	1	1	1		1		1	1	1			9		
Sandisfield	176	15	Loveland	Elijah	1	1	1	1	1	1		2		1			9		
Sandisfield	176	16	Smith	Stephen			1		1				1				3		
Sandisfield	176	17	Smith	Freelove Wido		1	3				3	2		1			10		
Sandisfield	176	18	Smith	Keisben	1	1	2		1		1	1		1			8		
Sandisfield	176	19	Buckman	Reuben			1			2			1				4		
Sandisfield	176	20	Granger	Elihu	1	1		1		1	1		1				6		
Sandisfield	176	21	Robbins	Solomon	5		1	1		1			1				9		
Sandisfield	176	22	Underwood	Silas	2			1		1			1				5		
Sandisfield	176	23	Smith	Jonathan 2nd		1	1		1			2	1	1			7		
Sandisfield	176	24	Smith	Freeman			4						1				5		
Sandisfield	176	25	Phelps	Levi C.			1						1	1			3		
Sandisfield	176	26	Robbins	Joshua	1		1						1				3		
Sandisfield	176	27	Fellows	Mary		1	1			1	1	1		1			6		
Sandisfield	176	28	Pease	Noadiah	1		1	1						2			5		
Sandisfield	176	29	Ayrault	James Esq				1					2	1			4		
Sandisfield	176	30	Ayrault	Nicholas	3	3		1		2			1				10		
Sandisfield	176	31	Deming	Elijah			2		1			1	1	1			6		
Sandisfield	176	32	Deming	Joel	1	1		1				1	1	1			6		
Sandisfield	176	33	Wright	Gideon				1				1	1	1			4		
Sandisfield	176	34	Lee	Isaac	1		1	1		1			1	1			6		
Sandisfield	176	35	Palmer	Stephen	2			1		1			1	1			6		
Sandisfield	176	36	Johnson	Samuel			1						1				2		
Sandisfield	176	37	Bozworth	Hannah	2	1			1		2		1	1			8		
Sandisfield	176	38	Kilborn	Jonathan			2	1		1	1	1	1				7		
Sandisfield	176	39	Wilcox	Rhoda								1					1		
Sandisfield	176	40	Parsons	Timothy 2nd			1										1		
Sandisfield	177	1	Slocum	Charles			1						1				2		
Sandisfield	177	2	White	Rev Levi				1					1		1		3		
Sandisfield	177	3	Kingsbery	Daniel				1		2			1				4		
Sandisfield	177	4	Adams	John		1	2		1	2	1	1	1				9		
Sandisfield	177	5	Churchill	John	2			1		2			1				6		
Sandisfield	177	6	Kilborn	Elisha & Son	1			1	1			1		1			5		
Sandisfield	177	7	Slate	Solomon			1										1		
Sandisfield	177	8	Mery	Truman			1										1		
Sandisfield	177	9	Stevens	Edward			1										1		
Sandisfield	177	10	Gillet	Marlin			1										1		
Sandisfield	177	11	Wilcox	John				1									1		
Sandisfield	177	12	Kingsbery	Benjamin			1										1		
Sandisfield	177	13	Horton	John	2				1	1	2		1				7		

TOWN	PG#	LN#	LAST NAME	FIRST NAME	FREE WHITE MALES					FREE WHITE FEMALES					TOTAL ALL OTHER	TOTAL SLAVES	TOTALS	DISTRICT/ TOWNSHIP	NOTES
					under 10	10 to 16	16 to 26	26 to 45	45 and over	under 10	10 to 16	16 to 26	26 to 45	45 and over					
Savoy	139	1	Bealey	Nathaniel	1				1	1	2	3		1			9		
Savoy	139	2	Carpenter	Benjamin	2			1		1		1	1				6		
Savoy	139	3	Babbett	Snellam		1	1	1		2			1				6		
Savoy	139	4	Bourne	John	2	3	1		1	1			1				9		
Savoy	139	5	Ingraham	William	3	1	1		1			1	1	1			9		
Savoy	139	6	Bliss	Ephraim	1	2	1		1	1		1	1				8		
Savoy	139	7	Carpenter	Ezra		3		1			1			1			6		
Savoy	139	8	Carpenter	Cyrel		1						1					2		
Savoy	139	9	Carpenter	Ezra Junr	1			1	1				1				4		
Savoy	139	10	Matthews	David		1			1	1		1	1				5		
Savoy	139	11	Bates	Comfort	1	1	1		1	2			1				7		
Savoy	139	12	Barber	Joseph	1	1		1	1	1		1		1			7		
Savoy	139	13	Hodges	Simeon	2		1	1						1			5		
Savoy	139	14	Hodges	Simeon Junr	1			1		1		1	1				5		
Savoy	139	15	Ingraham	John			1	1		1	1	1					5		
Savoy	139	16	Goff	Simeon	1	2	1		1	1	1	1					8		
Savoy	139	17	Haskins	Nathan	2	1	3	1	1	1	1	2	1	1			14		
Savoy	139	18	Haskins	Schradach	2		1						1				4		
Savoy	139	19	Hathaway	Peleg	1		1	1		2	2	2	1				10		
Savoy	139	20	Walker	Ethel	3			1				2					6		
Savoy	139	21	Dunham	Job	2			1					1				4		
Savoy	139	22	Dunham	Daniel	2					2		1	1				6		
Savoy	140	1	Jenks	David	2		1			1			1				5		
Savoy	140	2	Walker	Wilkes	1			1		1			1				4		
Savoy	140	3	Blanchard	Josiah		1											1		
Savoy	140	4	Waterman	Oliver	2	1		1		2	1	1					8		
Savoy	140	5	Shearman	Jacob	2		2		1	1				1			7		
Savoy	140	6	Bliss	David	4	1			1					1			7		
Savoy	140	7	Shearman	Seth	1			1		2			1				5		
Savoy	140	8	Fuller	Aaron					1		1			1			3		
Savoy	140	9	Fuller	Ebenezr	1			2		1			1				5		
Savoy	140	10	Francis	Isaac	1	1		1		1			1				5		
Savoy	140	11	Carpenter	Lewis	3			1					1				5		
Savoy	140	12	Carpenter	Abel	1			1		2			1				5		
Savoy	140	13	Martin	Joseph		3		1			1		1				6		
Savoy	140	14	Martin	Joseph Jr	3			1					1				5		
Savoy	140	15	Miller	Samuel	1	1	2		1	1	2			2			10		
Savoy	140	16	Hathaway	Joseph	1	1	2	1	1	1	2	1		1			11		
Savoy	140	17	Eddy	Loved		1		1			1	1		1			5		
Savoy	140	18	Bennett	Peter				1						1			2		
Savoy	140	19	Edson	Abiezer			2		1		1			1			5		
Savoy	140	20	Pierce	John	1			1		4	1			1			8		
Savoy	140	21	Shearman	James	1		1						1				3		
Savoy	140	22	Wilbour	William	2	1			1					1			5		
Savoy	140	23	Perkins	William			1						1				2		
Savoy	140	24	Paddleford	Zachariah		1	4		1	1			1	1			9		
Savoy	140	25	Williams	Joseph	1			1		1		2	1		1		7		
Savoy	140	26	Barney	Benjamin	3	1		1		2	2		1				10		
Savoy	140	27	Burden	Bethuel	1	1		1		1			1				5		
Savoy	140	28	Barney	William	1		1	1		1	1		1				6		
Savoy	140	29	Barney	George	1		1	1		1			1				5		
Savoy	140	30	Gelat	George	4	2		1				1	1				9		
Savoy	140	31	Gelat	John			1	1						1			3		
Savoy	140	32	Wescott	Stutely	1	1		1		1	1		1				6		
Savoy	140	33	Carpenter	Nathaniel				1						1			2		
Savoy	140	34	Spencer	Rhoda		1	1		1	1	1						5		
Savoy	140	35	Fuller	Eli	3			2	1		1		2				9		
Savoy	140	36	Kingman	Thomas			3					1					4		
Savoy	140	37	Howard	Edward	1	1	1		1				1	1			6		
Savoy	140	38	Carpenter	Elisha		1	1	1					1	1			5		
Savoy	140	39	Person	Jesse		1	1	1					1				4		
Savoy	140	40	Thatcher	Ebenezr	2	1		1		1	2	1		1			10		
Savoy	140	41	Fish	Thomas	4	1	1			1			1				8		
Savoy	140	42	Pierce	Constant	3			1		2			1				7		
Savoy	141	1	Nelson	James		1		1			1		1	1			4		
Savoy	141	2	Lewis	Dyer				1				1	1	1			3		
Savoy	141	3	Crapo	Consider	1	1	1		1			2	1				8		
Savoy	141	4	Burden	Lemuel	1		1	1		2	2	1	1				9		
Savoy	141	5	Crapo	Consider Jun	1			1		2			1				5		
Savoy	141	6	Hathaway	Lemuel		1	3		1			1		1			7		
Savoy	141	7	Hathaway	Nathaniel	1			1		1			1				4		
Savoy	141	8	Hathaway	Lemuel Jur	1		1	1					1				4		

TOWN	PG#	LN#	LAST NAME	FIRST NAME	M under 10	M 10 to 16	M 16 to 26	M 26 to 45	M 45 and over	F under 10	F 10 to 16	F 16 to 26	F 26 to 45	F 45 and over	TOTAL ALL OTHER	TOTAL SLAVES	TOTALS	DISTRICT/TOWNSHIP	NOTES
Sheffield	221	1	Austin	Gad		1	1	1						1	1		5		
Sheffield	221	2	Austin	Amos	1	1		1		1		1					5		
Sheffield	221	3	Sheldon	Dick											3		3		
Sheffield	221	4	Bush	Rachel		1						3	1		1		6		
Sheffield	221	5	Bush	Horace	1	2		1		1		1	1				7		
Sheffield	221	6	Bacon	William			2		1		1	2	1	1			8		
Sheffield	221	7	Austin	Augustus		1	1	1	1			2		1			7		
Sheffield	221	8	Hurlbut	John			1										1		
Sheffield	221	9	Buel	William			1	1		2		1			1		6		
Sheffield	221	10	Parmele	Eli	1			1		1			1				4		
Sheffield	221	11	Seymour	Josiah		1		1		2		1					5		
Sheffield	221	12	Fellows	William	1	1		1	1			2	1	1			8		
Sheffield	221	13	Lee	Elisha		1	2	1		1	1		1				7		
Sheffield	221	14	Raymond	Dan			2		1			1	2	1			7		
Sheffield	221	15	Thayer	Enoch W.			2						1	1			4		
Sheffield	221	16	Baxter	John	1			1		3			1				6		
Sheffield	221	17	Crawley	Ellis			1						1				2		
Sheffield	221	18	Johnson	Guy Negro											5		5		
Sheffield	221	19	Stewart	Philip			1			2			1				4		
Sheffield	222	1	Morse	Lemuel	1	2			1	2		2	1				9		
Sheffield	222	2	Goodrich	Amos	2		1	1		2			1				7		
Sheffield	222	3	Dewey	Silas	1	1		1		2		1	1				7		
Sheffield	222	4	Barnard	Lemll		1		1						1			3		
Sheffield	222	5	Root	Azariah	2	2	9	1				1	2				17		
Sheffield	222	6	Ensign	Freeman	2	1		1		1	1		1				7		
Sheffield	222	7	Dewey	Stephen	1	1		2		3	2		1				10		
Sheffield	222	8	Root	Aaron	1	1	2	1	1	1		2	1	1			11		
Sheffield	222	9	Ashley	William	1				1	2			1				5		
Sheffield	222	10	Pope	Rhoda	2							1	1				4		
Sheffield	222	11	Bush	Obadiah	1	1	1	2		1	1	1	1				9		
Sheffield	222	12	Dewey	Paul		2	1	2	1	1	1		2	1			11		
Sheffield	222	13	Day	Thomas		1	1			1	1	1					5		
Sheffield	222	14	Hubbell	John		1			1					1			4		
Sheffield	222	15	Marvin	Silas	3			1	1	1	1	1	1	1			10		
Sheffield	222	16	Goodail	Jonas H	1	1	1		1	2	1		1		1		9		
Sheffield	222	17	Stevens	Elijah	2			1		2			1				6		
Sheffield	222	18	Smith	Sarah									1				1		
Sheffield	222	19	Cawle	William	2	1		1		1			1				6		
Sheffield	222	20	Smith	Elisha		1	1	1					1				4		
Sheffield	222	21	Smith	Elijah	2			1					1				4		
Sheffield	222	22	Cawle	Elisha	1	1		1					1				4		
Sheffield	222	23	Ensign	Solomon	2			1					1				4		
Sheffield	222	24	Beman	Samll	2	1			1	1		1		1			7		
Sheffield	222	25	Benjamin	Nathan	1		1	1		2			1				6		
Sheffield	222	26	Hicock	Jeremiah		1	2		1		1	1	1	1			8		
Sheffield	222	27	Fellows	Daniel			1		1		1	1		1			5		
Sheffield	222	28	Peet	Arnold	1		1						1	1			4		
Sheffield	222	29	Pell	Tamer										1			1		
Sheffield	222	30	Bull	William	3			1				1	1				6		
Sheffield	222	31	Prince	Cyrus Negro											3		3		
Sheffield	222	32	Rogers	William											5		5		
Sheffield	222	33	Leonard	Nathll	1		1	1		1	1	1	1		1		8		
Sheffield	222	34	Fanning	John	2			1		1			1				5		
Sheffield	222	35	Noble	Jeremiah		1		1					1				3		
Sheffield	223	1	Hicock	Darling	3	1		1		3	1		1				10		
Sheffield	223	2	Leonard	Rice	1		2	1	1	1		2					8		
Sheffield	223	3	Holms	Lothrop		1		2	1		1	2	1	1			9		
Sheffield	223	4	Cawle	Nathanael				1		1	1		1	1			5		
Sheffield	223	5	Cawle	Joseph	1			1					1				3		
Sheffield	223	6	June	Benjamin		1	1			2	1		1				6		
Sheffield	223	7	Case	Ephraim		1		1				1		2			5		
Sheffield	223	8	Post	Gideon			1	1				1		1			4		
Sheffield	223	9	Forrest	Sylvester			1			3			1				5		
Sheffield	223	10	Bawen	Joseph	2	1		1		2	1		1				8		
Sheffield	223	11	Negro	Peter											4		4		
Sheffield	223	12	Negro	Isaac											5		5		
Sheffield	223	13	Sylva	Zilpha Widow											5		5		
Sheffield	223	14	Fanning	Shubael	2	1	1		1	3	1	2		1			12		
Sheffield	223	15	Stocking	Moses		1		1		1	1		1				5		
Sheffield	223	16	Austin	John	1	1	1		1	1	1			1			7		
Sheffield	223	17	Shilhousen	Conrad	1				1				1				3		
Sheffield	223	18	Manning	Thomas	1			1		4			1				7		
Sheffield	223	19	Gubbins	Humphry											5		5		
Sheffield	223	20	Martin	Jethro											2		2		
Sheffield	223	21	Sheldon	Benjamin	2			1	1	3	1	2					10		
Sheffield	223	22	Noble	Nathll Jun	3			1		2			1				7		
Sheffield	223	23	Noble	Oliver			1			1			1				3		
Sheffield	223	24	Noble	Nathll	1	1			1	1			1				5		
Sheffield	223	25	Noble	Silas			1			1			1				3		

TOWN	PG#	LN#	HEADS OF HOUSEHOLD		FREE WHITE MALES					FREE WHITE FEMALES					TOTAL ALL OTHER	TOTAL SLAVES	TOTALS	DISTRICT/ TOWNSHIP	NOTES
			LAST NAME	FIRST NAME	under 10	10 to 16	16 to 26	26 to 45	45 and over	under 10	10 to 16	16 to 26	26 to 45	45 and over					
Sheffield	223	26	Hubbard	Jonathan		1	3		1	1				1			7		
Sheffield	223	27	Shears	Zechariah	1	2			1			1	1	1			7		
Sheffield	223	28	Royce	Abner		1	2		2			1		2			8		
Sheffield	223	29	Royce	Isaac	1		1						1				3		
Sheffield	223	30	Austin	Bailey		1		1			1			1			4		
Sheffield	223	31	Griggs	Joseph		1		1		1		1	1	1			6		
Sheffield	223	32	Tuttle	Huldah	1					1	1		1				4		
Sheffield	223	33	Derry	George			1			1	1		1				4		
Sheffield	223	34	Andrews	Andrew	2	2	1	1		2		1	1				10		
Sheffield	224	1	Hezekiah	Knapp	1	1	3	1	1	1	1			1			10		
Sheffield	224	2	West	Josiah		1	1	1	1	2	1		1				8		
Sheffield	224	3	Bryan	Ezekiel	1			1			1						3		
Sheffield	224	4	Benton	Stephen	1	1	1			2			1				7		
Sheffield	224	5	Swift	Asahel			1				1						2		
Sheffield	224	6	Lawrence	Asa	1			1		1			1				4		
Sheffield	224	7	Cande	Zaccheus	1		1	1			1		1				5		
Sheffield	224	8	Cande	Theophilus		1	1		1			1		1			5		
Sheffield	224	9	Sparks	Lemuel	3		1			1		1					6		
Sheffield	224	10	Acton	Widow							1			1			2		
Sheffield	224	11	Witbeck	Ephraim				1					1				2		
Sheffield	224	12	Landon	Ezekiel	1	1		1		1			1				5		
Sheffield	224	13	Sparks	Asa	1	2	1		1	2	1	1		1			10		
Sheffield	224	14	Smith	David	1			1		3	1	1	1				8		
Sheffield	224	15	Royce	Ezra	2			1		1			1				5		
Sheffield	224	16	Stratton	Richard	3			1					1	1			6		
Sheffield	224	17	Austin	Leml1		1		1					1	1			4		
Sheffield	224	18	Burrows	Joseph			2		1	1				1			5		
Sheffield	224	19	Willougbee	Salmon		1		1		2	1		1				6		
Sheffield	224	20	Evertson	Austin			1			1			1				3		
Sheffield	224	21	Owen	Minor		1		1		1	1		1				5		
Sheffield	224	22	Matthews	Jabez	1	1	2	1		1			1				7		
Sheffield	224	23	Bush	Daniel	1		1		1	1	1		1				6		
Sheffield	224	24	Jenney	Abselm	1	1	1					1	1				5		
Sheffield	224	25	Sheldon	Whiting	2			1		1			1				6		
Sheffield	224	26	Bierce	Austin Jun	1	1	2	1		1			1				7		
Sheffield	224	27	Hamlin	David		2		1		1	2		1				7		
Sheffield	224	28	Hamlin	Eleazer		1	1					1	1				4		
Sheffield	224	29	Parks	John	2		1	1		1			1				6		
Sheffield	224	30	Holcombs	Michael				1					1				2		
Sheffield	224	31	Bullard	Asa	2								1				3		
Sheffield	224	32	Holcomb	Pliny			1						1				2		
Sheffield	224	33	Freeman	Casar											1		1		
Sheffield	224	34	Bierce	Winston	1		1			1		2					5		
Sheffield	224	35	Bierce	Austin		1	1	1				2		1			6		
Sheffield	224	36	Fellows	Nathan	2		1	1		1	1						6		
Sheffield	224	37	Rubelow	Thomas		1		1						1			3		
Sheffield	224	38	Lindsey	James		2		1				1		1			5		
Sheffield	225	1	Thacher	Pomp											6		6		
Sheffield	225	2	Lindsey	Aaron	1		1			1			1				4		
Sheffield	225	3	Eglestone	Moses	4			1		2	1		1				9		
Sheffield	225	4	Bryan	Timothy	2	1		1		2			1				7		
Sheffield	225	5	Root	Thaddeus	3			1		1	1	1					7		
Sheffield	225	6	Theley	Elisha				1				1		1			3		
Sheffield	225	7	Smith	Phinehas				1						1			2		
Sheffield	225	8	Dorrent	Henry		1		1		2			1				5		
Sheffield	225	9	Matthews	Jabez				1						1			2		
Sheffield	225	10	Barnam	Selah	2	1	1		1	2	2		1				10		
Sheffield	225	11	Holmes	Lothrop	3		2			1	1						7		
Sheffield	225	12	Gomm	Alexander	2		1			1			1				5		
Sheffield	225	13	Davis	Zaccheus											5		5		
Sheffield	225	14	Lebaran	Isaac	1	1		1		1			1	1			6		
Sheffield	225	15	Elithorp	Salmon	1		1			1			1				4		
Sheffield	225	16	Allen	Jesse		1				1		1	1				4		
Sheffield	225	17	Calder	Thomas											4		4		
Sheffield	225	18	Fellows	Ezra	1			1		1				1			4		
Sheffield	225	19	Dibble	Joseph	3			1		1			1	1			7		
Sheffield	225	20	Barnard	Sylvester				1									1		
Sheffield	225	21	Hubbard	Timothy	1	2	1		1			1	1				7		
Sheffield	225	22	Kellogg	Josiah	1	1	3	1		1	1		1				9		
Sheffield	225	23	Dimwell	William		1		1		2				1			5		
Sheffield	225	24	Merrills	Seth				1									1		
Sheffield	225	25	Austin	Bailey Jun		2		1		1	2		2				8		
Sheffield	225	26	Hubbard	Moses	1	1	1						1				5		
Sheffield	225	27	Jordon	Ephraim				1				1		1			3		
Sheffield	225	28	Curtiss	Jeptha		1	1			3			1		1		7		
Sheffield	225	29	Hubbard	Noah E.		1	2		1	1	1	1	1		1		9		
Sheffield	225	30	Fellows	John		2		1					1				4		
Sheffield	225	31	Baker	Abonjah		1	3						1				5		
Sheffield	225	32	Hubbard	John		1	2						2				5		

TOWN	PG#	LN#	LAST NAME	FIRST NAME	M under 10	M 10 to 16	M 16 to 26	M 26 to 45	M 45 and over	F under 10	F 10 to 16	F 16 to 26	F 26 to 45	F 45 and over	TOTAL ALL OTHER	TOTAL SLAVES	TOTALS	DISTRICT/TOWNSHIP	NOTES
Sheffield	225	33	Fellows	Edmund B	2		1				1	2					6		
Sheffield	225	34	Holcomb	Ira			1					1					2		
Sheffield	225	35	Jackson	Reuben			1		1	2		1	1				6		
Sheffield	225	36	Durston	John									1				1		
Sheffield	225	37	Chatfield	Joel	1			1		2		1	1				6		
Sheffield	226	1	Holcomb	Joel	1				1		1	1		1			5		
Sheffield	226	2	Fox	Jeremiah					1	3	1	1	1				7		
Sheffield	226	3	Westover	Oliver					1		2			1			4		
Sheffield	226	4	Sparks	William	3			1		1			1				6		
Sheffield	226	5	Kellogg	Pliny	1	1			1	2		1	1		1		8		
Sheffield	226	6	Amsden	Henry				1						1			2		
Sheffield	226	7	Kellogg	Homer	1	1		1		2		1		1			7		
Sheffield	226	8	McNiel	Wm				1					1				2		
Sheffield	226	9	Bushnall	Samll		1	3	1	1		1	1		1			9		
Sheffield	226	10	Vosburgh	Isaac	2	1	1	1		1		2	1	1			10		
Sheffield	226	11	Rainsford	Solomon	1			1			2		1				5		
Sheffield	226	12	Rainsford	Archa	1		1			1		1					4		
Sheffield	226	13	Curtiss	Joseph	1	1	1	1					1				5		
Sheffield	226	14	Kellogg	Nehemiah	1	2		1				2	1	1			9		
Sheffield	226	15	Bushnall	Samll Jr	1		1			1	1	1					5		
Sheffield	226	16	Vosburgh	Henry			1			2	1		1				5		
Sheffield	226	17	Harmon	Samll Jun			1			2		1					4		
Sheffield	226	18	Harmon	Samll		1		1		1	2		1				6		
Sheffield	226	19	Noble	Hezekiah	1	2		1			1	1		2			8		
Sheffield	226	20	Rawley	Hiel	4	1	1	1		2	1		1				11		
Sheffield	226	21	Curtiss	Jonathan		1	3	1	1	3	2			1			12		
Sheffield	226	22	Curtiss	Abijah	3			1		1		1					6		
Sheffield	226	23	Woodworth	William	2			1						1			4		
Sheffield	226	24	Seeley	Seth	1			1		1	1	1	1				6		
Sheffield	226	25	Spoor	Dirch		1	1		1		1	2		1			7		
Sheffield	226	26	Spoor	Isaac		2	1		1	1		1	1	1			8		
Sheffield	226	27	Parmeter	Daniel	1		2	1	1	1				1			7		
Sheffield	226	28	Shears	Jeremiah	1			1		1			1				4		
Sheffield	226	29	Jacobs	Israel	3	1		1		1			1				7		
Sheffield	226	30	Shears	Samll		1		1					1				3		
Sheffield	226	31	Shears	Amos	1		1						1				3		
Sheffield	226	32	Jacobs	Richard		1		1				1		1			4		
Sheffield	226	33	Jammons	Peleg Negro											3		3		
Sheffield	226	34	Holms	Benjamin F	2	1		1		1			1				6		
Sheffield	226	35	Frisbie	Ezra	2		1					1					4		
Sheffield	226	36	Paxton	John	2	1		1		1	1	1	1				8		
Sheffield	227	1	Kellogg	Thomas H			3			2		1	1				6		
Sheffield	227	2	Harris	David		1		1		1		1	1				5		
Sheffield	227	3	Vosburgh	Eliakim	3	1		1		1		1	1				8		
Sheffield	227	4	Kellogg	Erastus	2		1	1				1	1				6		
Sheffield	227	5	Dedman	Lois						2			1				3		
Sheffield	227	6	Hopkins	Stephen	1	2		1		2		1	1				8		
Sheffield	227	7	Bills	Hosea	3			1		1		1	1	1			8		
Sheffield	227	8	Vosburgh	Martin	3	1		1		2	1		1				9		
Sheffield	227	9	Catlin	James	1		2					1	1				5		
Sheffield	227	10	Vosburgh	Isaac		1		1		1				1			4		
Sheffield	227	11	Foot	Bere	2	1		1		1	1		1				7		
Sheffield	227	12	Moss	Darby										2			2		
Sheffield	227	13	Foot	Aaron		1		1						1			3		
Sheffield	227	14	Foot	Amos	3			1		1			1				6		
Sheffield	227	15	Kellogg	Ephraim		2	2		2		1	1		1			9		
Sheffield	227	16	Kellogg	Ephraim Jun	1	1	1						1				4		
Sheffield	227	17	Dibble	Sirus				1		1	1		1				4		
Sheffield	227	18	Schalenger	Gideon	2	2	1		1	1		1	1				9		
Sheffield	227	19	Mason	Thaddeus	3	3	1						1				8		
Sheffield	227	20	Stevens	Thomas	3		1	1		2			1				8		
Sheffield	227	21	Goodrich	Zaccheus			1		1			1		1			4		
Sheffield	227	22	Goodrich	Zaccheus Jun	1		1	1		3	2	1					9		
Sheffield	227	23	Mason	Rufus			1			1		1					3		
Sheffield	227	24	Callender	Abner	2	1	1		1		1	1	1				8		
Sheffield	227	25	Callender	Aaron		1		1	1	2	1	1	1				8		
Sheffield	227	26	Callender	Comfort				1				1		1			3		
Sheffield	227	27	Roach	William				1		2	1	1		1			6		
Sheffield	227	28	Clark	David	1		1	1		1	1		1				6		
Sheffield	227	29	Clark	Joel			1	1					1				3		
Sheffield	227	30	Keep	Jabez		1			1		2		1				5		
Sheffield	227	31	Mason	Robert	1			1					1				3		
Sheffield	227	32	Mason	Asa			1			1		1		1			4		
Sheffield	227	33	Callender	Silas	1					1		2	1	1			7		
Sheffield	227	34	Gleason	Enoch	2		1						1				4		
Sheffield	227	35	Higgins	Joseph	1	1		1		2			1				6		
Sheffield	227	36	Pixley	Nathll	1			1				1		1			4		
Sheffield	227	37	Taylor	Stephen	1		1						1				3		
Sheffield	228	1	Gleason	Ariel	3		1			1		1	2				9		

67

TOWN	PG#	LN#	HEADS OF HOUSEHOLD		FREE WHITE MALES					FREE WHITE FEMALES					TOTAL ALL OTHER	TOTAL SLAVES	TOTALS	DISTRICT/ TOWNSHIP	NOTES
			LAST NAME	FIRST NAME	under 10	10 to 16	16 to 26	26 to 45	45 and over	under 10	10 to 16	16 to 26	26 to 45	45 and over					
Sheffield	228	2	Gleason	Rufus				1		1		1	1				4		
Sheffield	228	3	Gleason	Elijah			1				1						2		
Sheffield	228	4	Warn	Jacob		1	2		1		1	1		1			7		
Sheffield	228	5	Burrall	David	2	1	1	1		2		1	1				9		
Sheffield	228	6	Nichols	James	2			1		2			1				6		
Sheffield	228	7	Nichols	Samll	2				1					1			4		
Sheffield	228	8	Lovejoy	Palmer	4			1		1	1		1				8		
Sheffield	228	9	Dibble	Benjamin			1			4			1				6		
Sheffield	228	10	Johnson	Jared	2	1			1	2	1	1	1				9		
Sheffield	228	11	Bowes	Jacob					1				1				2		
Sheffield	228	12	Carter	Amos					1				1				2		
Sheffield	228	13	Nichols	Jonathan	2				1	1	1		1				6		
Sheffield	228	14	Austin	Philip	1	1		2		2		1	1				8		
Sheffield	228	15	Hawden	Alexander				1					1				2		
Sheffield	228	16	Johnson	John Jun			1			3		1					5		
Sheffield	228	17	Johnson	Benjamin	2			1		3	1		1				8		
Sheffield	228	18	Rainsford	Thomas		3		1		2		1		1			8		
Sheffield	228	19	Kellogg	Mary								2		1			3		
Sheffield	228	20	Kellogg	Silas	3	2		1		2		2	1	1	1		13		
Sheffield	228	21	Kellogg	Gideon				1									1		
Sheffield	228	22	Kellogg	Ebenezer	1	1	3		1		1	1		2			10		
Sheffield	228	23	Porter	Amos		1		1				1		1			4		
Sheffield	228	24	Porter	Oliver		1	1						1				3		
Sheffield	228	25	Kellogg	Jesse		1		1		1	1		1				5		
Sheffield	228	26	Kellogg	Amasa			1					1					2		
Sheffield	228	27	Ferry	Isaac	2	1		1		1	2		1				8		
Sheffield	228	28	Ferry	David	1	1		1	1	2	1		1				8		
Sheffield	228	29	Ferry	Joseph		1	1	1	1		1	1		1			7		
Sheffield	228	30	Noble	Ezekiel P	2	1			1	1		1					6		
Sheffield	228	31	Boardman	Charles	1			1		2		1					5		
Sheffield	228	32	Parson	Batholomew			1			3	1		1				6		
Sheffield	228	33	Davis	Ammi	2			1		3	1	1	1				9		
Sheffield	228	34	Stillman	David	1	1		1			1		1				5		
Sheffield	228	35	Hurlbut	Simeon	1			1				1		1			4		
Sheffield	228	36	Callender	Joseph		1		1		1		1		1			5		
Sheffield	228	37	Callender	Archibald	1		1			1		1					4		
Sheffield	229	1	Goodrich	Jonathan		2	1						1				4		
Sheffield	229	2	Noble	Zecharh		1		1				1		1			4		
Sheffield	229	3	Wright	James		1		1									2		
Sheffield	229	4	Wright	James Jun			1			1	1		1				4		
Sheffield	229	5	Sprague	Seth	4			1		1			1				7		
Sheffield	229	6	May	Lemuel	3			1		2		1	1				8		
Sheffield	229	7	Leonard	Ephraim				1					1				2		
Sheffield	229	8	Winchel	Josiah			1										1		
Sheffield	229	9	Spaulding	Aaron	1	1		1					1				4		
Sheffield	229	10	Johnson	John		1		1		1	1		1	1			6		
Sheffield	229	11	Peck	James	1			1			1			1			4		
Sheffield	229	12	Lovejoy	Timothy	1			1			1		1	1			5		
Sheffield	229	13	Warn	Samll	2	1	2		1	1							7		
Sheffield	229	14	Warn	William	3	2			1	3			1				10		
Sheffield	229	15	Bushnall	Ziba	2			1		2			1				6		
Sheffield	229	16	Carter	Robert	1			1		2			1				5		
Sheffield	229	17	Forrest	George			1		1		1			1			4		
Sheffield	229	18	Forrest	John	3			1		2	2		1				9		
Sheffield	229	19	Hitchcock	Samll				1					1				2		
Sheffield	229	20	Sears	Thomas	2	1		1		3	1		1				9		
Sheffield	229	21	Sears	Rebecca									2				2		
Sheffield	229	22	Thompson	Timothy	1			1		1			1				4		
Sheffield	229	23	Day	John	1	1		1		1		2	1		1		8		
Sheffield	229	24	Spaulding	Phinehas		3	1	1		4	3	1	1				14		
Sheffield	229	25	Spaulding	Zebulon	1			1				1	1				4		
Sheffield	229	26	Pierammi	Caesar											2		2		
Sheffield	229	27	Howland	Jabez	1	1		2		2			1				7		
Sheffield	229	28	Lebaran	Joshua	1	1	2		1			1		1			7		
Sheffield	229	29	Gill	Amos		1		1				1	1				4		
Sheffield	229	30	Dream	London											9		9		
Sheffield	229	31	Stevens	William	1	1	1		1		2	3	1	1	1		12		
Sheffield	229	32	Romney	Abijah		1	1		1	1		2		1			7		
Sheffield	229	33		Simon Negro											2		2		
Sheffield	229	34	Downing	Roswell		1		2	1	1				1			6		
Sheffield	230	1	Brown	Lewis											4		4		
Sheffield	230	2	Burrall	Jonathan	2		3	1		1	2		1				10		
Sheffield	230	3	Simmons	William			1					1					2		
Sheffield	230	4	Watson	John	1				1		1			1			4		
Sheffield	230	5	Chamberlin	Ebenezer		1			1					1			3		
Sheffield	230	6	Westover	Job	1	1	2		1			1	1	1			8		
Sheffield	230	7	Slater	John	2	1		1		1		1	1				7		
Sheffield	230	8	Burrall	Jabez	1	1	3		1	2	1	1	1				12		
Sheffield	230	9	Spaulding	Zachhah		1		1					1				3		
Sheffield	230	10	Spaulding	Theophilus	1		1		1				1	1			5		

TOWN	PG#	LN#	LAST NAME	FIRST NAME	FREE WHITE MALES					FREE WHITE FEMALES					TOTAL ALL OTHER	TOTAL SLAVES	TOTALS	DISTRICT/ TOWNSHIP	NOTES
					under 10	10 to 16	16 to 26	26 to 45	45 and over	under 10	10 to 16	16 to 26	26 to 45	45 and over					
Sheffield	230	11	Higgins	Samll			1			2		1					4		
Sheffield	230	12	Higgins	Zebediah			2			1		1					4		
Sheffield	230	13	Stannard	Jehiel	3			1		1	2		1		1		9		
Sheffield	230	14	Elky	Diamond												3	3		
Sheffield	230	15	Austin	Joab	1	1	1	1	1		1	2		1			9		
Sheffield	230	16	Jacobs	Jonathan	1	1			1		1	1		2			7		
Sheffield	230	17	Van Loven	Zacchariah		2		1		2			1				6		
Sheffield	230	18	Daybald	Jonathan	1	1			1					1			4		
Sheffield	230	19	Cook	Eli	1			1		1			1				4		
Sheffield	230	20	Ashley	John	1	2	2	1		3			2				11		
Sheffield	230	21	Stowe	Comfort	2	1		1		1	1	2	1				9		
Sheffield	230	22	Trescott	Ebenezer	2				1	1	1		1				6		
Sheffield	230	23	Trescott	Samll	3	2	1	1		2	1	1	1				12		
Sheffield	230	24	Stevens	Stephen	3			1	1	1	2		1				9		
Sheffield	230	25	Chamberlin	Solomon		1		1		2			1				5		
Sheffield	230	26	Newton	John	2				1	1	1		1				6		
Sheffield	230	27	Stowe	William	3		1				2		1				7		
Sheffield	230	28	Curtiss	Giles	4		1	1		2	2		1				11		
Sheffield	230	29	Curtiss	John	1			1			1			1			4		
Sheffield	230	30	Curtiss	David	1		1			2			1				5		
Sheffield	230	31	Newton	Theodore				1			1		1				3		
Sheffield	230	32	Baker	Ephraim	3		2	1	1			2	1				10		
Sheffield	230	33	Clark	Uzziel		1	3	1			2	2	2				11		
Sheffield	230	34	Segur	Ezekiel	1				1	2	1		1				6		
Sheffield	230	35	Welch	Vine	3		1						1				5		
Sheffield	230	36	Gunn	Alexander															
Sheffield	230	37	Gunn	Ariel	1		1	1		2			1				6		
Sheffield	230	38	Davis	Abraham	3		1			1			1				6		
Sheffield	231	1	Noble	Matthew				1		2	1		1				5		
Sheffield	231	2	Noble	Eli			1	1		1		1					4		
Sheffield	231	3	Ensign	Elisha				1			1			1			3		
Sheffield	231	4	Bennett	Asahel P	2		2		1	2	2		1				10		
Sheffield	231	5	Mimson	Daniel	1			1		3		1					6		
Sheffield	231	6	Peas	Allen				1		2	1		1				5		
Sheffield	231	7	Lyon	Asa	1	1	1			1		1					5		
Sheffield	231	8	Adams	Joseph			1	1		1	1		1				5		
Sheffield	231	9	Hubbard	Prosper	1			1					1				3		
Sheffield	231	10	Lawrence	Daniel			1						1				2		
Sheffield	231	11	Stevens	Aaron			1			2			1				4		
Sheffield	231	12	Tacher	Cyrus	3	1		1		2			1				8		
Sheffield	231	13	Lipaugh	John Emery			1					1					2		
Sheffield	231	14	Francis	John												2	2		
Sheffield	231	15	Ashley	William		1	1	2			1	2		1	3		11		
Sheffield	231	16	Ashley	John Esq		1	1	1						1	2		6		
Sheffield	231	17	Beard	Aaron				1						1			2		
Sheffield	231	18	Fitch	Ari	1			1				1					3		
Sheffield	231	19	Fellows	John Jun	2	1	1	1		1	1		1				8		

TOWN	PG#	LN#	HEADS OF HOUSEHOLD		FREE WHITE MALES					FREE WHITE FEMALES					TOTAL ALL OTHER	TOTAL SLAVES	TOTALS	DISTRICT/ TOWNSHIP	NOTES
			LAST NAME	FIRST NAME	under 10	10 to 16	16 to 26	26 to 45	45 and over	under 10	10 to 16	16 to 26	26 to 45	45 and over					
Southfield	182	1	Bond	Nicholas Jr	2	1		1		2			1	1			8		
Southfield	182	2	Bozworth	Constant			1	1		1			1				4		
Southfield	182	3	Bond	Nicholas Sen					1					1			2		
Southfield	182	4	Baxter	Moses	4			1		3			1				9		
Southfield	182	5	Thorp	Aron	2			1		3			1	1			8		
Southfield	182	6	Simons	Eli			1		1			2	1	1			6		
Southfield	182	7	Turner	Thomas	1			1		2			1				5		
Southfield	182	8	Beach	James Jr			1						1				2		
Southfield	182	9	Smith	Amos	2	3		1		3		1	1	1			12		
Southfield	182	10	Sears	Daniel	1	1		1		1			1				5		
Southfield	182	11	Kneeland	Isaac 2nd					2			2	1				5		
Southfield	182	12	Kneeland	Isaac 3rd	1			1			1		1				4		
Southfield	182	13	Smith	Matthew					1				1				2		
Southfield	182	14	Denning	Solomon	1		1		1		1	5	1				10		
Southfield	182	15	Hawley	Zina	2	1		1		1	1		1				7		
Southfield	182	16	Bettis	Thomas			1	1		1	1		1	1			6		
Southfield	182	17	Bettis	Leonard				1		3			1				5		
Southfield	182	18	Bettis	Nathaniel	1		1		1	4	1		1				9		
Southfield	182	19	Thompson	Isaac	1			1		3			1				6		
Southfield	182	20	Thorp	Peter				1						1			2		
Southfield	182	21	Adams	James Jr	1			1		3	1		1				7		
Southfield	182	22	Markham	Ambrose	2			1		3	2		1				9		
Southfield	182	23	Beach	James		1	1	1									3		
Southfield	183	1	Smith	Henry	2	1		1		1			1				6		
Southfield	183	2	James	Dick J											3		3		
Southfield	183	3	Chapel	Richard	1	1	3		1	1	1	1	1	1			11		
Southfield	183	4	Mesenger	Aron	1	1	1		1	3	2	1		1			11		
Southfield	183	5	Sackett	Solomon	1	1			1		1	3	1				8		/
Southfield	183	6	Loveland	Daniel			1	1		4	1		1				8		
Southfield	183	7	Smith	Isaiah	1			1		4			1				7		
Southfield	183	8	Webster	Jonathan	3	1		1		2	1		1				9		
Southfield	183	9	Smith	Silas		1	1	1			1	2	2	1			9		
Southfield	183	10	Smith	Austin	1			1				1					3		
Southfield	183	11	Smith	Joseph	1	2	2		1	1	1			1			9		

TOWN	PG#	LN#	LAST NAME	FIRST NAME	under 10	10 to 16	16 to 26	26 to 45	45 and over	under 10	10 to 16	16 to 26	26 to 45	45 and over	TOTAL ALL OTHER	TOTAL SLAVES	TOTALS	DISTRICT/ TOWNSHIP	NOTES
					FREE WHITE MALES					FREE WHITE FEMALES									
Stockbridge	252	1	Bush	Aaron		1		1		2		1					5		
Stockbridge	252	2	Bennitt	Isaac			2		1	1	1	2	1	1			9		
Stockbridge	252	3	Bullock	William	2	1		1		1	1		1				7		
Stockbridge	252	4	Ball	Perry		1						1					2		
Stockbridge	252	5	Bidwell	Barnas	1		2	1		1	1						6		
Stockbridge	252	6	Barton	Joseph	3		2	1		1	1	1	1				10		
Stockbridge	252	7	Barns	Reuben	4	1		1		1	1	1					9		
Stockbridge	252	8	Baldwin	Clarke	3	1	2		1		1	2	1				11		
Stockbridge	252	9	Bliss	Wm Sen		1	1		1					1			4		
Stockbridge	252	10	Bliss	Wm Junr		1					1						2		
Stockbridge	252	11	Bishop	Elkanah		1			1	1	1		1				5		
Stockbridge	252	12	Brown	Elijah		1		1	1		1	1	1		1		7		
Stockbridge	252	13	Bement	Asa		1	1		1					1	1		5		
Stockbridge	252	14	Bement	John	1		1			1		1					4		
Stockbridge	252	15	Byington	Isaiah	3	3	3	1		1		1	1				13		
Stockbridge	253	1	Brown	Elisha	1	1	1	1		2	1		2				9		
Stockbridge	253	2	Brown	Henry		1	1	1		1	1		2				7		
Stockbridge	253	3	Billings	Henry	1			1		1			1				4		
Stockbridge	253	4	Billings	Matthew Jr				1		1			1				3		
Stockbridge	253	5	Bingham	Anna									1				1		
Stockbridge	253	6	Billings	Matthew		1			1					1			3		
Stockbridge	253	7	Brown	Luther				1		1			1				3		
Stockbridge	253	8	Clarke	James	3				1	1		1					6		
Stockbridge	253	9	Childs	William				1									1		
Stockbridge	253	10	Curtiss	Elnathan	3	1	2		1	1	1	1	1				11		
Stockbridge	253	11	Curtiss	Abel	1	1	3		1	1	1	2	1				11		
Stockbridge	253	12	Center	Ebenezer	1	1		1		2		1	1				7		
Stockbridge	253	13	Codner	Abram				1		1	1	1	1				5		
Stockbridge	253	14	Collins	Oliver Jr	2	1	1	1				1					6		
Stockbridge	253	15	Curtiss	Samuel	2			1		2	1		1				7		
Stockbridge	253	16	Cobb	Elijah W.	1	1		1		3			1				7		
Stockbridge	253	17	Cogswell	Nathan				1									1		
Stockbridge	253	18	Cumstock	Rufus		1	1		1		1			1			5		
Stockbridge	253	19	Collins	John		1	1			2		1					5		
Stockbridge	253	20	Curtiss	Samuel 2d	2		1	1		3	2		2				11		
Stockbridge	253	21	Cook	Ebenezer	1		1		1		1		1				5		
Stockbridge	253	22	Curtiss	Isaac	2	4	2		1	1		2	1	1			14		
Stockbridge	253	23	Carpenter	Abner		2	2		1	3	1	4		1			14		
Stockbridge	253	24	Cadwell	Mathew		2		2					1				5		
Stockbridge	253	25	Churchill	Jacob	1	1	1		1	2	1		1				8		
Stockbridge	253	26	Chapman	Caleb Jr			1			2	1		1				5		
Stockbridge	253	27	Chapman	Caleb				1				1		1			3		
Stockbridge	253	28	Chapman	James		1		1					1				3		
Stockbridge	253	29	Carwell	Ezra	1	1			1	1	1						5		
Stockbridge	253	30	Churchill	Elihu															
Stockbridge	253	31	Crosby	Abner	1		1	1		1		1					5		
Stockbridge	254	1	Churchill	Samuel			2		1				1	1			5		
Stockbridge	254	2	Churchill	Daniel			1			1		1					3		
Stockbridge	254	3	Collins	Oliver			1	1		1			1				4		
Stockbridge	254	4	Colton	Andrew	2		2	1			1	2					8		
Stockbridge	254	5	Cooper	Jemima									1				1		
Stockbridge	254	6	Donnelly	John				1					1				2		
Stockbridge	254	7	Dickenson	Justus			1		1			1	1				4		
Stockbridge	254	8	Dudley	Martha	2	1		2						1			6		
Stockbridge	254	9	Dewey	Abner		2	4	1		1		1		1			10		
Stockbridge	254	10	Dresser	James	1	1		1		1	1	1	1				7		
Stockbridge	254	11	Dunnells	Sally									1				1		
Stockbridge	254	12	Dwight	Henry W	1	2		1				1	1		1		7		
Stockbridge	254	13	Dening	Josiah		1	1	1	1			2	1	1			8		
Stockbridge	254	14	Dresser	Benj		2	1		1	1			1				6		
Stockbridge	254	15	Dening	Elijah	1			1					1	1			3		
Stockbridge	254	16	Dunham	William				1		2		1	1				5		
Stockbridge	254	17	Dwight	Jonah	2	1		1		1		2	1		1		9		
Stockbridge	254	18	Day	Amasa		1			1			1	2		1		6		
Stockbridge	254	19	Day	Roderick			1			1			1				3		
Stockbridge	254	20	Edwards	Timothy		1	2	1	1			2		1	1		9		
Stockbridge	254	21	Foot	Adonijah		1	1			3		1					6		
Stockbridge	254	22	Fairchild	Daniel	2	2		1		1	1		2				9		
Stockbridge	254	23	Fenn	Daniel	3			1		1			3				8		
Stockbridge	254	24	Fairman	Ichabod		1		1		1		2		1			6		
Stockbridge	254	25	Fox	Hubbard	3				1	2	2		1				9		
Stockbridge	254	26	Fox	Daniel									1				1		
Stockbridge	254	27	Griswold	Ezekiel		2	1		1	1				1			6		
Stockbridge	254	28	Goodrich	David	1		1	1		2			1				6		
Stockbridge	254	29	Glezen	Solomon				1				1	1				3		
Stockbridge	254	30	Gains	Daniel		1						1					2		
Stockbridge	255	1	Humphry	Enoch											6		6		
Stockbridge	255	2	Humphry	Enoch Jr											5		5		
Stockbridge	255	3	Hill	John	1	1			1	1	1			1			6		

71

TOWN	PG#	LN#	HEADS OF HOUSEHOLD LAST NAME	FIRST NAME	FREE WHITE MALES under 10	10 to 16	16 to 26	26 to 45	45 and over	FREE WHITE FEMALES under 10	10 to 16	16 to 26	26 to 45	45 and over	TOTAL ALL OTHER	TOTAL SLAVES	TOTALS	DISTRICT/TOWNSHIP	NOTES
Stockbridge	255	4	Holmes	Ezra	3			1		2			1				7		
Stockbridge	255	5	Holmes	George	1			1		3			1				6		
Stockbridge	255	6	Hamilton	John					1				1	1			3		
Stockbridge	255	7	Hart	Comfort	1	1		1		2			1				6		
Stockbridge	255	8	Hart	Job	1	1		1					1				4		
Stockbridge	255	9	Holland	Joseph		1		1					1				3		
Stockbridge	255	10	Hatch	Benj			1	1	1				1				4		
Stockbridge	255	11	Hagar	Amos	3		1		1	2	2		1				10		
Stockbridge	255	12	Hopkins	Archibald		1		1									2		
Stockbridge	255	13	Hollenback	Andrew	2			1					1				4		
Stockbridge	255	14	Hand	Abel		1		1		1			1				4		
Stockbridge	255	15	Hammond	Thomas	2			1				1	1				5		
Stockbridge	255	16	Hall	Amos		1	1	1			2		1				6		
Stockbridge	255	17	Hoxce	Mrs	1					2			1				4		
Stockbridge	255	18	Hall	Job	1		1			1		1					4		
Stockbridge	255	19	Hutchinson	Daniel	1			1		3			1				6		
Stockbridge	255	20	Hamilton	Benj	1	1		1			2	1	1				7		
Stockbridge	255	21	How	Joseph	1	1		1		1	1		1				6		
Stockbridge	255	22	Hart	Simeon	1			1		3			1	1			7		
Stockbridge	255	23	Hull	Agrippa											4		4		
Stockbridge	255	24	Ingersoll	Jonathan	2	2	1		1	3	1	2	1				13		
Stockbridge	255	25	Ide	Nehemiah	2	3	1		1	1	1		1				10		
Stockbridge	255	26	Jacklin	Ebenezer								1			2		3		
Stockbridge	255	27	Jason	Deliverance											3		3		
Stockbridge	255	28	James	Stephen	2			1		1	2		1				7		
Stockbridge	255	29	James	Stephen W	2	1		1		1	1		1				7		
Stockbridge	255	30	James	John				1					1				2		
Stockbridge	255	31	Jones	Jonah	1	1	1	1		1		2		2			9		
Stockbridge	256	1	Judd	Ozias		1		1				1		2			5		
Stockbridge	256	2	Kingsley	Wido						1			1	1			2		
Stockbridge	256	3	Linden	Jedediah	4	1	1	1					1	2			10		
Stockbridge	256	4	Lynch	Lawrence		1	2	1									4		
Stockbridge	256	5	Lynch	Nathaniel	2			1		1			1				5		
Stockbridge	256	6	Lynch	Moses	1			1		1			1				4		
Stockbridge	256	7	Lusk	William			1	1					1				3		
Stockbridge	256	8	Morgan	Sylvia									1				1		
Stockbridge	256	9	Morrison	John				1					2				3		
Stockbridge	256	10	Mighlls	Elijah	2		1	1		1			1	1			7		
Stockbridge	256	11	Miller	Jonathan	3	2	1	1		1		1	1				10		
Stockbridge	256	12	McMullen	John	1	2		1		3			1				8		
Stockbridge	256	13	Mighlls	Lucretia									1				1		
Stockbridge	256	14	Nash	Stephen	2		2		1	2		1	1	1	2		12		
Stockbridge	256	15	Nelson	Moses	1			1					1				3		
Stockbridge	256	16	Nelson	William	1		1	1				1	1				5		
Stockbridge	256	17	Nelson	Oliver	2			1		2			1				6		
Stockbridge	256	18	Nichols	Joseph				1					1				2		
Stockbridge	256	19	Nash	Anna									1				1		
Stockbridge	256	20	Olmstead	Samuel	3			1		1	1		1				7		
Stockbridge	256	21	Pepoon	Daniel	3	1	1	5		2	1	1	1		1		16		
Stockbridge	256	22	Partridge	Oliver				1									1		
Stockbridge	256	23	Pease	Phineas	4	1	2	1		1	3	1	1				14		
Stockbridge	256	24	Patton	Jonathan	1		1	1		1	1						5		
Stockbridge	256	25	Peck	Salmon	1			1		1			1				4		
Stockbridge	256	26	Peck	Selah	2	1		1		1			1				6		
Stockbridge	256	27	Phelps	Ely		1			1	1				2			5		
Stockbridge	256	28	Parker	Abraham	1	2		1		1	1		1				7		
Stockbridge	256	29	Perry	Peter	2	1	2		1	1	1	1		1			10		
Stockbridge	256	30	Partridge	Samuel			1	1		2			1				5		
Stockbridge	256	31	Peck	Elisha	2			1					1				4		
Stockbridge	256	32	Pepoon	Silas Jr		1	1	1	1			1		2			8		
Stockbridge	256	33	Paddock	Joseph				1		3			1				5		
Stockbridge	256	34	Plumb	Ebenezer		1	2	1				1		1			6		
Stockbridge	257	1	Parker	Benjamin	1			1		1			1				4		
Stockbridge	257	2	Rice	Abraham	2	1		1		3	2		1				10		
Stockbridge	257	3	Reeves	John	1		1					1					3		
Stockbridge	257	4	Rick	Joseph			1	1		1	1		1				5		
Stockbridge	257	5	Rice	Moses			1	1					1				3		
Stockbridge	257	6	Simons	Pearly			1	1					1				3		
Stockbridge	257	7	Seymour	Natha	2	1	1	1				1	1				7		
Stockbridge	257	8	Smith	Russel		1		1				1	1				4		
Stockbridge	257	9	Sedgewick	Theod	1	3	1	2	1	1		1	1	1	1		13		
Stockbridge	257	10	Squires	Jonan			2		1	2	2		2				9		
Stockbridge	257	11	Seely	Jonas	3	1		1		2			1	1			9		
Stockbridge	257	12	Seely	Joseph		2		1		3			1				7		
Stockbridge	257	13	Smith	Gideon		1			1		1			1	2		6		
Stockbridge	257	14	Smith	Gideon	2		1	1									4		
Stockbridge	257	15	Smith	Enos			1	1		1	1	1	1				6		
Stockbridge	257	16	Stevens	Paul	2	2			1			1	1	1			8		
Stockbridge	257	17	Sergeant	Erastus	1	1	3		2			1	4	1	1		14		

72

| TOWN | PG# | LN# | HEADS OF HOUSEHOLD | | FREE WHITE MALES | | | | | FREE WHITE FEMALES | | | | | TOTAL ALL OTHER | TOTAL SLAVES | TOTALS | DISTRICT/ TOWNSHIP | NOTES |
			LAST NAME	FIRST NAME	under 10	10 to 16	16 to 26	26 to 45	45 and over	under 10	10 to 16	16 to 26	26 to 45	45 and over					
Stockbridge	257	18	Smith	Heman Jr		1						1		1			3		
Stockbridge	257	19	Swift	Owen	1			1		2			1				5		
Stockbridge	257	20	Swift	James	3	1	1	1		2			1				9		
Stockbridge	257	21	Shaw	Prudence	1								1				2		
Stockbridge	257	22	Smith	Sarah								1			1		2		
Stockbridge	257	23	Taylor	John				1							1		2		
Stockbridge	257	24	Solomon	Ephraim	2	1	1		1	1	1		3				10		
Stockbridge	257	25	Tolman	Ebenzr	1	2			1			4	1				9		
Stockbridge	257	26	Tucker	John		1		1		1							3		
Stockbridge	257	27	Trask	Jesse	4	2	1	1			1		1				10		
Stockbridge	257	28	Taylor	John 2d			1			1							2		
Stockbridge	257	29	Vallett	Jeremiah Jr	1	1	1						1				4		
Stockbridge	257	30	Vaughan	John	2	1			1	1	2	1	1				9		
Stockbridge	257	31	West	Stephen		1			1				1	1	1		5		
Stockbridge	257	32	Woodbridge	Joseph			2	1				1	1		2		7		
Stockbridge	257	33	Willard	Enoch	1		1	1					1	1			5		
Stockbridge	258	1	Williams	Daniel		1		1	1				1	1			5		
Stockbridge	258	2	Williams	Asa	1		2	1		1	1		1				7		
Stockbridge	258	3	Willcox	Seth	3			1		1			1				6		
Stockbridge	258	4	Ward	Nicholas	2			1					1				4		
Stockbridge	258	5	Warner	Daniel	1			1			1						3		
Stockbridge	258	6	Williams	Azariah				1			1	2	1				5		
Stockbridge	258	7	Williams	Abram	2			1		2			1	1			7		
Stockbridge	258	8	Whitney	Elisha	3	2		1		2	2	1	1				12		
Stockbridge	258	9	Williams	Stephen		3	1		1	1		2		1			9		
Stockbridge	258	10	Whiton	John	1	1	1	1		2	1	1	1				9		
Stockbridge	258	11	Whelpley	Samuel				1					1				2		
Stockbridge	258	12	Whelpley	Thomas	3	1		1		2	1		1				9		
Stockbridge	258	13	Whittley	Elphalet	2	2	3		1	1		2		1			12		
Stockbridge	258	14	Wallis	James	1			1		1			1				4		
Stockbridge	258	15	Willcox	Solomon	3			1		1		1	1				7		
Stockbridge	258	16	Whitney	Silas Jr	2		2	1		3	1	2	1				12		
Stockbridge	258	17	Woolford	James			1			1		1					3		
Stockbridge	258	18	Woodruff	Noadiah	2			1		1			1				5		
Stockbridge	258	19	Webster	Elihu		1							1				2		
Stockbridge	258	20	Wheeler	Charles			1										1		
Stockbridge	258	21	Kellis	Thomas											3		3		
Stockbridge	258	22		Rose											2		2		Last name blank
Stockbridge	258	23		Bett											2		2		Last name blank
Stockbridge	258	24	Hadad	Ben											4		4		
Stockbridge	258	25	Freeman	Betty											1		1		
Stockbridge	258	26	Newport	Betty											4		4		
Stockbridge	258	27	Peters	Thomas											3		3		
Stockbridge	258	28	Purden	Anthony											2		2		
Stockbridge	258	29		Lemon											6		6		Last name blank
Stockbridge	258	30		Tummons											1		1		Last name blank
Stockbridge	258	31	Sharp	Peter											1		1		

TOWN	PG#	LN#	LAST NAME	FIRST NAME	FREE WHITE MALES under 10	10 to 16	16 to 26	26 to 45	45 and over	FREE WHITE FEMALES under 10	10 to 16	16 to 26	26 to 45	45 and over	TOTAL ALL OTHER	TOTAL SLAVES	TOTALS	DISTRICT/ TOWNSHIP	NOTES
Tyringham	110	1	Gardner	James		3	1		1					1			6		
Tyringham	110	2	Jones	Eliphalet	2	1		1				1	1				6		
Tyringham	110	3	Russell	John				1						1			2		
Tyringham	110	4	Patten	Nathal	1	1			1	3	1		1				8		
Tyringham	110	5	Russell	Jacob	1			1				1					3		
Tyringham	110	6	Hall	Hannah								1	1				2		
Tyringham	110	7	Jones	Eliphalet		1	1		1				1				4		
Tyringham	110	8	Park	Joshua	1		1	1		1			1	1			6		
Tyringham	110	9	Jones	Silas	1	1		1		3	3		1	1			11		
Tyringham	110	10	Rice	Stephen	2	1			1	1	1			1			7		
Tyringham	110	11	Slater	Giles	2	2	1		1		1	2	1	3			13		
Tyringham	110	12	Garfield	Isaac		1	4	1	1					2			9		
Tyringham	110	13	Herrick	Francis	2			2		2			1				7		
Tyringham	110	14	Heath	Elisha	4			1		1	1		1	1			9		
Tyringham	110	15	Hale	William Jun	1				1		1		1				4		
Tyringham	110	16	Jones	Ephraim	1	1		1		2		1					6		
Tyringham	110	17	Steadman	William				1		1		1					3		
Tyringham	110	18	Clerk	Walter			2	1	1			1	1				6		
Tyringham	110	19	Spring	Ebenz	2	1			1	1	2	2		1			10		
Tyringham	110	20	Benedict	Abel	1				1	1	2	2		1			8		
Tyringham	110	21	Benedict	Isaac	1		1			1	1						4		
Tyringham	110	22	Bowdich	Abel Junr		1				1		1					3		
Tyringham	110	23	Morse	Peter		1		1					1				3		
Tyringham	111	1	Billings	William	1	1						1					3		
Tyringham	111	2	Millman	Briant	1		1	1		2		1					6		
Tyringham	111	3	Willson	Joseph		1	1	1			1		1				5		
Tyringham	111	4	Brown	Asa	2		1				1						4		
Tyringham	111	5	Clafford	John	2		1				1						4		
Tyringham	111	6	Diskill	John		1		1		2		1					5		
Tyringham	111	7	Brewer	Nathl	2	2		1		2	1		1				9		
Tyringham	111	8	Brewer	Davis				1			1						2		
Tyringham	111	9	Brewer	Parker			1				1						2		
Tyringham	111	10	Northrop	Barzillai	3		1			1		1					6		
Tyringham	111	11	Caulfield	Aaron			1				1						2		
Tyringham	111	12	Canfield	Thomas				1			1		1				3		
Tyringham	111	13	Canfield	Oliver			1				1						2		
Tyringham	111	14	Ricer	Amos	1	3	2		1	1		2	1	1			12		
Tyringham	111	15	Milliman	Ezekiel	1	1	1				1						4		
Tyringham	111	16	Milliman	Abiram	2		1			4	1						8		
Tyringham	111	17	Steadman	Thomas	2	1		1		1			1				6		
Tyringham	111	18	Churchill	Saml	2		1	1			1						5		
Tyringham	111	19	Stanley	Abisha	2			1	4		2	2	2	5			18		
Tyringham	111	20	Herrick	Henry		1	1	8	6			6	7	6			35		
Tyringham	111	21	Rathbun	Jona	3	1		1		2	1	1					9		
Tyringham	111	22	Moon	Abram	1	3			1			1					6		
Tyringham	111	23	Allen	Potter	3			1		2	1		1				8		
Tyringham	111	24	Whaly	John P.	2	2	1		1	3				2			11		
Tyringham	111	25	Kimball	Charles				1		2	1		1				5		
Tyringham	111	26	Baily	Clerk		1	3		1		2			2			9		
Tyringham	111	27	Battle	Ithiel	2	1	1		1	1	3	1		1			11		
Tyringham	111	28	Morey	Jesse			2	1					1				4		
Tyringham	111	29	Willcox	Matthew	2	1			1				1				5		
Tyringham	111	30	Northrup	Amose Jur	1			1		1		1					4		
Tyringham	111	31	Bassett	Benjamin				1					1				2		
Tyringham	111	32	Webster	Daniel	4			1		1	1		1				8		
Tyringham	111	33	Cooper	Matthew			1	1				1	1				4		
Tyringham	111	34	Cooper	Reuben			1					1					2		
Tyringham	111	35	Gleason	Joseph				1			2		1				4		
Tyringham	111	36	Rathbon	Mary							1		1				2		
Tyringham	111	37	Rathbon	Percy	2	1		1		2		1	1				8		
Tyringham	111	38	Wolf	Peter D.	2		3		1	1				1			8		
Tyringham	111	39	Gibbs	Jona				1					1				2		
Tyringham	111	40	Gibbs	Nathan	4			1		1			1				7		
Tyringham	111	41	Tanner	William	1	1		1		2			1				6		
Tyringham	111	42	Higby	Josiah	3	1		1		2	1		1				9		
Tyringham	111	43	Battle	Justus	2	1	1		1	1		1	1				8		
Tyringham	111	44	Cooley	Enos	1		1			1			1				5		
Tyringham	111	45	Harris	Champlin	2			1				1	1				5		
Tyringham	111	46	Heath	Solomon			1	1		1		1					4		
Tyringham	111	47	Tuttle	Jonathan	2			1		1		1	1				6		
Tyringham	111	48	Webster	John	3	2	1	1			1		1				9		
Tyringham	112	1	Austin	Thomas	2			1		2			1				6		
Tyringham	112	2	Webster	Stephen	2	2		1		1	1		1				8		
Tyringham	112	3	Davis	Benjamin				1					1				2		
Tyringham	112	4	Davis	Gardner	1	3		1		3			1				9		
Tyringham	112	5	Pierce	Lawrence		1		1		1		1		1			4		
Tyringham	112	6	Pierce	John	2			1		2			1				6		
Tyringham	112	7	Pierce	Langarthe	2	1		1		2	1		1				8		
Tyringham	112	8	Steadman	William	1			1		1			1				4		

TOWN	PG#	LN#	LAST NAME	FIRST NAME	FREE WHITE MALES					FREE WHITE FEMALES					TOTAL ALL OTHER	TOTAL SLAVES	TOTALS	DISTRICT/ TOWNSHIP	NOTES
					under 10	10 to 16	16 to 26	26 to 45	45 and over	under 10	10 to 16	16 to 26	26 to 45	45 and over					
Tyringham	112	9	Park	Nathan			1	1		2			1				5		
Tyringham	112	10	Milliman	Theodoria		1				1			1				3		
Tyringham	112	11	Jones	Heman			2	1				2					5		
Tyringham	112	12	Northrop	Amos			1	1				1		1			4		
Tyringham	112	13	Northrup	John	1		1						1				3		
Tyringham	112	14	Heath	William	3	1	1	1		1	2		1				10		
Tyringham	112	15	Hall	Simion				1		1		1		1			4		
Tyringham	112	16	Park	Nehemiah	1	2			1	1	1	1		1			8		
Tyringham	112	17	Hall	Thomas	1		1		1	2	2	2	2	1			12		
Tyringham	112	18	Heath	Eleazer	3	2	1	1		2	1		1				11		
Tyringham	112	19	Hill	Josiah				1		1		1	1				4		
Tyringham	112	20	Park	Matthias	1	1		1		1	1	1	1				7		
Tyringham	112	21	Johnson	Anna		1	1	1				1		1			5		
Tyringham	112	22	Bailey	Stephen	1		1			2		1					5		
Tyringham	112	23	Howe	Joseph	2	1			1		2	3		1			10		
Tyringham	112	24	Collins	Abram	2	2	1		1			1	1				8		
Tyringham	112	25	Chappell	William	1	1		1		1			1				5		
Tyringham	112	26	Johnson	Stephen			2	1					1				4		
Tyringham	112	27	Johnson	Stephen Jun	2			1		1			1				5		
Tyringham	112	28	Card	John		1	1	1	1	1	1			1			7		
Tyringham	112	29	Lewis	Benoni	2	1	2		1	1	2	1		1			11		
Tyringham	112	30	Green	Samuel	2		3	1		1			1				8		
Tyringham	112	31	Colver	Simon	3			1		2			1				7		
Tyringham	112	32	Tucker	John	2			1		2	1		1				7		
Tyringham	112	33	Webster	John	2	2		1			1		1				7		
Tyringham	112	34	Allen	Jonathan				1						1			2		
Tyringham	112	35	Porter	Samuel			1					1					2		
Tyringham	112	36	Heath	Isaac		2	2	1		1		1	2	1			10		
Tyringham	112	37	Knapp	Ephraim	2			1		2			1				6		
Tyringham	112	38	Jinks	William	1	1	1		1	2		1					7		
Tyringham	112	39	Peck	Miller	1	1		1		1			1				5		
Tyringham	112	40	Mansfield	Daniel	2		3	1					1				7		
Tyringham	112	41	Averill	Thomas	2			1		3			1				7		
Tyringham	112	42	Clerk	Silas	3			1		1			1				6		
Tyringham	112	43	Keyes	Ephraim	1			1					1				3		
Tyringham	112	44	Russell	James	3	1		1		1			1				7		
Tyringham	112	45	Thompson	James	1			1	1	3		1	1	2			10		
Tyringham	112	46	Brown	James	2	2		1		1		1	1				8		
Tyringham	112	47	Sweet	James	1			1		2		1	1	1			7		
Tyringham	112	48	Heath	Solomon			2			1		1					4		
Tyringham	112	49	Garfield	Solomon	3		2		1	2				1			9		
Tyringham	112	50	Knapp	Ira			1					1					2		
Tyringham	112	51	Chadwick	Ebenz	1	2			1	3	1			1			9		
Tyringham	113	1	Allen	Elihu	2			1		1			1				5		
Tyringham	113	2	Tillotson	Samuel	4			1		1			1				7		
Tyringham	113	3	Read	Benjamin		1		1						1			3		
Tyringham	113	4	Wadsworth	Asa	2			1	1	1			1	2			8		
Tyringham	113	5	Sigler	George	3			1		1			1				6		
Tyringham	113	6	Wheelock	Samuel		1	1		2		1	1	2	1			9		
Tyringham	113	7	Towsend	Samuel	1			1				1		1			4		
Tyringham	113	8	Towsend	Lemuel			1					1					2		
Tyringham	113	9	Hale	Josiah	2	2	1	1		1	1		1				9		
Tyringham	113	10	Dwight	Sereno	2			1					1	2			6		
Tyringham	113	11	Carrier	Thomas	3			1		1			1				6		
Tyringham	113	12	Gates	Gideon			1						1				2		
Tyringham	113	13	Smith	Samuel		1		1		1	1		1				4		
Tyringham	113	14	Smith	William		1							1				2		
Tyringham	113	15	Smith	Daniel	1	1							1				3		
Tyringham	113	16	Rewey	John		1		1					1				3		
Tyringham	113	17	Hulet	Nehemiah	3			1		1	1		1				7		
Tyringham	113	18	Carpenter	Amos	1	2	1	1		3	1	2	1				12		
Tyringham	113	19	Garfield	John	2			1		2			1				6		
Tyringham	113	20	Gregory	Seth				1						1			2		
Tyringham	113	21	Case	Manning	1			1		1		1					4		
Tyringham	113	22	Stebbins	Darius	3	1	2	1		2	3		1				13		
Tyringham	113	23	Markham	Asa	1	1		1		3	1		1				8		
Tyringham	113	24	Buell	Joseph	2	1		1		1	2	1	2				10		
Tyringham	113	25	Townsend	Jonan	4			1					1				6		
Tyringham	113	26	Chapin	Joseph	2	1	1	1		1	2	1	1	1			11		
Tyringham	113	27	Hurd	Robert	2	1			1		1	2	1				8		
Tyringham	113	28	Martin	Noah	2	1		1		2	2		1				9		
Tyringham	113	29	Warren	Benjamin Jr		1		1		2		1					5		
Tyringham	113	30	Warren	Benjamin				1				3		1			5		
Tyringham	113	31	Wheelock	Amariah	1			1		3		2	1				8		
Tyringham	113	32	Garfield	Elisha	2	1		1		2			1				7		
Tyringham	113	33	Dodge	Ozias	1		1	1		3	2	1	1				10		
Tyringham	113	34	Hall	Ebenz	1		1		1	2			1	1			7		
Tyringham	113	35	Alden	Israel	1	2	2		1	1		2		2			11		
Tyringham	113	36	Rewey	Ebenezer	1	1	1			2			1				9		

75

TOWN	PG#	LN#	LAST NAME	FIRST NAME	FWM under 10	10 to 16	16 to 26	26 to 45	45 and over	FWF under 10	10 to 16	16 to 26	26 to 45	45 and over	TOTAL ALL OTHER	TOTAL SLAVES	TOTALS	DISTRICT/ TOWNSHIP	NOTES
Tyringham	113	37	Allen	Noah					1					1			2		
Tyringham	113	38	Allen	Noah Jun	2		1			1			1				5		
Tyringham	113	39	Joslin	Asa	1		1		1	1	2	1		1			8		
Tyringham	113	40	Garfield	Daniel		1	1			3			1	1			7		
Tyringham	113	41	Markham	Aaron	2		1			1			1	1			6		
Tyringham	113	42	Ball	Joseph	1	1	1		1	1	2	1		1			9		
Tyringham	113	43	Warren	Joshua			1	1					1				3		
Tyringham	113	44	Jackson	Ebenz	1		2		1	2	1	1	1	1			10		
Tyringham	113	45	Townsend	Rufus	1		1			1			1				4		
Tyringham	113	46	Heath	Abijah	2	2		1	1	3	2		1				12		
Tyringham	113	47	Abbot	Nathan		1		1	1	1	1			1			6		
Tyringham	113	48	Hill	Elijah	1	1		1		1	2	1	1				8		
Tyringham	113	49	Brown	Moses	3	2	1		1	1		2		1			11		
Tyringham	114	1	Bedwell	Udonjah	5		1	1				1	1				9		
Tyringham	114	2	Morse	Moses		1		1		3	1		1	1			8		
Tyringham	114	3	Alden	Benjamin	1		1					1					3		
Tyringham	114	4	Upham	Nathan	1	2		1		4			1				9		
Tyringham	114	5	Upham	Moses				1		1	1						3		
Tyringham	114	6	Barber	Samuel Jun	1	1		1				1					4		
Tyringham	114	7	Pickett	Eli				1		2			1				4		
Tyringham	114	8	Warren	Elijah	3			1		2			1				7		
Tyringham	114	9	Binney	Thomas			1	1						1			3		
Tyringham	114	10	Taylor	Elisha	2	2	1	2			1			1			9		
Tyringham	114	11	Taylor	Alvin			1			1			1				3		
Tyringham	114	12	Graton	Thomas	2	2		1		1		1	1	1			9		
Tyringham	114	13	Graves	Elisha		1		1					1	1			4		
Tyringham	114	14	Baldwin	Samuel				1					1				2		
Tyringham	114	15	Rewey	John			1	1						1			3		
Tyringham	114	16	Barber	Samuel	1		1	1						2			5		
Tyringham	114	17	Rewey	Thomas		2		1		2				1			6		
Tyringham	114	18	Markham	William	1	1	1	1		3	1		1				9		
Tyringham	114	19	Curtis	Amasa		1	1	1		2	2			1			8		
Tyringham	114	20	Curtis	Amasa Jun	1		1			1			1				4		
Tyringham	114	21	Thompson	Jared	3			1				1					5		
Tyringham	114	22	Thompson	Samuel				1		4			1				6		
Tyringham	114	23	Thompson	Grace		1	1				1			1			7		
Tyringham	114	24	Langdon	Amos	2	2		1		2	1	1	1				10		
Tyringham	114	25	Langdon	Jesse	3		1		1	1	1	1		1			9		
Tyringham	114	26	Orton	Darius	2			1		3			1				7		
Tyringham	114	27	Brewer	Joseph			2		1			2	1	1			7		
Tyringham	114	28	Orton	Amariah	2	1		1		3			1				8		
Tyringham	114	29	Jackson	Giles		1	2		1	1	2			1			8		
Tyringham	114	30	Judd	Thos C.	2			1		1			1				5		
Tyringham	114	31	Markham	Benjm	2	1	1		1	2	1	1		1			10		
Tyringham	114	32	Heath	Joseph	2		1	1		4	1	1	1				11		
Tyringham	114	33	Wadsworth	Ezekiel	3	1		1		1	1		1				8		
Tyringham	114	34	Gardner	Richard											5		5		
Tyringham	114	35	Heath	Patience									1				1		
Tyringham	114	36	Fowler	Asa			2	1		2			1				6		
Tyringham	114	37	Fowler	Gideon	1			1					1				3		
Tyringham	114	38	Alden	Benjamin Jr	1			1					1				3		
Tyringham	114	39	Avery	Joseph	1				2	1	1	2		2			9		
Tyringham	114	40	Baldwin	Stephen	1		1					1	1				4		
Tyringham	114	41	Heath	Elijah	2	1	1	1		2	1	1	1				10		
Tyringham	114	42	Barber	Alexanr	1			1		2			1				5		
Tyringham	114	43	Ross	Peleg	1	1	1	1	1	1	1	1	1				9		
Tyringham	114	44	Hobbs	Daniel	1		1		1		1	2		1			7		
Tyringham	114	45	Wells	Benjm D			1	1		3			1				6		
Tyringham	114	46	Garfield	Isaac		2	3		1	1				2			9		
Tyringham	115	1	Hall	Abel		1		1		1			1				4		
Tyringham	115	2	Wintworth	John	1			1		1			1				4		
Tyringham	115	3	Brown	Richard	1		1	1					1				4		
Tyringham	115	4	Rockwood	Reuben	3	1	1	1		1			1				8		
Tyringham	115	5	Fargo	Thomas	3		1						1				5		
Tyringham	115	6	Wadsworth	Barnabas			1						1				2		
Tyringham	115	7	Fowler	Elijah	2			1		1			1				5		
Tyringham	115	8	Hill	Josiah	1	2	1	1		2	1		1				9		
Tyringham	115	9	Brewer	Jonas			1	1		1			1				4		
Tyringham	115	10	Brewer	Josiah Jun			1						1				2		
Tyringham	115	11	Brewer	John			1			1			1				3		
Tyringham	115	12	Doud	Noah	2	1		1		2			1	1			8		
Tyringham	115	13	Doud	Marcena	2	1		1		1	2		1				8		
Tyringham	115	14	Barter	John			1			1	1		1				4		
Tyringham	115	15	Hind	David		2		1		3			1				7		
Tyringham	115	16	Walker	Isaac	1		1	1	1			1	1	1			7		
Tyringham	115	17	Harrman	Isaac	1		1			1			1				4		
Tyringham	115	18	Heath	John	1			1		2	2		1				7		
Tyringham	115	19	Doud	Sylvanus	2			1		1			1				5		
Tyringham	115	20	Spring	Amos	1	3		1		1	2		1				9		

76

TOWN	PG#	LN#	LAST NAME	FIRST NAME	under 10	10 to 16	16 to 26	26 to 45	45 and over	under 10	10 to 16	16 to 26	26 to 45	45 and over	TOTAL ALL OTHER	TOTAL SLAVES	TOTALS	DISTRICT/ TOWNSHIP	NOTES
					FREE WHITE MALES					FREE WHITE FEMALES									
Tyringham	115	21	Judd	Oliver	1	2	1	1		1	2		1				9		
Tyringham	115	22	Clerk	Francis	3	4	1		1	2	1		1				13		
Tyringham	115	23	Willson	James	1			1		3			1				6		
Tyringham	115	24	Hale	William					1					1			2		
Tyringham	115	25	Hale	Salathiel		1		1				1					3		
Tyringham	115	26	Clerk	John		2	1			2			1				6		
Tyringham	115	27	Platt	Ebenezer			1			1		1					3		
Tyringham	115	28	Clerk	Eli			1			1		1		1			4		
Tyringham	115	29	Clerk	Reuben				1	1					1			3		
Tyringham	115	30	Braman	Samuel		1	1		1			2		1			6		
Tyringham	115	31	Braman	Nicholas			1					1					2		
Tyringham	115	32	Hale	John	1	1	1		1	2	2	1	2				11		
Tyringham	115	33	Herrick	Ezekiel					1			1		1			3		
Tyringham	115	34	Pratt	Elnathan	1	1		1		1		1					5		
Tyringham	115	35	Herrick	Francis	2		1	1		2		1					7		
Tyringham	115	36	Willson	Joseph			2		1			1		1			5		
Tyringham	115	37	Jones	Ephraim	1	1		1		2		1					6		
Tyringham	115	38	Role	Gideon	2			1		1		1					5		
Tyringham	115	39	Herrick	Hezekiah	1	1	1			1	1	1	1				7		
Tyringham	115	40	Heath	William	3	1	1	1		2	1	1	1	1			12		
Tyringham	115	41	Heath	Isaac	2	1	1	2		2	1		2	1			12		
Tyringham	115	42	Read	Nathal		1		1		3	2		1	1			9		
Tyringham	115	43	Collins	Abram	3	1	1	3	1		1		1				11		
Tyringham	115	44	Fuller	Peter	1	1	1		1	2			1				7		
Tyringham	115	45	Hall	Simeon				1		1		1	2	1			6		
Tyringham	115	46	Baker	Israel	1		1		1	1		1		1			6		
Tyringham	116	1	Kingsley	Elijah		1	1		1	2	1		1				7		
Tyringham	116	2	Brown	Azariah					1			1		1			3		
Tyringham	116	3	Brookens	Artemas		1			1	1	2		1				6		
Tyringham	116	4	Brookens	Chester		1	1					1					3		
Tyringham	116	5	Rhoads	William		1	1	1		3	1		1				8		
Tyringham	119	1	Winchel	Ephm 1st		1		1		2		1					5		
Tyringham	119	2	Calkins	Elisha			1	1					1				3		
Tyringham	119	3	Hamilton	Samuel		1	1	1					1				4		
Tyringham	119	4	Parker	John	1		1					1					3		
Tyringham	119	5	Swett	Abraham	2		1			1		1					5		
Tyringham	119	6	Dutton	Jonathan		1		1		1		1					4		
Tyringham	119	7	Miller	Newbury				1		1			1				3		
Tyringham	119	8	Messenger	George	1		1	1		2	2		1				8		
Tyringham	119	9	Heath	Bartholomew		1	1	1					1				4		
Tyringham	119	10	Woolcot	John				1		1		1					3		
Tyringham	119	11	Atwater	James	2		1	1		1		1					6		
Tyringham	119	12	Messenger	George Jun	1		1			1		1					4		
Tyringham	119	13	Crippen	Joel	3			1		1		1	1	1			8		
Tyringham	119	14	Pixley	Squire	1	2		1			1	1					6		
Tyringham	119	15	Loomis	Solomon	2			1					1				4		
Tyringham	119	16	Winchel	Jacob	1	1		1					1	1			4		
Tyringham	119	17	Daley	Samuel Jun	1		1			1		1					4		
Tyringham	119	18	Gibbs	Solomon			1			1		1					3		
Tyringham	119	19	Banner	Nicholas	1		1					1					3		
Tyringham	119	20	Newman	Samuel	1	1		1		1		1	1				6		
Tyringham	119	21	Newman	Seth	3			1				1					5		
Tyringham	119	22	Banner	Levi	?	1		1			1		1	1			7		
Tyringham	119	23	Joy	Samuel	1			1		1		1					4		
Tyringham	119	24	Laman	Cornelius	?			1		1		1					5		

TOWN	PG#	LN#	HEADS OF HOUSEHOLD		FREE WHITE MALES					FREE WHITE FEMALES					TOTAL ALL OTHER	TOTAL SLAVES	TOTALS	DISTRICT/ TOWNSHIP	NOTES
			LAST NAME	FIRST NAME	under 10	10 to 16	16 to 26	26 to 45	45 and over	under 10	10 to 16	16 to 26	26 to 45	45 and over					
Washington	213	1	Richmond	Elkanah		1		1		4			1				7		
Washington	213	2	Richmond	Gideon		2	1							1			5		
Washington	213	3	Leonard	Samuel		3		1		1		1		1			7		
Washington	213	4	Leonard	Elijah	2	2		1		1	1		1				8		
Washington	213	5	Coding	Cobb	2			1		2			1				6		
Washington	213	6	Lillie	Joseph				1			2	1	1				5		
Washington	213	7	Pool	Oliver	1					1			1				4		
Washington	213	8	Porter	Ebenz	2		2	1		2			1				8		
Washington	213	9	Merrick	Gideon	1	2			1			1	1	1			7		
Washington	213	10	Barns	Ezekiel	1		1	1		1			1	1			6		
Washington	213	11	Chappel	Jonathan	1		1						1				3		
Washington	213	12	Arnold	Timothy	1	1		1			1		1	1			6		
Washington	213	13	Fox	Bethiah	3			1		1			1	1			7		
Washington	213	14	Morehouse	John	1			1		5	2		1				10		
Washington	213	15	Wood	Mary	1					1		1	1	1			5		
Washington	213	16	Jones	Daniel		1	1		1	1	1	1		1			7		
Washington	213	17	Carrier	Levi	2		2			1			1				7		
Washington	213	18	Morehouse	Thomas	1	1	2	1			1	2	1				9		
Washington	213	19	Utley	Ebenz		1	1			1			1				4		
Washington	213	20	Brown	Asahel		1		1		1				1			4		
Washington	213	21	Hubbard	Thomas	2	3		1		2	1		1				10		
Washington	213	22	Ingales	James	1		1	1		1			1				5		
Washington	213	23	Philips	Peltiah			1			2	3		1				7		
Washington	213	24	Sears	Luther	1		2			1		2					6		
Washington	213	25	Chapple	Ebenezer	2		2			2	1	3		1			11		
Washington	213	26	Williams	Elezer	1	2		1		2	1		1				8		
Washington	213	27	Sikes	Stephen	1	2	1		1	2		3		1			11		
Washington	213	28	Kilburn	Benjm		1	2	1						1			5		
Washington	213	29	Williams	Isaac			2		1	1	1	1		1			7		
Washington	213	30	Hamlin	Isaac			1		1					1			3		
Washington	213	31	Williams	Jacob	2			1					1				4		
Washington	213	32	Williams	John	1			1		2				1			5		
Washington	213	33	Stanton	Latham	2	2	1	1	1	2	1	1	2	1			14		
Washington	213	34	Clark	Augustus	2			1		1		1	1				6		
Washington	213	35	Clark	Amos			1	1		3			1				6		
Washington	213	36	Kilburn	Benjm Jur	1			1		2		1					5		
Washington	214	1	McKnight	Robert	2			1		2			1	1			7		
Washington	214	2	McKnight	James	2	1	2	1		1	1		1				9		
Washington	214	3	McKnight	John	3	2	1		1	3		1		1			12		
Washington	214	4	Congdon	William	1	1	1		1			1	1	1			7		
Washington	214	5	Cornish	Elijah	1			1		1		1					4		
Washington	214	6	Warren	Ezra					1	4	1		1				7		
Washington	214	7	Warren	Ezra Jun	3		1	1		1			1				7		
Washington	214	8	Campbell	Nathan	2			1				1	1				5		
Washington	214	9	Watson	Hazard		1		1		1			2				5		
Washington	214	10	Chappel	William	1	1	1		1	2		2		1			9		
Washington	214	11	Holmes	Isaac	1		2		1	1	2	1		1			9		
Washington	214	12	Lankton	John				1			1		1				3		
Washington	214	13	Chappel	Joseph	2	2	2		1	1	1		1				10		
Washington	214	14	Chappel	Ebenezer 2d		1				1		1					3		
Washington	214	15	Gilmore	Silas			1			2		1					4		
Washington	214	16	Steal	Pitts	1			2					1	1			5		
Washington	214	17	Phelps	George	5	1			1		2		1		4		14		
Washington	214	18	Clark	Silas	1		1	1					1				4		
Washington	214	19	Clark	Frederick	1			1		2			1				5		
Washington	214	20	Chamberlin	Eli		1	2			1		2	1				7		
Washington	214	21	Williams	Abraham	1		1	1		1	1		1				6		
Washington	214	22	Webb	Nathan Jun	1	1		1		1	1		1				6		
Washington	214	23	Webb	Nathan		1	1		1			1	1		2		7		
Washington	214	24	Cornish	Amasiah				1		1	1		1		3		7		
Washington	214	25	Lamb	Dudley	1	1	2			4			2				10		
Washington	214	26	Church	Richard		1						1	1	1			5		
Washington	214	27	Wing	Elijah		1	1					1		1			4		
Washington	214	28	Hoskin	Amos	1			1		3			1				6		
Washington	214	29	Squires	Elijah				1		4			1				6		
Washington	214	30	Mattoon	Philip	1			2					1	1			5		
Washington	214	31	Mattoon	Rufus		2		1		2			1				6		
Washington	214	32	Sela	James				1					1				2		
Washington	214	33	Babcock	Elias	2	1		1		4	1	2	1				12		
Washington	214	34	Fowler	John	2			1	1				1				5		
Washington	214	35	Squires	Josiah	2			1		2			1				6		
Washington	214	36	Hardy	Nathl	2		1	1		3	3	1	1				12		
Washington	214	37	Eames	Anthony	1	2	1		1	1	1		1				8		
Washington	214	38	Witter	Amos	2		1	1		3	1	1	1				10		
Washington	214	39	Root	Jeremiah	2		1	1		2	1		1				8		
Washington	214	40	Dunwill	Stephen	3	1	1	1		1	2		1				10		
Washington	214	41	Martin	Thomas	2	1	1		1	1	2	1	1				10		
Washington	215	1	Brown	Asa	1				1	1	1	2		1			7		
Washington	215	2	Brown	Levi		1		1					1				3		

TOWN	PG#	LN#	LAST NAME	FIRST NAME	FREE WHITE MALES					FREE WHITE FEMALES					TOTAL ALL OTHER	TOTAL SLAVES	TOTALS	DISTRICT/ TOWNSHIP	NOTES
					under 10	10 to 16	16 to 26	26 to 45	45 and over	under 10	10 to 16	16 to 26	26 to 45	45 and over					
Washington	215	3	Merifield	John	1			1				1					3		
Washington	215	4	Campbell	Robert	1			1		1		1					4		
Washington	215	5	Olds	Isaac				1		1			1				3		
Washington	215	6	Morss	John Jun				1		2			1				4		
Washington	215	7	Ellis	Rowland	1			1		1		1					4		
Washington	215	8	Tagget	John	3	4	1	1				1	1				11		
Washington	215	9	Egleston	Darias	2			1		2		1					6		
Washington	215	10	Matthews	James	1		1		1			1	1				5		
Washington	215	11	Sloan	Norman	2	1	2	1		3	1	1					11		
Washington	215	12	Case	Ezekiel	2	2		1		4	1	1					11		
Washington	215	13	Thompson	Edde	1					3	4	1					9		
Washington	215	14	Haskin	Daniel		1	1		1			1		1			5		
Washington	215	15	Seagers	John	2	2	1	1		3	2	1					12		
Washington	215	16	Miller	Lewis	1			1		2		1					5		
Washington	215	17	Bill	William		1	2		1			1	2	1			8		
Washington	215	18	Sibley	Ezra	3			1			2	1					7		
Washington	215	19	Spring	Silvester	2			1		2		1					6		
Washington	215	20	Spring	Ciril	1		1					1					3		
Washington	215	21	Crane	Amos		1						1					2		
Washington	215	22	Deming	Gideon			2	1		1	1		1				6		
Washington	215	23	Huntley	Amos	3	2	2		1	4	2	1	1				16		
Washington	215	24	Cook	Cloe		1						1	1				3		
Washington	215	25	Eames	Mark	2	2		1				1					6		
Washington	215	26	Ladd	Jesse	1		1	1		1		2		1			7		
Washington	215	27	Morss	John			3	1		1	2	3		1			11		
Washington	215	28	Bruce	Comfort	1			1		2		1					5		
Washington	215	29	Smith	William	2			1		1		1	1				6		
Washington	215	30	Frost	Apollas	1			1		1		1					4		
Washington	215	31	Brewster	Jasper	2			1			1						4		
Washington	215	32	Leonard	Tilley	2			1		2		1					6		
Washington	215	33	Smith	George	1		2			1		1					5		
Washington	215	34	Henry	Simeon	3			1		2		1					7		
Washington	215	35	Jennins	Ephraim	1		2			2		2					7		
Washington	215	36	Kent	John	1		1						1				3		
Washington	215	37	Clark	Hubbard	2		2					1					5		
Washington	215	38	Millekin	Alexander	3			1		1		1	1	2			9		
Washington	215	39	Brooke	Isaac		1		1	2			1		1			6		
Washington	216	1	Millakin	William		1		1		2	1	2					7		
Washington	216	2	Clark	Dillingham			1	1				1					3		
Washington	216	3	Savery	Hiram	2			1				1					4		
Washington	216	4	Bruce	Abner		1	1					1					3		
Washington	216	5	Allen	Justus		1	1		1	2	1	1		1			8		
Washington	216	6	Bush	Gideon	1	2	2		1	2	1	3		1			13		
Washington	216	7	Moore	William				1				1		1			3		
Washington	216	8	Hunt	Samuel	3	1	1		1			2		1			9		
Washington	216	9	Williams	Larkin	4			1				1	1				7		
Washington	216	10	Wolcot	William				1		1	2		1				5		
Washington	216	11	Ballentine	William G.		1			2	1		1	1		1		7		
Washington	216	12	Stevens	John				1									1		
Washington	216	13	Laurence	Jeremiah	1	2		1		1	1		1				7		
Washington	216	14	Crane	Elijah	1	1	1		1		1	1					6		
Washington	216	15	Byxbe	Moses		1	2		1	2	1	1	1				9		
Washington	216	16	Smith	William			1	1			1			1			4		
Washington	216	17	Franklin	Dean	1		1	1		2			1	1			7		
Washington	216	18	Noble	Zenas	1		2	1				3		1			8		
Washington	216	19	Messenger	Nathan	1	1	3	1			2	1					9		
Washington	216	20	Miller	Isaac			2	1				1					4		
Washington	216	21	West	Abel	4	1	1	2		1			2				11		
Washington	216	22	Sprague	Dyer			2	1		3	2		1				9		

TOWN	PG#	LN#	LAST NAME	FIRST NAME	FREE WHITE MALES under 10	10 to 16	16 to 26	26 to 45	45 and over	FREE WHITE FEMALES under 10	10 to 16	16 to 26	26 to 45	45 and over	TOTAL ALL OTHER	TOTAL SLAVES	TOTALS	DISTRICT/ TOWNSHIP	NOTES
West Stockbridge	246	1	Ayer	Oliver	1			1		1	1		1				5		
West Stockbridge	246	2	Arnold	Jonah	1	1			1	2	1		1				7		
West Stockbridge	246	3	Andrews	Ebenezer		1			1	1	1	1		1			6		
West Stockbridge	246	4	Andrews	Theod	4	1		1		1		1		1			9		
West Stockbridge	246	5	Andrews	Elijah		1	2			1			1				5		
West Stockbridge	246	6	Andrews	Benajah				1									1		
West Stockbridge	246	7	Barstow	Samuel			1										1		
West Stockbridge	246	8	Boughton	Nathan Jr	1		1			1			1				4		
West Stockbridge	246	9	Boughton	Nathan	1	1	2	1			1	3		1			10		
West Stockbridge	246	10	Benedict	Thomas	1	1	1		1	1	1		2	1			9		
West Stockbridge	246	11	Benedict	John	1			1		2			1				5		
West Stockbridge	246	12	Brownson	Ira			1										1		
West Stockbridge	246	13	Burghart	Lamber	1	1	1		1	1	1	1		1			8		
West Stockbridge	246	14	Benton	Elijah	1	1	1						1				4		
West Stockbridge	246	15	Benton	John				1				1		1			3		
West Stockbridge	247	1	Bemis	Jonathan	1	1	1	1			1		1				6		
West Stockbridge	247	2	Booker	Samuel			1										1		
West Stockbridge	247	3	Bradley	David	3	1		1			1		1				7		
West Stockbridge	247	4	Boughton	Matthew		1		1				1		1			4		
West Stockbridge	247	5	Boughton	Azor				1		3			1				5		
West Stockbridge	247	6	Boughton	Enos				1		2			1				4		
West Stockbridge	247	7	Boughton	David	3	1		1		1	1		1				8		
West Stockbridge	247	8	Boynton	Caleb	1	1	2		1	3	2	1	1				12		
West Stockbridge	247	9	Barnes	Silas	2	2		1		1				1			7		
West Stockbridge	247	10	Barnes	Timothy	2		1	1	1		1	1		1			8		
West Stockbridge	247	11	Brown	Stephen	3	1			1	2	2	2	1				12		
West Stockbridge	247	12	Brown	John	1			1		4			2				8		
West Stockbridge	247	13	Bebee	Gamaliel		1											1		
West Stockbridge	247	14	Brown	Amos		1	1	1				2		1			6		
West Stockbridge	247	15	Baldwin	Samll	2			1		1	2						6		
West Stockbridge	247	16	Bartlett	Abraham		1		1						1			3		
West Stockbridge	247	17	Bartlett	Abraham Jr	1	1		1		3	1		1				8		
West Stockbridge	247	18	Brail	Joseph				1									1		
West Stockbridge	247	19	Brown	Joel			1										1		
West Stockbridge	247	20	Burlinson	Amos	1	1	1		1	3	1	2		1			11		
West Stockbridge	247	21	Brown	John	3			1		1	2		1				8		
West Stockbridge	247	22	Buckley	Billy	2			1		2			1				6		
West Stockbridge	247	23	Burghardt	Isaac	2			1		1			1				5		
West Stockbridge	247	24	Bedwell	Isaac		2		2			1	1	1				7		
West Stockbridge	247	25	Bloss	Joseph	1		1	1		3			1				7		
West Stockbridge	247	26	Campbell	Abigail						1				1			2		
West Stockbridge	247	27	Campbell	George			1						1				2		
West Stockbridge	247	28	Cone	Ashbel	2	1	1		1	1		1	1				8		
West Stockbridge	247	29	Cook	James	2		1						1				4		
West Stockbridge	247	30	Crane	Silas	3	1		1		1			2				8		
West Stockbridge	247	31	Crampton	Benjm	1			1		2			1				5		
West Stockbridge	247	32	Conant	Israel					1			2		1			4		
West Stockbridge	248	1	Conners	Solomon		1	1			1		1	1				4		
West Stockbridge	248	2	Decker	Ferris			1										1		
West Stockbridge	248	3	Dryar	William	3	1	1	1	1		1	1	2				11		
West Stockbridge	248	4	Dryar	Allen	1		2		1	3	2		1				10		
West Stockbridge	248	5	Dryar	Daniel	2			1		3			1	1			8		
West Stockbridge	248	6	Derning	John		1	1			1		1	1				6		
West Stockbridge	248	7	Durfee	John	1	1		1			2		1				6		
West Stockbridge	248	8	Easland	John	1		1	1		2	1		1				7		
West Stockbridge	248	9	Easland	John G.			1						1				2		
West Stockbridge	248	10	Edwards	Gamial	3			1				1	1				6		
West Stockbridge	248	11	Evarts	Isaac		1	1					3		1			6		
West Stockbridge	248	12	Evarts	Augustus	1			1		2		1					5		
West Stockbridge	248	13	Earland	James	2			1		3	1		1				8		
West Stockbridge	248	14	Earland	Francis			1				1		1				3		
West Stockbridge	248	15	Ford	John	2		2		1	1	2	1		1			10		
West Stockbridge	248	16	Fitch	Sanford	2			1					1				4		
West Stockbridge	248	17	Fowler	Amos		1	1		1	1	1	1	1				7		
West Stockbridge	248	18	Fleming	Jacob		1			1	2	1	1		1			7		
West Stockbridge	248	19	French	Nathan	1	1	1		1	2	1	1	1				9		
West Stockbridge	248	20	Freeman	Walter	4			1			2		1				8		
West Stockbridge	248	21	Freese	John			1										1		
West Stockbridge	248	22	French	Christopher	2	1	3		1	3	1			1			12		
West Stockbridge	248	23	Foot	Charles	3	1			1	1	2	1	1				10		
West Stockbridge	248	24	Fuller	Jeremiah			1										1		
West Stockbridge	248	25	Gooe	Peter	2		1	1	1			3	1				10		
West Stockbridge	248	26	Griswold	Frederick		1		1				1					3		
West Stockbridge	248	27	Galusha	Nathan			1		1	2	1			1			6		
West Stockbridge	248	28	Gillett	Joseph	2			1		2			1				6		
West Stockbridge	248	29	Hewins	Joseph				1		1	1	1	1				5		
West Stockbridge	248	30	Hurlbart	Ulysses				1		1			1				3		
West Stockbridge	248	31	Hutchinson	David	1	1	3	1				2	1	1			10		
West Stockbridge	248	32	Hull	Peter		1		1	1				1		1		5		

TOWN	PG#	LN#	HEADS OF HOUSEHOLD		FREE WHITE MALES					FREE WHITE FEMALES					TOTAL ALL OTHER	TOTAL SLAVES	TOTALS	DISTRICT/ TOWNSHIP	NOTES
			LAST NAME	FIRST NAME	under 10	10 to 16	16 to 26	26 to 45	45 and over	under 10	10 to 16	16 to 26	26 to 45	45 and over					
West Stockbridge	249	1	Hutchinson	Matthew		1	1	1		1	2		1				7		
West Stockbridge	249	2	Hutchinson	Samll	2				1	3	1		1	1			9		
West Stockbridge	249	3	Hamilton	Seth	1					1			1				4		
West Stockbridge	249	4	Hooper	Elisha		1	1	1	1		1			1			6		
West Stockbridge	249	5	Hooper	Elisha Jr	2			1		1			1				5		
West Stockbridge	249	6	Hinman	Enoch	3		2	1			2		1				9		
West Stockbridge	249	7	Hawley	Samll				1			1		1				3		
West Stockbridge	249	8	Hartwell	Abigail										1			1		
West Stockbridge	249	9	Johnson	Jonathan				1		3	1		1				6		
West Stockbridge	249	10	Johns	Peter	1	1		1				1					4		
West Stockbridge	249	11	Johns	Stephen	2	1	2		1	2		1	1	1			11		
West Stockbridge	249	12	Jacquins	John	2		1	1		2	1						7		
West Stockbridge	249	13	Johnson	Benjm				1									1		
West Stockbridge	249	14	Johnson	Robert				1					1				2		
West Stockbridge	249	15	Jones	Joseph	3			1		2	3	1					10		
West Stockbridge	249	16	Kesterbauk	John	2		1						1				4		
West Stockbridge	249	17	Liet	Nathanll		1							1				2		
West Stockbridge	249	18	Lane	John	1	1			2	1				1			6		
West Stockbridge	249	19	Lewis	Benjm	2		1	1		2	1		1	1			9		
West Stockbridge	249	20	Lewis	Benjm Jr	2			1		1			1				5		
West Stockbridge	249	21	Loomis	Lodawich	1			1		1			1				4		
West Stockbridge	249	22	Minilier	John		1			1					1			3		
West Stockbridge	249	23	Moffatt	Lemuel		1	1		1				1	1			5		
West Stockbridge	249	24	Minilier	Barnabas		1			1					1			3		
West Stockbridge	249	25	Mayham	Philip		1											1		
West Stockbridge	249	26	Munn	John	1	1		1	1	3	1		1				9		
West Stockbridge	249	27	Munn	John Junr	1			1				1					3		
West Stockbridge	249	28	Miles	Jonathan	3			1		1		1					6		
West Stockbridge	249	29	Menter	Elijah				1		3			1				5		
West Stockbridge	249	30	Norton	Joel	2			1		1			1				5		
West Stockbridge	249	31	Newell	Hart		1							1				2		
West Stockbridge	249	32	Newell	Sary						1			1	1			3		
West Stockbridge	250	1	Newell	John			1		1				2	1			5		
West Stockbridge	250	2	Newell	John Jr		1		1		3	2	1	1				9		
West Stockbridge	250	3	Piper	Ebenz M.			1			1			1				3		
West Stockbridge	250	4	Parmele	Charles	2	1	1		1	1		1	1				8		
West Stockbridge	250	5	Pomeroy	Grove	2	1		1		2	1		1				8		
West Stockbridge	250	6	Putnam	Jona	1			1		1		1	1				5		
West Stockbridge	250	7	Parmele	Joel			1										1		
West Stockbridge	250	8	Robinson	Joseph			1										1		
West Stockbridge	250	9	Root	Chauncey	1			2					1				4		
West Stockbridge	250	10	Rowell	Jacob	3				1		1		1				6		
West Stockbridge	250	11	Robinson	Noah	1			1		1			1				4		
West Stockbridge	250	12	Rathbun	Philander	2	2		1		2	1		1				9		
West Stockbridge	250	13	Robbins	Thos B	1			1		2	2		1				7		
West Stockbridge	250	14	Robbins	Lemll		1		1						1			3		
West Stockbridge	250	15	Rawson	Jonathan	1	1	2		2	5		1	2	1			15		
West Stockbridge	250	16	Rees	John		2	2		1				1	1			7		
West Stockbridge	250	17	Rees	Isaac	1			1		1			1				4		
West Stockbridge	250	18	Root	Isaac	2	2	1	1		2	2	1	1				12		
West Stockbridge	250	19	Rice	Moses		1		1						1			3		
West Stockbridge	250	20	Reed	Thomas	1		2	1	1	1	1	1		1			9		
West Stockbridge	250	21	Rowley	Jahn				1									1		
West Stockbridge	250	22	Rice	Phineas	1	2		1		2	1	1					8		
West Stockbridge	250	23	Stevens	John W	1		1			1		2					5		
West Stockbridge	250	24	Spencer	James	2			1		2			1	1			7		
West Stockbridge	250	25	Smith	Eliph		1	3	1			1		1				7		
West Stockbridge	250	26	Smith	Abijah	1			1		3			1				6		
West Stockbridge	250	27	Sherwood	Timothy				1		1		1	1				4		
West Stockbridge	250	28	Swift	Lot	2	1	1	1		1	1		1				8		
West Stockbridge	250	29	Slaughter	Ephraim	2		1		1	3	2		1				10		
West Stockbridge	250	30	Smith	Asa			1					1					2		
West Stockbridge	251	1	Spencer	Daniel	4	1	1	1		2			1				10		
West Stockbridge	251	2	Stevens	Jared		1	2		1	1	1	2		1			9		
West Stockbridge	251	3	Stone	Ezekiel	2	1	1		1	1	2		1				9		
West Stockbridge	251	4	Stevens	Hubbel	1	2	1	1				1	1				7		
West Stockbridge	251	5	Stevens	John		1	1		1				1	1			5		
West Stockbridge	251	6	Spencer	Amasa	1	1	2			1			1				6		
West Stockbridge	251	7	Slaughter	Elijah	1	1	1			2		1					6		
West Stockbridge	251	8	Shaver	Abram											4		4		
West Stockbridge	251	9	Sacket	Jesse				1									1		
West Stockbridge	251	10	Tobey	Abram	2			1		2			1				6		
West Stockbridge	251	11	Turner	Peter	3	2	1		1	2	1	2	1	1			14		
West Stockbridge	251	12	Taylor	Teahan	2	2		1		1			1				7		
West Stockbridge	251	13	Webster	Jonathan		1	1		1					1			4		
West Stockbridge	251	14	Williams	Elisha			1			1		1					3		
West Stockbridge	251	15	Witherell	Seth				1				1					2		
West Stockbridge	251	16	Woodruffe	Elisha	3	1			1	1	3	3		1			14		
West Stockbridge	251	17	Warren					1									1		First name blank
West Stockbridge	251	18	Woodruff	Asaph	3				1	1		1	1				7		

81

TOWN	PG#	LN#	LAST NAME	FIRST NAME	FREE WHITE MALES under 10	10 to 16	16 to 26	26 to 45	45 and over	FREE WHITE FEMALES under 10	10 to 16	16 to 26	26 to 45	45 and over	TOTAL ALL OTHER	TOTAL SLAVES	TOTALS	DISTRICT/ TOWNSHIP	NOTES
West Stockbridge	251	19	Woodruff	Amos	1		2	1		4	1		1				10		
West Stockbridge	251	20	Witmark	Susanna	1	1	1			1	1		1				6		
West Stockbridge	251	21	Wood	William	1			1						1			3		
West Stockbridge	251	22	Willson	Fairing	1	1	1	1		2			1				7		
West Stockbridge	251	23	Willson	Nathan	1	1	1		1		1	1		1			7		
West Stockbridge	251	24	Willson	Shubal	2	1		1		3	1		1				9		
West Stockbridge	251	25	Winter	John	1			1		4			1				7		
West Stockbridge	251	26	Williams	Elijah			1		1	1	1		1	1			6		
West Stockbridge	251	27	Youngs	Nathan			2		1	3			1				7		

TOWN	PG#	LN#	LAST NAME	FIRST NAME	M under 10	M 10 to 16	M 16 to 26	M 26 to 45	M 45 and over	F under 10	F 10 to 16	F 16 to 26	F 26 to 45	F 45 and over	TOTAL ALL OTHER	TOTAL SLAVES	TOTALS	DISTRICT/ TOWNSHIP	NOTES
Williamstown	125	1	Balch	Timothy	1			1		2	1		1				6		
Williamstown	125	2	Snow	John		1	1		1			1		1			5		
Williamstown	125	3	Horsford	Josiah	1			1		1	1	1	1				6		
Williamstown	125	4	Joslin	John	1	1	1	1		1	2	1	1				9		
Williamstown	125	5	Smith	William		1	2	1		2	1	1	1				9		
Williamstown	125	6	Townor	William	4			1			3	2	1				11		
Williamstown	125	7	Barden	Jacob			1			1		1					3		
Williamstown	125	8	Welles	Simon	1	1		1	1	1				1			6		
Williamstown	125	9	Greene	James				1		2	2	1		1			7		
Williamstown	125	10	Meacham	James		1		2	1	1	1	2	1	1			10		
Williamstown	125	11	Northum	Timothy	2	2	1		1		1	1	1				9		
Williamstown	125	12	Bordwell	Obadiah	1	2		1		2	1	1	1				9		
Williamstown	125	13	Bacon	Joel	4			1		1			1				7		
Williamstown	125	14	Swift	Seth Revd	3		1	1	1	1		2	1				10		
Williamstown	125	15	Bacon	Jacob	2	1	1		1			2	2	1			10		
Williamstown	125	16	Harrison	Almond	1	1	1	1		3	2		1				10		
Williamstown	125	17	Barton	Josiah	1			1		3			1				6		
Williamstown	125	18	Fenton	Jason	2			1				1					4		
Williamstown	125	19	Prowty	Francis				1				1					2		
Williamstown	125	20	Sherman	Elihu	1	1	1		1			1		1			6		
Williamstown	126	1	Stratton	Ebenezer	1	3		1		1	1	1		1			9		
Williamstown	126	2	Foster	Edward			1						1				2		
Williamstown	126	3	Cowen	Jonathan	1		2	2		4			3	3			15		
Williamstown	126	4	Reed	Benjamin		1	1	1				2		1			6		
Williamstown	126	5	Dumett	Cato											6		6		
Williamstown	126	6	Wright	Solomon	2	1	1		1	1	1	1	1				9		
Williamstown	126	7	Blair	Absalom		1		1			2		1				5		
Williamstown	126	8	White	Aaron	2		1			1	1	1					6		
Williamstown	126	9	Williams	Elisha		1		1			1		1				4		
Williamstown	126	10	Thomas	Elijah	2	1	1		1			2		1			8		
Williamstown	126	11	Fuller	Daniel	4			1		1	1		1				8		
Williamstown	126	12	Spencer	Jesse		1	1	1		1			1				5		
Williamstown	126	13	Kriger	Betsey Mrs.		1		1		2	1		1	1			7		
Williamstown	126	14	Kriger	William			1					1					2		
Williamstown	126	15	Lane	John				1		1		1					3		
Williamstown	126	16	Philips	William	1		1			1		1					4		
Williamstown	126	17	Wilcox	Heman		1	1			1			1				4		
Williamstown	126	18	Pratt	Isaac			1					1					2		
Williamstown	126	19	Wilmarth	Shubael	2		1	1		2		2	1				9		
Williamstown	126	20	Hudson	Aaron	1	1			1	2			1				6		
Williamstown	126	21	Coy	Cottrel			1			1		1					3		
Williamstown	126	22	Duning	Matthew Jr		1		2				1		3			7		
Williamstown	126	23	Birchard	Samuel				1			1			1			3		
Williamstown	126	24	Newton	Isaac	1		1			1			1				4		
Williamstown	126	25	Crofoot	Joseph	2	1	1	1	1	2	1		1	1			11		
Williamstown	126	26	Crofoot	Rhoda Mrs	1						1	1		1			4		
Williamstown	126	27	Comstock	Solon	2			1		1	1		1				7		
Williamstown	126	28	Lamb	Elijah	3			1	1	1	3		1				10		
Williamstown	126	29	Moon	Benjamin	3	1		1			1			1			7		
Williamstown	126	30	Perrey	Reuben				1				1					2		
Williamstown	126	31	Burges	Josiah	1	2	2		1		1			1			8		
Williamstown	126	32	Burges	Jacob				1						1			2		
Williamstown	126	33	Bryan	Jacob				1						1			2		
Williamstown	126	34	Brooks	Benjamin			1			3	1	1					6		
Williamstown	126	35	Watson	Lois Mrs		1				1				1			3		
Williamstown	126	36	Coon	Thomas		1				1	1						3		
Williamstown	126	37	Wright	Aaron	1	1		1		2	2	1	1				9		
Williamstown	126	38	Barr	Daniel				1					1				2		
Williamstown	126	39	Bacon	Stephen		1	1	1		1			1				5		
Williamstown	126	40	Harris	Eliphalet				1						1			2		
Williamstown	126	41	Luther	Hezekiath	3	2		1		2			1	1			10		
Williamstown	127	1	Cook	Abiel	2			1		4	1		1				9		
Williamstown	127	2	Comstock	Medad	3	1		1		3	2	1	1				12		
Williamstown	127	3	Roberts	Asa	1	1	1	1				2	1				7		
Williamstown	127	4	Young	Andrew	1				1	1	3	2	1				9		
Williamstown	127	5	Kelley	William	3			1				1					5		
Williamstown	127	6	Kenney	Daniel	1		1				2	1	2				7		
Williamstown	127	7	Pratt	Ebenezer	2			1		3			1				7		
Williamstown	127	8	Fox	Andrew		1	1	1				1	1				5		
Williamstown	127	9	Deming	Titus	2	1	1	1		3	2	1	1				12		
Williamstown	127	10	Wheelock		5			1			3	3	1				13		First name blank
Williamstown	127	11	Deming	Aaron	1	1	1		1			2	1				7		
Williamstown	127	12	Roe	Thomas	1			1	1			1	1	1			7		
Williamstown	127	13	Burbank	Daniel			1	2	1		1	2		1			8		
Williamstown	127	14	Day	Daniel		1		3	1	2	1	1	1	1			11		
Williamstown	127	15	Fuller	Stephen	1	2			1		1	1		1			7		
Williamstown	127	16	Smith	John	3	3		1		2		1	1				11		
Williamstown	127	17	Smith	Nathan	1			1	1	1		1		1			6		
Williamstown	127	18	Wells	William	1			1	1			2		1			6		
Williamstown	127	19	Wells	Seth			1	1		3			1				6		

TOWN	PG#	LN#	HEADS OF HOUSEHOLD		FREE WHITE MALES					FREE WHITE FEMALES					TOTAL ALL OTHER	TOTAL SLAVES	TOTALS	DISTRICT/ TOWNSHIP	NOTES
			LAST NAME	FIRST NAME	under 10	10 to 16	16 to 26	26 to 45	45 and over	under 10	10 to 16	16 to 26	26 to 45	45 and over					
Williamstown	127	20	Foote	John	2	2	1	1		3		1	1				11		
Williamstown	127	21	Wells	Enos	1		1	1		1			1				5		
Williamstown	127	22	Cowen	John	2		2		1	1	2		1				9		
Williamstown	127	23	Martindale	Justin	1	1		1		2			1				6		
Williamstown	127	24	Morgan	Nathaniel	2			1		2	1		1				7		
Williamstown	127	25	Kellogg	Samuel	3	1	1	2	1	2	1	3	1	1	1		17		
Williamstown	127	26	Foote	Aaron			1			1			1				3		
Williamstown	127	27	Smedley	Levi & Elijah	3		3	2		6	1	1	3				19		
Williamstown	127	28	Davis	Francis		1	1	1		3	2		1				9		
Williamstown	127	29	Leete	Jared		1			1			1		1			4		
Williamstown	127	30	Levingstone	John		2		1				1		1			5		
Williamstown	127	31	Coon	Timothy	1		1					1					3		
Williamstown	127	32	Morse	James		1	2		1	1	1	3		1			10		
Williamstown	127	33	Wright	Nabby	3			1		1			2				7		
Williamstown	127	34	Greene	William	2			1		2			1				6		
Williamstown	127	35	Robinson	Edmund	1			1					1				3		
Williamstown	127	36	Hindersass	John G.	1			1		2			1				5		
Williamstown	127	37	Bridges	Jonathan	1	2	1		1	1	1		1				8		
Williamstown	127	38	Smith	Daniel	2	1	1	1	1	2	2		1				11		
Williamstown	127	39	Stearns	Reuben	2	1			1	1	1	2	2	1			11		
Williamstown	127	40	King	John	2	2			1	4	1		2	1			13		
Williamstown	127	41	Dewey	Samuel		1		2						1			4		
Williamstown	127	42	Seelye	Ephraim	1	1	2		1	2	2	1		1			11		
Williamstown	128	1	Wright	Miles			1	1	1			1		1			5		
Williamstown	128	2	Fowler	James	1			2		2	2	2	1	1			11		
Williamstown	128	3	Seelye	Reuben		1	1		1	1				1			5		
Williamstown	128	4	Fowler	Michael	1	1	1	1		1	1		1				7		
Williamstown	128	5	Pratt	Noah				1					1				2		
Williamstown	128	6	Boynton	Daniel	1	1		2			2		1				7		
Williamstown	128	7	Buck	Ezekiel			1						1				2		
Williamstown	128	8	Childs	Penuel	2	1	1	1		2	2	1	1				11		
Williamstown	128	9	Simonds	Benjamin			1							1			2		
Williamstown	128	10	Skinner	Benjamin	2	2	2	1	1	1	1	1		1			12		
Williamstown	128	11	Starke	Abraham	2		1	1	1			1	1				7		
Williamstown	128	12	Wright	Josiah	1			1	1	2		1	1	1			8		
Williamstown	128	13	Wolcott	Solomon		2		1				3		1			7		
Williamstown	128	14	Bulkley	Robbins J		1		1		2	1		1		1		7		
Williamstown	128	15	Granger	William				1					1				2		
Williamstown	128	16	Talmage	Joseph	2		1	2	1	1	1	1	1	1			11		
Williamstown	128	17	Hill	Josiah		1	1	1		1		1		1			6		
Williamstown	128	18	Baldwin	Joel		1	1		1	1		1					5		
Williamstown	128	19	Beckwith	James		1	1	1		2		1					6		
Williamstown	128	20	Williams	Zabin			1			1		1					3		
Williamstown	128	21	Chamberlin	Nathaniel	1	3		1			2		1				8		
Williamstown	128	22	Williams	Stephen		1		1		3			1				6		
Williamstown	128	23	Danforth	Coe		1				1	1						3		
Williamstown	128	24	Tyler	Samuel	1	1	1		1	1	2			2			9		
Williamstown	128	25	Miller	Benjamin	1			1		1			1				5		
Williamstown	128	26	Keep	Jonathan			1			1			1				3		
Williamstown	128	27	Foster	William		1			1	1	1	1		1			6		
Williamstown	128	28	Newbree	Elias		1			1	1	2	1		2			8		
Williamstown	128	29	Welch	Elijah	3		1			1			1				6		
Williamstown	128	30	Kenney	Richard	1	1	2	1	1	2			1				9		
Williamstown	128	31	Ford	Zadock	2	2			1		1	1	1				8		
Williamstown	128	32	Barett	Peter	1	2	1		1			2		1			8		
Williamstown	128	33	Kellogg	Nathaniel	2	2		1		2	1	1	1				10		
Williamstown	128	34	Isbell	Peruda	1			1		2	1						5		
Williamstown	128	35	Davidson	Peter		2		1		2			1				6		
Williamstown	128	36	Barrett	Oliver	1	1		1					1		1		5		
Williamstown	128	37	Williams	Robert	1	1	1	1		2	1		1				8		
Williamstown	128	38	Robbins	William		1				1		1					3		
Williamstown	128	39	Grandison	Charles											2		2		
Williamstown	129	1	Landrus	Lemuel	2			1	1	1			1	1			7		
Williamstown	129	2	Prindle	Solomon		1	1			1			1		1		5		
Williamstown	129	3	Littlefield	Josiah	2	1		1		2	1		1				8		
Williamstown	129	4	Brownson	Asa	4			1		1			1				7		
Williamstown	129	5	Treadwell	Ager		1	1			4	2		1				9		
Williamstown	129	6	Foster	David		4	1	1		4		1	1				12		
Williamstown	129	7	Birchard	Amos	1	1	1			1	1	1					6		
Williamstown	129	8	Whippey	John				1					1				2		
Williamstown	129	9	Birchard	Joseph	2	1	1	1		1	2	1	1	1			11		
Williamstown	129	10	Rowland	Nehma		1		1				1		1			4		
Williamstown	129	11	Torrey	John Junr			1			1		1					3		
Williamstown	129	12	Nicholl	Josiah	2		1	1		1		1	1				7		
Williamstown	129	13	Wareing	Betsey Mrs.						1	1		1				3		
Williamstown	129	14	Vinson	Pardon	2	2		1		1				1			7		
Williamstown	129	15	White	John	2	2	1	1		2	1	1	1				11		
Williamstown	129	16	Grey	Edward	3			1		1		1					6		
Williamstown	129	17	Hickox	Stephen		2		1			1	3		1			8		

TOWN	PG#	LN#	LAST NAME	FIRST NAME	FWM under 10	FWM 10 to 16	FWM 16 to 26	FWM 26 to 45	FWM 45 and over	FWF under 10	FWF 10 to 16	FWF 16 to 26	FWF 26 to 45	FWF 45 and over	TOTAL ALL OTHER	TOTAL SLAVES	TOTALS	DISTRICT/ TOWNSHIP	NOTES
Williamstown	129	18	Bishop	Thomas	1		1	1		2		1					6		
Williamstown	129	19	Stewart	Samuel	2	1		1	1	1			1				7		
Williamstown	129	20	Mackay	Samuel	1		2	1		1					1		7		
Williamstown	129	21	Sutton	Beemal	1	1		1			1	1	1				6		
Williamstown	129	22	Bacon	Ezekiel		1	1				1	2					5		
Williamstown	129	23	Purrington	Sylvanus		1		1		2	1	1	1				7		
Williamstown	129	24	Chamberlin	Paoli				1					1	1			3		
Williamstown	129	25	Kilborn	John		1		2		1		1	1				6		
Williamstown	129	26	Putnam	Perley	1	1	2	2		1	1	1	1				10		
Williamstown	129	27	Swan	Asa					1	1			1				3		
Williamstown	129	28	Stone	Jed			1			1		1					3		
Williamstown	129	29	Fowler	Morris	3			1		1			1				6		
Williamstown	129	30	Havens	Barzilla	1			1				1					3		
Williamstown	129	31	Danforth	Jonathan		1	1		1		1	1		1			6		
Williamstown	129	32	Whiting	Nathan	2		1			1	1		1				6		
Williamstown	129	33	Spencer	John	1			1		1	1		1				5		
Williamstown	129	34	Smith	Nathan	1				1	2		1	1				6		
Williamstown	129	35	Skinner	Tompson J.	1	1	2	2	1	1		1	2				11		
Williamstown	129	36	Wright	Timothy	2		1					1					4		
Williamstown	129	37	Bromley	Barber	2	1		1		2		1					7		
Williamstown	129	38	Cox	John	1	1		1		1			1				5		
Williamstown	129	39	Smith	Stephen		1	1					1					5		
Williamstown	129	40	Gold	Ebenz B.				1		2	1		1				5		
Williamstown	129	41	Carey	Hezekiah	2	1		1			1		1				6		
Williamstown	130	1	Smith	Jeremiah	1		1	1		1			1		1		6		
Williamstown	130	2	Stewart	Lemuel	1	2	3	1	2	1	1			1			12		
Williamstown	130	3	Hayden	David	2			1			1		1				5		
Williamstown	130	4	Porter	Daniel			3					1					4		
Williamstown	130	5	Mann	Southwick			4					1					5		
Williamstown	130	6	Hayward	William	1			1		1	1		1				5		
Williamstown	130	7	Barnes	Joseph	1			1		2		1					5		
Williamstown	130	8	Solomon	Albert			3		1	1		1					7		
Williamstown	130	9	Galusha	Daniel	1			1			2	2	1				7		
Williamstown	130	10	Sweet	John				1				1					2		
Williamstown	130	11	Standish	Asa	1	1	1	1		3	1		1	1			10		
Williamstown	130	12	Torrey	John			2		1	1	1	1	1				7		
Williamstown	130	13	Rich	Elijah	1		1	1		1	1	2	1	1			9		
Williamstown	130	14	Torrey	William	2		1	1				1	1	1			7		
Williamstown	130	15	Hand	Joseph	2	2		1			1	2					9		
Williamstown	130	16	Rich	Philip	1			1					1				3		
Williamstown	130	17	Perkins		2	1		1			1	1		1			7		First name blank
Williamstown	130	18	Clarke	Noble			1					1					2		
Williamstown	130	19	Booth	Henry											7		7		
Williamstown	130	20	Simonds	Enoch											5		5		
Williamstown	130	21	Porter	Samuel		1	1		1	2	2		1				8		
Williamstown	130	22	Phelps	Daniel	1		1					1					3		
Williamstown	130	23	Baldwin	Elijah	3			1		1		1					6		
Williamstown	130	24	Johnson	David	2	2		1	1	1		3	1	1			12		
Williamstown	130	25	Bingham	Thomas			1	1				1					3		
Williamstown	130	26	Judd	Reuben	1	2		1		3	1		1				9		
Williamstown	130	27	Thayer	Baruch	2	1	1	1	1	2				1			9		
Williamstown	130	28	Woodwork	Nehemiah		1	1	1				1		2			6		
Williamstown	130	29	Roberts	Warren	2	1	1	1	1	3	2	2	1				14		
Williamstown	130	30	Rich	Moses	2			1	1	0			1	1			8		
Williamstown	130	31	McMaster	Robert		1	2		1			2		1			7		
Williamstown	130	32	Burdick	Thomas	2	1		1		2		1	1				9		
Williamstown	130	33	Holmes	Calvin	2	1		1		1		1	1	1			8		
Williamstown	130	34	Holmes	Isaac	2		2		1	2	3	1	2				13		
Williamstown	130	35	Holmes	Elnathan	1	1	1		1	2	1		1				8		
Williamstown	130	36	Standish	Moses			1			2		1					4		
Williamstown	130	37	Sabin	Charles		1	1	1		3		1	1				9		
Williamstown	130	38	Cook	John	3			1		1			1	1			7		
Williamstown	130	39	Beeman	Reuben	3			1		2			1				7		
Williamstown	130	40	Sherwood	Samuel			1					1		1			3		
Williamstown	131	1	Mills	Samuel	3	1	1		1		1	3	1				11		
Williamstown	131	2	Sabin	Timothy	3	1		1		3		1					9		
Williamstown	131	3	Johnson	David 2d		3						1		2			7		
Williamstown	131	4	Sherwood	Jona	1		1	1		3	2	1	1				10		
Williamstown	131	5	Vanderworker	James	2			1			1	1					5		
Williamstown	131	6	Thayer	Jona	1		1					1					3		
Williamstown	131	7	Sabin	Widow			1				1	1		1			4		
Williamstown	131	8	Henderson	Joseph	3	2		1		1	1	1		1			10		
Williamstown	131	9	Young	Moses	2	1	2	1	2		1	2		2			13		
Williamstown	131	10	Evett	Amos	3			1		3			1				8		
Williamstown	131	11	Eldridge	Nathan	3			1		1		1	1				7		
Williamstown	131	12	Bebee	Ezra	1			1		3			1				6		
Williamstown	131	13	Vaughn	Joseph					1		1	2					4		
Williamstown	131	14	Corbin	Amasa					2			2	1				5		
Williamstown	131	15	Nash	Shubael	3	1	1	1		2	1	2	1				12		
Williamstown	131	16	Philips	Zebulon	2		1	1		1			1				6		

TOWN	PG#	LN#	LAST NAME	FIRST NAME	under 10	10 to 16	16 to 26	26 to 45	45 and over	under 10	10 to 16	16 to 26	26 to 45	45 and over	TOTAL ALL OTHER	TOTAL SLAVES	TOTALS	DISTRICT/ TOWNSHIP	NOTES
					FREE WHITE MALES					FREE WHITE FEMALES									
Williamstown	131	17	Roe	Elisha	1		1			1	1	1					5		
Williamstown	131	18	Corbin	Asa	2	1	1		1	1	2		1				9		
Williamstown	131	19	Day	John 2d	1	1		1		2		1	1				7		
Williamstown	131	20	Curtis	Theoder		1	1	1				1					4		
Williamstown	131	21	Buckley	Charles	1	3	1		1	1	1		1				9		
Williamstown	131	22	Sherwood	Stephen	3	2		1				1	1				8		
Williamstown	131	23	Sherwood	Isaac					1		1		1	1			4		
Williamstown	131	24	Giles	Jonathan	1	1		1	1			2	1	1			8		
Williamstown	131	25	Young	William	1	1		1	1	1		1	1				7		
Williamstown	131	26	Codding	Robert			1		1	1	1			1			5		
Williamstown	131	27	Woodcock	Bartholomew		1	1	1	1		1		1	1			7		
Williamstown	131	28	Walker	James		1		1		1	1		1				5		
Williamstown	131	29	Vaughn	John			1					1					2		
Williamstown	131	30	Rosseter	Nathan	1	2	1	2			2		1		1		10		
Williamstown	131	31	Wolcott	Solomon Jr	1	1	1	1			1		1				6		
Williamstown	131	32	Turner	Zebedee	2	1	2		1		1	1		1			9		
Williamstown	131	33	Daniels	Sterling	4		1		1	1	3	2	1				13		
Williamstown	131	34	Eddy	Lebbens	4	2	2			3	2	2	1				16		
Williamstown	131	35	Reab	George	2		1	1			1		1		1		7		
Williamstown	131	36	Stebbens	Lewis	2	2			1	1	1			1			8		
Williamstown	131	37	Cone	David S.		1				1		1					3		
Williamstown	131	38	Starkweather	William	2			1	1	3		1	1	1	1		11		
Williamstown	131	39	Maladay	Thomas	2			1	1				1				5		
Williamstown	131	40	Balch	Joseph	2	2		1		2			1				8		
Williamstown	131	41	Higgins	Lemuel	2		2	1		1	1		1				8		
Williamstown	132	1	Marther	Elias	1		5	1		1			1				9		
Williamstown	132	2	Chapman	William	1			1					1				3		
Williamstown	132	3	Whitman	John P.				2				1	1				4		
Williamstown	132	4	Sloan	Samuel	3		3	1	1		1	1		1			11		
Williamstown	132	5	Fitch	Ebenezer	3	2	3	1		1	1	2	1		1		15		
Williamstown	132	6	Baker	Ezra	1	1	1	1		2		3					9		
Williamstown	132	7	Bulkley	Gershom	1		1			2		1					5		
Williamstown	132	8	Sheldon	Rema	1	1		1		1		1	1		1		7		
Williamstown	132	9	Eason	Oliver				1					1				2		
Williamstown	132	10	Noble	David		1		2			2	1	1				7		
Williamstown	132	11	Boardman	Theodore		1			1		1		1				4		
Williamstown	132	12	Town	David D.			2		1	1	1		1				6		
Williamstown	132	13	Granger	William	2	1		1					1				5		
Williamstown	132	14	Higgins	Samuel				1					1				2		
Williamstown	132	15	Shearman	Wm. B.	1		1	1		5	1		2				11		
Williamstown	132	16	Satterlee	Samuel				1			1	1	2				5		
Williamstown	132	17	Lasell	Elias	2			2					1				5		
Williamstown	132	18	Day	John			3		1		1		1				6		
Williamstown	132	19	Dewey	Daniel	3	1	1	1		1	1	1	1				10		
Williamstown	132	20	Blin	Ebenezer	1		1	1		2	1	1	1				8		
Williamstown	132	21	Sabin	Jesse			1	1				1					3		
Williamstown	132	22	Noble	Deodaties	1	1		1		1			1				5		
Williamstown	132	23	Bulkley	Charles Jr			2					1					3		
Williamstown	132	24	Doty	Asa	2			1					1				4		
Williamstown	132	25	Paine	Lebbens	3			1		1			1				6		
Williamstown	132	26	Tucker	Seth				1		2	1	1					5		
Williamstown	133	1	Roberts	Isaac	5	1		1		1		1	1				10		
Williamstown	133	2	King	Paul	1				1	1	1			1			5		
Williamstown	133	3	Greene	Henry	4	1	1	1		1	2	1		1			12		
Williamstown	133	4	Sabin	Erastus	1			1		1			1				4		
Williamstown	133	5	Comstock	Thomas	1		2	1	1		1	2		1			9		
Williamstown	133	6	Comstock	Ishmael		3	3		1		1	2		1			11		

| TOWN | PG# | LN# | HEADS OF HOUSEHOLD | | FREE WHITE MALES | | | | | FREE WHITE FEMALES | | | | | TOTAL ALL OTHER | TOTAL SLAVES | TOTALS | DISTRICT/ TOWNSHIP | NOTES |
			LAST NAME	FIRST NAME	under 10	10 to 16	16 to 26	26 to 45	45 and over	under 10	10 to 16	16 to 26	26 to 45	45 and over					
Windsor	164	1	Wright	Arahel	2	3	1	1		2	1	1	1				12		
Windsor	164	2	Chilion	Benjamin	2		2		1	1	2		1				9		
Windsor	164	3	Prince	David Jun	2			1		1			1				5		
Windsor	164	4	Prince	Alpheus	1	1		1	1		1		1				6		
Windsor	164	5	Prince	William	1			1					1				3		
Windsor	164	6	Prince	Samuel	1		1	1		3			1				7		
Windsor	164	7	Basset	William					1	1				1			3		
Windsor	164	8	Warren	Ezra	1	1	2		1	2		1	1				9		
Windsor	164	9	Stevens	Isaac			1			1		1					3		
Windsor	164	10	Stevens	Joseph	1	2			1	1				1			6		
Windsor	164	11	Morey	Nathaniel		1		1			2	1		1			6		
Windsor	164	12	Phillips	Asa	5	2			1	1		2		1			12		
Windsor	164	13	Belknap	Thomas	2				1	3		1		1			8		
Windsor	164	14	Skiner	Samuel			1	1			1			1			4		
Windsor	164	15	Read	William	1	1			1	3	1		1				8		
Windsor	164	16	Read	Jeremiah	1			1		2	1	1	1				7		
Windsor	164	17	Burrows	John Jun			1					1	1				3		
Windsor	164	18	Burrows	John				1									1		
Windsor	165	1	Fuller	Aaron	1	1	1	1		2			1				7		
Windsor	165	2	Merrill	Gad	4	1		1					1				7		
Windsor	165	3	Spalding	Jabez			1			3	2		1				7		
Windsor	165	4	Hall	Asa	2	1	1			1	1		1				8		
Windsor	165	5	Read	Simeon	3			1					2				6		
Windsor	165	6	Britton	Squire	2			1		2			1				6		
Windsor	165	7	White	Elijah	2			1		1			1				5		
Windsor	165	8	Humes	David Jun		1		1		4	1		1				8		
Windsor	165	9	Brown	Alpheus	3			1		1	2		1				8		
Windsor	165	10	Brown	John	3			1	1	1			1	1			8		
Windsor	165	11	Stone	Simon	4			1					1				6		
Windsor	165	12	Parsons	Gideon	2			1		1			1				5		
Windsor	165	13	Morse	Enos	2		1	1		2	2		1				9		
Windsor	165	14	Chaffen	Darius	1		1		1	1		1	1				6		
Windsor	165	15	Kenedy	Asa	1	1		1		3			1				7		
Windsor	165	16	Brewster	Henry	2		4	1		1	1		1	1			11		
Windsor	165	17	Wentworth	Sylvanus	1		1		1	1		2		1			7		
Windsor	165	18	Wallace	John	1			1					1	1			4		
Windsor	165	19	Tucker	Ephraim	2			1		1			1				5		
Windsor	165	20	Walker	Robert	1	1	2		1	5	2	1	1				14		
Windsor	165	21	Balding	Samuel		1	1		1	1		2		1			7		
Windsor	165	22	Johnson	Obadiah	1	1		1		3	1		1				8		
Windsor	165	23	Balding	Ephraim	1	1	1	1					1				5		
Windsor	165	24	Robbins	Elias	1					1				1			4		
Windsor	165	25	Mally	Timothy	2			1		1			1				5		
Windsor	165	26	Jobes	John	2	1	2		1	1							7		
Windsor	165	27	Woodard	Seth	1	1		1		2	1	1					7		
Windsor	165	28	Stockwell	Solomon	1			1		1			1				4		
Windsor	165	29	Seen	Charles			1						2				3		
Windsor	165	30	Sawyer	Cornelius	3			1	1	1	1	1	1	1			10		
Windsor	165	31	Thayer	William	1	2	1		1	1			2				8		
Windsor	165	32	Mally	Thomas	3			1					1				5		
Windsor	165	33	Pierce	Eben	1					1			1				4		
Windsor	165	34	Harwood	John			1		1			1		1			4		
Windsor	165	35	Beale	Joshua		1	2		1			1		1			6		
Windsor	165	36	Higgins	Benjamin			1						1				2		
Windsor	165	37	Harwood	Jason	3			1		4			1				9		
Windsor	165	38	Pool	Ahirah		1	3		1	1	?	2		1			11		
Windsor	166	1	Ripley	Joseph	2	2		1		1	1		1	1			9		
Windsor	166	2	Miner	Ephraim	1	1	1		1		1	1		1			7		
Windsor	166	3	Haney	Stephen		2	1	1		1	1			1			7		
Windsor	166	4	Balding	Samuel Jun	2	1	1	1		1	1		1				8		
Windsor	166	5	Holbrook	Amos	1			1		3	2	1	1				9		
Windsor	166	6	Erskine	Jeremiah	1			1		2			1				5		
Windsor	166	7	Whitman	Jeptha	4		1	1		1	1		1				9		
Windsor	166	8	Ford	Benjamin Jr			1		1		1						3		
Windsor	166	9	White	Danford	1			1		2			1				5		
Windsor	166	10	Norie	Samuel			1			1			1				3		
Windsor	166	11	Read	Nathan	1		2	1		1			1				7		
Windsor	166	12	Weaver	Joseph	1			1		2			1				5		
Windsor	166	13	Ford	Benjamin	3	2			1	1	1	3		1			12		
Windsor	166	14	Smith	William		1			1	2	1	1		1			7		
Windsor	166	15	Louden	Jacob	1		1			1		1					4		
Windsor	166	16	Louden	John	1			1		3			1				6		
Windsor	166	17	Allen	Zebulon	1	1		1		1			1				5		
Windsor	166	18	Bannister	Rafeal			1			2			1				4		
Windsor	166	19	Lamb	Chester	1	1	1					1					4		
Windsor	166	20	Howard	Solomon	1			1		2			1				5		
Windsor	166	21	Bird	Ebenezer	3		2		1	2	2	1	1				12		
Windsor	166	22	Whitman	Ebenezer	1	1	1	1			1		2				7		
Windsor	166	23	Waterman	James	2		1	1		1			1	1			7		

| TOWN | PG# | LN# | HEADS OF HOUSEHOLD | | FREE WHITE MALES | | | | | FREE WHITE FEMALES | | | | | TOTAL ALL OTHER | TOTAL SLAVES | TOTALS | DISTRICT/ TOWNSHIP | NOTES |
			LAST NAME	FIRST NAME	under 10	10 to 16	16 to 26	26 to 45	45 and over	under 10	10 to 16	16 to 26	26 to 45	45 and over					
Windsor	166	24	Stearns	Joseph	3			1		1			1				6		
Windsor	166	25	Vining	Israel	2	1		1		1	1		1				7		
Windsor	166	26	Nash	John			1			1		1					3		
Windsor	166	27	Leonard	Barnie	1			1		1			1				4		
Windsor	166	28	Dawes	Samuel	3			1			1		1				6		
Windsor	166	29	Ford	Amos				1		2			1				4		
Windsor	166	30	Snow	Jacob	1	1		1		2	2		1				8		
Windsor	166	31	Dawes	John	2			1		1			1				5		
Windsor	166	32	Whitman	Isaiah	1			1		2	1		1				6		
Windsor	166	33	Latham	Levi	3			1		1	1		1	1			8		
Windsor	166	34	Payson	Joseph	1	2			1				1				5		
Windsor	166	35	Fields	James	3			1		1	2		1				8		
Windsor	166	36	Waterman	Calvin	2			1		2			1				6		
Windsor	167	1	Bates	Jarum				1		1			1				3		
Windsor	167	2	Russel	Asa	2			1		1			1				5		
Windsor	167	3	Whitaker	William	1		1					1					3		
Windsor	167	4	Packard	Zebulon	1								1				3		
Windsor	167	5	Convers	James		1	1	1		1	2	2	1	1			10		
Windsor	167	6	Eddy	Samuel					1	1				1			3		
Windsor	167	7	Eddy	Caleb					1	1		2		1			5		
Windsor	167	8	Eddy	Smith	3			1					1				5		
Windsor	167	9	Geer	Ezra	1	2		1		2	1		1				8		
Windsor	167	10	Bowen	Peleg	1			1		3			1				6		
Windsor	167	11	Freeman	Jared	1	1	1		1	1	1			1			7		
Windsor	167	12	Ball	Moses	2	1		1		2			1	1			8		
Windsor	167	13	Sanger	Jonathan	2	1		1		2	1	1	1				9		
Windsor	167	14	Crane	Ebenezer	2	1		1		3			1				8		
Windsor	167	15	Smith	Thomas	1				1				1	1			4		
Windsor	167	16	Eddy	Israel		1		1		2			1				5		
Windsor	167	17	Calisle	James	1	1	1	1		1			2				7		
Windsor	167	18	Eddy	Samuel Jun				1		2			1				4		
Windsor	167	19	Bowen	Amos			1			1	1	1					4		
Windsor	167	20	Lamphier	Elijah		1			1		1	1		1			5		
Windsor	167	21	Dean	Walter				1		2			1	1			5		
Windsor	167	22	Leonard	Solomon	3	1		1		1	2		1				9		
Windsor	167	23	Leonard	Jesse					1					1			2		
Windsor	167	24	Phillips	Joshua			1	1		1	1		1				5		
Windsor	167	25	Blanchard	Josiah			2	1					2				5		
Windsor	167	26	Westcot	Rufus	2			1		3			1				7		
Windsor	167	27	Whitaker	Abel		1		1		3	2		1				8		
Windsor	167	28	Westcot	Shukely				1			1	1	1				4		
Windsor	167	29	White	Daniel		2		1		1	1	1	1				7		
Windsor	167	30	Cotton	Wait	2			1		1			1	1	1		7		
Windsor	167	31	Svetland	Jonah	1	1	2	1			1	1	1				8		
Windsor	167	32	Howard	Phinehas	2		2	1		1		1					7		
Windsor	167	33	Hall	John	1	1	2		1	2			1				8		
Windsor	167	34	Chapman	Samuel				1		1			1				3		
Windsor	168	1	Tyler	William	3			1		2	1		1				8		
Windsor	168	2	Chapman	Daniel	1			1		1			1	1			5		
Windsor	168	3	Griggs	Lemuel		1		1		3		1	1				7		
Windsor	168	4	Robinson	Denison		2			1	1		2	1				7		
Windsor	168	5	Bussy	Jesse	2			1		1			1				5		
Windsor	168	6	Morse	Daniel			3		1		1	1	1	1	1		9		
Windsor	168	7	Dorrame	Gordon	1	1		1			1		1	1			6		
Windsor	168	8	Cooper	Ebenezer	2	1			1				1				5		
Windsor	168	9	Cooper	Francis	1		2	1		1		1					6		
Windsor	168	10	Beal	Jonah	1			1		3			1				6		
Windsor	168	11	Hill	Thomas	3	2	2	1			2		1				11		
Windsor	168	12	Beal	Joshua	3	2	3	1		1		3	1				14		
Windsor	168	13	Barber	Thomas	2	1	1	1		2	1	1	1	1			11		
Windsor	168	14	Dana	Daniel	2	2			1	3	2		1				11		
Windsor	168	15	Green	Hezekiah		1		1						1			3		
Windsor	168	16	Green	Noah	2	1		1		1			1				6		
Windsor	168	17	Dunbar	Walter	1			1		1			1				4		
Windsor	168	18	Dunbar	Joseph				1					1				2		
Windsor	168	19	Convers	Amasa J	1			1					1				3		
Windsor	168	20	Convers	Amasa		1	1		1	1	2	2		1			9		
Windsor	168	21	Clark	William				1		2			1				4		
Windsor	168	22	Cole	John	1		2	1				1		1			6		
Windsor	168	23	Cady	Elias	1		1	1				1		1			5		
Windsor	168	24	Clark	Joshua	2	4		1		2		1		1			11		
Windsor	168	25	Robbins	Eli	1			1		1			1				4		
Windsor	168	26	Luther	Nathaniel	3	1		1					1				6		

TOWN	PG#	LN#	LAST NAME	FIRST NAME	FREE WHITE MALES					FREE WHITE FEMALES					TOTAL ALL OTHER	TOTAL SLAVES	TOTALS	DISTRICT/ TOWNSHIP	NOTES
					under 10	10 to 16	16 to 26	26 to 45	45 and over	under 10	10 to 16	16 to 26	26 to 45	45 and over					
Zoar	143	1	Tenney	James	3	1		1		1	2		1				9		
Zoar	143	2	Lock	James	4			1					1				6		
Zoar	143	3	Bassett	Lemuel	1		2		1	2	3		1	1			11		
Zoar	143	4	Knowlton	Paul				1									1		
Zoar	143	5	Loomis	John	2	2		1		2	1	1	1				10		
Zoar	143	6	Towne	Eli		1		1		2	1		1				6		
Zoar	143	7	King	Jesse	3	2	2	1		1	1	1	1	2			14		
Zoar	143	8	Butler	Isaiah Zada			1			2			1				4		
Zoar	143	9	Nelson	Daniel	3			1	1	1	3	1		1			11		
Zoar	143	10	Wheeler	James 1st	1	1		1		1	1	1	1	1			8		
Zoar	143	11	Negus	Samuel	1	1	3		1		1			1			8		
Zoar	143	12	Ames	Eleazer		1	1			1				1			4		
Zoar	143	13	Porter	Miles	1	1	2	1	1	3	1	1	1	1			14		
Zoar	143	14	Pierce	Samuel	1		2		1	1	2	1		1			9		
Zoar	143	15	Wheeler	John	3	1	1	1	1	1		2	1	1			12		
Zoar	143	16	Willard	Julias	2			1		1		1					5		
Zoar	143	17	Baldwin	Murray L	2	1		1					1				5		
Zoar	143	18	Boardwell	Job			1		1	2		2		1			7		
Zoar	143	19	Stearns	Isaac	2	1			1	2		1		1			8		
Zoar	143	20	Taller		1		1			1		1	1				5		First name blank
Zoar	143	21	Hines	Alverson	1		1			1		1					4		
Zoar	143	22	Goodenow	Stephen	3			1		1	1		1				7		
Zoar	143	23	Butler	Isaiah	3	1		1		1				1			7		
Zoar	143	24	Leonard	Andrew	1			1					1				3		
Zoar	143	25	Eldridge	Amos		2		1		2			1				6		
Zoar	143	26	Eddy	Samuel		1		1		1	1		1	1			6		
Zoar	143	27	Hutchinson	Elisha	1			1				1					3		
Zoar	143	28	Eddy	William			1						1				2		
Zoar	143	29	Clarke	Supply		1	1	1				1		1			5		
Zoar	143	30	Clarke	Sylvanus		1				2		1	1				5		
Zoar	143	31	Clarke	Supply 2d	2	1		1		1	1		1				7		
Zoar	143	32	Drury	Nathan			1				1		1				3		
Zoar	143	33	Loveman	George			2		1	2		1	1	1			8		

TOWN	PG#	LN#	LAST NAME	FIRST NAME	FREE WHITE MALES under 10	10 to 16	16 to 26	26 to 45	45 and over	FREE WHITE FEMALES under 10	10 to 16	16 to 26	26 to 45	45 and over	TOTAL ALL OTHER	TOTAL SLAVES	TOTALS	DISTRICT/ TOWNSHIP	NOTES
Pittsfield	202	32	a negro	Hagar											3		3		
Pittsfield	202	29	a negro	Hartford											4		4		
Pittsfield	202	24	a negro	Thomas											2		2		
Bethlehem	172	15	Abba	Thomas	2	2		1		2	1		1				9		
Partridgefield	185	4	Abbey	Obadiah			1	1				1		1			4		
Partridgefield	185	5	Abbey	Roger	2			1		3			1				7		
Tyringham	113	47	Abbot	Nathan		1		1	1	1	1			1			6		
Lenox	209	1	Abbot	Seth	2			1		1			1				5		
Sheffield	224	10	Acton	Widow							1			1			2		
Bethlehem	181	22	Adams	Amos	3			1		3			1				8		
Bethlehem	180	9	Adams	Asahel	2	1	1	1		1		1	1				8		
Becket	265	1	Adams	Barna	2			1			1		1				5		
New Marlborough	234	16	Adams	Davenport		1	2		1	2	2	3		2			13		
Bethlehem	180	10	Adams	Ebenezer	1		1			1		1					4		
Loudon	178	26	Adams	Ebenezer	1			1		2			1				5		
Becket	265	2	Adams	Ebenz			1										1		
Becket	265	5	Adams	Elijah				1									1		
Hancock	159	3	Adams	Jacob	1			1		1			1				4		
Sandisfield	172	17	Adams	James			2		1			1		1			5		
Southfield	182	21	Adams	James Jr	1			1		3	1		1				7		
Partridgefield	185	1	Adams	John	2			1		1			1				5		
Sandisfield	177	4	Adams	John		1	2		1	2	1	1					9		
Sheffield	231	8	Adams	Joseph			1	1		1	1			1			5		
Becket	265	8	Adams	Mary		1				1				1			3		
Sandisfield	172	4	Adams	Richard		1		1				2		1			5		
Bethlehem	181	23	Adams	Samuel Jun			1	1				1	1	1			5		
Hancock	161	26	Adams	Shubel	2			1		2			1				6		
Partridgefield	185	2	Adams	Thomas	1			1		2	1		1				6		
Bethlehem	181	38	Adams	William Son	1		1	1					1				4		
New Marlborough	241	3	Adams	Zebediah	3	1	2		1	1	1						10		
Egremont	119	20	Alcott	Jared	1		1	1		2	2		1				8		
Tyringham	114	3	Alden	Benjamin	1	1							1				3		
Tyringham	114	38	Alden	Benjamin Jr	1			1					1				3		
Bethlehem	181	42	Alden	Israel	3			1						1			5		
Tyringham	113	35	Alden	Israel	1	2	2		1	1			2	2			11		
New Marlborough	235	20	Alden	Noah	3		1			1			1				6		
Bethlehem	182	13	Alden	Timothy	2		1	1		3			1				8		
Loudon	177	6	Alderman	John	1	1	2		1	2	2	1	1				11		
Cheshire	156	24	Aldridge	Samuel		2	1		1	1	3	2	1				11		
New Marlborough	236	6	Alexander	William		2	1		1	1			1	1			7		
Becket	265	4	Alford	Elijah		2	1	1		2	1	1		1			9		
Hancock	160	9	Alger	Elijah	1			1		3	1		1				7		
Adams	136	2	Alger	James	1	1		1		3			1				7		
Adams	135	27	Allen	Ebenz		1		1		1				1			4		
Tyringham	113	1	Allen	Elihu	2			1			1		1				5		
Bethlehem	172	14	Allen	Elijah	2	1		1		2			1				7		
Egremont	118	15	Allen	Elijah	1	1			1	2	4		1				10		
Pittsfield	194	5	Allen	Horace	1		1				1	1					4		
Sheffield	225	16	Allen	Jesse			1			1		1	1				4		
Lanesborough	146	1	Allen	John	1		1						1				3		
Bethlehem	172	12	Allen	John H.	1	1		1		2	1		1				7		
Tyringham	112	34	Allen	Jonathan				1						1			2		
New Marlborough	240	10	Allen	Joseph	3			1		2			1				7		
Washington	216	5	Allen	Justus		1	1		1	2	1	1		1			8		
New Marlborough	240	33	Allen	Levi	1			1		2			1	1			6		
Egremont	120	30	Allen	Luke	1	1	1	1		3	2	3	1				13		
Tyringham	113	37	Allen	Noah				1						1			2		
Tyringham	113	38	Allen	Noah Jun	2		1			1			1				5		
Lanesborough	146	2	Allen	Peleg	1	1		1				2		1			6		
Tyringham	111	23	Allen	Potter	3			1		2			1				8		
New Marlborough	240	16	Allen	Rufus	2	2		1		2		1	1				10		
Pittsfield	194	3	Allen	Rufus	2	1			1		2			1	1		8		
Pittsfield	194	4	Allen	Sarah									1	1			2		
Partridgefield	185	6	Allen	Thomas			1			1	1						3		
Pittsfield	194	1	Allen	Thomas	2	1		1		2	1		1				8		
Pittsfield	194	2	Allen	Thomas Jun	1		1	2							1		5		
Windsor	166	17	Allen	Zebulon	1	1		1		1			1				5		
Zoar	143	12	Ames	Eleazer		1	1			1				1			4		
Loudon	179	29	Ames	Joshua	2			1		3			1				7		
Sheffield	226	6	Amsden	Henry				1						1			2		
Bethlehem	181	5	Anabel	Ebenezer	2			1		2			1				6		
Sheffield	223	34	Andrews	Andrew	2	2	1	1		2			1	1			10		
West Stockbridge	246	6	Andrews	Benajah			1										1		
West Stockbridge	246	3	Andrews	Ebenezer		1			1	1	1	1		1			6		
West Stockbridge	246	5	Andrews	Elijah		1	2			1		1					5		
Great Barrington	109	23	Andrews	Elisha		1	2	1					3	1			8		
Richmond	206	41	Andrews	Leonard			1			1			1				3		
Richmond	208	19	Andrews	Oliver		1							1				2		
Richmond	206	39	Andrews	Oziah		2	2	1			1	4		1			11		
New Marlborough	237	28	Andrews	Philo	1			1		1		1	1				5		

TOWN	PG#	LN#	LAST NAME	FIRST NAME	FREE WHITE MALES					FREE WHITE FEMALES					TOTAL ALL OTHER	TOTAL SLAVES	TOTALS	DISTRICT/ TOWNSHIP	NOTES
					under 10	10 to 16	16 to 26	26 to 45	45 and over	under 10	10 to 16	16 to 26	26 to 45	45 and over					
Richmond	206	40	Andrews	Selah				1		1		1	1				4		
Lenox	212	18	Andrews	Solmon	2	1			1	1				1			6		
West Stockbridge	246	4	Andrews	Theod	4	1		1		1	1		1				9		
Egremont	118	17	Andrus	Appleton	2	1		1		2	1		1				8		
Cheshire	154	3	Angel	James	1	1			1	1				1			5		
Adams	135	36	Anthony	David Junr	1	1			1	1	1		1				6		
Adams	136	20	Anthony	Humphrey	2		1	1		2		1	1				8		
Partridgefield	185	3	Apthorp	James	2	1			1	1	2	1		1			9		
Adams	133	1	Arnold	Comfort		2		1		1				1			5		
Adams	135	35	Arnold	Daniel	1		1			3		1	1				7		
New Marlborough	234	27	Arnold	David	1			1		1			1				4		
Adams	136	23	Arnold	Elisha	2			1		2	2	1	1		8		17		
Adams	136	15	Arnold	Isaac		1	1	1	1	1			1				6		
Great Barrington	106	33	Arnold	Jacob		3		1		2	1		1				8		
Adams	135	16	Arnold	Jesse	1		1			2			1				5		
Great Barrington	106	31	Arnold	John	1	1		1		2	1	2	1				9		
West Stockbridge	246	2	Arnold	Jonah	1	1			1	2	1		1				7		
Sandisfield	174	38	Arnold	Jonathan	2		1			2	1	2		1			10		
Cheshire	155	41	Arnold	Joseph	3		1	1		2		1	1				9		
Adams	135	28	Arnold	Nathaniel	1	1	1		1	1			1				6		
Cheshire	156	23	Arnold	Smith	1			1		3		1					6		
Adams	133	11	Arnold	Stakely		2		1		1	1						5		
Great Barrington	106	32	Arnold	Timothy	2			1		1			1				5		
Washington	213	12	Arnold	Timothy	1	1		1		1			1	1			6		
Pittsfield	194	6	Ashley	David Junr			1	1	1	4	1	1	1				10		
Sheffield	230	20	Ashley	John	1	2	2	1		3			2				11		
Sheffield	231	16	Ashley	John Esq			1	1	1					1	2		6		
Sheffield	222	9	Ashley	William	1				1		2		1				5		
Sheffield	231	15	Ashley	William		1	1	2		1	2		1		3		11		
Richmond	207	22	Atkins	Seth	3			1		1			1				6		
Tyringham	119	11	Atwater	James	2			1	1	1		1					6		
Becket	265	3	Atwell	Joseph	2			1		1			1	1			6		
Great Barrington	108	47	Atwood	Hezekiah				1					1				2		
Great Barrington	108	46	Atwood	Phineas	3			1		2			1				7		
Egremont	120	21	Austin	Amasa			1					1					2		
Sheffield	221	2	Austin	Amos	1	1		1		1		1					5		
Sheffield	221	7	Austin	Augustus		1	1	1	1		2		1				7		
Sheffield	223	30	Austin	Bailey		1		1		1			1				4		
Sheffield	225	25	Austin	Bailey Jun		2		1		1	2		2				8		
New Marlborough	240	34	Austin	Dan	2	1			1	2	2		1				9		
Hancock	160	23	Austin	Elizabeth						3	1		1				5		
Sheffield	221	1	Austin	Gad		1	1	1						1	1		5		
Lee	259	1	Austin	James	1		1			1		1					4		
Sheffield	230	15	Austin	Joab	1	1	1	1	1	1	2		1				9		
Sheffield	223	16	Austin	John	1	1	1		1	1	1		1				7		
Becket	265	7	Austin	John				1									1		
Becket	265	6	Austin	John Jr	1			1		2	1	1	1				7		
Egremont	120	20	Austin	Judah	1	1			1	1	1	1					6		
Sheffield	224	17	Austin	Leml1		1			1			1		1			4		
Richmond	205	21	Austin	Levi			2	2	1			2	1				8		
Sheffield	228	14	Austin	Philip	1	1		2		2		1	1				8		
Tyringham	112	1	Austin	Thomas	2			1		2			1				6		
Tyringham	112	41	Averill	Thomas	2			1		3			1				7		
Pittsfield	202	26	Avase	Benajah											2		2		
Tyringham	114	39	Avery	Joseph	1				2	1	1	2	2				9		
Great Barrington	109	10	Avery	Miles		3		1		1	1		1				7		
West Stockbridge	246	1	Ayer	Oliver	1			1		1	1		1				5		
Adams	134	33	Aylsworth	Anthony				1					1				2		
Adams	134	32	Aylsworth	Warner	3			1		2	1		1				8		
Sandisfield	176	29	Ayrault	James Esq				1				2	1				4		
Sandisfield	176	30	Ayrault	Nicholas	3	3			1	2			1				10		
Loudon	178	9	Babb	Benjamin	2	1		1		3			1				8		
Loudon	178	6	Babb	John	1		1		1	1	2	1		1			8		
New Marlborough	239	30	Babbett	Asa	1	1	1			1		1					5		
Savoy	139	3	Babbett	Snellam		1	1	1		2			1				6		
Lanesborough	147	7	Babbit	David	2	1		1		1			1	1			7		
Lanesborough	147	13	Babbit	John			1	1				1	1				4		
New Ashford	163	22	Babbit	Mary	2	1	3				1	2		1			10		
Lanesborough	146	9	Babbit	Samuel	1	2		1		1	1		1				7		
Washington	214	33	Babcock	Elias	2	1				4	1	2	1				12		
Pittsfield	194	17	Babcock	James	1	1	1		1	3	1		1				9		
Partridgefield	186	7	Babcock	John		2			1	2		1	1				8		
Richmond	208	37	Babcock	William	2		1		1	3	1	1		1			10		
Egremont	119	12	Bacon	Andrew	3		1	1		2	1		1				9		
Pittsfield	195	26	Bacon	Asa	2	2	1		1	2	1	1					10		
Williamstown	129	22	Bacon	Ezekiel		1	1			1	2						5		
Williamstown	125	15	Bacon	Jacob	2	1	1		1	2	2	1					10		
Williamstown	125	13	Bacon	Joel	4			1		1			1				7		
Richmond	207	1	Bacon	John	1	1		1	1	1		2		1			8		
Richmond	207	2	Bacon	John Junr	1			1		2		1	1				6		

TOWN	PG#	LN#	LAST NAME	FIRST NAME	FREE WHITE MALES under 10	10 to 16	16 to 26	26 to 45	45 and over	FREE WHITE FEMALES under 10	10 to 16	16 to 26	26 to 45	45 and over	TOTAL ALL OTHER	TOTAL SLAVES	TOTALS	DISTRICT/ TOWNSHIP	NOTES
Partridgefield	186	2	Bacon	Joseph	2		1	1	1	2	1	1	1				10		
Egremont	119	11	Bacon	Samuel		1	2	2		2	1		1				9		
Lanesborough	146	4	Bacon	Samuel	1	1	1	1		4	1	1	1				11		
Williamstown	126	39	Bacon	Stephen		1	1	1		1			1				5		
Sheffield	221	6	Bacon	William		2			1	1	2	1	1				8		
Partridgefield	185	23	Bad*	Henry	1			1		1			2	1			6		
Lanesborough	146	3	Bagg	Aaron	2		1		1	2	2		1				9		
Lanesborough	146	16	Bagg	Abner	1		1			1		1					4		
Pittsfield	195	21	Bagg	Elijah	2		2	1		3			1	1			10		
Lanesborough	146	15	Bagg	Joseph			1		1			2		1			5		
Pittsfield	195	13	Bagg	Martin		1	1		1	1	1	1		1			7		
Pittsfield	195	8	Bagg	Martin Jun	1		1			1			1				4		
Lanesborough	146	17	Bagg	Silas	1			1		1			1				4		
Lee	259	21	Baikus	Ichabod	2	2			1	1			1				7		
Lee	259	24	Baikus	Lydia								2	1	1			4		
Lee	259	31	Baikus	Marcy										1			1		
Lee	259	4	Baikus	Nathan			1										1		
Lee	259	3	Baikus	Seth	3	2	2		1		2		1				11		
Lee	259	28	Baikus	Wally	1			1		2		1					5		
Pittsfield	194	18	Bailey	Joseph			1					1					2		
Great Barrington	109	24	Bailey	Oliver			1		1	1	2		1				6		
Great Barrington	109	25	Bailey	Scoville			1			1		1					3		
Tyringham	112	22	Bailey	Stephen	1			1		2			1				5		
Lee	259	6	Bailey	Thomas	3			1		1		1					6		
Tyringham	111	26	Baily	Clerk		1	3		1		2			2			9		
Pittsfield	195	11	Baker	Aaron			1	1	1	3		1	1	2			10		
New Marlborough	232	29	Baker	Abel	1	1			1	1	1		1				6		
Sheffield	225	31	Baker	Abonjah		1	3						1				5		
Lanesborough	147	16	Baker	Benejab	2		1		1	2	2		1				9		
Lanesborough	147	14	Baker	Bethiel	1	1	1	1	1			1		1			7		
Alford	117	25	Baker	Calvin	1			1					1				3		
Sandisfield	170	14	Baker	Daniel			1		1	1	1		1				5		
Adams	137	10	Baker	David	1	1	1		1	1			1	1			7		
Lee	259	15	Baker	David	3	1		1		2	1	1					9		
Bethlehem	172	7	Baker	Eliphalet	1		2	1		3			1				8		
Pittsfield	195	29	Baker	Elisha	1	1		1		2			1				6		
Sheffield	230	32	Baker	Ephraim	3		2	1	1			2	1				10		
Williamstown	132	6	Baker	Ezra	1	1	1	1		1		3					9		
Lanesborough	147	15	Baker	Francis	1	1			1	1		1		1			6		
Tyringham	115	46	Baker	Israel	1			1		1		1		1			6		
Alford	117	24	Baker	James			1	1		1			1				4		
Pittsfield	195	27	Baker	John				1					1				2		
Pittsfield	195	12	Baker	Joshua	1			1		1			1				4		
Great Barrington	107	5	Baker	Nathan		1	4		1	1		1		1			9		
New Marlborough	234	13	Baker	Nelson		1			1	1	1	2		1			7		
Cheshire	154	17	Baker	Oney				1		1			1				3		
Lanesborough	147	10	Baker	Samuel		2		1		4	1	1	1				10		
Great Barrington	104	8	Baker	Thomas	2	1	1		1	1	1	1		1			9		
Williamstown	131	40	Balch	Joseph	2	2		1		2			1				8		
Williamstown	125	1	Balch	Timothy	1			1		2	1		1				6		
Windsor	165	23	Balding	Ephraim	1	1	1	1					1				5		
Windsor	165	21	Balding	Samuel		1	1		1	1		2		1			7		
Windsor	166	4	Balding	Samuel Jun	2	1	1	1		1	1		1				8		
Bethlehem	182	7	Baldwin	Benjamin		1		1		5	1		1				9		
Stockbridge	252	8	Baldwin	Clarke	3	1	2		1	1	2	1					11		
New Marlborough	238	2	Baldwin	David	2	1	1		1	1		1		1			8		
Williamstown	130	23	Baldwin	Elijah	3			1		1		1					6		
Egremont	120	39	Baldwin	James	4	1	2	1					1				10		
Williamstown	128	18	Baldwin	Joel		1	1		1	1			1				5		
Egremont	120	40	Baldwin	Joseph				1				1	1				3		
Zoar	143	17	Baldwin	Murray L	2	1		1					1				5		
West Stockbridge	247	15	Baldwin	Samll	2			1		1	2						6		
Loudon	179	18	Baldwin	Samuel			1			4			1				7		
Tyringham	114	14	Baldwin	Samuel			1						1				2		
Tyringham	114	40	Baldwin	Stephen	1		1			1	1						4		
Partridgefield	185	15	Baleau	Elias		1	2		1	1			1	1			7		
Lee	259	19	Ball	John		2	2			1	2		1				8		
Pittsfield	194	19	Ball	Jonas	1			1		2			1				5		
Tyringham	113	42	Ball	Joseph	1	1	1		1	1	2	1		1			9		
Windsor	167	12	Ball	Moses	2	1		1		2			1	1			8		
Lee	259	5	Ball	Nathan			1	1		2			1				5		
Stockbridge	252	4	Ball	Perry			1			1							2		
Washington	216	11	Ballentine	William G.		1			2			1	1		1		7		
Adams	138	6	Ballou	Aaron	1		2	2	1	1	1	2	1	1			12		
Adams	138	8	Ballou	Jonas	2		1			2			1				6		
Lenox	209	13	Bangs	Abner	3	2		1		1	1		1				9		
Lenox	209	14	Bangs	Elisha				1					1				2		
Tyringham	119	22	Banner	Levi	2	1		1			1		1	1			7		
Tyringham	119	19	Banner	Nicholas	1		1						1				3		
Windsor	166	18	Bannister	Rafeal				1		2			1				4		

TOWN	PG#	LN#	LAST NAME	FIRST NAME	FREE WHITE MALES under 10	10 to 16	16 to 26	26 to 45	45 and over	FREE WHITE FEMALES under 10	10 to 16	16 to 26	26 to 45	45 and over	TOTAL ALL OTHER	TOTAL SLAVES	TOTALS	DISTRICT/ TOWNSHIP	NOTES
New Ashford	163	11	Banter	David					1					1			2		
New Ashford	163	9	Banter	John	2	1	2	1		3	2	1	1				13		
New Ashford	163	3	Banter	Thadeus	1			1		2			1				5		
Loudon	179	17	Barber	Abel	1			1		2		1					5		
Tyringham	114	42	Barber	Alexanr	1			1		2		1					5		
Loudon	179	15	Barber	Benjamin		1		1		1		1	1				5		
Hancock	159	29	Barber	James	1		1						1				3		
Savoy	139	12	Barber	Joseph	1	1		1	1	1			1				7		
Pittsfield	194	10	Barber	Matthew		1		1				2	1	1			6		
Loudon	179	20	Barber	Roswell			1			2		1					4		
Tyringham	114	16	Barber	Samuel	1		1	1					2				5		
Tyringham	114	6	Barber	Samuel Jun	1	1						1					4		
Hancock	162	10	Barber	Silas	2		1			2		1					6		
Windsor	168	13	Barber	Thomas	2	1	1	1		2	1	1	1	1			11		
New Marlborough	239	27	Barber	Zachheus	3		1	1		2		1					8		
Cheshire	158	5	Barden	Isaac		1		1			1		1				4		
Cheshire	158	6	Barden	Isaac Jun	3			1				1					5		
Williamstown	125	7	Barden	Jacob		1				1		1					3		
Dalton	191	1	Barden	James		1	3	1		1	1	2		1			10		
Williamstown	128	32	Barett	Peter	1	2	1	1				2	1				8		
Bethlehem	172	6	Barker	Eleazer	2		2	1		2	1	1	1				10		
Cheshire	154	30	Barker	Ezra	2	1	1	1	1		2		1	1			10		
Sandisfield	172	12	Barker	Jairus		2		1		3		1	1				8		
Cheshire	154	8	Barker	James			2	1				1		1			5		
Sandisfield	172	13	Barker	Nathan	2		1					1					4		
Cheshire	154	10	Barker	Newell	1		1	1		3	1		1				8		
Lanesborough	146	13	Barker	Silas		1	1	3				1	1				7		
Lee	259	9	Barlow	Lemuel	3		1	1		1			1				7		
Lee	259	12	Barlow	Peleg			1			1			1		1		4		
Lee	259	22	Barlow	Reuben	1		1				1		1				4		
Lee	259	10	Barlow	Seth		1		1			1			1			4		
Partridgefield	186	4	Barnabe	Chandler	1	1	1	1		2	1	1	1				9		
Sheffield	225	10	Barnam	Selah	2	1	1				2	2		1			10		
Sheffield	222	4	Barnard	Lemll		1		1					1				3		
Pittsfield	195	2	Barnard	Richard	3			1		1			1				6		
Sheffield	225	20	Barnard	Sylvester			1										1		
Becket	265	11	Barnes	Comfort	1	1	1			1	1		1				7		
Lanesborough	146	10	Barnes	Joseph	3		1	1					1	1			7		
Williamstown	130	7	Barnes	Joseph	1		1			2		1					5		
Lanesborough	146	11	Barnes	Joseph Jr		2	2		1		1		1		3		10		
Becket	265	19	Barnes	Moses	1		1			2		1					5		
West Stockbridge	247	9	Barnes	Silas	2	2		1		1			1				7		
West Stockbridge	247	10	Barnes	Timothy	2		1	1	1		1	1		1			8		
Savoy	140	26	Barney	Benjamin	3	1		1		2	2		1				10		
Savoy	140	29	Barney	George	1		1	1		1			1				5		
Savoy	140	28	Barney	William	1	1		1		1	1		1				6		
Washington	213	10	Barns	Ezekiel	1		1	1		1		1	1				6		
Richmond	207	24	Barns	Jeremiah	4	1		1		1	1	1					10		
New Ashford	163	31	Barns	Moses	1		1	1	1	1	1		1				7		
Stockbridge	252	7	Barns	Reuben	4	1		1		1	1		1				9		
Richmond	206	43	Barns	William			3	1			1	1		1			7		
Alford	117	44	Barnum	Stephen	2	2		1		1	1		1				8		
Williamstown	126	38	Barr	Daniel			1						1				2		
Partridgefield	185	11	Barrett	Amos	1	2	1			3		1	1				9		
Alford	117	49	Barrett	Eleazer		1	1	2					2				6		
Pittsfield	194	16	Barrett	Jonathan		1		1	1			2	1				6		
Alford	117	48	Barrett	Mahitable		1							1				2		
Partridgefield	185	12	Barrett	Nathan	3	1		1		2		1	1				9		
Williamstown	128	36	Barrett	Oliver	1	1		1					1		1		5		
Pittsfield	194	15	Barrett	Solomon	2		1			2		1					6		
Great Barrington	110	9	Barrey	Jonathan	1		1						1				2		
Lenox	209	5	Barrot	Nathan	2		2	1					1				6		
West Stockbridge	246	7	Barstow	Samuel		1											1		
Tyringham	115	14	Barter	John		1				1	1		1				4		
Richmond	207	16	Bartlet	William	1	1	1	1				1	1	1			7		
West Stockbridge	247	16	Bartlett	Abraham		1		1					1				3		
West Stockbridge	247	17	Bartlett	Abraham Jr	1	1		1		3	1		1				8		
Dalton	191	2	Bartlett	Nicholas				1			1		1				3		
Dalton	191	3	Bartlett	Stephen	1			1		1		1	1				5		
New Ashford	163	16	Bartner	Pitt*	3		1	1			3		1				9		
Stockbridge	252	6	Barton	Joseph	3		2	1		1	1	1	1				10		
Williamstown	125	17	Barton	Josiah	1			1		3			1				6		
Pittsfield	194	14	Barton	Robert		1		1		1			1				4		
Partridgefield	185	14	Bass	Henry		1						1					2		
Partridgefield	185	21	Bass	Jonathan	2		1	1		2		1		1			8		
Windsor	164	7	Basset	William			1			1			1				3		
Adams	137	32	Bassett	Abel			1			3	3		1				8		
Lee	259	16	Bassett	Anne	1	1		1				1					4		
Tyringham	111	31	Bassett	Benjamin				1					1				2		

93

TOWN	PG#	LN#	HEADS OF HOUSEHOLD		FREE WHITE MALES					FREE WHITE FEMALES					TOTAL ALL OTHER	TOTAL SLAVES	TOTALS	DISTRICT/ TOWNSHIP	NOTES
			LAST NAME	FIRST NAME	under 10	10 to 16	16 to 26	26 to 45	45 and over	under 10	10 to 16	16 to 26	26 to 45	45 and over					
Lee	259	8	Bassett	Cornelius		2	1		1	3			1				8		
Lee	259	2	Bassett	Cornelius Jr	2	1			1	2			1				7		
Lee	259	7	Bassett	Isaac			1		1	1	1	1					5		
Egremont	118	6	Bassett	Justus	1			1		2		1					5		
Zoar	143	3	Bassett	Lemuel	1		2		1	2	3		1	1			11		
Dalton	191	4	Bassett	Nathan	3	1		1				1	1				7		
Lee	259	11	Bassett	Nathan	2	1		1		1	1	2	1				9		
Lee	259	29	Bassett	Nathan	1		1		1	1	2	2	1	1			10		
Lenox	209	3	Bateman	Luther	1	1		1		1	2	2		1			9		
Savoy	139	11	Bates	Comfort	1	1	1		1	2			1				7		
Pittsfield	195	7	Bates	Ezekiel			2			1		1					4		
Windsor	167	1	Bates	Jarum				1		1			1				3		
Great Barrington	106	24	Bates	Martin		2	1		1	2		3	1	1			11		
Tyringham	111	27	Battle	Ithiel	2	1	1		1	1	3	1		1			11		
Tyringham	111	43	Battle	Justus	2	1	1		1		1		1	1			8		
Sheffield	223	10	Bawen	Joseph	2	1		1		2	1		1				8		
Sandisfield	173	33	Baxter	John				1					1				2		
Sheffield	221	16	Baxter	John	1			1		3			1				6		
Southfield	182	4	Baxter	Moses	4			1		3			1				9		
Dalton	191	5	Baxter	Wm				1					1				2		
Dalton	191	6	Baxter	Wm Junr	4	2		1					1				8		
New Ashford	163	12	Beach	Archibald	4			1		2	1		1				9		
New Ashford	163	14	Beach	Hezekiah			2		1			1		1			5		
New Ashford	163	13	Beach	Hezekiah Jr	2			1		1			1				5		
Southfield	182	23	Beach	James		1	1		1								3		
Southfield	182	8	Beach	James Jr		1							1				2		
Great Barrington	108	36	Beach	Josiah	1			1		1			1				4		
New Marlborough	233	29	Beach	Nathll		2		1			2		1				6		
Sandisfield	173	34	Beach	Orra	1	1						1					3		
New Marlborough	233	31	Beach	Stiles	1			1		2			1				5		
New Ashford	163	10	Beach	Tyler	3			1		2	2		1				9		
Richmond	207	8	Beacher	Thomas	1		1		1				2				5		
Windsor	168	12	Beal	Joshua	3	2	3		1	3			3	1			14		
Windsor	168	10	Beal	Jonah	1			1		3			1				6		
Windsor	165	35	Beale	Joshua		1	2		1			1		1			6		
Savoy	139	1	Bealey	Nathaniel	1			1		1	2	3		1			9		
Bethlehem	180	8	Beard	Aaron				1					1				2		
Sheffield	231	17	Beard	Aaron				1					1				2		
Bethlehem	180	7	Beard	Asa	3		2	1		2	1		1				10		
Bethlehem	180	5	Beard	Kindol	2			1		1			1				5		
Bethlehem	180	6	Beard	Moses	3	2		1		1	1	2	1				11		
Partridgefield	186	12	Beaton	Jacob	3	1		1		1	1		1	1			9		
Williamstown	131	12	Bebee	Ezra	1			1		3			1				6		
West Stockbridge	247	13	Bebee	Gamaliel			1										1		
Richmond	206	33	Bebee	Levi		2	1	1					1				5		
Williamstown	128	19	Beckwith	James		1	1	1		2		1					6		
Dalton	191	16	Beckwith	Jonah	2	2		1		2			1				8		
Pittsfield	195	23	Beckwith	Reynolds	1	2	1		1	1	1		1				8		
Alford	116	24	Beckwith	Richard	1			1		1			1				4		
West Stockbridge	247	24	Bedwell	Isaac		2		2		1	1	1					7		
Tyringham	114	1	Bedwell	Udonjah	5		1	1				1	1				9		
Great Barrington	107	31	Beebee	Joseph		1	1		1	1			1				5		
Williamstown	130	39	Beeman	Reuben	3			1		2			1				7		
Loudon	178	32	Belamy	Simeon Sen			1		1	1	2		1				6		
Partridgefield	186	6	Belcher	Andrew			1		1	1	2	1	1				7		
Partridgefield	186	17	Belcher	Calvin				1		3			1		*		5		
Hancock	158	20	Beldin	Daniel	1		1			1		1	1				5		
Lenox	209	6	Beldin	Oliver	1		1	1		1			1				5		
Lenox	209	2	Beldin	Oliver Jun	1	1	1	1		2	1		2				9		
Sandisfield	173	23	Belding	Daniel	1			1					1				3		
Sandisfield	173	22	Belding	David			1			2		1					4		
Sandisfield	173	21	Belding	James		1	2		2	2	2		2				12		
Windsor	164	13	Belknap	Thomas	2			1		3			1				7		
New Marlborough	238	30	Beman	Reuben		1	2		1	1	1		1				7		
Sheffield	222	24	Beman	Samll	2	1		1		1		1		1			7		
Stockbridge	252	13	Bement	Asa		1	1		1					1	1		5		
Stockbridge	252	14	Bement	John	1			1		1			1				4		
West Stockbridge	247	1	Bemis	Jonathan	1	1	1	1			1		1				6		
New Marlborough	240	12	Bence	Rory		2		1		1			1				5		
Tyringham	110	20	Benedict	Abel	1			1		1	2	2		1			8		
New Marlborough	239	31	Benedict	Francis			1			1		1					3		
Tyringham	110	21	Benedict	Isaac	1		1			1		1					4		
West Stockbridge	246	11	Benedict	John	1			1		2			1				5		
Egremont	118	3	Benedict	Peter	1			1		1		1					4		
West Stockbridge	246	10	Benedict	Thomas	1	1	1		1	1	1		2	1			9		
New Marlborough	237	14	Benedict	William	1	1		2		1			1	2			8		
Egremont	120	12	Benjamin	Joseph	3	1		2		1			1	1			9		
Sheffield	222	25	Benjamin	Nathan	1		1	1		2			1				6		
Sheffield	231	4	Bennett	Asahel P	2		2		1	2	2		1				10		
Lee	259	17	Bennett	George		1			1	2			1				5		

94

TOWN	PG#	LN#	LAST NAME	FIRST NAME	FREE WHITE MALES					FREE WHITE FEMALES					TOTAL ALL OTHER	TOTAL SLAVES	TOTALS	DISTRICT/ TOWNSHIP	NOTES
					under 10	10 to 16	16 to 26	26 to 45	45 and over	under 10	10 to 16	16 to 26	26 to 45	45 and over					
Cheshire	155	6	Bennett	John	2	1	1	1		1	1	1	1	1	1		11		
Savoy	140	18	Bennett	Peter				1						1			2		
Stockbridge	252	2	Bennitt	Isaac			2		1	1	1	2	1	1			9		
Partridgefield	185	19	Benson	Noah		1		1		1				1			4		
Bethlehem	172	10	Benton	Abraham		1	2	2	1			2		1			9		
Lenox	209	11	Benton	Amos			1		1				1				3		
Bethlehem	182	16	Benton	Elijah	1			1		1		1					4		
West Stockbridge	246	14	Benton	Elijah	1	1	1					1					4		
West Stockbridge	246	15	Benton	John				1				1	1				3		
Richmond	205	23	Benton	Stephan			2	2	1			1		1			7		
Sheffield	224	4	Benton	Stephen	1	1	1	1		2			1				7		
Mount Washington	232	26	Berazee	Case	2	2	3		1	2	1		1				12		
Mount Washington	232	27	Berazee	Frederick	1			1	1	3	1		1				7		
Hancock	159	23	Berry	William		2	1		1	2	1	2		1			10		
Dalton	191	7	Beslow	Job	2	1		1		3	1	1					9		
Southfield	182	17	Bettis	Leonard			1			3		1					5		
Southfield	182	18	Bettis	Nathaniel	1		1			4	1		1				9		
Southfield	182	16	Bettis	Thomas				1	1	1	1		1	1			6		
Richmond	207	43	Betts	Aaron	1	1	1	1			2	2	1				9		
Richmond	208	6	Betts	Comstock				1						1			2		
Richmond	207	37	Betts	Uriah		1	1	1		2		2					7		
Richmond	207	42	Betts	Zebulon	2	1	1	1		3			1				9		
Great Barrington	107	24	Bevins	James			1			1		1					3		
Dalton	191	8	Bicknell	Otis	1			1		2			1				5		
Stockbridge	252	5	Bidwell	Barnas	1		2	1		1	1						6		
Sheffield	224	35	Bierce	Austin		1	1		1			2		1			6		
Sheffield	224	26	Bierce	Austin Jun	1	1	2	1		1							7		
Sheffield	224	34	Bierce	Winston	1		1			1		2					5		
Adams	133	5	Bigabee	William	1		1		1	1	2		1				7		
Dalton	191	10	Bill	Rhoda	1					1			1				3		
Washington	215	17	Bill	William		1	2		1			1	2	1			8		
Lanesborough	146	6	Billings	Daniel	1		2		1	1	3	2	1	1			12		
Stockbridge	253	3	Billings	Henry	1			1		1			1				4		
Stockbridge	253	6	Billings	Matthew		1		1						1			3		
Stockbridge	253	4	Billings	Matthew Jr			1			1			1				3		
Great Barrington	109	2	Billings	Samuel				1				1					2		
Tyringham	111	1	Billings	William	1	1							1				3		
Lenox	209	4	Billins	N*1	1	1	1	1		1	1		1				7		
Sheffield	227	7	Bills	Hosea	3			1		1		1	1	1			8		
Hancock	160	40	Bills	Jabez	2	1			1	1	1		1				7		
Stockbridge	253	5	Bingham	Anna										1			1		
Lanesborough	147	12	Bingham	Eliphalet	2			1		1			1	1			6		
Pittsfield	195	4	Bingham	Septimus	1		1	1		1			1				5		
Williamstown	130	25	Bingham	Thomas			1	1					1				3		
Tyringham	114	9	Binney	Thomas			1		1				1				3		
New Ashford	162	2	Birch	Gideon	4	1		1		1			1				8		
Williamstown	129	7	Birchard	Amos	1	1	1			1	1	1					6		
New Marlborough	232	2	Birchard	David					2			1	1				5		
Becket	265	12	Birchard	James & James Jr	2		1	1	1	2	1		1	1			10		
Williamstown	129	9	Birchard	Joseph	2	1	1	1		1	2	1	1	1			11		
Becket	265	10	Birchard	Nathan	1			1		3			2				7		
Williamstown	126	23	Birchard	Samuel					1	1			1				3		
Windsor	166	21	Bird	Ebenezer	3		2	1		2	2	1	1				12		
New Marlborough	234	31	Bird	Nathll		2		1		4			1				8		
Pittsfield	195	14	Bishop	Charles	2			1	1	2			1	1			8		
Stockbridge	252	11	Bishop	Elkanah		1			1		1	1		1			5		
Richmond	205	20	Bishop	Leonard	2			1				1		1			5		
Richmond	207	26	Bishop	Nathaniel	1		2		1			1	1				6		
Richmond	208	16	Bishop	Richard		1		1		4		1					8		
Williamstown	129	18	Bishop	Thomas	1		1	1		2		1					6		
Bethlehem	182	21	Black	Isaac	2	2		1		1	1		1				8		
Partridgefield	185	17	Blackman	Abraham		1	1		1			1		1			5		
Partridgefield	185	10	Blackman	Abraham Jr	3			1		1			1				6		
Pittsfield	195	3	Blackman	Dan	3	1	1	1		2	1		1				10		
Partridgefield	186	9	Blackman	Eleazer						3			1				4		
Pittsfield	194	12	Blackman	Isbon											6		6		
Richmond	208	39	Blackman	James	1			1		2		1					6		
Lee	259	18	Blackman	Jonathan					1				1	1			3		
Partridgefield	185	16	Blackman	Nathl	2			1					1				4		
New Marlborough	233	19	Blackman	Paul	1	1	2	1	1		1	2	1				11		
Pittsfield	195	6	Blackman	Samuel	2	1			1	2			1				7		
New Marlborough	232	25	Blackman	Titus	3			1		1	2		1				8		
Great Barrington	109	31	Blackney	Eldad	1			1		1		1					4		
Hancock	159	18	Blading	Ephraim	2	1			1					1			5		
Williamstown	126	7	Blair	Absalom			1		1			2		1			5		
Becket	265	13	Blair	David & David Jr		2	1	1	1	1		1	2	1			10		
Becket	265	16	Blair	Luther			1			1		1					3		
Becket	265	14	Blair	Thompson	1			1		3			1				6		
Adams	137	33	Blakeley	Elizabeth	1		1						1				4		

TOWN	PG#	LN#	HEADS OF HOUSEHOLD		FREE WHITE MALES					FREE WHITE FEMALES					TOTAL ALL OTHER	TOTAL SLAVES	TOTALS	DISTRICT/ TOWNSHIP	NOTES
			LAST NAME	FIRST NAME	under 10	10 to 16	16 to 26	26 to 45	45 and over	under 10	10 to 16	16 to 26	26 to 45	45 and over					
New Marlborough	233	23	Blakely	Stephen			1			1		1					3		
Egremont	118	8	Blakesley	Jared	6	3		1			1		1				12		
Savoy	140	3	Blanchard	Josiah			1										1		
Windsor	167	25	Blanchard	Josiah			2		1				2				5		
Williamstown	132	20	Blin	Ebenezer	1		1	1		2	1	1	1				8		
Cheshire	155	20	Bliss	Benjamin	2		1	1		3		1	1				9		
Savoy	140	6	Bliss	David	4	1			1				1				7		
Lanesborough	147	1	Bliss	Ebenezer				1				1	1				3		
Cheshire	158	10	Bliss	Elkanah				1		1		1					3		
Savoy	139	6	Bliss	Ephraim	1	2	1		1	1		1	1				8		
Lanesborough	147	3	Bliss	Levi				1					1				2		
Cheshire	154	5	Bliss	Nathaniel	1	3	1			1		1	1				9		
Cheshire	153	6	Bliss	Samuel	2			1		2			1				6		
Cheshire	153	8	Bliss	Timothy	2			1		2			1				6		
Great Barrington	109	3	Bliss	William	2	1			1	1	1	1		1			8		
Stockbridge	252	10	Bliss	Wm Junr			1					1					2		
Stockbridge	252	9	Bliss	Wm Sen		1	1		1					1			4		
Alford	117	3	Bloss	James	2	1		1		1			1	1			7		
West Stockbridge	247	25	Bloss	Joseph	1		1	1		3			1				7		
Lenox	209	12	Blossom	Enos	1	2	2		1	3			1				10		
Lenox	212	8	Blossom	Ezra	2			1		2	2	1	1				9		
Sheffield	228	31	Boardman	Charles	1			1		2			1				5		
Bethlehem	181	40	Boardman	Edward	2		1						1				4		
Williamstown	132	11	Boardman	Theodore		1			1			1		1			4		
Zoar	143	18	Boardwell	Job			1		1	2		2		1			7		
Great Barrington	109	18	Bolles	Hezekiah	1			1		2			1				5		
Southfield	182	1	Bond	Nicholas Jr	2	1		1		1		1	1	1			8		
Southfield	182	3	Bond	Nicholas Sen				1					1				2		
West Stockbridge	247	2	Booker	Samuel		1											1		
Williamstown	130	19	Booth	Henry											7		7		
Partridgefield	186	14	Booth	Isaiah		1						1					2		
Partridgefield	186	15	Booth	Jacob	1		1	1		1		1		1			6		
Partridgefield	186	13	Booth	Jesse	1		1					1					3		
Lenox	209	16	Booth	Lemuel				1		1	2		1				5		
Adams	135	38	Booth	Peter	1			1		2	3	1	1				9		
Richmond	206	17	Booth	Samuel		2		1		2	1		1				7		
Dalton	191	11	Bordman	Danl				1					1				2		
Dalton	191	12	Bordman	Danl Jr	1	1		1		3		1					7		
Williamstown	125	12	Bordwell	Obadiah	1	2		1		2	1	1	1				9		
Hancock	161	40	Boss	John	2	1	1	1		1		1	1				8		
Great Barrington	107	17	Bostwick	Adolphus	1			1		2			1				5		
West Stockbridge	247	5	Boughton	Azor			1			3			1				5		
West Stockbridge	247	7	Boughton	David	3	1		1		1	1		1				8		
West Stockbridge	247	6	Boughton	Enos			1			2			1				4		
West Stockbridge	247	4	Boughton	Matthew		1		1				1		1			4		
West Stockbridge	246	9	Boughton	Nathan	1	1	2	1			1	3	1				10		
West Stockbridge	246	8	Boughton	Nathan Jr	1		1			1		1					4		
Cheshire	158	13	Bourn	Francis		1		1		2	2	1	1				8		
Savoy	139	4	Bourne	John	2	3	1		1	1			1				9		
Dalton	191	9	Bow	Jacob	3	1		1			1		1				7		
Pittsfield	202	25	Bow	Simon											5		5		
Tyringham	110	22	Bowdich	Abel Junr		1				1		1					3		
Cheshire	155	23	Bowen	Aaron	1			1		2		1	1				6		
Windsor	167	19	Bowen	Amos		1				1	1	1					4		
Partridgefield	186	3	Bowen	Christopher		1	2		2	1		1		2			9		
Adams	136	18	Bowen	David	1	1		1		1		1		1			6		
Cheshire	155	18	Bowen	Hezekiah		1	1	1		2		1		1			7		
Cheshire	157	37	Bowen	Joseph	5	1		1		1		1	1				10		
Cheshire	157	57	Bowen	Joseph	5	1		1		1		1	1				10		
Becket	265	15	Bowen	Joshua	1	1		1		3	2	1	1	1			11		
Cheshire	155	17	Bowen	Nathan		2	2		1	1	1	1	1				10		
Windsor	167	10	Bowen	Peleg	1			1		3			1				6		
Partridgefield	186	1	Bowen	Peter	1		1	1			1		1	1			6		
Adams	136	19	Bowen	Samuel	2			1		2		1	1				7		
Sheffield	228	11	Bowes	Jacob				1					1				2		
Adams	135	17	Boyd	Samuel											6		6		
Pittsfield	194	11	Boyndon	Joshua		1	1			2		2	1				7		
West Stockbridge	247	8	Boynton	Caleb	1	1	2		1	3	2	1	1				12		
Williamstown	128	6	Boynton	Daniel	1	1		2			2		1				7		
Sandisfield	173	31	Bozworth	Constant		1			1			1		1			4		
Southfield	182	2	Bozworth	Constant			1	1		1			1				4		
Lenox	209	10	Bozworth	David	1	1	2		2	1		2		2			11		
Sandisfield	176	37	Bozworth	Hannah	2	1			1		2		1	1			8		
Bethlehem	181	20	Bozworth	Ichabod	3			1		1			1				6		
Bethlehem	173	21	Bozworth	Jabez		1	1		1			1	1	1			6		
Sandisfield	175	13	Bozworth	John	2	1	1		1	2		3	1				11		
Bethlehem	181	19	Bozworth	Osborn	1	1		1		1			1				6		
New Ashford	162	17	Bracee	Christopher	2		1	1		1	1	1	1				8		
Cheshire	156	33	Bradford	Elisha	3	3			1	1		3	1				12		
Lanesborough	147	2	Bradley	Asahel	1	2		1		1		1	2				8		

TOWN	PG#	LN#	LAST NAME	FIRST NAME	FWM under 10	FWM 10 to 16	FWM 16 to 26	FWM 26 to 45	FWM 45 and over	FWF under 10	FWF 10 to 16	FWF 16 to 26	FWF 26 to 45	FWF 45 and over	TOTAL ALL OTHER	TOTAL SLAVES	TOTALS	DISTRICT/ TOWNSHIP	NOTES
West Stockbridge	247	3	Bradley	David	3	1		1			1		1				7		
Great Barrington	106	35	Bradley	Dimon	1	2		1	1	4	2		1				12		
Lee	259	23	Bradley	Eli	2	1	2	1		1	3		1				11		
Lanesborough	146	12	Bradley	Ephraim	1		1		1	1			1	1			6		
Lee	259	25	Bradley	Jared	2		1	1		1	2	1	1				9		
Lee	259	27	Bradley	Jesse & Jesse Jr		1		1	1	4	1		1	1			10		
Lanesborough	146	8	Bradley	Joel		1		2	1	1		1	1	1			8		
Lanesborough	147	8	Bradley	Joel 2d		1		1				1	1	1			5		
Lee	259	26	Bradley	Joseph	1		1	1		3			1				7		
Great Barrington	109	21	Bradley	Josiah	2	1	1		1	2	2	1	1				11		
Lee	259	20	Bradley	Stephen	2			1			1		1				5		
Lanesborough	146	7	Bradley	Uri	1	1	2	1	1				3	1			10		
West Stockbridge	247	18	Brail	Joseph									1				1		
Bethlehem	181	27	Brakenridge	James	2	2		1		1			1	1			8		
Adams	137	5	Braley	Caleb	3		2		1	1	1	1	1		1		11		
Pittsfield	194	13	Braley	Nathl		2		1		1							4		
Tyringham	115	31	Braman	Nicholas			1					1					2		
Tyringham	115	30	Braman	Samuel		1	1	1				2		1			6		
Richmond	207	7	Branch	Cyprian	1	1		1		1			1				5		
Richmond	207	4	Branch	Levi			1			2	1	1					5		
Richmond	209	6	Branch	Wine		1	2	1		1	1	1		1			8		
Pittsfield	194	9	Brattle	James	1	1		2		1		1	1	2			9		
Pittsfield	194	8	Brattle	William	1		1	1		2	1		1		1		8		
Cheshire	156	11	Brayton	Arnold		1				2		1					4		
Clarkesburg	142	12	Brayton	David	2	1		1		2	2		1				9		
Cheshire	156	6	Brayton	Isaac	2	1	1	1		1		2	1				9		
Cheshire	156	10	Brayton	Stephen		1		1				1		1			4		
Cheshire	156	12	Brayton	Stephen Jun	1			1					1				3		
Tyringham	111	8	Brewer	Davis				1				1					2		
Lenox	209	9	Brewer	Eliab	4			1					1				6		
New Marlborough	238	33	Brewer	Elisha		1		2		1			1				5		
New Marlborough	235	13	Brewer	Isaac	1	1		1			1		1				5		
Tyringham	115	11	Brewer	John			1			1		1					3		
Tyringham	115	9	Brewer	Jonas	1			1		1			1				4		
Tyringham	114	27	Brewer	Joseph			2		1			2	1	1			7		
New Marlborough	235	15	Brewer	Joseph Jun	1	1		1		2	2		1				8		
New Marlborough	235	14	Brewer	Joshua	1			1		1	1	1		1			6		
Tyringham	115	10	Brewer	Josiah Jun			1					1					2		
Tyringham	111	7	Brewer	Nathl	2	2		1		2	1		1				9		
Tyringham	111	9	Brewer	Parker			1				1						2		
Windsor	165	16	Brewster	Henry	2		4	1		1	1		1	1			11		
Washington	215	31	Brewster	Jasper	2			1		1							4		
Becket	265	9	Brewster	Oliver		2		1		3	1	1	2				10		
Loudon	177	13	Bridgen	John	1			1		3			1				6		
Dalton	191	13	Bridges	Edmund		1		1		1			1				4		
Williamstown	127	37	Bridges	Jonathan	1	2	1		1	1	1		1				8		
Adams	135	20	Briggs	Allen	3	1	1	1		1	1	1	1				10		
Adams	137	2	Briggs	Benjamin	1	6	3		1		1	1		1			14		
Hancock	160	21	Briggs	Carey			2	1		1	2	1	1		1		9		
Adams	137	3	Briggs	Elisha	2	2		1	1	3		1	1				11		
Cheshire	155	16	Briggs	Harmon	1		1	1				1		1			5		
New Marlborough	237	2	Brigham	Francis		1	1					1	1				4		
New Marlborough	237	3	Brigham	Jedediah			1			2		1					4		
New Marlborough	235	2	Brigham	Joel	2	1		1		1		1	1				7		
Alford	117	53	Brigham	John				1						1			2		
New Marlborough	237	4	Brigham	John	3			1					1				5		
New Marlborough	236	25	Brigham	Mary	3		1			2	3	1	1				11		
Alford	116	17	Brinsmade	Daniel	1		1						1				3		
Alford	116	29	Brinsmade	Hubbel			1						1				2		
Alford	116	18	Brinsmade	Samuel			1	1				1		1			4		
New Marlborough	238	10	Bristol	Chloe	2		1			2	2	1	1				10		
Alford	117	50	Brittain	William		1		1		1				1			4		
Windsor	165	6	Britton	Squire	2			1		2			1				6		
Hancock	159	8	Broad	Amos	1	1		1		1	2		1				7		
Cheshire	153	10	Broadway	Jeremiah	2		1			1		1					5		
Becket	265	20	Broga	Andrew	1			1		2	2		1				7		
Williamstown	129	37	Bromley	Barber	2		1	1		2			1				7		
Washington	215	39	Brooke	Isaac		1		1	2			1		1			6		
Tyringham	116	3	Brookens	Artemas		1		1			1	2		1			6		
Tyringham	116	4	Brookens	Chester		1	1					1					3		
Williamstown	126	34	Brooks	Benjamin			1			3	1		1				6		
New Marlborough	240	5	Brooks	David			1	1		2	3		1				8		
New Marlborough	238	14	Brooks	Elizabeth	1						1		1				3		
New Marlborough	240	8	Brooks	Jabez	1	1		1				2		1			6		
Pittsfield	195	28	Brooks	Jabez	1	1	2		1	1	2			1			9		
Richmond	207	5	Brooks	Jabez	2	2		1		2			1	1			9		
New Marlborough	232	15	Brooks	James	2	2		1				1		1			7		
New Marlborough	240	4	Brooks	Luther	1		1	1		3			1	1			8		
Pittsfield	195	9	Brooks	Reuben	3			1		1	1		1				7		

97

TOWN	PG#	LN#	LAST NAME	FIRST NAME	\<10	FREE WHITE MALES 10–16	16–26	26–45	45+	\<10	FREE WHITE FEMALES 10–16	16–26	26–45	45+	TOTAL ALL OTHER	TOTAL SLAVES	TOTALS	DISTRICT/ TOWNSHIP	NOTES
Adams	134	13	Brown	Abraham		1	2		1		1			1			6		
Pittsfield	195	24	Brown	Abraham C	1			1		2	2	1					7		
Cheshire	155	36	Brown	Allen	2	1		1	1	1		2					8		
Windsor	165	9	Brown	Alpheus	3			1		1	2	1					8		
West Stockbridge	247	14	Brown	Amos		1	1		1			2	1				6		
Tyringham	111	4	Brown	Asa	2			1				1					4		
Washington	215	1	Brown	Asa	1			1		1	1	2		1			7		
Washington	213	20	Brown	Asahel			1	1		1			1				4		
Tyringham	116	2	Brown	Azariah				1			1		1				3		
Cheshire	155	1	Brown	Benjamin	1	2		2		3	1	1					10		
Cheshire	157	11	Brown	Caleb	1	2	1		1	3		1	1				10		
Adams	135	43	Brown	Chas			3	1		1		2	1				8		
Cheshire	154	24	Brown	Daniel		1	1	3	2	3		1	2	2			15		
Becket	265	21	Brown	David				1					1				2		
Partridgefield	186	19	Brown	David 2d	2	1	1	1		2	1		1				9		
Cheshire	155	11	Brown	Dexter		1	2			4	1		1				9		
Adams	136	7	Brown	Eleazer	1		1		1			1		1			5		
Adams	138	25	Brown	Elijah	3	2		1		1	1		1				9		
Hancock	161	31	Brown	Elijah		1				2		1					4		
Stockbridge	252	12	Brown	Elijah		1		1	1		1	1	1		1		7		
Cheshire	154	40	Brown	Elisha		1	1	1	1	1	1	2		1			9		
Stockbridge	253	1	Brown	Elisha	1	1	1		1	2	1		2				9		
Becket	265	18	Brown	Elkhanah	1	1			1	3	1		1				8		
Cheshire	155	7	Brown	Ezech	1		1	1		2	2		1				8		
Stockbridge	253	2	Brown	Henry		1	1	1		1	1		2				7		
New Marlborough	234	4	Brown	Horatio		1					1			1			3		
Adams	134	20	Brown	Jacob	1	3		1		1	1		1				8		
Pittsfield	194	7	Brown	James	1		2	2		1	1						7		
Tyringham	112	46	Brown	James	2	2		1		1	1		1				8		
Clarkesburg	141	17	Brown	Jesse Jrn		1	1		1	2		1		1			7		
West Stockbridge	247	19	Brown	Joel				1									1		
Cheshire	156	22	Brown	John	2	1		1		1		1	1				7		
West Stockbridge	247	12	Brown	John	1			1		4		2					8		
West Stockbridge	247	21	Brown	John	3			1		1	2		1				8		
Windsor	165	10	Brown	John	3			1	1	1			1	1			8		
Cheshire	155	12	Brown	Joseph			1						1				2		
Cheshire	157	10	Brown	Levi	1		1	1			1		1				5		
Washington	215	2	Brown	Levi		1		1			1						3		
Sheffield	230	1	Brown	Lewis											4		4		
Adams	134	11	Brown	Luke	2			1		1	2		1				7		
Stockbridge	253	7	Brown	Luther			1			1			1				3		
Tyringham	113	49	Brown	Moses	3	2	1		1	1		2		1			11		
Hancock	161	33	Brown	Nathan			1			3	2		1				7		
Cheshire	156	16	Brown	Nicholas	1	1	2	1		2	1	1	1		1		11		
New Marlborough	238	9	Brown	Perez	1	1		1		3	1	2	1				10		
New Marlborough	232	35	Brown	Rhoda	1					1			1				3		
Tyringham	115	3	Brown	Richard	1			1	1				1				4		
Sandisfield	174	15	Brown	Sanford	2		1	1		1	1	1					8		
Lenox	209	7	Brown	Thomas	2	1		1		2		1	1				8		
Pittsfield	194	21	Brown	Thomas	3			1		1	1		1	1			8		
Richmond	208	35	Brown	Tristram	1			1		1			1	1			5		
Adams	135	37	Brown	William	4		1	1		2		1					9		
Cheshire	155	2	Brown	William	2	1	1	1	1	2	2		1				11		
West Stockbridge	247	11	Brown	Stephen	3	1			1	2	2	2	1				12		
Partridgefield	186	16	Brown	Daniel	1		1			2		1					5		
Adams	135	23	Browne	Ichabod	1		1		1	2	1		1				7		
Partridgefield	186	10	Browning	David		1		1					1				3		
Partridgefield	185	9	Browning	Joseph	1			1		2	1		1				6		
Partridgefield	185	20	Browning	Solomon	1			1		1		1					4		
Partridgefield	186	11	Browning	Tristram	2	1		1		2	2	1	2				11		
Williamstown	129	4	Brownson	Asa	4			1		1		1					7		
West Stockbridge	246	12	Brownson	Ira			1										1		
Washington	216	4	Bruce	Abner		1	1						1				3		
Washington	215	28	Bruce	Comfort	1			1		2			1				5		
Lanesborough	147	6	Brundige	Nathan		1				1		1					3		
Lanesborough	147	9	Brundige	Nathan	1			1				1					3		
Egremont	120	11	Brunson	John	2	1		1		3			1				8		
Alford	116	31	Brunson	Nathan				1					1				2		
Alford	117	6	Brunson	William		1	1		1	1		1	1	1			7		
New Marlborough	238	28	Bryan	Elizabeth		1							1				2		
Sheffield	224	3	Bryan	Ezekiel	1			1				1					3		
Williamstown	126	33	Bryan	Jacob			1						1				2		
New Marlborough	240	30	Bryan	Reuben	2			1		3			1				7		
Sheffield	225	4	Bryan	Timothy	2	1		1		2			1				7		
Cheshire	154	26	Bryant	David		1				1		1					3		
Pittsfield	195	22	Bryant	John	2	1		1		1		1					6		
Dalton	191	15	Buchard	Matthew	1	1	1		1	1	1	1		1			8		
Lanesborough	146	14	Buck	Ebenezer	3	1			1	1	2		1				9		
New Marlborough	235	6	Buck	Ebenezer	2			1		2			1				7		

TOWN	PG#	LN#	LAST NAME	FIRST NAME	FREE WHITE MALES					FREE WHITE FEMALES					TOTAL ALL OTHER	TOTAL SLAVES	TOTALS	DISTRICT/ TOWNSHIP	NOTES
					under 10	10 to 16	16 to 26	26 to 45	45 and over	under 10	10 to 16	16 to 26	26 to 45	45 and over					
Williamstown	128	7	Buck	Ezekiel			1						1				2		
Cheshire	157	32	Buck	Asahel	2	3		1		1		1	1				9		
West Stockbridge	247	22	Buckley	Billy	2		1			2			1				6		
Williamstown	131	21	Buckley	Charles	1	3	1		1	1	1		1				9		
Cheshire	156	14	Bucklin	Darius	1		2		1				2				6		
Adams	136	9	Bucklin	Jeremiah		1	3	1	1	2	1	2		1			12		
Cheshire	154	25	Bucklin	John				1					1				2		
Sandisfield	176	19	Buckman	Reuben			1			2		1					4		
Great Barrington	108	22	Budd	John		1	1	2		1		2	1				8		
Becket	265	17	Buel	Ichabod		1		1					1				3		
Sheffield	221	9	Buel	William		1	1			2		1			1		6		
Tyringham	113	24	Buell	Joseph	2	1		1		1	2	1	2				10		
Clarksburg	141	14	Buerall	Isaac			1			3			1				5		
Williamstown	132	23	Bulkley	Charles Jr		2							1				3		
Williamstown	132	7	Bulkley	Gershom	1		1			2		1					5		
Williamstown	128	14	Bulkley	Robbins J		1		1		2	1		1		1		7		
Lanesborough	147	17	Bull	Nehemiah		2			1				2				5		
Partridgefield	185	8	Bull	Seth			1			1			1				3		
Sheffield	222	30	Bull	William	3		1					1	1				6		
Sheffield	224	31	Bullard	Asa	2								1				3		
New Marlborough	235	5	Bullard	Benjamin	3		1	1		1			1				7		
New Marlborough	235	7	Bullard	Eleazer		1	1		1		1	2		1			7		
New Marlborough	235	10	Bullard	Elijah	1		1			1			1				4		
Partridgefield	185	18	Bullard	Lemuel	1	1		1		2			1				6		
Stockbridge	252	3	Bullock	William	2	1		1		1	1		1				7		
Egremont	120	14	Bunts	Ephraim Jr	3	1		1		1	1		1				8		
Williamstown	127	13	Burbank	Daniel			1	2	1		1	2		1			8		
Becket	265	22	Burdell	John			1		1			1	1				4		
Savoy	140	27	Burden	Bethuel	1	1		1		1			1				5		
Savoy	141	4	Burden	Lemuel	1		1	1		2	2	1	1				9		
Lee	259	13	Burden	Lot		1		1		3			1				6		
Lee	259	30	Burden	Noah		1			1				2				4		
Lee	259	14	Burden	Seth	2			1		1			1				5		
Pittsfield	195	20	Burdich	Francis			1			2			1				4		
Hancock	159	2	Burdick	Asa		1		1		3		1	1				7		
Hancock	159	30	Burdick	Hasard	3			1		1	1		1				7		
Williamstown	130	32	Burdick	Thomas	2	1		1		3		1	1				9		
Hancock	159	1	Burdick	Wait			1					1		1			3		
Williamstown	126	32	Burges	Jacob				1					1				2		
Williamstown	126	31	Burges	Josiah	1	2	2		1	1			1				8		
Pittsfield	195	25	Burgess	Joseph	1	1		1		1			1				5		
Great Barrington	106	16	Burghardt	Andrew	1	1		1		1		1	1	1			6		
Great Barrington	107	46	Burghardt	Hendrick			3	1	2	2	1	1	1	1			11		
West Stockbridge	247	23	Burghardt	Isaac	2		1			1			1				5		
Great Barrington	108	7	Burghardt	Jack											11		11		
Great Barrington	106	17	Burghardt	John				1					2		1		4		
Great Barrington	105	44	Burghardt	John 2d		1	1		1			1	2				6		
Great Barrington	107	19	Burghardt	Lambert	1	2		1		2			1	1			8		
Great Barrington	104	25	Burgharot	John 3d	2	1	1		2		1		1	1			9		
West Stockbridge	246	13	Burghart	Lamber	1	1	1		1	1	1	1		1			8		
Lanesborough	147	5	Burgin	Benjamin		1		1					1				3		
Lanesborough	146	5	Burhance	Henry	1			1				1					3		
Lanesborough	147	11	Burhance	Henry				1					1				2		
Cheshire	155	13	Burlingame	Charles	2	1			1		1	1		1			7		
Cheshire	155	26	Burlingame	Elisha	1	1		1		2	2	1		1			9		
Cheshire	155	15	Burlingame	Jeremiah	4			1		2	1		1				9		
West Stockbridge	247	20	Burlison	Amos	1	1	1		1	3	1	2		1			11		
Partridgefield	185	13	Burnett	Daniel	3					2			1				7		
Partridgefield	186	8	Burnham	Elizeer			1	1					1				3		
Sheffield	228	5	Burrall	David	2	1	1	1		2	1		1				9		
Sheffield	230	8	Burrall	Jabez	1	1	3	1		2	1	1	1	1			12		
Sheffield	230	2	Burrall	Jonathan	2		3	1		1	2		1				10		
Windsor	164	18	Burrows	John				1									1		
Windsor	164	17	Burrows	John Jun			1					1	1				3		
Sheffield	224	18	Burrows	Joseph			2		1	1			1				5		
Pittsfield	195	17	Burt	Ebenezer	1			1		3			1				6		
Richmond	208	3	Burt	Henry	1	1	1		1				1				5		
Pittsfield	195	15	Burt	Oliver			1					1	1				4		
Pittsfield	195	16	Burt	Thomas		1	1	1		4	1		1				9		
Cheshire	153	15	Burton	Amos		1		1		1		1		1			5		
Cheshire	156	1	Burton	Anthony		1						1	1				3		
Cheshire	155	21	Burton	Elijah	2	2			1		1	1	1		1		9		
Cheshire	154	34	Burton	William	2	1		1		1	1	1					7		
Stockbridge	252	1	Bush	Aaron		1		1			2		1				5		
Sheffield	224	23	Bush	Daniel	1		1		1	1	1			1			6		
Pittsfield	195	1	Bush	David	2	1	1	1	1	1			1	1			9		
Pittsfield	194	22	Bush	David Junr	3	2	2	1			1		2				11		
Washington	216	6	Bush	Gideon	1	2	2	1		2	1	3		1			13		
Sheffield	221	5	Bush	Horace	1			1		1			1				7		

99

TOWN	PG#	LN#	LAST NAME	FIRST NAME	FREE WHITE MALES under 10	10 to 16	16 to 26	26 to 45	45 and over	FREE WHITE FEMALES under 10	10 to 16	16 to 26	26 to 45	45 and over	TOTAL ALL OTHER	TOTAL SLAVES	TOTALS	DISTRICT/ TOWNSHIP	NOTES
Sheffield	222	11	Bush	Obadiah	1	1	1	2		1	1	1	1				9		
Sheffield	221	4	Bush	Rachel		1						3		1	1		6		
Sheffield	226	9	Bushnall	Samll		1	3	1	1		1	1		1			9		
Sheffield	226	15	Bushnall	Samll Jr	1		1			1	1	1					5		
Sheffield	229	15	Bushnall	Ziba	2			1		2			1				6		
Cheshire	157	52	Busk	Asahel	2	3		1		1		1	1				9		
Windsor	168	5	Bussy	Jesse	2		1			1		1					5		
Pittsfield	194	20	Butler	George	4	1		1			1		1				8		
Zoar	143	23	Butler	Isaiah	3	1		1		1			1				7		
Zoar	143	8	Butler	Isaiah Zada			1			2		1					4		
Lenox	209	8	Butler	Jethro	2		3		1	2	2		1				11		
Pittsfield	195	18	Butler	Joseph		1	1	1	1	1	1		1				7		
Pittsfield	195	19	Butler	Josiah		1	1		1	1		1	1				6		
Great Barrington	107	4	Butler	Martin			1			2		2					5		
Lenox	209	15	Butler	Matthew		1	1		1	1	2	2	1				9		
New Marlborough	238	1	Butler	Nathan	2			2	1	1	1		2				9		
Lanesborough	147	4	Butler	Silas	1			1		1		1					4		
Pittsfield	195	10	Butler	Simeon			1					1					2		
Loudon	177	17	Butter	Isaac			1			1		1					3		
Great Barrington	108	10	Buttolph	Roger		1		1					1				3		
Dalton	191	14	Butts	Josiah	1			1		2	1		1				6		
Partridgefield	185	22	Butts	Rufus		2	1		1	3	1	1		1			10		
Stockbridge	252	15	Byington	Isaiah	3	3	3	1		1		1	1				13		
Partridgefield	186	5	Byxbe	Aaron				2					1				3		
Washington	216	15	Byxbe	Moses		1	2		1	2	1	1	1				9		
Partridgefield	185	7	Byxbe	Solomon	1		1					1					3		
Alford	117	35	Cabler	Hendrick	1	1	1	1	1	1			1				7		
Partridgefield	186	27	Cad	Phineas		2	1	1		1	2		1				8		
Mount Washington	232	6	Cade	Thomas				1		1			1				3		
Pittsfield	195	40	Cadwell	Abigail		1	1			1	1		1				5		
Pittsfield	196	1	Cadwell	Eliar	3		1	1		1	1		1				8		
Becket	266	8	Cadwell	Jeremiah	1		1						1				3		
Stockbridge	253	24	Cadwell	Mathew			2		2				1				5		
Pittsfield	195	39	Cadwell	Timothy	2	1		1	1		1	4	1				11		
Dalton	191	20	Cady	Chester	2		1				1						4		
Partridgefield	186	31	Cady	Eleazer	3			1	1	1	2						8		
Windsor	168	23	Cady	Elias	1		1		1		1		1				5		
Partridgefield	186	29	Cady	Philip	1		1	1				1	1				5		
Great Barrington	107	12	Cady	Reuben	1	1		1		1	1		1				6		
Dalton	191	17	Cady	Rufus	2	1	1		1	1	2	2		1			11		
Dalton	191	19	Cady	Wm. Waterman	1			1		1			1				4		
Hancock	159	10	Cain	William O.	2			1					1				5		
Sheffield	225	17	Calder	Thomas											4		4		
Adams	138	1	Caldwell	James	2	1		1		2	1	1	1				9		
Windsor	167	17	Calisle	James	1	1	1	1		1			2				7		
Tyringham	119	2	Calkins	Elisha		1	1						1				3		
Sheffield	227	25	Callender	Aaron		1		1		2	1	1	1				8		
Sheffield	227	24	Callender	Abner	2	1	1		1	1	1	1					8		
Sheffield	228	37	Callender	Archibald	1		1			1			1				4		
Sheffield	227	26	Callender	Comfort				1			1		1				3		
Sheffield	228	36	Callender	Joseph		1		1	1		1			1			5		
Sheffield	227	33	Callender	Silas	1			1		2	1	1	1				7		
Lanesborough	150	34	Camp	Daniel											3		3		
New Marlborough	241	1	Camp	Hannah	2					1		1	2				6		
New Marlborough	239	19	Camp	John	1		1			2		1					5		
Clarkesburg	142	6	Camp	Jonah	1		1					1					3		
New Ashford	163	15	Campbel	William	2	1	1		2				1				8		
West Stockbridge	247	26	Campbell	Abigail						1			1				2		
Pittsfield	196	5	Campbell	David	2	1	2	1		2	2		1				11		
West Stockbridge	247	27	Campbell	George			1					1					2		
Adams	138	26	Campbell	Joseph	1		1						1				3		
Washington	214	8	Campbell	Nathan	2		1				1	1					5		
Mount Washington	232	16	Campbell	Robert		2	1			1		1					5		
Washington	215	4	Campbell	Robert	1		1			1		1					4		
Sheffield	224	8	Cande	Theophilus		1	1		1		1		1				5		
Sheffield	224	7	Cande	Zaccheus	1		1	1		1		1					5		
New Marlborough	240	1	Canfield	Daniel	4	1	1	1		2			1				10		
New Marlborough	236	30	Canfield	Gideon	1		1			1		1					4		
New Marlborough	237	26	Canfield	Gideon	2	1		1		1		1					6		
Sandisfield	175	17	Canfield	John Esq	2		2		1	3	2	3		1			14		
Sandisfield	175	16	Canfield	John Jr	2		1					1					4		
Tyringham	111	13	Canfield	Oliver			1					1					2		
New Marlborough	237	15	Canfield	Oran		1				2		1					4		
New Marlborough	240	2	Canfield	Samuel				1		1			1				3		
New Marlborough	239	5	Canfield	Samuel Jun	2		1			2		1					6		
Tyringham	111	12	Canfield	Thomas				1			1		1				3		
Hancock	160	19	Capron	Danfield	1	1		1		1			1				5		
Tyringham	112	28	Card	John		1	1	1	1	1			1				7		
Lanesborough	149	20	Card	William	1		1			2			1				5		

TOWN	PG#	LN#	LAST NAME	FIRST NAME	FREE WHITE MALES under 10	10 to 16	16 to 26	26 to 45	45 and over	FREE WHITE FEMALES under 10	10 to 16	16 to 26	26 to 45	45 and over	TOTAL ALL OTHER	TOTAL SLAVES	TOTALS	DISTRICT/TOWNSHIP	NOTES
Williamstown	129	41	Carey	Hezekiah	2	1		1			1		1				6		
Savoy	140	12	Carpenter	Abel	1			1		2			1				5		
Stockbridge	253	23	Carpenter	Abner		2	2		1	3	1	4		1			14		
Tyringham	113	18	Carpenter	Amos	1	2	1	1		3	1	2	1				12		
Savoy	139	2	Carpenter	Benjamin	2			1		1			1	1			6		
Adams	138	31	Carpenter	Calvin			2					1					3		
Savoy	139	8	Carpenter	Cyrel		1						1					2		
Savoy	140	38	Carpenter	Elisha		1	1		1			1		1			5		
Savoy	139	7	Carpenter	Ezra		3		1			1			1			6		
Savoy	139	9	Carpenter	Ezra Junr	1			1	1				1				4		
Lenox	209	19	Carpenter	Joshua	2			1		3			1				7		
Savoy	140	11	Carpenter	Lewis	3			1					1				5		
Adams	136	4	Carpenter	Nathaniel	3	1		2		4	1	1	2				14		
Savoy	140	33	Carpenter	Nathaniel				1					1				2		
Cheshire	154	9	Carpenter	Rufus			1			3	2		1		1		8		
Richmond	208	31	Carpenter	Simeon		1		1				1		1			4		
Cheshire	156	30	Carpenter	Stephen	1		2			1		1		1			6		
Adams	137	25	Carpenter	Uriah	1			1				1	1				4		
Dalton	191	18	Carrier	Elisha	1			1		1			1				4		
Washington	213	17	Carrier	Levi	2	2		1		1			1				7		
Tyringham	113	11	Carrier	Thomas	3			1		1			1				6		
Lenox	209	17	Carrol	James	1			1	1	3			1	2			9		
Sheffield	228	12	Carter	Amos				1					1				2		
New Marlborough	233	11	Carter	Lyman		1				1		1					3		
Becket	266	7	Carter	Marcus	1		1						1				3		
Lanesborough	147	22	Carter	Peter B.	2	2	1		1	2	1	2		2			13		
Sheffield	229	16	Carter	Robert	1			1		2			1				5		
Lanesborough	153	4	Carven	James		2	1		1			1		1			6		
Adams	134	1	Carver	Peter	1			1					1				3		
Stockbridge	253	29	Carwell	Ezra	1	1			1	1	1						5		
Sheffield	223	7	Case	Ephraim		1		1				1		2			5		
Washington	215	12	Case	Ezekiel	2	2		1		4	1		1				11		
Loudon	179	19	Case	Farran			1					1					3		
Becket	265	34	Case	Hannah Wid	1					1				1			3		
Loudon	178	8	Case	James	2	1	1		1	2		3	1				11		
New Marlborough	239	15	Case	Lemuel	1	1		1				1					4		
Tyringham	113	21	Case	Manning	1			1		1		1					4		
Loudon	179	13	Case	Ozias	2	1	1	1		2	1		1				9		
Loudon	179	31	Case	Ozias Jr		1				2		1					4		
New Marlborough	238	24	Case	Seth		1			1			2		1			5		
Loudon	179	16	Case	Timothy	3	1		1		1	3	1	1				11		
Loudon	179	12	Case	Truman				1		4	1		1				7		
Lanesborough	152	20	Casey	Edward	2	1		1		2	1		1				8		
Richmond	206	18	Castle	Ebenezer			1		1		1	1	1				5		
Richmond	206	19	Castle	Samuel	1			1		1	1						4		
New Marlborough	234	22	Catlin	Elijah	3	1	1	1		1	1		1	1			10		
New Marlborough	234	26	Catlin	Elijah	1			1		4		1	1				8		
Sheffield	227	9	Catlin	James			2					1	1				5		
Tyringham	111	11	Caulfield	Aaron				1				1					2		
Sheffield	222	22	Cawle	Elisha	1	1		1					1				4		
Sheffield	223	5	Cawle	Joseph	1			1					1				3		
Sheffield	223	4	Cawle	Nathanael				1		1	1		1	1			5		
Sheffield	222	19	Cawle	William	2	1		1		1			1				6		
Stockbridge	253	12	Center	Ebenezer	1	1		1		2		1	1				7		
Cheshire	157	16	Chace	John		1		1	1	1			1	1			6		
Cheshire	157	39	Chace	Nehemiah		1		1		1		1		1			5		
Cheshire	157	59	Chace	Nehemiah	3			1		2			1				7		
Lee	260	1	Chadwick	Abiatha	2	1			1	3	1	1	1				10		
Lee	260	21	Chadwick	Archelaus	2	2		1		1	1			1			8		
Great Barrington	109	48	Chadwick	Caleb	3	1			1		1			1			7		
Tyringham	112	51	Chadwick	Ebenz	1	2			1	3	1			1			9		
Lee	260	18	Chadwick	Sama			2	1						2			5		
Lee	260	24	Chadwick	Thomas			1						1				2		
Becket	266	2	Chaffee	Thomas Jr	5			1					1				7		
Windsor	165	14	Chaffen	Darius	1		1		1	1		1	1				6		
Becket	265	33	Chaffer	Benja	3	1		1			2		1				8		
Becket	265	28	Chaffer	Jonathan 2d	4			1					1				6		
Becket	265	32	Chaffer	Jonathan 2d	1		1			2		1					5		
Becket	265	23	Chaffer	Nathan			1			1		1					3		
Becket	265	31	Chaffer	Thomas		2		1			1		1				5		
Great Barrington	108	19	Chamberlain	Joel	2	1		1		1	2		1				8		
Bethlehem	172	1	Chamberlain	Samuel	1			1		3	1			1			7		
Partridgefield	186	30	Chamberlin	Asa	2			1		1	1		1				6		
Dalton	191	23	Chamberlin	Benja		2			1	1	1	1		1			7		
Sheffield	230	5	Chamberlin	Ebenezer		1			1					1			3		
Washington	214	20	Chamberlin	Eli		1	2			1		2	1				7		
Dalton	191	22	Chamberlin	Eliph		2		1				1	1	1			6		
Dalton	191	27	Chamberlin	Elisha	1			1		3			1				6		
Dalton	191	25	Chamberlin	Jacob	3		1	1		1			1				7		

101

TOWN	PG#	LN#	LAST NAME	FIRST NAME	\<10	10-16	16-26	26-45	45+	\<10	10-16	16-26	26-45	45+	TOTAL ALL OTHER	TOTAL SLAVES	TOTALS	DISTRICT/ TOWNSHIP	NOTES
Pittsfield	196	8	Chamberlin	John			1		2					1			4		
Dalton	191	26	Chamberlin	John Jr		1	3	1									5		
Dalton	191	21	Chamberlin	Joseph					1			2		1			4		
Dalton	191	24	Chamberlin	Martin	2	1	1	1		1	1	1	1				9		
Williamstown	128	21	Chamberlin	Nathaniel	1	3		1			2		1				8		
Williamstown	129	24	Chamberlin	Paoli				1					1	1			3		
Sheffield	230	25	Chamberlin	Solomon		1		1		2			1				5		
Alford	116	5	Champeon	Lynd	3	2	1			1	1		1				9		
Lee	260	10	Chanter	George		1	1		1					1			4		
Lee	260	11	Chanter	William	1		1		1					1			4		
New Marlborough	235	18	Chapel	Amos	1				1	2	1	2		1			8		
New Marlborough	233	3	Chapel	Giles	1		1			1		1					4		
New Marlborough	233	2	Chapel	Joseph		1	1		1					1			4		
Southfield	183	3	Chapel	Richard	1	1	3		1	1	1	1	1	1			11		
New Marlborough	236	2	Chapin	Amos	1	1	1		1	1	2	1	1				9		
Richmond	207	40	Chapin	David	1	2	2		1	1	2			1			10		
Tyringham	113	26	Chapin	Joseph	2	1	1	1		1	2	1	1	1			11		
New Marlborough	236	3	Chapin	Joshua				1						1			2		
New Marlborough	237	16	Chapin	Rachel			1				1			1			3		
New Marlborough	234	33	Chapin	Aaron	1			1		1			1				4		
New Marlborough	232	6	Chapins	Jonathan	1			1		2			1				5		
New Marlborough	233	33	Chapins	Nathan	1	1		1	1	1		2	1	1			9		
New Marlborough	236	5	Chapins	Peter	2	1	2			2	2		1				11		
New Marlborough	233	10	Chapins	Phinehas	3	1		1		2	1		1				9		
Hancock	159	6	Chapman	Amasa	4	2	1		2	2	4	2		2			19		
Great Barrington	108	23	Chapman	Barnabas		1		1		1		1	2				6		
Stockbridge	253	27	Chapman	Caleb				1			1		1	1			3		
Stockbridge	253	26	Chapman	Caleb Jr			1			2	1	1					5		
Windsor	168	2	Chapman	Daniel	1		1			1			1	1			5		
Pittsfield	195	41	Chapman	David		1			1	1	1	3		1			8		
Great Barrington	109	7	Chapman	Ezra	1		2		1	2	3			1			10		
Stockbridge	253	28	Chapman	James		1						1					3		
Great Barrington	109	14	Chapman	Jebediah	2			1		1			1				5		
Lenox	209	20	Chapman	Jesse	3	1	1	1	1	1			1				9		
New Marlborough	238	18	Chapman	John	3	1	2		1	2	2			1			12		
Pittsfield	195	33	Chapman	Olcutt	3	1		1					1				6		
Windsor	167	34	Chapman	Samuel			1			1			1				3		
Alford	117	42	Chapman	Stephen				1						1			2		
Williamstown	132	2	Chapman	William	1			1					1				3		
Washington	214	14	Chappel	Ebenezer 2d			1			1		1					3		
Bethlehem	173	12	Chappel	Edgecomb			1					1					2		
Richmond	207	27	Chappel	James				1		1							5		
Washington	213	11	Chappel	Jonathan	1		1					1					3		
Washington	214	13	Chappel	Joseph	2	2	2		1	1	1		1				10		
Bethlehem	173	11	Chappel	Samuel	2		2		1	1	2		1				9		
Washington	214	10	Chappel	William	1	1	1		1	2		2		1			9		
Great Barrington	105	24	Chappell	Dan	2	2	1	1		1	1		2				10		
Tyringham	112	25	Chappell	William	1	1				2				1			5		
Washington	213	25	Chapple	Ebenezer	2		2			2	1	3		1			11		
Adams	134	24	Chase	Benjamin		2	1		1	1	1		1	1			8		
Lee	260	6	Chase	Levi		1	1		1	2				1			6		
Becket	266	9	Chase	Richard				1		2	3	1		1			8		
Sheffield	225	37	Chatfield	Joel	1			1		2	1		1				6		
Adams	134	28	Cheesborough	Elisha	3	1		1		1	1		1				8		
Adams	134	37	Cheesborough	Nathl	2	1		1		2		1					7		
Adams	134	29	Cheesborough	Oliver	2		1	1		1			1				6		
Adams	134	27	Cheesborough	Silvester				1		1			1	1			4		
Great Barrington	109	8	Cheney	William	1					1			1				3		
Great Barrington	107	39	Cherrytree	John	1			1		3			1				6		
Great Barrington	107	22	Cherrytree	Reuben	3	1		1		2			1				8		
Becket	265	25	Childs	Daniel	4		1		1			2					8		
Becket	265	30	Childs	Isaac	1	1	1			1			2				6		
Lee	260	15	Childs	Job	2			1	1			1		1			6		
Becket	265	29	Childs	Jonas				1						1			2		
Williamstown	128	8	Childs	Penuel	2	1	1	1		2	2	1	1				11		
Pittsfield	195	31	Childs	Timothy	2		1	1	1	2	3		1				11		
Lee	260	16	Childs	William			1										1		
Stockbridge	253	9	Childs	William								1					1		
Windsor	164	2	Chilion	Benjamin	2		2		1	1	2		1				9		
Lanesborough	149	1	Chilson	Louise			1		1	1	2	1					6		
Richmond	206	4	Chittenden	William		1	1							1			3		
Richmond	208	30	Chittendin	Calvin	2			1		1			1				5		
Lee	260	13	Church	Anna							1	1		1			3		
Becket	266	1	Church	Anthony	1	1		1		1	1		1				6		
Great Barrington	105	1	Church	Joseph		1		1			1			1			4		
Lee	260	14	Church	Levi		1	1						1				3		
New Marlborough	234	28	Church	Noah		3	1			1	1	1	1				8		
Washington	214	26	Church	Richard		1		1		1	1	1					5		
Great Barrington	108	33	Church	Samuel	2	2	1	1		2			1	1			10		
Lanesborough	147	21	Church	Samuel W.	1			1		1			1				4		

TOWN	PG#	LN#	LAST NAME	FIRST NAME	FREE WHITE MALES under 10	10 to 16	16 to 26	26 to 45	45 and over	FREE WHITE FEMALES under 10	10 to 16	16 to 26	26 to 45	45 and over	TOTAL ALL OTHER	TOTAL SLAVES	TOTALS	DISTRICT/TOWNSHIP	NOTES
Stockbridge	254	2	Churchill	Daniel			1			1		1					3		
Stockbridge	253	30	Churchill	Elihu															
Stockbridge	253	25	Churchill	Jacob	1	1	1		1	2	1		1				8		
Pittsfield	195	34	Churchill	John		2			1		1	1		1			6		
Sandisfield	177	5	Churchill	John	2			1		2			1				6		
Pittsfield	195	35	Churchill	John 2d	1	1		1		4	1		1				9		
Tyringham	111	18	Churchill	Saml	2		1	1					1				5		
Stockbridge	254	1	Churchill	Samuel			2		1				1	1			5		
Sandisfield	174	6	Claffen	Joshua	1			1		3			1				6		
Sandisfield	173	12	Claffen	Robert	3			1		1			1				6		
Tyringham	111	5	Clafford	John	2			1					1				4		
New Marlborough	235	22	Claflin	Abner			1	1	1	1		2		1			7		
Cheshire	155	14	Claflin	Allen				1		1	2		1				5		
Cheshire	154	27	Claflin	George		1				1		1					3		
Washington	213	35	Clark	Amos			1	1		3			1				6		
Washington	213	34	Clark	Augustus	2			1		1			1	1			6		
Cheshire	154	12	Clark	Benjamin		1	1		1		2	1		1			7		
Sandisfield	171	6	Clark	Benjamin					1	1	1	2	1	1			7		
Hancock	160	32	Clark	Caleb	3	1				1	1		1				8		
Loudon	178	5	Clark	Comfort	2			1		4			1	1			9		
New Marlborough	238	22	Clark	Daniel	4	2		1			1		1				9		
Sheffield	227	28	Clark	David	1		1		1	1	1			1			6		
Washington	216	2	Clark	Dillingham		1	1						1				3		
Dalton	191	30	Clark	Ephraim	3	1		1		1			1				7		
Washington	214	19	Clark	Frederick	1			1		2			1				5		
New Marlborough	232	30	Clark	George	2		1			1	1		1				6		
Cheshire	153	13	Clark	Hannah	1								1	1			3		
Lanesborough	147	18	Clark	Hezekiah	3	1		1		2	2		1				10		
Washington	215	37	Clark	Hubbard	2			2					1				5		
Pittsfield	195	38	Clark	Ichabod	1	1			1	1	3			1			8		
New Marlborough	238	7	Clark	Jacob		1		1			1		1				4		
Lanesborough	151	11	Clark	Jahleel	1	1	1	1	1		1	1	1	1			9		
Loudon	178	11	Clark	James	1	1		1		3	1		1				8		
Sandisfield	171	7	Clark	James	1	1		1		1		1					5		
Sheffield	227	29	Clark	Joel			1	1					1				3		
New Marlborough	232	34	Clark	John			1										1		
Dalton	191	29	Clark	John Cook	3			1			1		2				7		
Partridgefield	186	26	Clark	Joseph	1				1	2	1	1	1	1			8		
Loudon	178	12	Clark	Joseph W.			1	1						1			3		
Windsor	168	24	Clark	Joshua	2	4			1	2		1		1			11		
Lanesborough	147	19	Clark	Levi	1	2	4		1	2	1	2		1			14		
Pittsfield	196	3	Clark	Nathan		1				1			1				3		
New Marlborough	236	11	Clark	Phebe	1								1				2		
Great Barrington	109	43	Clark	Rodman	2	2	1			1			1				7		
Lenox	212	2	Clark	Samuel			1	1		1	3	1	1				8		
Sandisfield	172	18	Clark	Samuel			1										1		
Washington	214	18	Clark	Silas	1		1	1					1				4		
Dalton	191	28	Clark	Solomon	3	1		1		1	1		1				8		
New Marlborough	232	21	Clark	Thomas	1	1		1					1				4		
Pittsfield	196	9	Clark	Thomas	1	1	1		1	1	1		1				7		
Sheffield	230	33	Clark	Uzziel		1	3	1			2	2	2				11		
Windsor	168	21	Clark	William		1				2			1				4		
New Marlborough	232	12	Clark	Winthrop		1							1				2		
Lee	260	19	Clarke	Jabez	4	2	3	1		1	1	2	1				15		
Stockbridge	253	8	Clarke	James	3				1		1		1				6		
Lee	260	12	Clarke	Jesse	3	1		1		2	2	1	1				11		
Adams	136	32	Clarke	John	1			1					1				3		
Lee	260	20	Clarke	Jonathan	2	3		1		2			1				9		
Becket	265	26	Clarke	Joseph	3			1		1		1					6		
Becket	266	4	Clarke	Keziah		1	1				1			1			4		
Adams	139	8	Clarke	Moses	3				1	2	2		1				9		
Clarkesburg	141	10	Clarke	Nicolas	1	2	3	2	1		1	1		2			13		
Williamstown	130	18	Clarke	Noble			1					1					2		
Clarkesburg	141	8	Clarke	Stephen			1		1	1	1			1			5		
Zoar	143	29	Clarke	Supply		1	1		1				1	1			5		
Zoar	143	31	Clarke	Supply 2d	2	1		1		1	1		1				7		
Zoar	143	30	Clarke	Sylvanus			1			2		1	1				5		
Becket	266	5	Clarke	Thomas	1			1		2			1				5		
Great Barrington	105	43	Cleaveland	Lemuel	1				1		1		3	1			7		
Tyringham	115	28	Clerk	Eli			1			1		1		1			4		
Tyringham	115	22	Clerk	Francis	3	4	1		1	2	1		1				13		
Tyringham	115	26	Clerk	John		2	1			2							6		
Tyringham	115	29	Clerk	Reuben				1	1					1			3		
Tyringham	112	42	Clerk	Silas	3			1		1			1				6		
Tyringham	110	18	Clerk	Walter		2	1	1			1	1					6		
Dalton	191	35	Cleveland	Aaron	3		1				2		1				7		
Dalton	191	36	Cleveland	Asahel			1					1					2		
Dalton	191	32	Cleveland	Henry		2			1			3		1			7		
Dalton	191	34	Cleveland	Jedediah	3	1		1		1	2	2	1				11		
Dalton	191	33	Cleveland	Sarah	2		1				2	1	1				7		

103

TOWN	PG#	LN#	LAST NAME	FIRST NAME	FREE WHITE MALES					FREE WHITE FEMALES					TOTAL ALL OTHER	TOTAL SLAVES	TOTALS	DISTRICT/ TOWNSHIP	NOTES
					under 10	10 to 16	16 to 26	26 to 45	45 and over	under 10	10 to 16	16 to 26	26 to 45	45 and over					
Mount Washington	231	14	Cline	Frederick	1			1		1		1					4		
New Ashford	163	29	Clother	Jesse	1	1	1	1		1	1	1					7		
Mount Washington	232	21	Coan	David	1	1		1		1		1					5		
Stockbridge	253	16	Cobb	Elijah W.	1	1		1		3		1					7		
Williamstown	131	26	Codding	Robert			1		1	1	1		1				5		
Washington	213	5	Coding	Cobb	2			1		2			1				6		
Stockbridge	253	13	Codner	Abram					1		1	1	1	1			5		
Mount Washington	232	14	Coe	Amos	1	1	1			2		1					6		
Egremont	119	7	Coe	Jesse	2			1		1			2				6		
Mount Washington	232	23	Coe	Seth			1			2		1					4		
Adams	134	35	Coffin	Laban	2		1	1		2		1	1				8		
Loudon	178	16	Coft	Eliphalet	1			1		2		1					5		
Pittsfield	195	32	Cogswell	Benja		1	1	1		2	1	1	1				8		
Becket	266	10	Cogswell	Daniel				1									1		
Hancock	158	2	Cogswell	Daniel				9	1			3	7				20		
Stockbridge	253	17	Cogswell	Nathan			1										1		
Pittsfield	196	2	Cogswell	Rufus		1			1	1		2	1				6		
Richmond	208	22	Cogswell	Samuel	1	1		1		1		1		2			7		
Hancock	161	6	Cogswell	Solomon	1		1	1		1				1			5		
Adams	136	11	Colbourn	Eleanor				1	1				1				3		
Adams	138	37	Coldgrove	Jeremiah		1	2	1		1	1	1	1				8		
New Marlborough	232	14	Cole	Asa	2	1	1	1		3		1	1	1			11		
Adams	136	33	Cole	Barnet	2			1					1				4		
Richmond	207	9	Cole	Benjamin			1			1		1					3		
New Ashford	163	25	Cole	Ebenezer	1		2			1		1					5		
Partridgefield	186	28	Cole	Ezra	4		1	1		3	1	1					11		
Cheshire	156	34	Cole	Israel			2		1			1		1			5		
Cheshire	156	36	Cole	Israel 2d		1	1	1				2					7		
New Ashford	163	21	Cole	Jacob	1	1		1		2			2				7		
New Ashford	163	37	Cole	James	1	1	1	1		3	2		1				10		
Windsor	168	22	Cole	John	1		2		1			1		1			6		
Dalton	191	37	Cole	Justin		2			1	4	1		1	2			11		
Richmond	207	10	Cole	Timothy	3			1		2			1				7		
New Marlborough	240	18	Collar	Asa	1			1		3			1				6		
New Marlborough	240	13	Collar	John	1	2	1	1		3	1	1	1				11		
New Marlborough	240	25	Collar	Moses	2	1		1			1		1				6		
New Marlborough	240	7	Collar	Silas	1			1		1			1				4		
Tyringham	112	24	Collins	Abram	2	2	1		1			1	1				8		
Tyringham	115	43	Collins	Abram	3	1	1	3	1		1		1				11		
Richmond	208	18	Collins	Dan			1		1	1	1	3	1	1			9		
Lanesborough	147	20	Collins	Daniel	2			1		1	1		1				6		
Great Barrington	110	5	Collins	Jacob				1		1		1					3		
Stockbridge	253	19	Collins	John		1	1			2		1					5		
Lenox	209	18	Collins	Lemuel		1	1		1	1	3		1				8		
Richmond	208	9	Collins	Menarah	1	1	1		1	1		1		1			7		
Stockbridge	254	3	Collins	Oliver			1	1		1			1				4		
Stockbridge	253	14	Collins	Oliver Jr	2	1	1						1				6		
Richmond	208	20	Collins	Ralph			1	1				1					3		
Lanesborough	152	12	Collins	William	1			1		1			1				4		
Pittsfield	195	42	Colt	Jabez		1		1		2		1					5		
Richmond	207	13	Colt	Jabez			2		1				1				5		
Pittsfield	195	37	Colt	James D	2	2		1	1	1	2	1	1		3		14		
Pittsfield	196	10	Colt	James D Junr	3		2	1		1		1	1		1		10		
Pittsfield	196	12	Colt	John		1							1				2		
Partridgefield	186	20	Colt	Richard			1			1	1	*	*	*			3		image torn
Pittsfield	195	30	Colt	William		1	1			1		1					4		
Stockbridge	254	4	Colton	Andrew	2		2	1			1	2					8		
Tyringham	112	31	Colver	Simon	3			1		2			1				7		
Great Barrington	109	17	Comstock	Ebenz		1		1		4	1		1				8		
Richmond	208	24	Comstock	Ezekiel		1	1						1				3		
Williamstown	133	6	Comstock	Ishmael		3	3		1		1	2					11		
Bethlehem	173	8	Comstock	Jeremiah	1			1		3			1				6		
Great Barrington	109	15	Comstock	Lancaster				1					1				2		
Williamstown	127	2	Comstock	Medad	3	1		1		3	2	1	1				12		
Great Barrington	109	16	Comstock	Perrygrine	2	2	1		1	1	1	1	1				10		
Adams	135	22	Comstock	Seth		1	1			1			1	1	8		13		
Williamstown	126	27	Comstock	Solon	2			1		1	1		1				7		
Great Barrington	107	43	Comstock	Thomas	3			1		1	1		1				7		
Williamstown	133	5	Comstock	Thomas	1		2	1	1		1	2		1			9		
Becket	265	24	Conant	George		2		1		3	2		1				9		
West Stockbridge	247	32	Conant	Israel				1			2		1				4		
Becket	266	6	Conant	Thatcher	2			1		3	1		1				9		
West Stockbridge	247	28	Cone	Ashbel	2	1	1		1	1	1		1				8		
Sandisfield	175	31	Cone	Cornelius & Son		1		1			2	2	1				7		
Partridgefield	186	21	Cone	Daniel	1			1	*	*	*	*	*	*			2		image torn
Williamstown	131	37	Cone	David S.		1				1		1					3		
New Marlborough	232	16	Cone	Frederick	1		1			1			1				4		
Sandisfield	175	30	Cone	Joseph	1		1			4			1				7		
Washington	214	4	Congdon	William	1	1	1		1	1	1		1				7		
New Marlborough	240	3	Conn	Robert	4			1		2	1		1				9		

TOWN	PG#	LN#	LAST NAME	FIRST NAME	FWM <10	FWM 10-16	FWM 16-26	FWM 26-45	FWM 45+	FWF <10	FWF 10-16	FWF 16-26	FWF 26-45	FWF 45+	TOTAL ALL OTHER	TOTAL SLAVES	TOTALS	DISTRICT/TOWNSHIP	NOTES
Great Barrington	108	6	Conner	Daniel	1				1	3			1	1			7		
Great Barrington	105	46	Conner	John				1				1					2		
West Stockbridge	248	1	Conners	Solomon		1	1			1		1					4		
Windsor	168	20	Convers	Amasa		1	1		1	1	2	2		1			9		
Dalton	191	44	Convers	Edward	2	1		1		1		1		1			7		
Windsor	167	5	Convers	James		1	1	1		1	2	2	1	1			10		
Windsor	168	19	Convers	Amasa J	1			1					1				3		
Williamstown	127	1	Cook	Abiel	2			1		4	1		1				9		
Clarkesburg	141	6	Cook	Abraham	1			1		1			1				4		
Washington	215	24	Cook	Cloe		1						1	1				3		
Stockbridge	253	21	Cook	Ebenezer	1		1	1				1		1			5		
Sheffield	230	19	Cook	Eli	1			1		1			1				4		
Loudon	179	10	Cook	Elisha	3	2	1	1			2	1	1	1			12		
Richmond	206	34	Cook	Erastus			1						1				2		
Bethlehem	173	20	Cook	Eunice									1				1		
Richmond	208	7	Cook	Isaac	1			2		2			1	1			7		
West Stockbridge	247	29	Cook	James	2		1						1				4		
Loudon	179	11	Cook	John	1	1		1				2	1				6		
Williamstown	130	38	Cook	John	3			1		1			1	1			7		
Adams	138	20	Cook	Joshua	1		2	1		2	3	1	1				11		
Loudon	178	37	Cook	Josiah	3	3	1		1	1				1			10		
New Marlborough	240	22	Cook	Levi	2		1	1		1		1		1			7		
Clarkesburg	142	2	Cook	Martin	1		1			1		1					4		
New Marlborough	240	35	Cook	Mary									2				2		
Loudon	178	23	Cook	Moses	1			1				2					4		
Loudon	179	21	Cook	Moses H.	1			1				1					3		
Richmond	205	3	Cook	Philip		1	2	1			1	3		1	1		10		
New Marlborough	240	26	Cook	Russell	2		1	1		1	1		2	1			9		
Adams	138	19	Cook	Silas				1		1		1		1			4		
New Marlborough	240	21	Cook	Solomon	1		1	1		1	1		1				6		
Loudon	179	32	Cook	Thomas			1			1		1					3		
Richmond	206	37	Cook	Walter		1		1		3			1				6		
Great Barrington	107	48	Cook	Jesse				1					1				2		
Great Barrington	108	1	Cook	Serad	3	2		1		1	2	1	1				11		
Tyringham	111	44	Cooley	Enos	1			1		1			1				4		
Cheshire	153	12	Coomer	Daniel	1	1	3	1		1	2		2				11		
Williamstown	126	36	Coon	Thomas			1			1			1				3		
Williamstown	127	31	Coon	Timothy	1		1						1				3		
Windsor	168	8	Cooper	Ebenezer	2	1		1						1			5		
Windsor	168	9	Cooper	Francis	1		2	1		1		1					6		
Stockbridge	254	5	Cooper	Jemima									1				1		
Adams	133	2	Cooper	Jeremiah	2	1	1	1				1					6		
Tyringham	111	33	Cooper	Matthew			1	1				1	1				4		
Tyringham	111	34	Cooper	Reuben			1						1				2		
Great Barrington	104	19	Cooper	Simeon	1	1	1	2		3	1	1	2				12		
Williamstown	131	14	Corbin	Amasa				2				2	1				5		
Williamstown	131	18	Corbin	Asa	2	1	1	1		1	2		1				9		
Hancock	161	2	Corey	Abel	2		1			2			1				6		
Hancock	160	10	Corey	Benjamin	1		1			1		1					4		
Hancock	161	22	Corey	Caleb		1				2		1					4		
Hancock	161	23	Corey	John	1		1			1		1					4		
Hancock	160	7	Corey	Reuben		2	1			1			1				5		
Bethlehem	180	13	Corfin	Solomon			1			1		1					3		
Lanesborough	151	33	Corhal	Thomas				1						1			2		
Washington	214	24	Cornish	Amasiah			1			1	1		1		3		7		
Washington	214	5	Cornish	Elijah	1		1			1		1					4		
Sandisfield	175	5	Cornish	John & Son			1	1		1	1	2					6		
Cheshire	156	29	Cornwall	Joseph		1	1						1				3		
Cheshire	157	13	Corwall	William	1	1	1	1		2	1	2	1				10		
Adams	135	15	Cote	James	3			1		1			1				6		
Pittsfield	196	4	Cottin	Jonathan	1			1		1		1					4		
Windsor	167	30	Cotton	Wait	2			1		1			1	1	1		7		
Loudon	178	7	Cotton	Walter				1		1		1					3		
Loudon	177	15	Cotton	William	3	1	1	1					1				7		
Dalton	191	31	Couch	John	1	2		1		3	1		1				9		
Lee	260	4	Couch	John Jr	1	1	1	1		2	1	1	1				9		
Lee	260	2	Couch	Samuel		1		1		2			1				5		
Sandisfield	175	29	Couch	Samuel	3	1		2			1	1	1	2			11		
Lee	260	3	Couch	Stephen	1		1	1		2	2		1				8		
Bethlehem	181	39	Couch	William	5			1				1		1			8		
Lanesborough	151	37	Covell	William	1			1		2			1				5		
Mount Washington	231	16	Covey	Luther			1			3		1					5		
Hancock	162	11	Cowan	Isaac	1			1		3	2		1				8		
Williamstown	127	22	Cowen	John	2		2	1		1	2		1				9		
Williamstown	126	3	Cowen	Jonathan	1			2	2	4			3	3			15		
Bethlehem	180	15	Cowl	Timothy	1	1		1		1			1				5		
Williamstown	129	38	Cox	John	1	1		1		1				1			5		
Williamstown	126	21	Coy	Cottrel				1				1					3		
Great Barrington	105	13	Coy	Eddy	1	2		1		4		1					9		
Great Barrington	106	42	Crain	William			2		1	1		2	2		1		9		

TOWN	PG#	LN#	LAST NAME	FIRST NAME	Free White Males under 10	10 to 16	16 to 26	26 to 45	45 and over	Free White Females under 10	10 to 16	16 to 26	26 to 45	45 and over	TOTAL ALL OTHER	TOTAL SLAVES	TOTALS	DISTRICT/ TOWNSHIP	NOTES
West Stockbridge	247	31	Crampton	Benjm	1			1		2			1				5		
Pittsfield	195	36	Crandal	Ezekiel	1	1			1	2		1					6		
Becket	266	3	Crane	Abel	3	1			1	1	2		1				9		
Washington	215	21	Crane	Amos			1					1					2		
Sandisfield	175	2	Crane	David				1									1		
Windsor	167	14	Crane	Ebenezer	2	1		1		3			1				8		
Washington	216	14	Crane	Elijah	1	1	1		1	1	1						6		
Sandisfield	174	40	Crane	Elijah & Son	1		4		1	5	1	1	2	1			16		
West Stockbridge	247	30	Crane	Silas	3	1		1		1			2				8		
Pittsfield	196	11	Crane	Stephen						1			1				2		
Hancock	159	38	Cranstone	John	1	2		1		1	1	1	1				8		
Savoy	141	3	Crapo	Consider	1	1	1		1	2	1		1				8		
Savoy	141	5	Crapo	Consider Jun	1			1		2			1				5		
Adams	136	14	Crapo	Noah			1			1		1					3		
Partridgefield	186	32	Crary	Christopher	1	1		1		3	1	1	1				9		
Sheffield	221	17	Crawley	Ellis		1						1					2		
Tyringham	119	13	Crippen	Joel	3			1		1		1	1	1			8		
Egremont	119	9	Crippen	Reuben	2		1			1		1					6		
Egremont	120	10	Crippin	David	3		1	1			1			1			7		
Egremont	120	28	Crippin	Nathaniel		1				1		1					3		
Richmond	208	15	Crittenden	Levi	2		2	1		2		4	1				12		
Lee	260	23	Crocker	Elisha	2	2			1	2		3	1				11		
Lee	259	32	Crocker	Jedediah		2	1	1		3	1			1			9		
Richmond	208	8	Crocker	John	1			1				1		1			4		
Lee	260	17	Crocker	Joseph	3		1		1	2	3		1				11		
Lee	260	5	Crocker	Josiah	3			1			1	1	1				7		
Williamstown	126	25	Crofoot	Joseph	2	1	1	1	1	2	1		1	1			11		
Williamstown	126	26	Crofoot	Rhoda Mrs	1					1	1	1					4		
Lee	260	8	Crosby	Abijah	2			1					1				4		
Stockbridge	253	31	Crosby	Abner	1		1	1		1			1				5		
Lee	260	9	Crosby	John		1		1	1			1		1			5		
Lee	260	7	Crosby	John Jr	1		2	1		1			1				6		
Pittsfield	196	7	Crowfoot	Simeon			2		1	1			1				5		
Partridgefield	186	25	Crozier	John	1	2		1		2	1		1				8		
Sandisfield	170	8	Cruttenden	Ichabod Sen	2		3	1		1	1	2		1			11		
Bethlehem	182	17	Cruttendon	Wm S	1	1			1	4			1				8		
Loudon	179	9	Cuff	Sampson											1		1		
Pittsfield	196	6	Culver	Henry	1			1		3			1				6		
Lee	260	22	Culver	Simon	2			1		3			1				7		
Hancock	158	15	Cummins	Nathan		1		1			1		1				4		
Stockbridge	253	18	Cumstock	Rufus		1	1	1			1		1				5		
Hancock	160	37	Cunningham	John	1	1		1		3	1		1				8		
Dalton	191	43	Curtis	Alford	2			1				1					4		
Tyringham	114	19	Curtis	Amasa		1	1	1		2	2		1				8		
Tyringham	114	20	Curtis	Amasa Jun	1		1			1		1					4		
Dalton	191	41	Curtis	Ebenezer	1	1		1		2			1				6		
Dalton	191	38	Curtis	Elijah				1			2			1			4		
Dalton	191	39	Curtis	Elijah Jr	1		1	1		2	2		1				8		
Dalton	191	42	Curtis	Epaphras	2					1			1				4		
Dalton	191	40	Curtis	John	1			1		2		1					5		
Hancock	159	33	Curtis	Jonah		1		1			1		1				4		
Egremont	120	19	Curtis	Joseph	1	1	3	1		1	1	1					9		
Lenox	212	16	Curtis	Justus		1				2		1					4		
Lanesborough	147	23	Curtis	Peter	1	1						1					3		
Bethlehem	182	11	Curtis	Sarah									1				1		
Williamstown	131	20	Curtis	Theoder		1	1	1				1					4		
Stockbridge	253	11	Curtiss	Abel	1	1	3	1		1	1	2	1				11		
Sheffield	226	22	Curtiss	Abijah	3		1		1	1		1					6		
Partridgefield	186	24	Curtiss	Amasa	2			1		1							4		
Partridgefield	186	23	Curtiss	Comfort	1		1			1	1						4		
Sheffield	230	30	Curtiss	David	1		1			2			1				5		
Stockbridge	253	10	Curtiss	Elnathan	3	1	2		1	1	1	1	1				11		
Partridgefield	186	22	Curtiss	Francis	1		1			1							3		
Sheffield	230	28	Curtiss	Giles	4			1	1	2	2		1				11		
Stockbridge	253	22	Curtiss	Isaac	2	4	2		1	1		2	1	1			14		
Sheffield	225	28	Curtiss	Jeptha		1	1			3		1			1		7		
Sheffield	230	29	Curtiss	John	1			1			1		1				4		
Sheffield	226	21	Curtiss	Jonathan		1	3	1	1	3	2		1				12		
Sheffield	226	13	Curtiss	Joseph	1	1	1	1					1				5		
New Marlborough	239	16	Curtiss	Nathanael		1			1				1				3		
Stockbridge	253	15	Curtiss	Samuel	2			1		2	1		1				7		
Stockbridge	253	20	Curtiss	Samuel 2d	2		1	1		3	2	2					11		
Cheshire	155	37	Cushington	David	2	1	1	1		1			1				7		
Becket	265	27	Cushman	Jonah				1		3	2		1				7		
Alford	117	16	D*ey	Peleg			1			2	1		1				5		
Loudon	179	25	Daily	Jeremiah	1			1		1			1				4		
Egremont	118	10	Daley	Absalom		1		1		1		2					5		
Egremont	120	8	Daley	Ammon	1			1		1		1					4		
Tyringham	119	17	Daley	Samuel Jun	1			1		1		1					4		
Egremont	120	34	Daley	William	2	1		1		1	1		1				7		

TOWN	PG#	LN#	HEADS OF HOUSEHOLD		FREE WHITE MALES					FREE WHITE FEMALES					TOTAL ALL OTHER	TOTAL SLAVES	TOTALS	DISTRICT/ TOWNSHIP	NOTES
			LAST NAME	FIRST NAME	under 10	10 to 16	16 to 26	26 to 45	45 and over	under 10	10 to 16	16 to 26	26 to 45	45 and over					
Egremont	119	2	Daly	Mary			2					1		1			4		
Windsor	168	14	Dana	Daniel	2	2			1	3	2		1				11		
Williamstown	128	23	Danforth	Coe			1			1			1				3		
Williamstown	129	31	Danforth	Jonathan		1	1		1		1	1		1			6		
Pittsfield	196	16	Danforth	Joshua	1		1	1		3		1	2				9		
Becket	266	14	Daniels	Amariah			1										1		
Cheshire	155	35	Daniels	Moses			1			3		1					5		
Hancock	159	15	Daniels	Reuben			1			3		1					5		
Williamstown	131	33	Daniels	Sterling	4		1		1	1	3	2	1				13		
Partridgefield	186	35	Daniels	Walter	2			1		3			1				7		
New Ashford	162	18	Danley	Esther	1	1	1			2	1	1	1				8		
Alford	117	14	Darby	Abner	2	2		1					1				6		
Alford	117	15	Darby	George				2			1			1			4		
Alford	117	13	Darby	George Junr				1		1				1			3		
Adams	138	22	Darby	Joseph	1	1		1		4			1				8		
Adams	134	8	Darling	David Junr	3	2	1	1		3		1	2				13		
Adams	134	15	Darling	David Junr	1	2	1		1	1		1		1			7		
Lanesborough	150	15	Darwin	Ephraim		1			1		1		1				4		
Partridgefield	186	37	Davenport	Joseph		1		1		1		1	1				5		
Sandisfield	173	13	David	Nathaniel B. & S	1		2		1	1	1		1				7		
Williamstown	128	35	Davidson	Peter		2			1	2			1				6		
Lee	260	29	Davies	Calvin	1			1				1					3		
Lee	260	33	Davies	Hope					1					1			2		
Lee	260	28	Davies	Isaac					1				2				3		
Lee	260	27	Davies	Nathan	2	1		1		2	1	2	1				10		
Lee	260	26	Davies	Samuel	3	1	1	1		1	1	1	1				10		
Sheffield	230	38	Davis	Abraham	3			1		1			1				6		
Sheffield	228	33	Davis	Ammi	2			1		3	1	1		1			9		
Tyringham	112	3	Davis	Benjamin				1						1			2		
Pittsfield	196	24	Davis	Cyrus			2					1					3		
Williamstown	127	28	Davis	Francis		1	1	1		3	2		1				9		
Tyringham	112	4	Davis	Gardner	1	3			1	3			1				9		
Alford	116	36	Davis	Jabez	2			1		2			1				6		
Pittsfield	196	18	Davis	James				2		5			2				9		
Great Barrington	110	14	Davis	Samuel	3	2		1		2			1				9		
Great Barrington	108	3	Davis	William	2	3	1		1	2	1	2	1	1			14		
Sheffield	225	13	Davis	Zaccheus											5		5		
Loudon	177	10	Davison	Benjamin	3			1			2		1				7		
Loudon	179	1	Davison	John	3			1		1	1		1				7		
Loudon	178	39	Davison	Samuel	3			1		1			1				6		
Loudon	178	41	Davison	Thomas	1	2		1				1	1				6		
Loudon	178	40	Davison	Zepheniah	1			1					1	1			4		
Windsor	166	31	Dawes	John	2			1		1			1				5		
Windsor	166	28	Dawes	Samuel	3			1			1		1				6		
Hancock	161	8	Dawley	Job		1	1		1	1	1	1	1				7		
Dalton	192	3	Day	Amasa	1	2	1	1	1	1	1		1	1			10		
Stockbridge	254	18	Day	Amasa		1			1			1		2	1		6		
Dalton	192	2	Day	Charles	1	1	1		1	2	4		1	1			12		
Dalton	192	1	Day	Daniel	3	1			1	2		3		1			11		
Williamstown	127	14	Day	Daniel		1		3	1	2	1	1	1	1			11		
Sheffield	229	23	Day	John	1	1		1		1		2	1		1		8		
Williamstown	132	18	Day	John			3		1		1			1			6		
Williamstown	131	19	Day	John 2d	1	1		1		2		1	1				7		
Lanesborough	150	12	Day	Nehemiah	3			1		1			1				6		
Stockbridge	254	19	Day	Roderick			1			1			1				3		
Lanesborough	150	13	Day	Thomas	1	1	1						1				4		
Sheffield	222	13	Day	Thomas		1	1			1	1	1					5		
Great Barrington	106	36	Day	William		1		1		1	1			1			5		
Sheffield	230	18	Daybald	Jonathan	1	1		1						1			4		
Egremont	119	17	Days	Samuel	3	1	1	1			1	1	1				9		
Adams	135	10	Dean	Asa	3		1	1					1	1			7		
Cheshire	157	3	Dean	Eliphalet			1			1			1				3		
Cheshire	155	25	Dean	Joseph	2	1		1		1	3	1	1				10		
New Marlborough	238	25	Dean	Walter	1	1	2		1	2		1	1				9		
Windsor	167	21	Dean	Walter			1			2			1	1			5		
New Marlborough	233	1	Dean	Zebediah				1					1	1			3		
Pittsfield	196	22	Deane	Pearl		1				1		1					3		
Pittsfield	196	17	Deane	Solomon		1		1			1		1				4		
West Stockbridge	248	2	Decker	Ferris		1											1		
Sheffield	227	5	Dedman	Lois						2			1				3		
Sandisfield	173	7	Deland	John	2			1		1		1					5		
Sandisfield	173	6	Deland	Obadiah		2	1			1	1	1		1			8		
Richmond	209	1	Delano	Amos	2	1			1	2	1	3	1				11		
Williamstown	127	11	Deming	Aaron	1	1	1	1					2	1			7		
Sandisfield	174	7	Deming	David	1			1			1		1				4		
Great Barrington	109	28	Deming	Elijah				1						1			2		
Sandisfield	176	31	Deming	Elijah		2		1				1	1	1			6		
Washington	215	22	Deming	Gideon		2	1			1	1			1			6		
Sandisfield	176	32	Deming	Joel	1	1		1				1	1	1			6		
Sandisfield	175	1	Deming	John			1		1			2		1			5		

107

TOWN	PG#	LN#	HEADS OF HOUSEHOLD LAST NAME	FIRST NAME	FREE WHITE MALES under 10	10 to 16	16 to 26	26 to 45	45 and over	FREE WHITE FEMALES under 10	10 to 16	16 to 26	26 to 45	45 and over	TOTAL ALL OTHER	TOTAL SLAVES	TOTALS	DISTRICT/ TOWNSHIP	NOTES
Bethlehem	181	36	Deming	Jonathan	1		1			1		1					4		
Great Barrington	109	4	Deming	Justus	1	1		1		2			1				6		
Sandisfield	174	21	Deming	Solomon	2			1		2	1		1				7		
Williamstown	127	9	Deming	Titus	2	1	1	1		3	2	1	1				12		
Stockbridge	254	15	Dening	Elijah	1			1					1	1			3		
Stockbridge	254	13	Dening	Josiah		1	1	1	1			2	1	1			8		
Sandisfield	171	16	Dening	Ozias	2	1		1		2	1		1				8		
Sandisfield	170	19	Denning	Benjamin	4	1		1		2			1	1			10		
Southfield	182	14	Denning	Solomon	1		1		1			1	5	1			10		
Becket	266	12	Dennison	Boswell	2			1		1			1				5		
Sandisfield	174	20	Denslow	Bartemas			1										1		
Sandisfield	174	18	Denslow	Joseph Jr			1						1				2		
Sandisfield	174	19	Denslow	Joseph Sen					1			1		1			3		
Great Barrington	109	34	Denton	William	1		1		1	1	3		1				8		
Great Barrington	109	35	Denton	William Jr			1			2			1				4		
Pittsfield	196	20	Derning	John		1	2	3	7	1		3	6	3			26		
West Stockbridge	248	6	Derning	John		1	1		1	1		1	1				6		
Sheffield	223	33	Derry	George		1				1	1		1				4		
Becket	266	11	Dewey	Abel	2	1		1	1	1		1	1				8		
Stockbridge	254	9	Dewey	Abner		2	4		1	1			1	1			10		
Richmond	207	44	Dewey	Asaph	2	4		1		1			1	1			10		
Williamstown	132	19	Dewey	Daniel	3	1	1	1		1	1	1	1				10		
Hancock	158	5	Dewey	David		1	1		1	1		1		1			6		
New Ashford	163	7	Dewey	Henry	1		1			1		1					4		
Great Barrington	105	31	Dewey	Hugo	4	1	1		1	1	1	2	1				12		
Great Barrington	107	18	Dewey	Josiah	2	2		1			1	1	1				8		
Great Barrington	105	32	Dewey	Justin	3	3	1		1	1			1				10		
Sheffield	222	12	Dewey	Paul		2	1	2	1	1	1		2	1			11		
Great Barrington	106	20	Dewey	Roswell			1			1		1					3		
Richmond	207	12	Dewey	Samuel	1		1	1		1		1					5		
Williamstown	127	41	Dewey	Samuel			1		2					1			4		
Sheffield	222	3	Dewey	Silas	1	1		1		2		1	1				7		
Sheffield	222	7	Dewey	Stephen	1	1		2		3	2		1				10		
Lee	260	34	Dexter	Stephen	1		1	1		2		1					6		
Partridgefield	186	33	Diball	Eritha	1		1			1		1					4		
Sheffield	228	9	Dibble	Benjamin			1			4		1					6		
Mount Washington	231	12	Dibble	Daniel			1			2		1					4		
Loudon	178	15	Dibble	Heman	2	1		1		2			1				7		
Mount Washington	231	11	Dibble	John	1		1		1		2			1			6		
Sheffield	225	19	Dibble	Joseph	3			1		1			1	1			7		
Mount Washington	232	9	Dibble	Samll		1			1		2			1			5		
Sheffield	227	17	Dibble	Sirus				1		1	1		1				4		
Partridgefield	186	34	Dibol	Eli	1		1			1		1					4		
Stockbridge	254	7	Dickenson	Justus		1		1				1	1				4		
Lee	260	30	Dickinson	Elizar		1	1	1				1	2	1			7		
Pittsfield	196	19	Dickinson	John		2	1	1		1		1					6		
Great Barrington	109	27	Dickinson	Lodowick	1			1	1	2		1					6		
Pittsfield	196	15	Dickinson	Olr P.		1	1	1		2	1		2	1	1		10		
New Marlborough	233	4	Dickinson	Thomas	2	2		1		2	1	1	1				10		
Pittsfield	196	25	Dighton	John B	2	3			1	2			1				9		
Clarkesburg	142	3	Dillingham	George		1							1				2		
Lee	260	32	Dillingham	Nathan	4		1	1		1	2	1	1				11		
Loudon	179	34	Dimick	Isaac		1	1		1		1	3		1			8		
Lee	260	25	Dimmick	Sylvanus				1			1		1				3		
Sheffield	225	23	Dimwell	William		1		1		2				1			5		
Tyringham	111	6	Diskill	John		1		1			2		1				5		
Great Barrington	109	22	Dobill	John	1	2		1		3		3	1				11		
Lee	260	31	Dodge	Elisha		1											1		
Bethlehem	173	15	Dodge	Francis			2		1					1			4		
New Marlborough	233	6	Dodge	John		2	2		2	2		2		1			11		
Tyringham	113	33	Dodge	Ozias	1		1	1		3	2	1	1				10		
New Marlborough	235	27	Doland	Elijah		1							1				2		
Alford	117	41	Dolin	Thomas	2	1		1		2	1		1				8		
Alford	116	15	Dollsur	John			1			1		1					3		
Egremont	118	24	Done	Jane	2	1					1		1				5		
Stockbridge	254	6	Donnelly	John				1						1			2		
New Marlborough	239	4	Dorchester	Daniel			1					1					2		
Richmond	208	36	Dorchester	Stephen			1	1						1			3		
Windsor	168	7	Dorrame	Gordon	1	1		1			1		1	1			6		
Sheffield	225	8	Dorrent	Henry		1		1		2			1				5		
Williamstown	132	24	Doty	Asa	2			1					1				4		
Tyringham	115	13	Doud	Marcena	2		1	1		1	2		1				8		
Tyringham	115	12	Doud	Noah	2		1	1		2		1	1				8		
Tyringham	115	19	Doud	Sylvanus	2			1		1		1					5		
Great Barrington	108	31	Douglas	Samuel	1			1					1				3		
Great Barrington	107	9	Douglas	Thos James		1	1		1	4	2	1	1	1			12		
Lenox	212	17	Dove	John		2			1	1		2		1			7		
Cheshire	155	3	Dow	Benjamin	1	1		1		1	2		1				7		
Sheffield	229	34	Downing	Roswell		1		2	1	1				1			6		

TOWN	PG#	LN#	LAST NAME	FIRST NAME	FREE WHITE MALES					FREE WHITE FEMALES					TOTAL ALL OTHER	TOTAL SLAVES	TOTALS	DISTRICT/ TOWNSHIP	NOTES
					under 10	10 to 16	16 to 26	26 to 45	45 and over	under 10	10 to 16	16 to 26	26 to 45	45 and over					
Sandisfield	171	13	Downs	Abraham	1		2		1	1	1		1	1			8		
Sheffield	229	30	Dream	London											9		9		
Stockbridge	254	14	Dresser	Benj		2	1		1		1			1			6		
Great Barrington	109	12	Dresser	David	1	1	1	1		1	1			1			7		
Partridgefield	186	36	Dresser	Isaac	1	1		1		2	1		1				7		
Stockbridge	254	10	Dresser	James	1	1		1		1	1	1	1				7		
Zoar	143	32	Drury	Nathan				1			1		1				3		
Lenox	209	24	Drury	Paul	1	1	1	1	1	2	2	1	1	1			12		
Lenox	209	25	Drury	Paul Junr	1	1		1		1	1		1				6		
West Stockbridge	248	4	Dryar	Allen	1		2		1	3	2			1			10		
West Stockbridge	248	5	Dryar	Daniel	2			1		3			1	1			8		
West Stockbridge	248	3	Dryar	William	3	1	1	1	1		1	1	2				11		
Richmond	206	26	Dryer	John	2		1		1	2	1	1	1				9		
Richmond	207	38	Dudley	John			2	1			1	1					5		
Richmond	207	41	Dudley	John Jun	2	1	2	1		1		1	1				9		
Stockbridge	254	8	Dudley	Martha	2	1		2					1				6		
Richmond	207	14	Dudley	William		3		1				1	2				7		
Williamstown	126	5	Dumett	Cato											6		6		
Pittsfield	196	13	Dunbar	Calvin	1	1	2	1			1	1		1			8		
Lenox	209	23	Dunbar	Daniel			1			1		1	1				4		
Lenox	209	21	Dunbar	David	3		1	1		2	1	1	1				10		
Windsor	168	18	Dunbar	Joseph			1						1				2		
Lenox	209	22	Dunbar	Samuel				1				1		1			3		
Windsor	168	17	Dunbar	Walter	1			1		1			1				4		
Great Barrington	108	18	Dunham	Benajah				2		1				2			5		
Savoy	139	22	Dunham	Daniel	2						2		1	1			6		
Savoy	139	21	Dunham	Job	2			1					1				4		
Lenox	209	26	Dunham	Joseph	2	2	1	1		1	1	1					9		
Sandisfield	171	14	Dunham	Joseph			1		1			2		2			6		
Stockbridge	254	16	Dunham	William				1		2		1	1				5		
Williamstown	126	22	Duning	Matthew Jr			1	2				1		3			7		
Stockbridge	254	11	Dunnells	Sally									1				1		
Pittsfield	202	23	Dunton	David	3	1		1		1	1		1				8		
Lanesborough	151	2	Dunton	Nathaniel	2			1		2			1				6		
Washington	214	40	Dunwill	Stephen	3	1	1	1		1	2		1				10		
West Stockbridge	248	7	Durfee	John	1	1		1		2		1					6		
Pittsfield	196	23	Durfey	John				1					1				2		
Cheshire	153	14	Durfy	Robert				1					1				2		
Dalton	192	4	Durkee	Henry	2			1					1				4		
Cheshire	153	18	Durphy	David	2			1		2			1				6		
Sheffield	225	36	Durston	John									1				1		
Pittsfield	196	21	Durwin	Abner	1			1		3			1				6		
Lanesborough	152	22	Durwin	Ephraim Jr		1	1	1			1		1				5		
Lanesborough	152	33	Durwin	Hannah	1	1	1			3	1		1				8		
Lanesborough	152	34	Durwin	Russel	3	2		1		3			1				10		
Lanesborough	150	11	Durwin	Thomas		1	1		2	1	1		1				7		
Tyringham	119	6	Dutton	Jonathan		1			1	1		1					4		
Lee	264	14	Duzen	Matthew	1		1		1	1	2			1			7		
Stockbridge	254	12	Dwight	Henry W	1	2		1				1	1		1		7		
Stockbridge	254	17	Dwight	Jonah	2	1		1		1		2	1		1		9		
Tyringham	113	10	Dwight	Sereno	2			1					1	2			6		
Becket	266	13	Dwolf	Horace			1										1		
Pittsfield	196	14	Dyke	Elias	2			1				1					5		
Becket	266	16	Eames	Abner		1		1		1				1			4		
Becket	266	20	Eames	Amos	2	1		1		1			1				6		
Washington	214	37	Eames	Anthony	1	2	1		1	1	1		1				8		
Becket	266	15	Eames	David				1						1			2		
Becket	266	17	Eames	Joel	3			1					1				5		
Becket	266	19	Eames	Leml	1			1		1			1				4		
Washington	215	25	Eames	Mark	2	2		1					1				6		
Becket	266	18	Eames	Zephariah				1				1					2		
West Stockbridge	248	14	Earland	Francis				1			1		1				3		
West Stockbridge	248	13	Earland	James	2			1		3	1		1				8		
West Stockbridge	248	8	Easland	John	1		1	1		2	1		1				7		
West Stockbridge	248	9	Easland	John G.				1						1			2		
Pittsfield	196	34	Eason	Joseph	1	1		1		2	1		1				7		
Williamstown	132	9	Eason	Oliver				1					1				2		
Great Barrington	108	15	Eddy	Briant	1			1		1		1	1				6		
Pittsfield	196	28	Eddy	Caleb	1			2	3				6	4			16		
Windsor	167	7	Eddy	Caleb				1	1	1		2		1			5		
Adams	134	12	Eddy	Eliakim	2			1		1	1		1				6		
Adams	134	4	Eddy	Elisha	1		1		1	3	1	2	1				10		
Windsor	167	16	Eddy	Israel		1		1		2			1				5		
Adams	133	6	Eddy	James	3	1		1		1	1	1	1				9		
Williamstown	131	34	Eddy	Lebbens	4	2	2			3	2	2	1				16		
Savoy	140	17	Eddy	Loved		1		1			1	1		1			5		
Windsor	167	6	Eddy	Samuel				1		1				1			3		
Zoar	143	26	Eddy	Samuel			1		1	1	1		1				5		
Windsor	167	18	Eddy	Samuel Jun			1			2			1				4		
Windsor	167	8	Eddy	Smith	3			1					1				5		

TOWN	PG#	LN#	LAST NAME	FIRST NAME	FREE WHITE MALES					FREE WHITE FEMALES					TOTAL ALL OTHER	TOTAL SLAVES	TOTALS	DISTRICT/ TOWNSHIP	NOTES
					under 10	10 to 16	16 to 26	26 to 45	45 and over	under 10	10 to 16	16 to 26	26 to 45	45 and over					
Zoar	143	28	Eddy	William				1					1				2		
Pittsfield	196	26	Edgerton	Ebenezer	3		1	1		1			1				7		
Cheshire	155	8	Edmonds	Edward	2	2	2		1	2	2	1	1				13		
Savoy	140	19	Edson	Abiezer			2		1		1		1				5		
Adams	138	28	Edwards	Benjamin		3		1		1	2	2		1	1		11		
Richmond	207	33	Edwards	Daniel		1	1		1			1		1			5		
West Stockbridge	248	10	Edwards	Gamial	3			1					1	1			6		
Stockbridge	254	20	Edwards	Timothy		1	2	1	1				2		1	1	9		
Loudon	179	26	Egelston	Aaron	3	2		1		2			1				9		
Lenox	209	27	Egleston	Azariah	1		1	1		3			2		2		10		
Washington	215	9	Egleston	Darias	2			1		2		1					6		
Sheffield	225	3	Eglestone	Moses	4			1		2	1			1			9		
Zoar	143	25	Eldridge	Amos		2		1		2		1					6		
Hancock	161	38	Eldridge	Griffin	2			1		2			1				6		
Williamstown	131	11	Eldridge	Nathan	3			1		1			1	1			7		
Hancock	161	7	Eldridge	Rebecca	3	1		1		1	2	1	1				10		
Hancock	161	9	Eldridge	Thomas	1		2		1			1		1			6		
Sheffield	225	15	Elithorp	Salmon	1		1			1			1				4		
Sheffield	230	14	Elky	Diamond											3		3		
Hancock	162	12	Ellis	Gideon	1	1			1	1	1			1			6		
Lee	260	36	Ellis	John	1			1		2			1				5		
Pittsfield	196	33	Ellis	John	1		2		1			1		1	1		7		
Becket	266	21	Ellis	Manoah		1	2		1	2	4		1				11		
Washington	215	7	Ellis	Rowland	1			1		1		1					4		
Pittsfield	196	29	Ellithorp	Ichabod	1				1	1		1	1	1	1		6		
Pittsfield	196	27	Ells	John	1			1		1			1				4		
Sandisfield	174	4	Elmer	Joel		2		1		1	1	1					6		
Bethlehem	180	12	Elmer	Solomon			1			2			1				4		
Hancock	161	15	Ely	John		1	4			1	1	2		1			10		
Hancock	161	5	Ely	Reuben		1	2		1	1				1			6		
Sandisfield	176	7	Emms	Joshua		1	1		1				1	1			5		
Pittsfield	196	31	Ensign	Elijah	1	3	1	1		2	1	1	1				11		
Sheffield	231	3	Ensign	Elisha				1			1			1			3		
Sheffield	222	6	Ensign	Freeman	2	1		1		1	1		1				7		
Pittsfield	196	30	Ensign	Jacob		2		1						1			4		
Pittsfield	196	32	Ensign	Polly	1	1				2	1	1	1				7		
Sheffield	222	23	Ensign	Solomon	2			1					1				4		
Dalton	192	5	Ensign	William	2	2	2		1			1	1				9		
Pittsfield	202	33	Erskine	Christian											3		3		
Windsor	166	6	Erskine	Jeremiah	1			1		2			1				5		
Adams	138	33	Estes	David	2			1	1				1				5		
Clarkesburg	142	13	Estes	Elijah	2			1		1			1				5		
Adams	137	29	Estes	Israel	1			1		1			1				4		
Clarkesburg	142	15	Estes	John				1	1					1			3		
Clarkesburg	142	16	Estes	John Jr	3	2		1		1	1	1	1				10		
Adams	135	9	Estes	Peter	1			1		2		2	1				7		
Adams	137	28	Estes	Samuel		1	1		1	1			1	1			6		
Clarkesburg	142	17	Estes	Samuel	1			1		2		1	1				6		
West Stockbridge	248	12	Evarts	Augustus	1			1		2		1					5		
Richmond	208	10	Evarts	Eli				1		1		1					3		
West Stockbridge	248	11	Evarts	Isaac		1	1					3		1			6		
Partridgefield	186	38	Everett	Andrew		1	2	1		1			1				6		
Sheffield	224	20	Everton	Austin			1			1			1				3		
Williamstown	131	10	Evett	Amos	3			1		3			1				8		
Lee	260	35	Ewer	Paul	3	1			1	1	1		1				8		
Stockbridge	254	22	Fairchild	Daniel	2	2		1		1	1		2				9		
Alford	116	8	Fairchild	Moses	2	1		1		5	1	1	1				12		
Great Barrington	107	37	Fairchild	Zacharia	2	1	1		1	2	3	1					11		
Pittsfield	196	39	Fairfield	Enoch	3		1	1					1				6		
Pittsfield	196	38	Fairfield	John	1			1				1			1		4		
Pittsfield	196	36	Fairfield	Joseph	1			1		1			1	1			6		
Pittsfield	196	37	Fairfield	Joseph Jr	1		1	1		2		1	1				7		
Pittsfield	196	35	Fairfield	Nathll		2	3	1	1		1	1		1			10		
Stockbridge	254	24	Fairman	Ichabod		1		1	1	1		2		1			6		
Sheffield	222	34	Fanning	John	2			1		1			1				5		
Pittsfield	196	41	Fanning	Orionel	2	3	1			2			1	1			10		
Sheffield	223	41	Fanning	Shubael	2	1	1		1	3	1	2		1			12		
Sandisfield	173	11	Fargo	Ezekiel	2				1			3	2		2		10		
Sandisfield	173	14	Fargo	Jabez	1	1		1		2			1				6		
Sandisfield	173	15	Fargo	Moses Jr	3			1		1	1		1				7		
Sandisfield	173	16	Fargo	Moses Sen				1						1			2		
Great Barrington	109	11	Fargo	Nehemiah	2	1		1		1	1			1			8		
Sandisfield	173	17	Fargo	Samuel	1			1		2		1					5		
Tyringham	115	5	Fargo	Thomas	3		1						1				5		
Lanesborough	149	7	Farnam	Benjamin		1			1	1			1	1			5		
Dalton	192	6	Farnam	Isaiah	1			1		1			1				4		
Lanesborough	150	2	Farnham	John	1			1		1	1		1				5		
Adams	134	41	Farnham	Thomas			1						2				3		
Cheshire	155	27	Farnsworth	John	1			1		3			1				6		
Great Barrington	106	12	Farnum	John	2		2	1		2	1		1				9		

TOWN	PG#	LN#	LAST NAME	FIRST NAME	FREE WHITE MALES					FREE WHITE FEMALES					TOTAL ALL OTHER	TOTAL SLAVES	TOTALS	DISTRICT/ TOWNSHIP	NOTES
					under 10	10 to 16	16 to 26	26 to 45	45 and over	under 10	10 to 16	16 to 26	26 to 45	45 and over					
Cheshire	156	2	Farnum	Jonathan	2			1		3	1		1				8		
Lanesborough	148	34	Farnum	Joseph		1			1				1	1			4		
Lanesborough	148	35	Farnum	Joseph Jun			1					1					2		
Pittsfield	196	40	Farr	Joseph		1		1		2		1		1			6		
Becket	266	25	Farrar	Joseph					1	3		1		1			6		
Loudon	179	2	Fay	John	2	1		1		1	1		1				7		
Sheffield	222	27	Fellows	Daniel			1		1	1	1		1				5		
Sheffield	225	33	Fellows	Edmund B	2		1				1	2					6		
Sheffield	225	18	Fellows	Ezra	1				1	1				1			4		
Sheffield	225	30	Fellows	John		2			1			1					4		
Sheffield	231	19	Fellows	John Jun	2	1	1	1		1	1		1				8		
Sandisfield	176	27	Fellows	Mary		1	1			1	1	1					6		
Sheffield	224	36	Fellows	Nathan	2		1	1		1	1						6		
Egremont	119	10	Fellows	Samuel			2	3			1						6		
Sheffield	221	12	Fellows	William	1	1		1	1			2	1	1			8		
Adams	138	34	Felton	David	1			1		1			1				4		
Stockbridge	254	23	Fenn	Daniel	3			1		1			3				8		
Adams	133	10	Fenner	Thomas		1			1		2		1				5		
Adams	138	35	Fenton	Asaph	3			1				1					5		
Williamstown	125	18	Fenton	Jason	2			1				1					4		
Partridgefield	186	39	Ferguson	James				1					1				2		
Cheshire	156	35	Ferrington	Ephraim	2		1	1					1				5		
Sheffield	228	28	Ferry	David	1	1		1	1	2	1		1				8		
Sheffield	228	27	Ferry	Isaac	2	1		1		1	2		1				8		
Sheffield	228	29	Ferry	Joseph		1	1	1	1		1		1	1			7		
Pittsfield	202	30	Fethergill	Joseph				1							2		3		
Adams	134	21	Fetteplace	William	1	1		1		3	1	1	1				9		
Cheshire	158	7	Fetterman	Charles	1			1	1	2		1	1	1			8		
Adams	136	1	Field	Nehemiah		1	2	1				1	1				6		
Windsor	166	35	Fields	James	3			1		1	2		1				8		
Alford	117	51	Fin	John	1			1				1					3		
Loudon	178	3	Finch	Isaac			1		1	1	1		1				5		
Becket	266	26	Finney	Abram	2			1		1		1					5		
Dalton	192	7	Finney	Benja	1			1		3			1				6		
Lee	261	11	Finney	Calvin			1										1		
Pittsfield	197	3	Finney	David	2		1		1			1		1			6		
Egremont	119	4	Finney	Joseph				1		2	1		1				5		
Becket	266	27	Finney	Sylvanus			1										1		
Partridgefield	186	41	Fish	Ervin			1			1		1					2		
Cheshire	157	36	Fish	Isaac				1		1			1	1			4		
Cheshire	157	34	Fish	Jonathan		1	1	1		4	1		1	1			10		
New Ashford	163	26	Fish	Matthew			1			3			1				5		
Savoy	140	41	Fish	Thomas	4	1	1			1			1				8		
Cheshire	157	33	Fish	William		1	1		1	1	1		1				6		
Cheshire	154	18	Fisk	Caleb	2			1		1			1				5		
Lanesborough	152	31	Fisk	Charles	2	1		1		2			1				7		
Cheshire	156	20	Fisk	Ephraim		1	3		1		2	1		1			9		
Cheshire	157	56	Fisk	Isaac				1		1			1	1			4		
Adams	135	29	Fisk	John	2		1	1		1		1	1				7		
Cheshire	157	54	Fisk	Jonathan		1	1	1		4	1		1	1			10		
Cheshire	157	53	Fisk	William		1	1			1	1		1				6		
Sheffield	231	18	Fitch	Ari	1			1				1					3		
Pittsfield	197	4	Fitch	Dyar	2	1	1	1		2			1				8		
Williamstown	132	5	Fitch	Ebenezer	3	2	3	1		1	1	2	1		1		15		
Alford	117	33	Fitch	Elijah	1	1	1	1		2	1		1				8		
New Marlborough	239	6	Fitch	Joseph			1		1				1				3		
New Marlborough	239	32	Fitch	Joseph Jun	1	1		1					1				4		
Hancock	159	11	Fitch	Prentice	2	2		1		2	2		1				10		
West Stockbridge	248	16	Fitch	Sanford	2			1					1				4		
New Marlborough	240	6	Flannards	John	1	1	1			4			1				9		
West Stockbridge	248	18	Fleming	Jacob		1			1			2	1	1			7		
Great Barrington	106	38	Fleming	William	2		1	1		2	2		1				9		
Pittsfield	196	43	Fletcher	John	2	1		1		2			1				7		
Partridgefield	187	2	Fletcher	William	1		1	1				1		1			6		
Richmond	208	28	Flowers	John	3			1		1			1				6		
Dalton	192	10	Follett	Roger	2	1		1		1			1				6		
Sheffield	227	13	Foot	Aaron		1			1					1			3		
Stockbridge	254	21	Foot	Adonijah		1	1			3			1				6		
Lee	261	5	Foot	Alvin	1		1					1					3		
Sheffield	227	14	Foot	Amos	3			1		1			1				6		
Lee	261	1	Foot	Asahel	2		1	1		2			2	1			10		
Sheffield	227	11	Foot	Bere	2	1		1		1	1		1				7		
West Stockbridge	248	23	Foot	Charles	3	1			1	1	2	1	1				10		
Dalton	192	8	Foot	Daniel	1	1			1	1	1		1	1			7		
Lee	261	2	Foot	David		2		1		2	1		1				7		
Lee	261	9	Foot	Elisha	1		1			1	1	2					6		
Lee	261	3	Foot	Fenner	3		2	1		2	1	1	1				11		
Lee	261	4	Foot	Jonathan Jr		2	1		1		1	1		1			7		
Lanesborough	149	8	Foot	Joseph		1	1			1		1					4		
Lee	261	10	Foot	William		1		1		2		1					5		

TOWN	PG#	LN#	LAST NAME	FIRST NAME	M under 10	M 10 to 16	M 16 to 26	M 26 to 45	M 45 and over	F under 10	F 10 to 16	F 16 to 26	F 26 to 45	F 45 and over	TOTAL ALL OTHER	TOTAL SLAVES	TOTALS	DISTRICT/ TOWNSHIP	NOTES
Williamstown	127	26	Foote	Aaron				1		1			1				3		
Williamstown	127	20	Foote	John	2	2	1	1		3		1	1				11		
Pittsfield	197	13	Forbes	Alexander		1	2		1		1	1	1				7		
Partridgefield	187	6	Forbes	Elisha			1						1				2		
New Marlborough	239	23	Ford	Abel				1		1				1			3		
Richmond	208	41	Ford	Absalom				1		3	1	2	1				8		
Windsor	166	29	Ford	Amos				1		2			1				4		
Windsor	166	13	Ford	Benjamin	3	2			1	1		1	3	1			12		
Windsor	166	8	Ford	Benjamin Jr			1	1					1				3		
Partridgefield	186	42	Ford	Charles	2			1		2			1				6		
Lenox	210	2	Ford	Ichabod	1		1	1					1	1			5		
Lenox	212	1	Ford	Ichabod Jun	2			1		2			1				6		
Richmond	209	5	Ford	James		1		1	1	3			3	1			10		
New Marlborough	239	24	Ford	Joel		1	3			1			1				6		
West Stockbridge	248	15	Ford	John	2		2		1	1	2	1		1			10		
Great Barrington	106	40	Ford	Jonathan	1	1	2	1	1	1				1			8		
Pittsfield	197	2	Ford	Rhoda									2				2		
Hancock	160	24	Ford	Simeon	3	1		1		2			1				8		
Partridgefield	187	4	Ford	Sybil						1			1				2		
Williamstown	128	31	Ford	Zadock	2	2			1	1	1	1					8		
Lee	261	13	Fordick	Ezeka				1						1			2		
Sheffield	229	17	Forrest	George		1		1		1			1				4		
Sheffield	229	18	Forrest	John	3			1		2	2			1			9		
Sheffield	223	9	Forrest	Sylvester		1				3			1				5		
New Marlborough	235	17	Forsyth	Abigail		1				2	1		2				6		
New Marlborough	232	4	Fosket	Ebenezer	1		1	1	1	1			1	1			7		
New Marlborough	232	10	Fosket	Ephraim	3		1	1		3	2	1					11		
Adams	139	6	Foster	Chillings				1		1				1			3		
Williamstown	129	6	Foster	David		4	1	1		4		1	1				12		
Williamstown	126	2	Foster	Edward			1						1				2		
Adams	139	5	Foster	Elnath	1		1		1	2	1	1	1		3		11		
New Marlborough	240	24	Foster	Ezekiel	1		2	1		1		1	2				9		
Lenox	209	28	Foster	Jedidiah	1	1	2	1				2	1				8		
Hancock	160	36	Foster	John			3	1		1			1				6		
Lenox	209	29	Foster	Jonathan			1	1				1		1	1		5		
Hancock	160	27	Foster	Joshua	1	1	1	1	1	3			1				9		
Great Barrington	104	16	Foster	Melaneton	2			1		1		1					5		
Williamstown	128	27	Foster	William			1	1		1	1	1		1			6		
Pittsfield	197	12	Foulton	John	2		1			1			1				5		
Alford	117	46	Fowler	Abiattier		1	1	1		1			1	1			6		
West Stockbridge	248	17	Fowler	Amos		1	1		1	1	1	1					7		
Tyringham	114	36	Fowler	Asa			2	1		2		1					6		
Hancock	161	24	Fowler	Caleb	3	1		1		1	1		1				8		
Bethlehem	182	4	Fowler	Daniel	5			1	1		2		1	1	2		13		
Tyringham	115	7	Fowler	Elijah	2			1		1				1			5		
Tyringham	114	37	Fowler	Gideon	1			1						1			3		
Williamstown	128	2	Fowler	James	1			2		2	2	2	1	1			11		
Washington	214	34	Fowler	John	2		1	1					1				5		
Williamstown	128	4	Fowler	Michael	1	1	1	1		1	1		1				7		
Williamstown	129	29	Fowler	Morris	3			1		1			1				6		
Pittsfield	197	8	Fowler	Stephen		2	1		1			1		1			6		
Dalton	192	9	Fox	Abiah			1					1		1			3		
Williamstown	127	8	Fox	Andrew		1	1	1				1	1				5		
Washington	213	13	Fox	Bethiah	3			1		1			1	1			7		
Stockbridge	254	26	Fox	Daniel									1				1		
Stockbridge	254	25	Fox	Hubbard	3			1		2	2		1				9		
Sheffield	226	2	Fox	Jeremiah				1		3	1	1	1				7		
Mount Washington	232	28	Fox	Jona	2			1		3			1				8		
Becket	266	24	Framan	Benja		1					1						2		
Loudon	178	18	Francis	Hosea		1		1					1				3		
Savoy	140	10	Francis	Isaac	1	1		1		1			1				5		
Pittsfield	197	11	Francis	John	1			1		1	2	1	1				7		
Sheffield	231	14	Francis	John											2		2		
Pittsfield	197	9	Francis	Josiah		1		1	1				1	1			5		
Pittsfield	197	10	Francis	Josiah Jun	1	1		1		1			1	1			6		
Pittsfield	197	5	Francis	Luke	1			1					1				3		
Pittsfield	197	7	Francis	Robert	2		1		1	2	2		1				9		
Pittsfield	197	6	Francis	William	1		1	1		2			1	1			8		
Washington	216	17	Franklin	Dean	1			1	1	2			1	1			7		
Cheshire	156	28	Franklin	Oliver				1						1			2		
Becket	266	23	Frarey	Eleazer	2	2		1		1			1				7		
Becket	266	22	Frarey	John	3			1		1			1				6		
Becket	266	28	Frarey	Joseph		1		1						1			3		
Becket	266	29	Frarey	Joseph Jr	1			1		1				1			4		
Adams	137	21	Frazier	John		1		1						1			3		
Stockbridge	258	25	Freeman	Betty											1		1		
Sheffield	224	33	Freeman	Casar											1		1		
Great Barrington	105	12	Freeman	Ceasar											6		6		
Partridgefield	187	3	Freeman	Ebenezer	1			1		1			1				4		
Lee	261	6	Freeman	Elisha	1	1	1		1		1	2		1			8		

112

TOWN	PG#	LN#	LAST NAME	FIRST NAME	M under 10	M 10 to 16	M 16 to 26	M 26 to 45	M 45 and over	F under 10	F 10 to 16	F 16 to 26	F 26 to 45	F 45 and over	TOTAL ALL OTHER	TOTAL SLAVES	TOTALS	DISTRICT/TOWNSHIP	NOTES
New Marlborough	232	18	Freeman	James	1		1					1					3		
Windsor	167	11	Freeman	Jared	1	1	1		1	1	1			1			7		
Lee	261	8	Freeman	John		1	2		1			3		1			8		
New Marlborough	236	19	Freeman	Paul											9		9		
Pittsfield	202	27	Freeman	Pomp											3		3		
New Marlborough	232	17	Freeman	Silas		2	1		1	1	1		1	2			9		
New Marlborough	232	20	Freeman	Silas	3			1			1	1					6		
West Stockbridge	248	20	Freeman	Walter	4			1			2		1				8		
Lee	261	7	Freeman	William	2			1		2			1				6		
West Stockbridge	248	21	Freese	John			1										1		
West Stockbridge	248	22	French	Christopher	2	1	3		1	3	1			1			12		
Alford	117	47	French	Enos				1			1		1				4		
Sandisfield	174	28	French	Joseph	1	1	1		1	1	1	1		1			8		
West Stockbridge	248	19	French	Nathan	1	1	1		1	2	1	1	1				9		
Partridgefield	186	43	Frink	Israel	1		2		1	1			1				6		
Cheshire	153	19	Frink	Minor	1			1		2			1				5		
Sheffield	226	35	Frisbie	Ezra	2		1						1				4		
Pittsfield	196	44	Frisby	Edward	1		6			2	1		1				11		
Partridgefield	186	40	Frissel	Amasa	2			1		1			1				5		
Partridgefield	187	1	Frissel	William			3	1	1				1				6		
Partridgefield	187	5	Frissel	William Jr	2	1		1					1				5		
Dalton	192	11	Frost	Amasa	1			1		2			1				5		
Washington	215	30	Frost	Apollas	1			1		1			1				4		
Dalton	192	12	Frost	Nehemiah	2	1		1		2	1		1				8		
Great Barrington	108	17	Fullar	Joel	2	2	1	1					1				7		
Egremont	120	17	Fullar	Seneca	1		2		1	1	1		1				7		
Cheshire	156	26	Fuller	Aaron	1			1		2			1				5		
Savoy	140	8	Fuller	Aaron				1			1		1				3		
Windsor	165	1	Fuller	Aaron	1	1	1	1		2			1				7		
Pittsfield	196	42	Fuller	Asa	3	1		1		2	1	3	1				12		
Williamstown	126	11	Fuller	Daniel	4			1		1	1		1				8		
Savoy	140	9	Fuller	Ebenezr	1		2			1			1				5		
Savoy	140	35	Fuller	Eli	3		2	1		1			2				9		
West Stockbridge	248	24	Fuller	Jeremiah			1										1		
Lee	261	12	Fuller	Jethro	2	1		1		1			1				6		
Egremont	119	13	Fuller	John		1	2	2	1	2	1		1				10		
Bethlehem	172	8	Fuller	Judah	3	1		1	1	1	1		1				9		
Bethlehem	172	9	Fuller	Lot	1	1	1		1	2		2		1			9		
Richmond	208	13	Fuller	Matthias	3	1		1				2		1			8		
Pittsfield	197	1	Fuller	Oliver		1				1	1						3		
Tyringham	115	44	Fuller	Peter	1	1	1		1	2			1				7		
Williamstown	127	15	Fuller	Stephen	1	2			1	1	1		1				7		
Lanesborough	150	33	Fuller	Zadock	3		1	1		1			1				8		
Becket	266	34	Gabriel	Thomas	1												1		
Stockbridge	254	30	Gains	Daniel		1							1				2		
Bethlehem	181	32	Gallop	Samuel				1				1		1			3		
Dalton	192	13	Gallup	Benja			1	1			1	2	1				6		
Dalton	192	15	Gallup	Olive		2				2		1	1	1			7		
Dalton	192	14	Gallup	Urrial	1			1		1			1				4		
Williamstown	130	9	Galusha	Daniel	1				1	2	2		1				7		
West Stockbridge	248	27	Galusha	Nathan		1		1		2	1		1				6		
Hancock	159	36	Gardner	Caleb		1	2		1	1	1	2		1			9		
Hancock	162	8	Gardner	Daniel				2		2	2		1				6		
Tyringham	110	1	Gardner	James		3	1		1				1				6		
Hancock	159	37	Gardner	John	1			1					1				3		
Lee	261	22	Gardner	John			1						1				2		
Lee	261	21	Gardner	Lodwick				1		1			1				3		
Hancock	162	1	Gardner	Nathaniel		1	1		1	1	1		1				6		
Tyringham	114	34	Gardner	Richard											5		5		
Hancock	162	2	Gardner	Robert	2	1	1	1		2	1		1	1			10		
Hancock	161	18	Gardner	Sylvester		2	1			1	2		1				7		
Lee	261	26	Gardner	Varnum	1			1		2			1				5		
Hancock	161	19	Gardner	Willet	1			1		1	1						4		
Lee	261	25	Gardner	William			1						1				2		
Tyringham	113	40	Garfield	Daniel			1	1		3		1	1				7		
Tyringham	113	32	Garfield	Elisha	2	1		1		2			1				7		
Lee	261	23	Garfield	Enoch		2	1		1	1	1			1			7		
Tyringham	110	12	Garfield	Isaac		1	4		1	1				2			9		
Tyringham	114	46	Garfield	Isaac		2	3		1	1				2			9		
Tyringham	113	19	Garfield	John	2			1		2			1				6		
Tyringham	112	49	Garfield	Solomon	3		2		1	2				1			9		
Lanesborough	152	3	Garlick	Henry	2			1		2			1	1			9		
Lanesborough	151	32	Garlick	Seth				1		1			1				3		
Lanesborough	151	34	Garlick	Seth Jun		1				2		1					4		
Hancock	160	28	Garr	Caleb	2	2		1			1		1				7		
Hancock	160	26	Garr	Robert	2	1	1	1	1	2	1		1	1	1		12		
Partridgefield	187	12	Gasper	Joseph	1			1		1			1				6		
Richmond	206	20	Gaston	Alexander	1	2	1	1		3	1		1				10		
Richmond	206	14	Gaston	John	1	2	1		1	2	1	2		1			11		
Richmond	206	22	Gaston	Naomi			3			2	1		1				7		

TOWN	PG#	LN#	LAST NAME	FIRST NAME	under 10	10 to 16	16 to 26	26 to 45	45 and over	under 10	10 to 16	16 to 26	26 to 45	45 and over	TOTAL ALL OTHER	TOTAL SLAVES	TOTALS	DISTRICT/ TOWNSHIP	NOTES
					FREE WHITE MALES					FREE WHITE FEMALES									
Richmond	206	16	Gaston	Robert	1		1		1		1	2		1			7		
Richmond	206	27	Gaston	William			1			1							2		
Lenox	210	4	Gates	Elijah	1		2		1	2	2		1				11		
Tyringham	113	12	Gates	Gideon			1					1					2		
Richmond	206	15	Gates	James O.	3	1	1	1		2		1	1				10		
New Marlborough	234	29	Gates	Levi	1		2	1		1		1					6		
Lenox	211	37	Gates	Luke			2	1		3			2				8		
Richmond	206	1	Gates	Samuel		1	4	1			1		1	2			10		
Lenox	210	5	Gates	Thomas		1			1			1		1			4		
New Marlborough	239	25	Gaylord	Munson		1	1			1		1					4		
Egremont	118	13	Geed	Isaac	1				1				1				3		
Alford	117	23	Geed	Joseph		1			1				1				3		
Windsor	167	9	Geer	Ezra	1	2		1		2	1		1				8		
Pittsfield	197	19	Geer	Hezekiah	3		1	1		3			1				9		
Partridgefield	187	9	Geer	John	2	3	1	1		2	1		1				11		
Savoy	140	30	Gelat	George	4	2		1				1	1				9		
Savoy	140	31	Gelat	John			1		1				1				3		
Egremont	120	18	Gerralds	Hyder			1		1	1	2		1				6		
Loudon	177	7	Gibbins	Peter		2	2		1		1		1				7		
Tyringham	111	39	Gibbs	Jona				1					1				2		
Tyringham	111	40	Gibbs	Nathan	4			1	1			1					7		
Tyringham	119	18	Gibbs	Solomon			1		1	1		1					3		
Great Barrington	105	8	Gibron	John		1		2	2	1		3		1			10		
Becket	266	30	Gibs	Saml				1					1				2		
Becket	266	31	Gibs	Saml Jr	3	1		1		1			1				7		
Great Barrington	108	37	Gibson	John 2d	2		1			1	2		1				7		
Alford	117	1	Gickner	Daniel				1					1				2		
Alford	117	2	Gickner	Daniel Junr	2		1					1					4		
Lee	261	16	Gifford	Cornell				1					1				2		
Pittsfield	197	21	Gifford	Eliab		1		1		1		2					5		
Lee	261	18	Gifford	James	2			1		1			1				5		
Lee	261	15	Gifford	Jesse	1	2			1	1	2	3		1			11		
Lee	261	17	Gifford	John	1	1	1	1		1	1	1					8		
Lee	261	14	Gifford	Sylvanus				1					1				2		
Lanesborough	150	8	Giffords	Rufus			1			1			1				3		
Alford	116	40	Gilbert	Asahel	4		1	1		2	2	1	1				12		
Great Barrington	105	20	Gilbert	Ebenezer					1				1				2		
Partridgefield	187	8	Gilbert	Elijah			2		1	1	2		1				7		
Partridgefield	187	14	Gilbert	Elizabeth								1	1				2		
Partridgefield	187	15	Gilbert	Henry		1			1	3	2		1				8		
Becket	266	32	Gilbert	Oreemus	2			1					1				4		
Williamstown	131	24	Giles	Jonathan	1	1		1	1			2	1	1			8		
Sheffield	229	29	Gill	Amos		1		1				1	1				4		
Sandisfield	177	10	Gillet	Marlin			1										1		
West Stockbridge	248	28	Gillett	Joseph	2			1		2			1				6		
Washington	214	15	Gilmore	Silas			1			2	1						4		
Sheffield	228	1	Gleason	Ariel	3			1		1	1	2		1			9		
Sheffield	228	3	Gleason	Elijah			1					1					2		
Sheffield	227	34	Gleason	Enoch	2		1					1					4		
Tyringham	111	35	Gleason	Joseph				1			2		1				4		
Sheffield	228	2	Gleason	Rufus			1			1		1	1				4		
New Marlborough	232	13	Gleason	Uriel	1		1					1					3		
Adams	134	7	Gleazon	Abner		2		1		2		1	1				7		
Becket	266	33	Glezan	Ezekiel		1	2	1			3		1				8		
Lenox	210	7	Glezen	Amasa	1		1	1		1	1		1				6		
Stockbridge	254	29	Glezen	Solomon				1		1		1	1				3		
Hancock	161	36	Glother	Asa	1		1	1		1		1					5		
Adams	135	24	Godfrey	Caleb		1		1			1		1				4		
Adams	134	34	Godfrey	Joseph	1		1				1						3		
Lanesborough	150	24	Godwin	Moses			1	1					1				3		
Savoy	139	16	Goff	Simeon	1	2	1		1	1	1	1					8		
Williamstown	129	40	Gold	Ebenz B.				1		2	1		1				5		
Pittsfield	197	25	Gold	Thomas	1	2	3	2		3	4	2	1				18		
Partridgefield	187	10	Goldthwait	Daniel	1			1		1			1				4		
Partridgefield	187	7	Goldthwait	Joseph			2		1		1		1	1			6		
Partridgefield	187	13	Goldthwait	Nathan	3			1					1				5		
Sheffield	225	12	Gomm	Alexander	2			1		1			1				5		
Pittsfield	197	26	Good	Charles	2	2	1		1		1	3		1			11		
Sheffield	222	16	Goodail	Jonas H	1	1	1		1	2	1		1		1		9		
New Ashford	162	5	Goodale	Elijah		1		2			1		1				5		
Pittsfield	197	17	Goodale	Isaac	2	2		1		2	1	1	1				10		
New Ashford	162	6	Goodale	Stephen	3			1			1		1				6		
New Marlborough	240	27	Goodenough	Solomon	1	1		1		1	1		1				6		
Zoar	143	22	Goodenow	Stephen	3			1		1	1		1				7		
Pittsfield	197	22	Goodrich	Abigail	1	1	3			1	1	2	2				11		
Sheffield	222	2	Goodrich	Amos	2		1	1		2			1				7		
Partridgefield	187	32	Goodrich	Asa		2		1		2	1		1				7		
Richmond	207	15	Goodrich	Benjamin			2	1		1	1		1				6		
Pittsfield	197	16	Goodrich	Butler	4		1	1					1	1			8		

114

TOWN	PG#	LN#	LAST NAME	FIRST NAME	FREE WHITE MALES under 10	10 to 16	16 to 26	26 to 45	45 and over	FREE WHITE FEMALES under 10	10 to 16	16 to 26	26 to 45	45 and over	TOTAL ALL OTHER	TOTAL SLAVES	TOTALS	DISTRICT/ TOWNSHIP	NOTES
Hancock	158	1	Goodrich	Daniel			2	5	7			3	7	6			30		
Hancock	159	28	Goodrich	Daniel	3			1		1			1				6		
Stockbridge	254	28	Goodrich	David	1		1	1					1				6		
Hancock	159	25	Goodrich	Elijah		2			2	2	2		1	1			10		
Partridgefield	187	11	Goodrich	Elijah	2			1		2			1				6		
Lanesborough	151	21	Goodrich	James					1		1			1			3		
Pittsfield	197	15	Goodrich	Jesse	2			1		2	2		1	1			9		
Hancock	159	24	Goodrich	John				2				3		1			6		
Sheffield	229	1	Goodrich	Jonathan			2	1					1				4		
Hancock	159	27	Goodrich	Justus	2			1			1		1				5		
Sandisfield	175	36	Goodrich	Michael	1	1	1		1	2	1		1				8		
Pittsfield	197	14	Goodrich	Moses	1	2			1	1		1	1				7		
Pittsfield	197	18	Goodrich	Orionel	2		2	1		1			1				7		
Dalton	192	16	Goodrich	Sela	1			1		3			1				6		
Hancock	158	12	Goodrich	Seth				1		1	1						3		
Hancock	159	31	Goodrich	Solomon	1		1	1		2		1	1				7		
Lanesborough	151	20	Goodrich	Thomas	1	2	1		1	2		1	1				9		
Hancock	158	11	Goodrich	Timothy	2			1		2			1				6		
Hancock	159	26	Goodrich	Uriah	2			1		2			1				6		
Sheffield	227	21	Goodrich	Zaccheus			1		1			1		1			4		
Sheffield	227	22	Goodrich	Zaccheus Jun	1		1	1		3	2	1					9		
Lenox	210	8	Goodspead	William		1	1		1			1		1			5		
Lanesborough	150	36	Goodwich	Ashbel	1	2			1	2	1	2		1			10		
Lenox	210	3	Goodwin	Joseph	3	1		1		2	3	1	1				12		
West Stockbridge	248	25	Gooe	Peter	2	1	1	1	1			3	1				10		
Adams	135	4	Gorton	John	1	1	2		1	1	2	1		1			10		
Egremont	118	16	Goulbourn	William				1			1		1				3		
Partridgefield	186	18	Grace	Sybil	2					2	1		1	1			7		
Hancock	159	22	Gracher	Peter	1	1	1	1		2	1		1	1			9		
Great Barrington	109	13	Graham	Aaron	1			1	1	1			1	1			6		
Sandisfield	174	16	Graham	James				1		3	1		1				6		
Williamstown	128	39	Grandison	Charles											2		2		
Sandisfield	176	20	Granger	Elihu	1	1		1		1	1		1				6		
New Marlborough	239	33	Granger	Phinehas		1		1		2			1				5		
Bethlehem	180	4	Granger	Thadeus	3	1		1					1				6		
Sandisfield	174	11	Granger	Thadeus	1			1		2			1				5		
Sandisfield	175	8	Granger	William	1	1		1		3			1				7		
Williamstown	128	15	Granger	William					1					1			2		
Williamstown	132	13	Granger	William	2	1		1					1				5		
Lee	261	20	Grant	Elisha	1	1	1		1		1	1		1			7		
Great Barrington	105	21	Grant	Hezekiah	1			1		1	1	1					5		
Mount Washington	232	25	Grant	John		1			1	2	1	1	1	1			8		
Great Barrington	105	17	Grant	Sylvester	2			1		2			1				6		
Pittsfield	202	28	Grant	Titus												5	5		
Tyringham	114	12	Graton	Thomas	2	2		1		1		1	1	1			9		
Tyringham	114	13	Graves	Elisha		1		1					1	1			4		
Richmond	207	39	Graves	Rufus		1	1		1		1	1	2				7		
Great Barrington	107	35	Gray	Hezekiah					1					1			2		
Egremont	120	43	Gray	Jaduthan	2	2	1		1	2	1		1				10		
Hancock	159	32	Green	Archibald	2			1		2			1				6		
Hancock	160	22	Green	Benjamin	1				1	1			1	1			5		
Cheshire	157	2	Green	Eli		1	1					1					3		
Cheshire	154	23	Green	Eli			1					1	2				4		
Cheshire	156	8	Green	Henry	?			1		1		1	1				6		
Windsor	168	15	Green	Hezekiah		1			1					1			3		
Lanesborough	149	21	Green	Jeremiah F.			?					1					3		
Lee	261	19	Green	John	4			1		1			1				7		
Lanesborough	151	13	Green	Nathan	1			1		1	1	1					5		
Windsor	168	16	Green	Noah	2	1		1		1			1				6		
Cheshire	154	33	Green	Oliver		1	1			1		1					4		
Cheshire	154	37	Green	Peleg	2	1	1	1		2		2	1				10		
Hancock	162	4	Green	Russel	3	2		1			1		1				8		
Tyringham	112	30	Green	Samuel	2		3	1		1			1				8		
Williamstown	133	3	Greene	Henry	4	1	1	1		1	2	1		1			12		
Williamstown	125	9	Greene	James					1	2	2	1		1			7		
Williamstown	127	34	Greene	William	2			1		2			1				6		
Lanesborough	149	15	Gregory	Elnathan	2	1	3	1		1	1	1	1				11		
New Ashford	163	5	Gregory	Esbon	2			1		1			1				6		
Lenox	210	6	Gregory	John	2		1	2		1		1	1				8		
Tyringham	113	20	Gregory	Seth					1					1			2		
Williamstown	129	16	Grey	Edward	3			1		1		1					6		
Richmond	209	4	Griffey	Jasper	1	2		1		1	1		1				7		
Lee	261	24	Griffin	Samuel	1			1		1			1				4		
Richmond	205	13	Griffing	Russel					1	1	3	2		1			8		
Richmond	208	29	Griffing	Timothy	2	1	1	1				1	1				7		
New Ashford	163	34	Griffiths	Paul	2	1		1		1			1				6		
Sheffield	223	31	Griggs	Joseph		1		1		1		1	1	1			6		
Windsor	168	3	Griggs	Lemuel		1		1		3			1				7		
Hancock	160	16	Grippin	Silas	2			1		1			1				5		
Stockbridge	254	27	Griswold	Ezekiel		2	1		1	1				1			6		

TOWN	PG#	LN#	LAST NAME	FIRST NAME	FREE WHITE MALES under 10	10 to 16	16 to 26	26 to 45	45 and over	FREE WHITE FEMALES under 10	10 to 16	16 to 26	26 to 45	45 and over	TOTAL ALL OTHER	TOTAL SLAVES	TOTALS	DISTRICT/ TOWNSHIP	NOTES
West Stockbridge	248	26	Griswold	Frederick			1		1					1			3		
Pittsfield	197	23	Griswold	Samuel	2			1				1					4		
Pittsfield	197	20	Griswold	Simeon		1	1		1	3	1		1				8		
Mount Washington	231	10	Groat	Philip	1			1				1					3		
Cheshire	154	31	Grosvenor	Caleb	1		2		1	1		2	1				8		
New Ashford	163	32	Grover	David S.	1			1			1		1				4		
Clarksburg	142	10	Grover	Jona	3			1		1	2		1				8		
Sheffield	223	19	Gubbins	Humphry											5		5		
Lanesborough	150	21	Guiteau	Francis	1	1	2		1			2	1				8		
Sheffield	230	36	Gunn	Alexander															
Sheffield	230	37	Gunn	Ariel	1			1	1	2			1				6		
Pittsfield	197	27	Gunn	Calvin			1			1			1				3		
Pittsfield	197	24	Gunn	Gideon				1				1	1				3		
Richmond	205	10	Hackley	Peter		1		1		2	1		1				6		
Richmond	205	9	Hackley	Samuel				1					1	1	1		3		
Stockbridge	258	24	Hadad	Ben											4		4		
Lenox	210	1	Hadley	Samuel		2		2		1	3		1				11		
Hancock	160	12	Hadrdel	Elijah	1			1		2			1				5		
Hancock	160	18	Hadrdel	Isaac	3			1					1				5		
Hancock	160	3	Hadrdel	Joseph			3		1	2		3	2	1			12		
Hancock	162	5	Hadsdel	Nathan	1			1		3	1		1				7		
Stockbridge	255	11	Hagar	Amos	3		1		1	2	2		1				10		
Great Barrington	106	5	Haight	Elijah	2		3			2		1					8		
Tyringham	115	32	Hale	John	1	1	1		1	2	2	1	2				11		
Tyringham	113	9	Hale	Josiah	2	2	1	1		1	1		1				9		
New Marlborough	235	21	Hale	Nathll	3	1	1	1		1		1	1				9		
Tyringham	115	25	Hale	Salathiel		1		1					1				3		
Dalton	192	17	Hale	William	2		1		2	1	2	1	1				10		
Tyringham	115	24	Hale	William				1				1		1			2		
Tyringham	110	15	Hale	William Jun	1			1			1		1				4		
Great Barrington	110	13	Hall	Abel		1	2		1	2	1		1	1			9		
Tyringham	115	1	Hall	Abel		1		1		1			1				4		
Lanesborough	148	31	Hall	Ambrose	1	2	3	1	1			2		2	1		13		
Sandisfield	176	8	Hall	Amos	3	1		1		2			1				8		
Stockbridge	255	16	Hall	Amos		1	1		1	2			1				6		
Windsor	165	4	Hall	Asa	2	1	1		1	1		1	1				8		
Hancock	160	35	Hall	Benjamin	1	1		1		2			1				6		
Cheshire	154	20	Hall	Calvin			1	1		3			1		1		7		
Lee	261	30	Hall	David		1											1		
Richmond	207	11	Hall	David		1		1		1		1		1			5		
New Marlborough	232	22	Hall	Ebenezer	1	1	1		1	2	2	1	1				10		
Tyringham	113	34	Hall	Ebenz	1		1		1	2			1	1			7		
Adams	138	3	Hall	Elisha	1	1		1				1	1				5		
New Marlborough	235	25	Hall	Elisha	1	1	1		1	1	1	1		1			8		
Lanesborough	149	13	Hall	Ezra	2		1	1		1			1				6		
Hancock	160	6	Hall	George	3	1	2		1	2	1		1				11		
Tyringham	110	6	Hall	Hannah								1	1				2		
Stockbridge	255	18	Hall	Job	1		1			1		1					4		
Hancock	162	3	Hall	John			1						1				2		
Lanesborough	151	18	Hall	John	1	2	1	1					1	1			7		
Lee	262	2	Hall	John			1										1		
Richmond	208	14	Hall	John			3		1	1	1	2	1	1			10		
Windsor	167	33	Hall	John	1	1	2		1	2			1				8		
New Marlborough	235	26	Hall	Luke	1		1					1					3		
Lanesborough	148	11	Hall	Lyman	1	1	2	1		2	1		1				9		
Lee	261	29	Hall	Moses	4	1				2	1		1				10		
Dalton	192	21	Hall	Nathan			1			2			1				4		
Pittsfield	198	10	Hall	Nathan				1			1			1			3		
Cheshire	156	5	Hall	Nicholas	1		1	1		1	1						5		
Hancock	158	19	Hall	Noah				2					4	4			10		
Partridgefield	187	19	Hall	Parker	1	1	2		1	1	1	1					8		
Tyringham	115	45	Hall	Simeon			1		1			1	2	1			6		
Tyringham	112	15	Hall	Simion			1		1			1		1			4		
Mount Washington	231	5	Hall	Smith	3		1		2				1				7		
Tyringham	112	17	Hall	Thomas	1		1		1	2	2	2	2	1			12		
Lee	261	35	Hamblin	Cornelius	2			1					1				4		
Lee	261	36	Hamblin	David		1		1		2		1		1			6		
Lee	261	34	Hamblin	Job		1		1					1				3		
Stockbridge	255	20	Hamilton	Benj	1	1		1		2	1	1					7		
Stockbridge	255	6	Hamilton	John				1				1	1				3		
Tyringham	119	3	Hamilton	Samuel		1	1	1					1				4		
West Stockbridge	249	3	Hamilton	Seth	1			1		1			1				4		
Sheffield	224	27	Hamlin	David		2		1		1	2		1				7		
Sheffield	224	28	Hamlin	Eleazer		1	1					1	1				4		
Lenox	210	12	Hamlin	Ichabod	2	1			1	1	2		1				8		
Washington	213	30	Hamlin	Isaac			1						1				3		
Alford	117	36	Hamlin	Jabez		1			1	1		1	1				5		
Lenox	210	14	Hamlin	Nathaniel		1	1		1			1	1				5		
New Ashford	163	30	Hammond	Gaius	1		2		1			1	1				6		
Pittsfield	198	1	Hammond	James	3			1			1		1				6		

TOWN	PG#	LN#	LAST NAME	FIRST NAME	FREE WHITE MALES					FREE WHITE FEMALES					TOTAL ALL OTHER	TOTAL SLAVES	TOTALS	DISTRICT/ TOWNSHIP	NOTES
					under 10	10 to 16	16 to 26	26 to 45	45 and over	under 10	10 to 16	16 to 26	26 to 45	45 and over					
Stockbridge	255	15	Hammond	Thomas	2			1					1	1			5		
Hancock	159	17	Hamton	Henry	1		1	1					1	1			5		
Pittsfield	197	33	Hanchit	Simeon		1	1		1		1		1				5		
Stockbridge	255	14	Hand	Abel		1		1		1			1				4		
Richmond	207	28	Hand	Daniel			1	1					1	1			4		
Hancock	161	4	Hand	Edmond	1		1						1				3		
Williamstown	130	15	Hand	Joseph	2	2			1	1	2		1				9		
Lee	262	1	Handy	Joseph & Seth			1	1					1				3		
Windsor	166	3	Haney	Stephen		2	1	1		1	1		1				7		
Adams	135	32	Hanis	Benjamin				1		3		1	1				6		
Sandisfield	174	23	Hanley	Flavel	3	1		1		2			1				8		
Sandisfield	174	26	Hanley	William Jr	3		2	1		1	2	2	1				12		
Pittsfield	197	35	Hanmer	Alenson	2	1		1		1	1		1				7		
Partridgefield	187	21	Hapall	Roger	1	2	1		1	3			1	1			10		
Washington	214	36	Hardy	Nathl	2		1	1		3	3	1	1				12		
Clarkesburg	142	14	Harington	Jefferson		1		1					1				3		
Adams	137	7	Harkness	Daniel		1		1	1	2	1	1	1	1			9		
New Marlborough	235	12	Harmon	Aran	1	1			1			2	1	1	1		8		
New Marlborough	235	11	Harmon	Aran Jun			1			1			1				3		
New Marlborough	236	28	Harmon	Asa		1			1	1		2	1	1			7		
New Marlborough	232	5	Harmon	David			1		1	2				1			5		
New Marlborough	232	7	Harmon	Eli		1			1					1			3		
New Marlborough	236	29	Harmon	Elisha			1	1		2	1		1				6		
New Marlborough	238	5	Harmon	Jehiel	2	1	2	1	1	1	1	1	1				11		
New Marlborough	236	22	Harmon	Jonathan	1			1		1			1				4		
New Marlborough	236	21	Harmon	Jonth				1			1			1			3		
New Marlborough	238	17	Harmon	Joseph	4	1		1		2			1				9		
New Marlborough	236	27	Harmon	Josiah	1			1		2			1				5		
New Marlborough	238	20	Harmon	Mark			1			3		1					5		
New Marlborough	238	19	Harmon	Moses		1		1					1				3		
New Marlborough	236	26	Harmon	Rufus	1		1	1				1	1				5		
New Marlborough	236	24	Harmon	Samll		1											1		
Sheffield	226	18	Harmon	Samll			1		1		1	2		1			6		
Sheffield	226	17	Harmon	Samll Jun			1			2		1					4		
New Marlborough	236	13	Harmon	Uriah			1	1					1	1			4		
New Marlborough	236	20	Harmon	William			1						1				2		
Adams	137	16	Harrington	Abraham	3	1		1			1		1				7		
Adams	137	27	Harrington	Daniel	1	1	3		1	1	1	1		1			10		
Adams	137	18	Harrington	James	1				1	1		1		1			5		
Adams	137	23	Harrington	Nathaniel			1	1		1			1	1			5		
Adams	137	24	Harrington	Nicodemus	1	2	2	1					1	1			8		
Tyringham	111	45	Harris	Champlin	2				1	1			1				5		
Becket	267	3	Harris	Daniel	2	1	2		1	1	1		1				9		
Sheffield	227	2	Harris	David			1		1	1		1	1				5		
Great Barrington	109	19	Harris	Elijah	2		2		1	2	2	2		1			12		
Great Barrington	109	20	Harris	Elisha			1					1					2		
Hancock	160	1	Harris	George	2	1		1		1			1				6		
Becket	267	2	Harris	James & James Jr		1			1	3	2		1				8		
Becket	267	4	Harris	Nathan		1			1		2	1		1			6		
Clarkesburg	141	2	Harris	Robert	2			1					1				4		
Richmond	206	8	Harris	William H.	1	1		1		3			1				7		
Williamstown	126	40	Harris	Eliphalet					1					1			2		
Richmond	208	5	Harrison	Abel	1	1		1	2	1			2	1			9		
Williamstown	125	10	Harrison	Almond	1	1	1	1		3	2		1				10		
New Marlborough	237	1	Harrison	Isaac	1		1		1	2	1		1				7		
Tyringham	115	17	Harriman	Isaac	1		1			1		1					4		
Stockbridge	255	7	Hart	Comfort	1	1		1		2			1				6		
Stockbridge	255	8	Hart	Job	1	1		1					1				4		
Lanesborough	149	37	Hart	John		2		1				1	2	1			7		
Great Barrington	106	37	Hart	Martin	1			1		3	1	1	1				8		
Stockbridge	255	22	Hart	Simeon	1			1		3			1	1			7		
New Marlborough	233	30	Hart	Solomon	2	1	1	1		3	2						11		
West Stockbridge	249	8	Hartwell	Abigail										1			1		
Sandisfield	173	10	Hartwell	Jesse	3			1		2			1				7		
Windsor	165	37	Harwood	Jason	3			1		4			1				9		
Windsor	165	34	Harwood	John			1		1			1		1			4		
Partridgefield	187	23	Hascal	Jeremiah	1	4	2		1	2			1	1			12		
Washington	215	14	Haskin	Daniel		1		1		1		1		1			5		
Adams	135	30	Haskin	George		1	1	1		2	1	3		1			10		
Savoy	139	17	Haskins	Nathan	2	1	3	1	1	1	1	2	1	1			14		
Savoy	139	18	Haskins	Schradach	2			1					1				4		
Stockbridge	255	10	Hatch	Benj			1	1	1					1			4		
Great Barrington	107	34	Hatch	Benjamin	3	1			1	1	2		1				10		
Egremont	118	9	Hatch	Ebenezer	1			1		2	1		1				6		
Alford	117	22	Hatch	Isaac				1	1				1	1			4		
Lee	262	6	Hatch	Jonah					1					1			2		
Lee	261	37	Hatch	Wait					1					1			2		
Lanesborough	148	32	Hatcher	Gamaliel	1			1		1	1		1				5		
Adams	134	19	Hathaway	Arnold	3			1		2			1				7		

117

TOWN	PG#	LN#	LAST NAME	FIRST NAME	FREE WHITE MALES under 10	10 to 16	16 to 26	26 to 45	45 and over	FREE WHITE FEMALES under 10	10 to 16	16 to 26	26 to 45	45 and over	TOTAL ALL OTHER	TOTAL SLAVES	TOTALS	DISTRICT/ TOWNSHIP	NOTES
Adams	134	25	Hathaway	Jonah	1	1	1		1		1	1	1				7		
Savoy	140	16	Hathaway	Joseph	1	1	2	1	1	1	2	1		1			11		
Savoy	141	6	Hathaway	Lemuel		1	3		1		1		1				7		
Savoy	141	8	Hathaway	Lemuel Jur	1		1	1				1					4		
Cheshire	157	20	Hathaway	Maletiah			1	1		1			1				4		
Savoy	141	7	Hathaway	Nathaniel	1			1		1			1				4		
Savoy	139	19	Hathaway	Peleg	1		1	1		2	2	2	1				10		
Cheshire	156	39	Hathaway	William	1			1		1		1					4		
Adams	134	38	Hathaway	Zach*		2	2	1	1	2		2		1			11		
Partridgefield	187	18	Hatheway	John	1			1				1					3		
Partridgefield	187	20	Hatheway	Seth		1		1		1		1					4		
Williamstown	129	30	Havens	Barzilla	1			1				1					3		
Sandisfield	170	7	Havens	Nathan	1			1		2	2	2					8		
Sheffield	228	15	Hawden	Alexander				1					1				2		
Sandisfield	171	19	Hawley	Elijah				1					1				2		
Sandisfield	172	3	Hawley	John Jr	1			1		4	1		1				8		
Loudon	177	1	Hawley	Ozias	1	1		1		3	1		1				8		
West Stockbridge	249	7	Hawley	Samll				1		1		1					3		
Loudon	178	38	Hawley	Thomas	2		1	1		1	1		1				7		
Southfield	182	15	Hawley	Zina	2	1		1		1	1		1				7		
Sandisfield	172	2	Hawley	John Sen				1			1	1	1				4		
Egremont	118	11	Haws	Benjamin	1	2		1		2	1	1	1				9		
Williamstown	130	3	Hayden	David	2			1				1	1				5		
Sandisfield	172	1	Hayes	Elisha		1		1		2			1				5		
Pittsfield	197	36	Hayes	William	3		1			1	1						6		
Lenox	210	10	Hayward	Moses			1	1			1		1				4		
Williamstown	130	6	Hayward	William	1			1	1	1	1		1				5		
Hancock	160	31	Hazard	Henry				1			1		1				3		
Hancock	160	30	Hazard	Rodman	2	1	1			2		1					7		
Pittsfield	202	31	Hazel	Bathsheba											2		2		
Adams	134	16	Head	William	3			1		1							5		
Egremont	120	16	Heare	Francis	1	1	2		1	1	2	1					9		
Egremont	120	15	Heare	Nicholas	2			1		1		2	1				7		
Pittsfield	197	44	Hearich	Jason	4	1		1		1			1				8		
Pittsfield	198	2	Hearich	Zebulon	1				1				1				3		
Pittsfield	198	4	Hearich	Zebulon Jr	2	1		1		1		1	1				7		
Sandisfield	173	18	Heath	Aaron	2	1	1		1	3	2	1	1	1			13		
Tyringham	113	46	Heath	Abijah	2	2		1	1	3	2		1				12		
Lee	261	31	Heath	Abraham	1			1		2			1				5		
Tyringham	119	9	Heath	Bartholomew		1	1	1					1				4		
Tyringham	112	18	Heath	Eleazer	3	2	1	1		2	1		1				11		
Tyringham	114	41	Heath	Elijah	2	1	1	1		2	1	1	1				10		
Tyringham	110	14	Heath	Elisha	4			1		1	1		1	1			9		
Great Barrington	109	41	Heath	George	1			1		2	2	1	1				8		
Tyringham	112	36	Heath	Isaac		2	2	1		1	1		2	1			10		
Tyringham	115	41	Heath	Isaac	2	1	1	2		2	1		2	1			12		
Sandisfield	171	20	Heath	Jacob	4			1					1				6		
Lee	261	32	Heath	John	1	1		1		3	1		1				9		
Tyringham	115	18	Heath	John	1				1	2	2		1				7		
Tyringham	114	32	Heath	Joseph	2		1	1		4	1	1	1				11		
Sandisfield	173	19	Heath	Levi	1		2		1	1		1	1	1			8		
Tyringham	114	35	Heath	Patience									1				1		
Bethlehem	173	6	Heath	Roswell	1			1		2		1					5		
Bethlehem	173	5	Heath	Samuel		1	2		1	1			1				6		
Tyringham	111	46	Heath	Solomon		1	1			1		1					4		
Tyringham	112	48	Heath	Solomon			2			1		1					4		
Bethlehem	180	19	Heath	Stephen	2			1		2	3		1				9		
Tyringham	112	14	Heath	William	3	1	1	1		1	2		1				10		
Tyringham	115	40	Heath	William	3	1	1	1		2	1	1	1	1			12		
Richmond	208	44	Hedges	Jonathan	1	1			1	2		1	1				7		
Williamstown	131	8	Henderson	Joseph	3	2			1	1	1		1				10		
Great Barrington	107	11	Hendrick	Daniel	2			1		3	1		1				8		
Partridgefield	187	27	Hening	Samuel				1									1		
Partridgefield	187	22	Henry	John	4			1		2	1		1				9		
Dalton	192	22	Henry	Malcom	1		1	1			1		1				5		
Becket	267	5	Henry	Robt						2		1					3		
Washington	215	34	Henry	Simeon	3			1		2		1					7		
Pittsfield	198	3	Henry	William		1		1		1			1				4		
Clarkesburg	141	5	Herrenden	Daniel			1			1			1				3		
Clarkesburg	141	1	Herrenden	Isaiah		1	1	1			2		1				6		
Clarkesburg	141	3	Herrenden	Seth	2			1					1				4		
Sandisfield	176	4	Herrick	Daniel	3			1		1	1	1	1				8		
Tyringham	115	33	Herrick	Ezekiel				1			1		1				3		
Tyringham	110	13	Herrick	Francis	2			2		2			1				7		
Tyringham	115	35	Herrick	Francis	2		1	1		2			1				7		
Tyringham	111	20	Herrick	Henry		1	1	8	6		6	7	6				35		
Tyringham	115	39	Herrick	Hezekiah	1	1	1			1	1	1	1				7		
Adams	138	2	Hewet	John	1			1		1	1		1				5		
Adams	133	4	Hewett	Achas	1			1		2			1				5		
Adams	133	3	Hewett	Caleb	1		1				1						3		

TOWN	PG#	LN#	LAST NAME	FIRST NAME	M under 10	M 10 to 16	M 16 to 26	M 26 to 45	M 45 and over	F under 10	F 10 to 16	F 16 to 26	F 26 to 45	F 45 and over	TOTAL ALL OTHER	TOTAL SLAVES	TOTALS	DISTRICT/ TOWNSHIP	NOTES
West Stockbridge	248	29	Hewins	Joseph				1		1	1	1	1				5		
Sheffield	224	1	Knapp	Hezekiah	1	1	3	1	1	1	1			1			10		
Partridgefield	187	26	Hibbard	Nathan	1	1	1		1			1		1			6		
Pittsfield	198	6	Hibbard	Nathan	4			1		1	1		1				8		
Loudon	177	2	Hickland	Daniel				1		2		1					4		
Williamstown	129	17	Hickox	Stephen			2		1		1	3		1			8		
Pittsfield	197	34	Hicock	Aaron	1			1		2		2					6		
Sheffield	223	1	Hicock	Darling	3	1		1		3		1		1			10		
Pittsfield	197	40	Hicock	Ichabod		1	2		1					1			5		
Sheffield	222	26	Hicock	Jeremiah		1	2		1	1	1	1	1				8		
Pittsfield	197	37	Hicock	John	1		2					1					4		
Sandisfield	170	17	Hide	Agur				1									1		
Becket	266	37	Higby	Benja		1											1		
Becket	266	36	Higby	Joseph		1	1	1		1	1			1			6		
Tyringham	111	42	Higby	Josiah	3	1		1		2	1		1				9		
Becket	267	1	Higby	Ozias	2			1		2							5		
Windsor	165	36	Higgins	Benjamin				1					1				2		
Sheffield	227	35	Higgins	Joseph	1	1				2			1				6		
Williamstown	131	41	Higgins	Lemuel	2		2	1		1	1		1				8		
Sheffield	230	11	Higgins	Samll			1			2		1					4		
Williamstown	132	14	Higgins	Samuel				1					1				2		
Sheffield	230	12	Higgins	Zebediah			2			1		1					4		
Adams	133	12	Hill	Amos	1	2			1	1		1		1			7		
Lenox	212	3	Hill	Arunah	2	1	1		1	1	2		1				9		
Lenox	210	16	Hill	Ashbel	1		1	1		2			1				6		
Tyringham	113	48	Hill	Elijah	1	1		1		1	2	1	1				8		
Adams	134	3	Hill	Isaac		1		1		1	1	1	1				6		
Adams	136	6	Hill	James	1			1				1	1				5		
Adams	137	22	Hill	James		1	1		1					1			4		
Stockbridge	255	3	Hill	John	1	1			1	1	1			1			6		
Tyringham	112	19	Hill	Josiah				1		1		1	1				4		
Tyringham	115	8	Hill	Josiah	1	2	1		1	2	1		1				9		
Williamstown	128	17	Hill	Josiah			1	1	1	1		1		1			6		
Alford	117	45	Hill	Lemuel	1	1		1	1				1				5		
Adams	133	14	Hill	Levi	3		1			1	2	1	1				9		
Dalton	192	18	Hill	Nathl	3			2					1				6		
Windsor	168	11	Hill	Thomas	3	2	2	1				2	1				11		
Cheshire	154	13	Hilliard	Henry		2	2		1	1		2		1			9		
Richmond	206	12	Hillock	Robert		1		1		1			1				4		
Sandisfield	174	27	Hills	Drake Esq	4	1	1	1		1	2	3	1				14		
Tyringham	115	15	Hind	David		2		1		3			1				7		
Williamstown	127	36	Hindersass	John G.	1			1		2			1				5		
Zoar	143	21	Hines	Alverson	1		1			1		1					4		
Lee	262	14	Hinkley	Benja	1	1		1			1		1				5		
Lee	262	5	Hinkley	Edmund			1			1				1			3		
Lee	262	3	Hinkley	Heman	2	2	1	1	1	1	1	1	1				11		
Lee	262	4	Hinkley	Joseph			1			2		1					4		
West Stockbridge	249	6	Hinman	Enoch	3		2	1			2		1				9		
Lenox	210	15	Hinsdale	Jonathan			1	1				1					3		
Dalton	192	24	Hinsdale	Theodore		3	2	1	1		1	1		1	1		11		
Lanesborough	148	10	Hirch	Asher	2	3		1			1		1				8		
New Marlborough	236	7	Hitchcock	Abner		1		1			1			1			4		
New Marlborough	237	20	Hitchcock	Cornish	1	1		1		2			2				7		
Great Barrington	105	33	Hitchcock	David	1			1				1					3		
Pittsfield	198	7	Hitchcock	Eli	1	2		1		1			1				6		
Lanesborough	151	28	Hitchcock	Jesse	2	1		1		1	2		1				8		
New Marlborough	238	4	Hitchcock	Jonathan			1			3			1				5		
Sheffield	229	19	Hitchcock	Samll				1					1				2		
Cheshire	153	20	Hix	Amos		1	1						1				3		
Cheshire	153	9	Hix	Eliphalet	1	3	1	1		4	1		1				12		
Cheshire	153	2	Hix	Thomas		1	1			1		1					4		
Pittsfield	197	42	Hoadley	Jacob		1		1					1				3		
Tyringham	114	44	Hobbs	Daniel	1		1		1		1	2		1			7		
New Marlborough	232	32	Hobbs	Humphry			1			1	1						3		
Richmond	209	3	Hochkin	Ebenezer	2		1	1		1			1				6		
Richmond	206	29	Hochkin	Joseph		1	1			1	1		1				5		
New Marlborough	239	29	Hockley	Asahel	1	1	1	1	1	2		1	2	2			12		
Adams	136	40	Hodge	David			1	1					1	1			4		
Adams	136	39	Hodge	George	1			1		3			1				6		
Adams	136	44	Hodge	Nehemiah				1		3			1				5		
Adams	138	17	Hodge	Otis	2			1		2	2		1				8		
Savoy	139	13	Hodges	Simeon	2		1		1					1			5		
Savoy	139	14	Hodges	Simeon Junr	1			1		1		1	1				5		
Great Barrington	105	40	Hogets	Emanuel				1					1				2		
Sandisfield	170	3	Holbert	Eliphalet	2	1			1	3	1		1				9		
Windsor	166	5	Holbrook	Amos	1			1		3	2	1	1				9		
Partridgefield	187	17	Holbrook	Benajah			1						1				2		
Sheffield	225	34	Holcomb	Ira			1						1				2		
Sheffield	226	1	Holcomb	Joel	1			1			1	1		1			5		

TOWN	PG#	LN#	LAST NAME	FIRST NAME	FREE WHITE MALES					FREE WHITE FEMALES					TOTAL ALL OTHER	TOTAL SLAVES	TOTALS	DISTRICT/ TOWNSHIP	NOTES
					under 10	10 to 16	16 to 26	26 to 45	45 and over	under 10	10 to 16	16 to 26	26 to 45	45 and over					
Sandisfield	171	3	Holcomb	Noadiah			1						1				2		
Sandisfield	171	2	Holcomb	Oliver	1			1		4		1					7		
Richmond	206	35	Holcomb	Richard	3			1					1				5		
Sheffield	224	32	Holcomb	Pliny				1					1				2		
Sheffield	224	30	Holcombs	Michael					1					1			2		
Sandisfield	175	20	Holden	Samuel	1	2			1	2	2		1				9		
Great Barrington	109	6	Holdridge	Israel	3			1		1			1				6		
Stockbridge	255	9	Holland	Joseph		1		1					1				3		
Stockbridge	255	13	Hollenback	Andrew	2			1					1				4		
Egremont	120	7	Hollenbeck	Darius			1			1		1					3		
Egremont	120	3	Hollenbeck	Domick	1				1			1		1			4		
New Marlborough	234	19	Hollister	Benjamin	2	2		1		2	1		1				9		
Lanesborough	151	36	Hollister	George				1					1				2		
Lenox	210	13	Hollister	Gurdin	2			1		2			1				6		
Pittsfield	198	8	Hollister	William	5			1		1	1	1	1		1		11		
Bethlehem	173	18	Holman	Thomas Junr	1	1			2	3		1	1	1			10		
Egremont	119	18	Holmes	Alpheus		1		1									2		
Williamstown	130	33	Holmes	Calvin	2	1		1		1		1	1	1			8		
Williamstown	130	35	Holmes	Elnathan	1	1	1		1	2	1		1				8		
Stockbridge	255	4	Holmes	Ezra	3			1		2			1				7		
Stockbridge	255	5	Holmes	George	1			1		3			1				6		
Washington	214	11	Holmes	Isaac	1		2		1	1	2		1				9		
Williamstown	130	34	Holmes	Isaac	2		2		1	2	3	1	2				13		
Sheffield	225	11	Holmes	Lothrop	3			2		1			1				7		
Egremont	120	6	Holmes	William		1				1			1				3		
Sheffield	226	34	Holms	Benjamin F	2	1		1		1			1				6		
Sheffield	223	3	Holms	Lothrop		1		2	1		1	2	1	1			9		
Sandisfield	173	37	Holt	Ebenezer			1	1	1				1	1			5		
Becket	266	35	Hooker	Nathana			1										1		
Pittsfield	197	32	Hooper	Archelaus	1			1		3			1				6		
West Stockbridge	249	4	Hooper	Elisha		1	1	1	1		1			1			6		
West Stockbridge	249	5	Hooper	Elisha Jr	2			1		1			1				5		
Pittsfield	197	31	Hooper	Zalonanna	1			2		1		1					5		
Stockbridge	255	12	Hopkins	Archibald		1		1									2		
Great Barrington	108	11	Hopkins	Daniel	2			1		2			1				6		
Adams	134	17	Hopkins	Gid	1			1		1			1				4		
Great Barrington	105	9	Hopkins	Ichabod		2			1		1		1				5		
Great Barrington	104	2	Hopkins	Moses	1	2	2		1		1	2		1			10		
Great Barrington	105	28	Hopkins	Samuel	1	1		1		1			1				5		
Adams	133	22	Hopkins	Seth			1		1	1			1				4		
Sheffield	227	6	Hopkins	Stephen	1	2		1		2		1	1				8		
Clarkesburg	141	18	Horich	Daniel	1	1	2	1		2	3			1			11		
Cheshire	155	31	Horsford	Eri			1	1		2			2				6		
Williamstown	125	3	Horsford	Josiah	1			1		1	1	1	1				6		
Mount Washington	232	22	Horton	Andrew			1		1					1			3		
Lanesborough	149	36	Horton	Asa	4	1		1		1			1				8		
Cheshire	153	7	Horton	Isaac	3	1			1	3		2	1				11		
Sandisfield	177	13	Horton	John	2			1		1	2		1				7		
Cheshire	157	40	Horton	Moses		1		1		1		1		1			5		
Cheshire	157	60	Horton	Moses		1		1		1		1		1			5		
Washington	214	28	Hoskin	Amos	1			1		3			1				6		
Richmond	205	22	Hough	Simon			1					1		1			4		
Adams	137	36	Houghton	Elisha			1	2						1			4		
Great Barrington	107	13	Houk	John	4	2		1		2			1				10		
Great Barrington	107	14	Houk	Martin	2	2		1		2			1				8		
Bethlehem	172	5	House	Benijah		1			1	1			2				5		
New Marlborough	240	17	House	Sarah	2								1	1			4		
Dalton	192	23	Hovey	John	1	1		1		2	1		1				7		
Dalton	192	20	Hovey	Jonathan	2	1	1	1		3			1				9		
Dalton	192	19	Hovey	Luke	1		1		2	1			1	1			7		
Stockbridge	255	21	How	Joseph	1	1		1		1	1		1				6		
Partridgefield	187	24	Howard	Artemas	1			1		2			1				5		
Savoy	140	37	Howard	Edward	1	1	1		1			1		1			6		
Partridgefield	187	16	Howard	Henry			2			1	1	1		1			6		
Hancock	161	3	Howard	Jesse	3	1		1		1	2		1				9		
Windsor	167	32	Howard	Phinehas	2		2	1		1		1					7		
Windsor	166	20	Howard	Solomon	1			1		2			1				5		
New Marlborough	240	36	Howe	Bates	1		1						1				3		
New Marlborough	240	20	Howe	Bowers	2			1		1			1				5		
Cheshire	156	9	Howe	Isaac G.	1	2	1		1				1	1			7		
New Marlborough	233	7	Howe	James			1						1				2		
Hancock	161	21	Howe	Jonathan		1		1		1			1				5		
Adams	139	7	Howe	Joseph	1		2			1			1				5		
Tyringham	112	23	Howe	Joseph	2	1			1	2	3		1				10		
New Marlborough	233	21	Howe	Lemll		1	1		1	1	1	1		1			7		
New Marlborough	234	6	Howe	Nathll			1						1				2		
New Marlborough	233	20	Howe	Uriah	1		1			1			1				4		
Lee	261	33	Howk	Isaac	3	1		1		1	1		1		1		9		
Adams	136	36	Howland	Abraham	1	1	2	2	1	2		2		2			13		

TOWN	PG#	LN#	HEADS OF HOUSEHOLD — LAST NAME	FIRST NAME	FREE WHITE MALES under 10	10 to 16	16 to 26	26 to 45	45 and over	FREE WHITE FEMALES under 10	10 to 16	16 to 26	26 to 45	45 and over	TOTAL ALL OTHER	TOTAL SLAVES	TOTALS	DISTRICT/ TOWNSHIP	NOTES
Sheffield	229	27	Howland	Jabez	1	1		2		2			1				7		
Pittsfield	198	5	Howland	Joseph	2			1			1		1				5		
Lee	262	16	Howland	Nathanll		1			1			2		1			5		
Stockbridge	255	17	Hoxce	Mrs	1						2		1				4		
Adams	135	26	Hoxey	Stephen	4				1	1	1		1				8		
Lanesborough	151	35	Hoyt	David H.				1		3			1				5		
Lanesborough	152	25	Hoyt	Jonathan L.	1		2	1		2	1	1					8		
Egremont	120	22	Hubbard	Booker	2			1	1	1		1	1	1			7		
Pittsfield	197	30	Hubbard	Daniel	1		1					1					3		
Dalton	192	27	Hubbard	Enoch	3		1	1					1	1			7		
Partridgefield	187	25	Hubbard	Ephraim		1			1	1				1			4		
Great Barrington	109	40	Hubbard	Hezekiah	2	1		1		2			1				7		
Sandisfield	173	9	Hubbard	Jadimer	3		1		1	1	2	1	1	1			11		
Pittsfield	197	28	Hubbard	James		2			1	1		2		1			7		
Pittsfield	197	29	Hubbard	James Jr	2			1		2			1				6		
Sheffield	225	32	Hubbard	John		1	2						2				5		
Sandisfield	173	4	Hubbard	John & Son		1		1	1	3	1	2	1	1			11		
Sandisfield	173	5	Hubbard	John Jr			1			1			1				3		
Sheffield	223	26	Hubbard	Jonathan		1	3		1	1				1			7		
Sheffield	225	26	Hubbard	Moses	1	1	1		1				1				5		
Bethlehem	173	10	Hubbard	Nathaniel		1		1					1	1			4		
Sheffield	225	29	Hubbard	Noah E.		1	2		1		1	1	1	1	1		9		
Sheffield	231	9	Hubbard	Prosper	1			1					1				3		
Sandisfield	175	3	Hubbard	Seth & Son	2		2		1	4	3	4	1				17		
Sandisfield	173	2	Hubbard	Theophhilas			1			1	1		1				4		
Washington	213	21	Hubbard	Thomas	2	3		1		2	1		1				10		
Sheffield	225	21	Hubbard	Timothy	1	2		1		1	1		1				7		
Lenox	210	21	Hubbard	Zadoch			3		1	1	1	3		1			10		
Pittsfield	197	41	Hubbard	Zadoch Jr		1	1			1		1					4		
Lenox	210	11	Hubbard	Zadoch P.	1			1		3			1				6		
Lanesborough	150	4	Hubbel	Diah				1						1			2		
Lanesborough	150	5	Hubbel	Hicock	3	2		1		1			1				8		
Lanesborough	148	33	Hubbel	Calvin	1	4	4	2		2	1	1	1				16		
Sheffield	222	14	Hubbell	John		1		1		1				1			4		
Lanesborough	148	4	Hubbell	Wolcott	2	1	2	1	1	2	1	2	2				14		
Pittsfield	197	43	Hubby	Hardes			1	1					1	1			4		
Williamstown	126	20	Hudson	Aaron	1	1		1		2			1				6		
New Marlborough	233	8	Huff	Josiah	1		1			1			1				4		
Great Barrington	108	13	Huggins	John			1				1	1					3		
New Marlborough	232	11	Huggins	Medad		1		1		1	2		1				6		
New Marlborough	234	3	Huggs	Daniel			1			1			1				3		
Dalton	192	25	Hulbert	John	2		1			1		1					5		
Pittsfield	198	9	Hulbert	John			1			2			1				4		
Great Barrington	107	2	Hulbert	Russell	3		2		1	2		1	1	1			11		
Dalton	192	26	Hulbert	Thaddeus				1		1			1				3		
Pittsfield	197	39	Hulbert	Timothy	1	2		1		3	1		1				9		
Tyringham	113	17	Hulet	Nehemiah	3			1		1	1		1				7		
Sandisfield	172	8	Hulet	Obadiah			1										1		
Lee	262	9	Hulett	Asa	3		1			1			1				6		
Lee	262	8	Hulett	John	3		1			1	1	1	1	1			9		
Lee	262	7	Hulett	Samuel	1	1		1		2			1				6		
Lee	262	10	Hulett	Sylvanus	1	1		1		3	1		1				8		
Stockbridge	255	23	Hull	Agrippa											4		4		
Great Barrington	105	36	Hull	Cornelius				1		1	1	2					5		
Richmond	205	15	Hull	David				1						1			2		
Sandisfield	175	12	Hull	Eliakim & Arnold	1	1		2		2		1	1				8		
West Stockbridge	248	32	Hull	Peter		1		1	1			1	1				5		
Windsor	165	8	Humes	David Jun		1		1		4	1		1				8		
Lee	262	15	Humphrey	Elias	1		1			1	1	1					5		
Stockbridge	255	1	Humphry	Enoch											6		6		
Stockbridge	255	2	Humphry	Enoch Jr											5		5		
Lanesborough	152	6	Hungerford	Thomas	1	2			1	1	2			1			8		
Lenox	210	18	Hunt	Benjamin	1			1	1	3			1	1			8		
Lenox	210	9	Hunt	John	2	2	1	1		1			1				8		
Washington	216	8	Hunt	Samuel	3	1	1		1		2			1			9		
Bethlehem	181	1	Hunter	Isaac	1			1					1	1			4		
Bethlehem	181	2	Hunter	John				1		3	1		1				6		
Washington	215	23	Huntley	Amos	3	2	2		1	4	2	1	1				16		
Sandisfield	175	6	Hurd	Jabez	2			1		3			1				7		
Great Barrington	108	4	Hurd	Josiah		1			1	2	1		1				6		
Tyringham	113	27	Hurd	Robert	2	1				1	2	1					8		
West Stockbridge	248	30	Hurlbart	Ulysses			1			1		1					3		
Great Barrington	108	35	Hurlbat	William		1		1		1		1		1			5		
Alford	117	12	Hurlbert	John		1	1		1	1		1	2				7		
Alford	117	10	Hurlbert	Philander	2	1		1		1			1				6		
Lee	262	11	Hurlburt	Christopher		1	1	1		1		1	1				6		
Lee	262	12	Hurlburt	Nathanl	2		1		1			2	1	1			8		
Lee	262	13	Hurlburt	Royal	1			1					1				3		
Lee	261	27	Hurlburt	William		1	1					1					3		
Alford	116	6	Hurlbut	Abijah		1	1	1	1				1				5		

TOWN	PG#	LN#	LAST NAME	FIRST NAME	FREE WHITE MALES					FREE WHITE FEMALES					TOTAL ALL OTHER	TOTAL SLAVES	TOTALS	DISTRICT/ TOWNSHIP	NOTES
					under 10	10 to 16	16 to 26	26 to 45	45 and over	under 10	10 to 16	16 to 26	26 to 45	45 and over					
Alford	116	9	Hurlbut	Hubbard		1	1	1		1		1					5		
Alford	116	7	Hurlbut	Isaac		1	1					1					3		
Sheffield	221	8	Hurlbut	John			1										1		
Egremont	118	12	Hurlbut	Samuel	1	3	1	1		2	1		1				10		
Sheffield	228	35	Hurlbut	Simeon	1				1			1		1			4		
Alford	116	12	Husted	Nathl	1		1	1		1	1	1					6		
Stockbridge	255	19	Hutchinson	Daniel	1			1		3			1				6		
West Stockbridge	248	31	Hutchinson	David	1	1	3	1			2	1	1				10		
Zoar	143	27	Hutchinson	Elisha	1			1				1					3		
New Marlborough	233	24	Hutchinson	Joel	1			1		1			1				4		
West Stockbridge	249	1	Hutchinson	Matthew		1	1	1		1	2		1				7		
New Marlborough	233	17	Hutchinson	Paul	1		1	1		2		1	1	1			8		
Pittsfield	197	38	Hutchinson	Paul				1			1		1	2			5		
West Stockbridge	249	2	Hutchinson	Samll	2			1		3	1		1	1			9		
Alford	116	16	Hutchinson	Shubiel	2		1						1				4		
New Marlborough	238	32	Huxley	Dan		2	1				1		1				5		
Lee	261	28	Hyde	Alvan	3		1	1			1		1	1			8		
Lenox	210	17	Hyde	Andrew				1				1		1			3		
Lenox	210	19	Hyde	Andrew Junr	1		2	1		3			1				8		
Lenox	210	20	Hyde	Caleb			2	1		1			1		1		6		
New Marlborough	234	14	Hyde	Ebenezer			1			1			1	1			4		
New Marlborough	234	15	Hyde	Freeman	1			1					1				3		
New Marlborough	234	7	Hyde	John	1		3		1	2	1	1	1	2			12		
New Marlborough	235	31	Hyde	John 2d	1	1	1	1		1			1	2			8		
New Marlborough	234	12	Hyde	Mercy									1				1		
New Marlborough	234	11	Hyde	Zenas	1			1		2			1		1		6		
Partridgefield	187	29	Ide	David	3			1		1			1				6		
Stockbridge	255	25	Ide	Nehemiah	2	3	1		1		1	1		1			10		
Partridgefield	187	28	Ide	Oliver				1					1	1			3		
Washington	213	22	Ingales	James	1		1	1		1			1				5		
New Ashford	162	11	Ingalls	William	1	2							1				4		
Cheshire	158	15	Ingals	Stephen	1	1							1				3		
Lee	262	21	Ingersoll	Calvin	4			1		1	1	1	1				9		
Lee	262	19	Ingersoll	David	2	1	1	1		4	1	1	1	1			13		
Alford	117	5	Ingersoll	Deodat	1	1	1		1	2	3		1				10		
Lee	262	20	Ingersoll	Elijah	5		1	1		2	2	1					12		
Great Barrington	106	1	Ingersoll	Horton			1			1							2		
Lee	262	22	Ingersoll	Jared	3	2		1		2	2		1				11		
Pittsfield	198	12	Ingersoll	Jared			1		1	1	2		1				6		
Stockbridge	255	24	Ingersoll	Jonathan	2	2	1		1	3	1	2	1				13		
Lee	262	23	Ingersoll	Moses	1		1	1		1			1				5		
Lee	262	17	Ingersoll	William			1						1				2		
Lee	262	18	Ingersoll	William Jr	3	2		1		1	1	1	1				10		
Adams	135	12	Ingesham	Samuel	1			1		2			1				5		
Egremont	119	24	Ingraham	Benjamin	1		2	1				1	1				6		
Savoy	139	15	Ingraham	John			1	1		1	1	1					5		
New Ashford	162	8	Ingraham	Jonathan	2		1			5	1		1				10		
Adams	135	33	Ingraham	Obadiah			1	1		1			1				4		
Savoy	139	5	Ingraham	William	3	1	1		1		1	1		1			9		
Dalton	192	31	Isaacs	Chloe						1	1	1					3		
Adams	138	29	Isbell	Garner	2	1	3	2		2	1	3	1				15		
Williamstown	128	34	Isbell	Peruda	1			1		2	1						5		
Pittsfield	198	15	Isham	Lemuel	1	1		1					1				4		
Adams	138	4	Ives	Amasa			1		1	2	2	2		1			9		
Great Barrington	105	14	Ives	Samuel	2			1		1			1				5		
Adams	138	5	Ives	Stephen		1		1	1	1	1			1			6		
Great Barrington	104	14	Ives	Thomas	1	1	2		1	5	1	1	2				14		
Stockbridge	255	26	Jacklin	Ebenezer									1		2		3		
New Marlborough	233	28	Jackson	Azar	1			1		1			1				4		
New Marlborough	232	23	Jackson	David				1		2		1					4		
Tyringham	113	44	Jackson	Ebenz	1		2		1	2	1	1	1				10		
Tyringham	114	29	Jackson	Giles		1	2		1	1	2			1			8		
Bethlehem	180	16	Jackson	Jacob	2			1		2	2		1				8		
Partridgefield	187	30	Jackson	Joshua		1	1		1	1	1		1				6		
Sheffield	225	35	Jackson	Reuben		1		1		2		1	1				6		
Cheshire	156	19	Jacob	Moses	1	1		1		2	1		1				7		
Sheffield	226	29	Jacobs	Israel	3	1		1		1			1				7		
Sheffield	230	16	Jacobs	Jonathan	1	1		1			1	1		2			7		
Sheffield	226	32	Jacobs	Richard		1		1					1	1			4		
West Stockbridge	249	12	Jacquins	John	2		1	1		2	1						7		
Becket	267	8	Jager	Elias		2	1	1						1			5		
Southfield	183	2	James	Dick J											3		3		
Stockbridge	255	30	James	John				1					1				2		
Lanesborough	150	1	James	Jonathan				1		1	1			1			4		
Stockbridge	255	28	James	Stephen	2			1		1	2			1			7		
Stockbridge	255	29	James	Stephen W	2	1		1		1	1			1			7		
Sheffield	226	33	Jammons	Peleg Negro											3		3		
Pittsfield	198	16	Janes	Seth	1	1	1	2		1		1					7		
Alford	117	27	Jaquins	Peter	1			1		2	1			1			6		

TOWN	PG#	LN#	LAST NAME	FIRST NAME	FREE WHITE MALES					FREE WHITE FEMALES					TOTAL ALL OTHER	TOTAL SLAVES	TOTALS	DISTRICT/ TOWNSHIP	NOTES
					under 10	10 to 16	16 to 26	26 to 45	45 and over	under 10	10 to 16	16 to 26	26 to 45	45 and over					
Pittsfield	198	11	Jarrett	Stephen			1		1	1				1			4		
Pittsfield	198	19	Jarvis	John				1		1				1			3		
Lanesborough	149	18	Jarvis	Joseph	2	2	1		1	2	1		2				11		
Stockbridge	255	27	Jason	Deliverance											3		3		
Lanesborough	152	1	Jecocks	Samuel	1	1		1			1		1				5		
Pittsfield	198	17	Jeffords	Amasa	1			1		1			1				4		
Pittsfield	198	18	Jeffords	John					1	1		2		1			5		
Lee	262	24	Jenkins	Ebenezer		1			1					1			3		
Lee	262	25	Jenkins	Ebenz Junr	4			1		1			1				7		
Savoy	140	1	Jenks	David	2		1			1			1				5		
Adams	136	8	Jenks	Edmund	3	1	1	1	1	2	1	1	2				13		
Adams	136	3	Jenks	George	2	2		1			1		2				8		
Cheshire	156	15	Jenks	George	1			1		3				1			6		
Adams	137	11	Jenks	Jacob	1		4	1		2	1	3	1				13		
Cheshire	156	18	Jenks	Jesse	2	1	2	1		3		1	1				11		
Adams	137	14	Jenks	Peter	3	2		1		1		1		1			9		
Adams	135	19	Jenks	Samuel	2			1		1			1				5		
Adams	136	21	Jenks	Stephen	3	2		1		1	1	1	1				10		
Adams	135	18	Jenks	Thomas	1		2	1		2		1					7		
Sheffield	224	24	Jenney	Abselm	1	1	1			1	1						5		
Adams	136	10	Jennings	Sylvester			1			2			1				4		
Washington	215	35	Jennins	Ephraim	1			2		2		2					7		
Alford	116	23	Jewell	Eliphalet		1		1				1	1				4		
Adams	134	2	Jewell	Jonathan		1	2	1		2	1		1				8		
Egremont	119	14	Jewit	Joseph	1	1		1		3			1		1		8		
Lanesborough	150	14	Jewitt	David		1		1		1			1				4		
Tyringham	112	38	Jinks	William	1	1	1	1		2		1					7		
Windsor	165	26	Jobes	John	2	1	2	1		1							7		
Alford	116	25	Johns	Aaron	2		1			1		1					5		
West Stockbridge	249	11	Johns	Stephen	2	1	2		1	2		1	1	1			11		
West Stockbridge	249	10	Johns	Peter	1	1	1					1					4		
Tyringham	112	21	Johnson	Anna		1	1	1				1		1			5		
Sheffield	228	17	Johnson	Benjamin	2			1		3	1	1					8		
West Stockbridge	249	13	Johnson	Benjm			1										1		
Williamstown	130	24	Johnson	David	2	2		1	1	1		3	1	1			12		
Williamstown	131	3	Johnson	David 2d		3			1			1		2			7		
Becket	267	10	Johnson	Dyer	1		1			2		1					5		
Lanesborough	148	12	Johnson	George		2		1		1	1	1					7		
Sheffield	221	18	Johnson	Guy Negro											5		5		
Pittsfield	198	14	Johnson	Isaac			1	1		1		1	1				5		
Great Barrington	105	34	Johnson	Jacob			1				2						3		
Sheffield	228	10	Johnson	Jared	2	1			1	2	1	1	1				9		
Becket	267	9	Johnson	Jesse	1		1			1		1					4		
Dalton	192	32	Johnson	John											7		7		
Sheffield	229	10	Johnson	John			1		1	1	1		1	1			6		
Sheffield	228	16	Johnson	John Jun			1			3		1					5		
West Stockbridge	249	9	Johnson	Jonathan			1			3	1		1				6		
Richmond	206	11	Johnson	Lemuel	1		2		1	1	2	1	1				9		
Richmond	206	44	Johnson	Lewis			2					1	1				4		
Becket	267	11	Johnson	Moody	1			1		2		1	1				6		
Windsor	165	22	Johnson	Obadiah	1	1		1		3	1		1				8		
West Stockbridge	249	14	Johnson	Robert				1					1				2		
Pittsfield	198	13	Johnson	Rufus		1	1			1			1			1	6		
Becket	267	6	Johnson	Runnels			2	1					1				4		
New Marlborough	238	6	Johnson	Samll	1			1		3	2	1	1				9		
Sandisfield	176	36	Johnson	Samuel		1						1					2		
Tyringham	112	26	Johnson	Stephen			2	1					1				4		
Tyringham	112	27	Johnson	Stephen Jun	2			1		1			1				5		
Becket	267	7	Johnson	William	2			1		1			1				5		
Egremont	120	36	Joiner	Octavus	2		1	1	1	4	2		1	1			13		
Bethlehem	181	33	Jones	Adonijah	2	1	1			1		2	1		1		9		
Hancock	160	39	Jones	Amos	3			1					1				5		
Adams	137	38	Jones	Baker	3			1		2			1				7		
Dalton	192	29	Jones	Benajah			1	1						1			3		
Hancock	160	15	Jones	Benjamin	4	1		1			1		1				8		
Sandisfield	170	4	Jones	Benoni	4			1		1			1				7		
Cheshire	157	14	Jones	Daniel	1	1		1		2	2		1				8		
Hancock	161	28	Jones	Daniel	1				1				1	1			6		
Washington	213	16	Jones	Daniel		1	1		1	1	1	1		1			7		
Dalton	192	30	Jones	Eli	2			1			1		1				5		
Adams	139	3	Jones	Elias	1	1	1	1	1	1	1	1		1			9		
Tyringham	110	2	Jones	Eliphalet	2	1		1					1	1			6		
Tyringham	110	7	Jones	Eliphalet		1	1	1					1				4		
Dalton	192	28	Jones	Elkanah		1		1		1			1				4		
Tyringham	110	16	Jones	Ephraim	1	1		1		2		1					6		
Tyringham	115	37	Jones	Ephraim	1	1		1		2		1					6		
Tyringham	112	11	Jones	Heman			2		1			2					5		
Adams	138	41	Jones	Isaac	1	2	1	1	1	1	3		1	1			12		
Cheshire	158	9	Jones	Isaac	1			1		2			1				5		

TOWN	PG#	LN#	LAST NAME	FIRST NAME	FREE WHITE MALES					FREE WHITE FEMALES					TOTAL ALL OTHER	TOTAL SLAVES	TOTALS	DISTRICT/ TOWNSHIP	NOTES
					under 10	10 to 16	16 to 26	26 to 45	45 and over	under 10	10 to 16	16 to 26	26 to 45	45 and over					
Sandisfield	170	5	Jones	Israel	2				2	1	3	1		2			11		
Mount Washington	232	3	Jones	John	3		1						1				5		
Bethlehem	173	14	Jones	John	1	2		1		3			1		1		9		
Stockbridge	255	31	Jones	Jonah	1	1	1	1		1		2		2			9		
Bethlehem	173	3	Jones	Joseph			1			1		1		1			4		
West Stockbridge	249	15	Jones	Joseph	3			1		2	3	1					10		
Adams	138	36	Jones	Marshal	1		2	1			2				1		7		
Bethlehem	181	24	Jones	Milles	2	1		1		2			1				7		
Loudon	177	5	Jones	Phinehas	1	1			1	4			1				8		
Lee	262	26	Jones	Samuel	1			1		3			1				6		
Partridgefield	187	31	Jones	Samuel	1					1			1				3		
Bethlehem	182	19	Jones	Sarah Daughter								1	1				2		
Cheshire	158	8	Jones	Seth		1	4	1	1	3		3		1			14		
Tyringham	110	9	Jones	Silas	1	1		1		3	3		1	1			11		
Great Barrington	104	4	Jones	Solomon	3				1	3	2	1					10		
Mount Washington	231	15	Jones	Thomas	3	2	1		1			1		1			9		
New Marlborough	235	8	Jones	Thomas	2	2				1	1	2	1				10		
Sheffield	225	27	Jordon	Ephraim				1				1		1			3		
Lanesborough	149	4	Joseph	Cud (Negro)											4		4		
Richmond	207	18	Joseph	Edward	1			1		1			1				4		
Richmond	207	19	Joseph	Nathaniel			1	1	2				1				5		
Tyringham	113	39	Joslin	Asa	1		1		1	1	2	1		1			8		
Williamstown	125	4	Joslin	John	1	1	1	1		1	2	1	1				9		
New Ashford	163	20	Jourdan	Francis	1	2		1	1			3		1			9		
Great Barrington	110	15	Joy	Ceasar											5		5		
Tyringham	119	23	Joy	Samuel	1			1		1		1					4		
Lenox	210	24	Jubell	Nathan	2	1		1	1	2	1		1				9		
Great Barrington	108	39	Judd	Elnathan	1			1		1	1		1				5		
Lenox	210	26	Judd	Keziah		1				1	3		1				6		
Bethlehem	182	10	Judd	Oliver		2	1	1		1		1	1				7		
Tyringham	115	21	Judd	Oliver	1	2	1	1		1	2		1				9		
Sandisfield	170	6	Judd	Orange	3	1		1		1	2		1				9		
Stockbridge	256	1	Judd	Ozias			1		1			1		2			5		
Williamstown	130	26	Judd	Reuben	1	2		1		3	1		1				9		
Lenox	210	25	Judd	Samuel		1	1		1	1	2		1				7		
Lenox	210	23	Judd	Seymour	1			1					1				3		
Tyringham	114	30	Judd	Thos C.	2			1		1			1				5		
Bethlehem	182	14	Judd	Timothy Son			1	1					1				3		
Lenox	210	22	Judd	Uriah	1	2		1		1			1				6		
Great Barrington	104	24	June	Benjamin	1	1		1		1	1		1				6		
Sheffield	223	6	June	Benjamin			1	1		2	1		1				6		
Egremont	119	3	Kaline	Jacob		1		1					1				3		
Egremont	119	22	Karner	Felix	2			1		3			1				7		
Egremont	119	15	Karner	Jacob			1		1	1		1		1			5		
Egremont	119	16	Karner	Stephen			1					1					2		
Pittsfield	198	23	Keeler	Benjamin		1	2		1	1	1		1				7		
Pittsfield	198	22	Keeler	Elias	2		1	1	1	1		2					8		
Sheffield	227	30	Keep	Jabez		1			1	2			1				5		
Lee	262	27	Keep	John	3	2			1	1		1					8		
Williamstown	128	26	Keep	Jonathan				1		1			1				3		
New Marlborough	235	16	Kelcey	David	1	1		1		3			1				7		
Hancock	162	14	Kelley	Benjamin		1	1		1			1		1			5		
Adams	134	40	Kelley	Isaac		1	1	1	1			1	1	1			7		
Williamstown	127	5	Kelley	William	3			1					1				5		
Stockbridge	258	21	Kellis	Thomas											3		3		
Alford	117	11	Kellogg	Abner		1	2		1	2	1		1				8		
Sheffield	228	26	Kellogg	Amasa		1							1				2		
Sandisfield	176	9	Kellogg	Asahel	1		1		1	1	1		1				6		
Sheffield	228	22	Kellogg	Ebenezer	1	1	3		1	1	1		2				10		
Sheffield	227	15	Kellogg	Ephraim		2	2		2	1	1		1				9		
Sheffield	227	16	Kellogg	Ephraim Jun	1	1	1						1				4		
Sheffield	227	4	Kellogg	Erastus	2		1	1				1	1				6		
Great Barrington	104	10	Kellogg	Ezra		1		1		3	3	2	1		1		12		
Sheffield	228	21	Kellogg	Gideon				1									1		
Sheffield	226	7	Kellogg	Homer	1	1		1		2	1		1				7		
Sheffield	228	25	Kellogg	Jesse		1		1		1	1		1				5		
New Marlborough	234	2	Kellogg	Joel	2			1		1	1		1				6		
Great Barrington	108	32	Kellogg	John		1	3		1			1		1			7		
Alford	116	33	Kellogg	Jonah	2		1			1			1				5		
Becket	267	22	Kellogg	Joseph			1					1					2		
Sheffield	225	22	Kellogg	Josiah	1	1	3	1		1	1		1				9		
Sheffield	228	19	Kellogg	Mary								2		1			3		
Williamstown	128	33	Kellogg	Nathaniel	2	2		1		2	1	1					10		
Dalton	192	33	Kellogg	Nathl	1	1			1	1	1		2				7		
Dalton	192	34	Kellogg	Nathl Jr	1			1					1				3		
Sheffield	226	14	Kellogg	Nehemiah	2		2		1	2	1		1				9		
Sheffield	226	5	Kellogg	Pliny	1	1		1		2	1	1					8		
Williamstown	127	25	Kellogg	Samuel	3	1	1	2	1	2	1	3	1	1	1		17		
Sheffield	228	20	Kellogg	Silas	3	2		1		2		2	1	1	1		13		

TOWN	PG#	LN#	LAST NAME	FIRST NAME	FREE WHITE MALES under 10	10 to 16	16 to 26	26 to 45	45 and over	FREE WHITE FEMALES under 10	10 to 16	16 to 26	26 to 45	45 and over	TOTAL ALL OTHER	TOTAL SLAVES	TOTALS	DISTRICT/ TOWNSHIP	NOTES
Sheffield	227	1	Kellogg	Thomas H			3			2		1	1				6		
Alford	116	39	Kelsey	Abel	1	1	3		1	1				1			8		
Alford	116	37	Kelsey	Daniel			2		1	1	1		1				6		
Alford	116	35	Kelsey	Daniel Junr		1		1				1					3		
Alford	116	3	Kelsey	Reuben		1	1		1	2	1	3	1	1			11		
Becket	267	18	Kendrick	Polly											3		3		
Windsor	165	15	Kenedy	Asa	1	1		1		3			1				7		
Pittsfield	198	24	Kennedy	Andrew		1	1			1		1					4		
Williamstown	127	6	Kenney	Daniel	1		1			2	1	2					7		
Williamstown	128	30	Kenney	Richard	1	1	2	1	1	2			1				9		
Pittsfield	198	25	Kent	Benjamin	1	1		1		1			1	1			6		
Washington	215	36	Kent	John	1			1					1				3		
New Ashford	163	4	Kent	Nathaniel	2	1			1	2	1			1			8		
West Stockbridge	249	16	Kesterbauk	John	2			1					1				4		
Clarkesburg	141	13	Ketchum	David	3			1		1			1				6		
Clarkesburg	141	12	Ketchum	Eleazer	4			1		1		1					7		
Clarkesburg	141	11	Ketchum	Epenetus			1	2	1					2			6		
Clarkesburg	141	16	Ketchum	Samuel			1			1		1	1				4		
New Marlborough	232	24	Keyes	Elias	1			1					1				3		
Tyringham	112	43	Keyes	Ephraim	1			1					1				3		
New Marlborough	240	28	Keyes	Thaddeus	3		1	1	1		1		1	1			9		
Sandisfield	175	28	Kibbe	Ebenezer	1	1			1		1	2	1				7		
Hancock	161	20	Kibbe	Samuel						4	1		1				6		
Loudon	178	33	Kibbee	Daniel	1			1		3		1					6		
Loudon	179	8	Kibbee	Ebenezer	2			1				1		1			5		
Loudon	178	35	Kibbee	John	2	3		1		2		2	1				11		
Loudon	179	7	Kibbee	William	1			1	1	1		1					5		
Richmond	207	34	Kidington	Jacob		2	1		1			3		1			8		
Great Barrington	105	38	Kilborn	Charles		1		1					1				3		
Great Barrington	109	45	Kilborn	Elijah		1				2			1				4		
Sandisfield	177	6	Kilborn	Elisha & Son	1			1	1			1		1			5		
Williamstown	129	25	Kilborn	John		1			2	1		1	1				6		
Sandisfield	176	38	Kilborn	Jonathan			2	1		1	1	1	1				7		
Great Barrington	110	7	Kilborn	Richard		1		1		1			1	1			5		
Bethlehem	173	7	Kilborn	Robbins	3			1		2			1				7		
Great Barrington	105	35	Kilborn	Robert	2		1	1		1			1				6		
Washington	213	28	Kilburn	Benjm		1	2	1					1				5		
Washington	213	36	Kilburn	Benjm Jur	1			1		2		1					5		
Bethlehem	181	15	Kimbal	Edmond		1											1		
Tyringham	111	25	Kimball	Charles				1		2	1			1			5		
Adams	136	43	Kimball	David		1	1			1	1	1					5		
Adams	138	13	Kimball	Isaac	2		2					2					6		
Adams	138	12	Kimball	Noah		1		1		4	3		1				10		
Adams	138	14	Kimball	Samuel	2	1		1		3	1	1	1				10		
Great Barrington	108	49	King	Asahel	2			1					1				4		
Cheshire	157	1	King	Curtis			1			1			1				3		
Egremont	120	32	King	Elijah	2		2	1		3	2	1	1	1			13		
Mount Washington	232	31	King	Fenner	4	2		1		2			1				10		
Zoar	143	7	King	Jesse	3	2	2	1		1	1	1	1	2			14		
Mount Washington	232	30	King	John		1			1		1	1		1			5		
Williamstown	127	40	King	John	2	2			1	4	1		2	1			13		
Great Barrington	105	18	King	Lucius	1	2			1		1	2		1			8		
Cheshire	156	40	King	Medad		1		1	1	1		1		2			7		
Cheshire	156	41	King	Noble	1			1		1		1	1				5		
Pittsfield	198	20	King	Paul				1			2		1				4		
Williamstown	133	2	King	Paul	1			1		1	1		1				5		
Great Barrington	106	11	King	Reuben	1		1						1				3		
Hancock	161	17	King	Reuben	2	1		1		2	1		1				8		
Becket	267	19	King	Solomon				1					1				2		
Hancock	161	13	King	Ward	1			1		1			1				4		
Great Barrington	106	4	King	William				1						2			3		
Becket	267	17	King	Reuben		1				1		1					3		
New Marlborough	236	16	Kingman	Amos		1						1					2		
New Marlborough	240	19	Kingman	Caleb	2		2	1		1	2		1	1			10		
New Marlborough	234	5	Kingman	Samll	1			1		2			1				5		
Savoy	140	36	Kingman	Thomas			3					1					4		
Sandisfield	177	12	Kingsbery	Benjamin		1											1		
Sandisfield	177	3	Kingsbery	Daniel				1			2		1				4		
Bethlehem	181	37	Kingsbery	Jabez	2			1					1				4		
Bethlehem	181	35	Kingsbery	Joseph	2			1		2	1		1				7		
Sandisfield	172	9	Kingsbery	Lemuel				1		1	1		1				4		
Becket	267	14	Kingsley	Amos	3			1		2		1	1				8		
Tyringham	116	1	Kingsley	Elijah		1	1		1		2	1		1			7		
Adams	135	25	Kingsley	Elisha	2		1	1		1		1	1	1			8		
Becket	267	12	Kingsley	Enos	3		1	1		2	1	2	1				11		
Becket	267	16	Kingsley	Isaiah		1	2	1		1		1		1			7		
Partridgefield	187	33	Kingsley	Jedidiah		2	1	1		2		1		1			9		
Pittsfield	198	21	Kingsley	Jona	4			1		1			1	1			8		
Becket	267	21	Kingsley	Joseph				1		3			1				5		

TOWN	PG#	LN#	LAST NAME	FIRST NAME	FREE WHITE MALES					FREE WHITE FEMALES					TOTAL ALL OTHER	TOTAL SLAVES	TOTALS	DISTRICT/ TOWNSHIP	NOTES
					under 10	10 to 16	16 to 26	26 to 45	45 and over	under 10	10 to 16	16 to 26	26 to 45	45 and over					
Becket	267	13	Kingsley	Martin	1	1	1	1		1	1	1	1				8		
Becket	267	20	Kingsley	Mary			1					1	1				3		
Becket	267	15	Kingsley	Nathan		1			1		1			1			4		
Becket	267	23	Kingsley	Sarah				1				2					3		
Bethlehem	180	20	Kingsley	Seth		2			1	3	1		1				8		
Partridgefield	187	34	Kingsley	Silas	1			1		2			1				5		
Stockbridge	256	2	Kingsley	Wido							1		1	1			2		
Dalton	192	35	Kittridge	Abel	1	1		1		1		2					6		
Pittsfield	198	27	Kittridge	William		1	1	4		2	2	1	2				13		
Great Barrington	107	47	Kline	Conrad			1				2						3		
Mount Washington	231	8	Kline	John Jun			1			2			1				4		
Great Barrington	107	40	Knapp	Daniel	2	1		1		3	1	1	1				10		
Mount Washington	232	15	Knapp	David	2		1				1						4		
Tyringham	112	37	Knapp	Ephraim	2		1			2		1					6		
New Marlborough	238	8	Knapp	Ezra	2		2	1		2	1	1	2				11		
Tyringham	112	50	Knapp	Ira			1					1					2		
New Marlborough	239	9	Knapp	Mary	1		1	1		1	1		1				6		
Pittsfield	198	26	Knealand	John	1			1		2			1				5		
Pittsfield	198	28	Knealand	Polly									1				1		
Sandisfield	175	34	Kneeland	Dudley	1			1		1			1				4		
Southfield	182	11	Kneeland	Isaac 2nd				2			2		1				5		
Southfield	182	12	Kneeland	Isaac 3rd	1			1		1	1						4		
Bethlehem	181	4	Knight	Lydia Wid									1				1		
Adams	138	40	Knight	Richard		1		1		2		1	1				6		
Great Barrington	108	29	Knight	Samuel		1		1		1		1					4		
Sandisfield	170	1	Knowles	Paul	2	3		1	1	3			1				11		
Loudon	177	14	Knowles	Seth	1	1		1		2			1				6		
Sandisfield	173	30	Knowles	Willard Jr	2			1		1			1				5		
Sandisfield	175	33	Knowles	Willard Sen				1						2			3		
Zoar	143	4	Knowlton	Paul			1										1		
Williamstown	126	13	Kriger	Betsey Mrs.		1		1		2	1		1	1			7		
Williamstown	126	14	Kriger	William			1						1				2		
Bethlehem	181	28	Kyes	Ephraim	1			1		1			1				4		
Washington	215	26	Ladd	Jesse	1			1	1	1		2		1			7		
Great Barrington	108	38	Laird	Joseph	2	2	2	1		1	2		1				11		
Egremont	120	23	Laman	Clement		2	1	1	1	1		1		1			8		
Tyringham	119	24	Laman	Cornelius	2			1			1	1					5		
Alford	116	28	Laman	Jacob		1		1				1		1			4		
Alford	116	26	Laman	William				1						1			2		
Windsor	166	19	Lamb	Chester	1	1	1					1					4		
Washington	214	25	Lamb	Dudley	1	1		2		4			2				10		
Williamstown	126	28	Lamb	Elijah	3		1	1		1	3		1				10		
Alford	116	30	Lambert	Samuel	2		3	1		2	1		1				10		
Windsor	167	20	Lamphier	Elijah		1		1		1	1		1				5		
Lanesborough	148	28	Lamphier	Phinehas		1	2	1			2		1				7		
Lenox	210	27	Landers	Asael	2	1		1		2		1	1				8		
Lenox	210	28	Landers	Thomas				1						1			2		
Sheffield	224	12	Landon	Ezekiel	1	1		1		1			1				5		
Williamstown	129	1	Landrus	Lemuel	2		1	1		1			1	1			7		
New Marlborough	240	15	Lane	Isaac	3	1	1	1		1	2	1	1				11		
West Stockbridge	249	18	Lane	John	1	1		2		1			1				6		
Williamstown	126	15	Lane	John			1			1		1					3		
Cheshire	153	17	Lane	William		1	1		1	1	1		1				6		
Tyringham	114	24	Langdon	Amos	2	2		1		2	1	1	1				10		
Lee	262	29	Langdon	Christopher	1					1		1					3		
Tyringham	114	25	Langdon	Jesse	3		1	1		1	1		1	1			9		
Lee	262	28	Langdon	John	1	1		1			1	2					6		
Washington	214	12	Lankton	John				1			1		1				3		
Great Barrington	105	15	Lantman	James											4		4		
Adams	136	28	Lapham	David	2	1	1		1	1			1	1			8		
Adams	136	29	Lapham	George	4	2	1	2		2	1	2	2	2			18		
Adams	134	39	Lapham	John		1	3	2		2		4	2				14		
Loudon	177	11	Larkum	Paul	3	1		1		2		1					9		
Loudon	177	12	Larkum	Silas	2		1			1		1					5		
Pittsfield	198	33	Larned	Simon	5		1		1		2	1	1				11		
Williamstown	132	17	Lasell	Elias	2			2					1				5		
Lanesborough	152	5	Lasell	Joshua	1		1	1	1	1			1				7		
Windsor	166	33	Latham	Levi	3			1		1	1		1	1			8		
Pittsfield	198	34	Lathrop	Uriah	1	2			1	4	2		1				11		
Washington	216	13	Laurence	Jeremiah	1	2		1		1	1		1				7		
Hancock	159	13	Lawrence	Aaron	3		2		1			1	1				8		
Sheffield	224	6	Lawrence	Asa	1		1			1			1				4		
Dalton	192	38	Lawrence	Daniel	2		1			1		1					5		
Sheffield	231	10	Lawrence	Daniel		1							1				2		
Dalton	192	39	Lawrence	Jona	2		1					1					4		
Dalton	192	36	Lawrence	Joseph		2		1		1		1		1			6		
Dalton	192	40	Lawrence	Josiah				1					1				2		
Pittsfield	198	31	Lawrence	Josiah	2	2			1	1	1	1	1				9		
Dalton	192	37	Lawrence	Thomas		2	1	1				1		1			6		
Pittsfield	198	29	Leach	Elijah		1			1	2	1	2		1			8		

126

TOWN	PG#	LN#	LAST NAME	FIRST NAME	FREE WHITE MALES under 10	10 to 16	16 to 26	26 to 45	45 and over	FREE WHITE FEMALES under 10	10 to 16	16 to 26	26 to 45	45 and over	TOTAL ALL OTHER	TOTAL SLAVES	TOTALS	DISTRICT/ TOWNSHIP	NOTES
Richmond	206	3	Leadbetter	Israel	1				1					2			4		
Richmond	205	11	Leadbetter	Thomas	1			1		3			1	1			7		
Richmond	206	9	Leadbetter	William S.			3						2				5		
Partridgefield	187	35	Lealand	John		1		1		1	1		1				5		
Partridgefield	187	36	Lealand	John Jun			1					1					2		
Partridgefield	187	37	Lealand	Moses	1			1		1			1				4		
Great Barrington	110	6	Leaming	Jeremiah	2			1		3			1				7		
Sheffield	225	14	Lebaran	Isaac	1	1		1		1			1	1			6		
Sheffield	229	28	Lebaran	Joshua	1	1	2		1				1	1			7		
New Marlborough	240	11	Lee	Abner	1			1				1	1				4		
New Marlborough	240	29	Lee	Elias	2	1			2	1	1	1	1				9		
Sheffield	221	13	Lee	Elisha		1	2	1		1	1		1				7		
Great Barrington	105	7	Lee	Henry	2			1				1	1				5		
Sandisfield	176	34	Lee	Isaac	1		1	1		1		1	1				6		
Pittsfield	198	30	Lee	Jonathan				1		1				1			3		
Loudon	179	24	Lee	Samuel	2			1		1			1	1			6		
Great Barrington	105	5	Lee	Solomon N	2		2					1	1				7		
Mount Washington	232	20	Lee	William	1	1	1		1	2	1	2		1			10		
Adams	139	9	Leeman	Andrew	1	1			1	1	1			1			6		
Williamstown	127	29	Leete	Jared			1		1				1	1			4		
Cheshire	156	17	Leland	John	1		1		1	3	3			1			10		
Zoar	143	24	Leonard	Andrew	1			1					1				3		
Windsor	166	27	Leonard	Barnie	1			1		1			1				4		
Becket	267	30	Leonard	Elijah			1										1		
Washington	213	4	Leonard	Elijah	2	2			1	1	1		1				8		
Sheffield	229	7	Leonard	Ephraim					1					1			2		
Windsor	167	23	Leonard	Jesse					1					1			2		
Sheffield	222	33	Leonard	Nathll	1		1	1		1	1	1	1		1		8		
Sheffield	223	2	Leonard	Rice	1		2	1	1	1		2					8		
Lee	262	30	Leonard	Samll			1										1		
Washington	213	3	Leonard	Samuel		3			1	1		1		1			7		
Windsor	167	22	Leonard	Solomon	3	1		1		1	2		1				9		
Washington	215	32	Leonard	Tilley	2			1		2		1					6		
New Marlborough	239	21	Leonard	Timothy										1			1		
Clarkesburg	142	9	Lessure	Isaiah	1		1	2	1	1				2			8		
Becket	267	27	Lester	John		1		1					1				3		
Becket	267	25	Lester	Lemuel				1						1			2		
Great Barrington	105	16	Lester	Silas	2			1		2			1				6		
Becket	267	26	Lester	Steward		1				3		1					5		
Williamstown	127	30	Levingstone	John			2	1				1	1				5		
Richmond	205	16	Lewis	Abel	1	1		1		4		1					8		
West Stockbridge	249	19	Lewis	Benjm	2		1	1		2	1		1	1			9		
West Stockbridge	249	20	Lewis	Benjm Jr	2		1					1	1				5		
Tyringham	112	29	Lewis	Benoni	2	1	2	1		1	2	1		1			11		
Richmond	208	1	Lewis	David			1					1					2		
Savoy	141	2	Lewis	Dyer				1				1	1				3		
New Marlborough	240	9	Lewis	Ebenezer	1	1	2	1		2	2		1				12		
New Ashford	162	19	Lewis	Gideon			1	1		2	1			1			5		
New Ashford	162	14	Lewis	James			1			1		1	1				4		
Pittsfield	198	41	Lewis	Joseph			1			1		1		1			4		
Sandisfield	174	5	Lewis	Joseph	1	2	1		1	2				1			8		
New Marlborough	239	14	Lewis	Oliver	2	1	1	1		3	3		1				12		
Adams	136	37	Lewis	Richard	2			1					1	1			5		
Lenox	210	30	Lewis	Eldad	3		2		1	1			1	1			9		
West Stockbridge	249	17	Liet	Nathanll			1						1				2		
Egremont	120	33	Lightbody	John	3	1			1	1	1		1				8		
Washington	213	6	Lillie	Joseph			1			2	1	1					5		
Hancock	159	7	Lilly	Benjamin	2			1		1			1				5		
Adams	138	11	Lincoln	Apollos	3	1	1						1				6		
Lanesborough	151	16	Lincoln	Jonathan	2		1	1		1			1				6		
Stockbridge	256	3	Linden	Jedediah	4	1	1	1				1	2				10		
Sheffield	225	2	Lindsey	Aaron	1		1			1			1				4		
Sheffield	224	38	Lindsey	James			2		1			1		1			5		
Sheffield	231	13	Lipaugh	John Emery			1					1					2		
Cheshire	155	30	Lipit	John				1				2		1			4		
Pittsfield	198	32	Little	Woodbridge	1	1		1		1			1	2			7		
Williamstown	129	3	Littlefield	Josiah	2	1		1		2	1			1			8		
Loudon	178	29	Lloyd	David	1			1		2		1					5		
Zoar	143	2	Lock	James	4			1					1				6		
New Marlborough	233	5	Lockwood	Gershom		1		1		1	1	1	1				6		
Lanesborough	151	8	Lockwood	Jeremiah	3	1		1		1			1				7		
Bethlehem	173	23	Logan	William			1			1		1					3		
Pittsfield	198	38	Longworthy	Willard	1		1					1					3		
Partridgefield	187	41	Loomer	Charles	3	1		1			2	1	1				9		
Partridgefield	187	38	Loomer	Darius	3			1					1	1			6		
Egremont	120	29	Loomis	Andrew	4	1	2	1					1	1			10		
Lenox	210	29	Loomis	Andrew	1	1		1	1	1				1			6		
Egremont	118	22	Loomis	Daniel			1		1	1	1		1				5		
Partridgefield	187	42	Loomis	Eleazer		3		1		2		1	1				8		
Lanesborough	151	15	Loomis	Elijah	1			1		3			1				6		

127

TOWN	PG#	LN#	LAST NAME	FIRST NAME	FREE WHITE MALES under 10	10 to 16	16 to 26	26 to 45	45 and over	FREE WHITE FEMALES under 10	10 to 16	16 to 26	26 to 45	45 and over	TOTAL ALL OTHER	TOTAL SLAVES	TOTALS	DISTRICT/ TOWNSHIP	NOTES
Zoar	143	5	Loomis	John	2	2		1		2	1	1	1				10		
Pittsfield	198	37	Loomis	Jonathan	1	1		1		1	1			1			7		
Becket	267	28	Loomis	Jonathan	1		2			2	2			1			9		
Egremont	119	1	Loomis	Josiah		1		2						2			5		
West Stockbridge	249	21	Loomis	Lodawich	1			1		1			1				4		
Tyringham	119	15	Loomis	Solomon	2			1					1				4		
Richmond	208	17	Loomis	Timothy		2	1	1		1	1	2	1				9		
Mount Washington	232	35	Lord	Daniel	1	1			1	1	2		1				7		
Adams	135	39	Lord	Prudence	1								1				2		
Windsor	166	15	Louden	Jacob	1		1			1		1					4		
Windsor	166	16	Louden	John	1			1		3			1				6		
Great Barrington	108	25	Louis	Ebenz	1	1			1	1	2		1				7		
Sheffield	228	8	Lovejoy	Palmer	4			1		1	1		1				8		
Sheffield	229	12	Lovejoy	Timothy	1			1		1		1	1	1			5		
Loudon	177	20	Loveland	Amos	3	2		1		2			1	1			10		
Southfield	183	6	Loveland	Daniel			1	1		4	1		1				8		
Sandisfield	176	15	Loveland	Elijah	1	1	1	1		1	1	2		1			9		
Loudon	178	1	Loveland	Isaac		1		1		1		2		1			6		
Partridgefield	187	40	Loveland	Levi	2			1		1	2			1			7		
Partridgefield	188	1	Loveland	Philip		1		1		4			1				7		
Zoar	143	33	Loveman	George		2		1		2		1	1	1			8		
Dalton	192	41	Lovernan	George		1				1		1					3		
Sandisfield	171	8	Lucas	William	2			1		1			1	1			6		
Pittsfield	198	39	Luce	Benjamin	1	2	1	3			1	2	1				11		
Pittsfield	199	1	Luce	Cornelius	2			1		2			1				6		
Pittsfield	198	42	Luce	David	1	1			1				2				5		
Pittsfield	198	40	Luce	Hezekiah	2		1	2	1	2		1	1	1			11		
Pittsfield	198	35	Luce	Joshua	2		2	1		1	2	1	1				10		
Becket	267	24	Luer	Simeon	5		1	1		1			1				9		
Stockbridge	256	7	Lusk	William			1	1					1				3		
Adams	138	21	Luther	Eber	2			1		1	2		1		10		17		
Williamstown	126	41	Luther	Hezekiath	3	2		1		2		1	1				10		
Windsor	168	26	Luther	Nathaniel	3	1		1					1				6		
Adams	135	40	Luther	Seth	1			1		2		1					5		
Partridgefield	187	44	Lyman	Isaac	1			1		3			1				6		
Becket	267	29	Lyman	Jeremiah	1			1		2			2	1			7		
Partridgefield	187	39	Lyman	Joel	3			1				1	1				6		
Pittsfield	198	36	Lyman	Miles			1						1				2		
Cheshire	158	12	Lyman	Moses		1			1	1				1			4		
Richmond	208	43	Lyman	Noah				1						1			2		
Richmond	208	42	Lyman	Noah Jun	1			1				1	1				4		
Partridgefield	187	43	Lyman	Samuel	1			1		2	1		1				6		
Stockbridge	256	4	Lynch	Lawrence		1	2	1									4		
Stockbridge	256	6	Lynch	Moses	1			1		1			1				4		
Stockbridge	256	5	Lynch	Nathaniel	2			1		1			1				5		
Sheffield	231	7	Lyon	Asa	1	1	1			1		1					5		
Cheshire	154	14	Lyon	Ruth			1						1				2		
Lanesborough	151	24	Lyon	Seth	1		1			2			1				5		
Lanesborough	151	31	Lyon	Thomas	1	1	1		1	1	1	1		1			8		
Cheshire	154	19	Lyons	John		1		1		1	2		1				6		
Williamstown	129	20	Mackay	Samuel	1		2	1					1		1		7		
Alford	117	30	Macklin	Mary	1								1				2		
Williamstown	131	39	Maladay	Thomas	2			1	1				1				5		
Lanesborough	149	5	Malby	Frederick		1				1		2			2		6		
New Ashford	162	16	Mallery	Eli	2	1			1	1	1	1	1				8		
New Ashford	163	17	Mallery	Uriah		1	1	1		1		1	1	1			7		
Lenox	210	31	Malloon	Charles		1	1		1	1	1	2	1				8		
Lenox	211	20	Malloon	John	3			1		1	1	1	1				8		
Partridgefield	188	7	Malloon	Ruth		1	3			1	3			1			9		
Windsor	165	32	Mally	Thomas	3			1					1				5		
Windsor	165	25	Mally	Timothy	2			1					1	1			5		
Lee	262	31	Maltby	Zacherus	1		1	1		1		1	1				6		
Loudon	178	2	Man	William	2	1		1		2			1				7		
Cheshire	155	42	Manchester	Isaac	1		1	3		3	1		2				11		
Adams	136	30	Manchester	Waterman	1		1	1				1					4		
Bethlehem	181	18	Manley	Daniel		1		1		2	3		1				8		
Bethlehem	172	11	Manley	George & David	2	2		1	1				1	1			8		
Bethlehem	173	19	Manley	John	1	2		1	1				1				8		
Bethlehem	181	30	Manley	Martin	2			1		2		1					6		
Bethlehem	181	14	Manley	Shubael	1			1		2			1				5		
Becket	268	6	Mann	Joseph		2	1		1	1	1	1					7		
Williamstown	130	5	Mann	Southwick		4							1				5		
Sheffield	223	18	Manning	Thomas	1			1		4			1				7		
Great Barrington	110	11	Manning	William			3		1		1			1			6		
Great Barrington	105	25	Mansfield	Abijah	1			1									2		
Great Barrington	105	26	Mansfield	Daniel			1	1					1				3		
Tyringham	112	40	Mansfield	Daniel	2		3	1					1				7		
Great Barrington	107	10	Mansfield	Lydia		1							1				2		
Alford	117	29	Mansfield	Thomas	2			1				1					4		
Loudon	179	4	Marcy	Howland	2			1		2			1				6		

TOWN	PG#	LN#	LAST NAME	FIRST NAME	FREE WHITE MALES					FREE WHITE FEMALES					TOTAL ALL OTHER	TOTAL SLAVES	TOTALS	DISTRICT/ TOWNSHIP	NOTES
					under 10	10 to 16	16 to 26	26 to 45	45 and over	under 10	10 to 16	16 to 26	26 to 45	45 and over					
Loudon	179	6	Marcy	Lawton		1		1		3			1				6		
Loudon	179	3	Marcy	Smith		1			1	1	1		1	1	1		6		
Loudon	179	5	Marcy	Thomas	2			1		1	1	1					6		
Tyringham	113	41	Markham	Aaron	2			1		1		1	1				6		
Southfield	182	22	Markham	Ambrose	2				1	3	2		1				9		
Tyringham	113	23	Markham	Asa	1	1		1		3	1		1				8		
Tyringham	114	31	Markham	Benjm	2	1	1		1	2	1	1		1			10		
Tyringham	114	18	Markham	William	1	1	1	1		3	1		1				9		
Dalton	193	1	Marsh	Henry	3	1	1	1		1	1	2	1	1			12		
Partridgefield	188	4	Marsh	Lemuel		1		1				3	1				6		
Partridgefield	188	5	Marsh	Lemuel Jun	1		1					1					3		
Lee	262	34	Marsh	Reuben	3			1		1			1				6		
Partridgefield	188	6	Marsh	Samuel		1				2	2		1				6		
Williamstown	132	1	Marther	Elias	1		5	1		1			1				9		
Adams	133	16	Martin	Benjamin	1		1	1		1	1	1		1			7		
Cheshire	156	37	Martin	Ebenezer		2	1		1	2		1	2				9		
Adams	133	17	Martin	George				1				1		1			3		
Hancock	159	21	Martin	Gideon	1	1			1		1	2	1				7		
Great Barrington	108	48	Martin	Jesse			1										1		
Sheffield	223	20	Martin	Jethro											2		2		
Savoy	140	13	Martin	Joseph		3		1			1		1				6		
Savoy	140	14	Martin	Joseph Jr	3			1				1					5		
Tyringham	113	28	Martin	Noah	2	1		1		2	2		1				9		
Hancock	159	20	Martin	Simeon	2	1	1		1	3		2	1				11		
Washington	214	41	Martin	Thomas	2	1	1		1	1	2	1	1				10		
Loudon	179	37	Martin	William											4		4		
Lenox	210	32	Martindale	Edward	1	1	2		1	1	1	1	1	1			10		
Williamstown	127	23	Martindale	Justin	1	1		1		2			1				6		
Sandisfield	171	18	Marvin	Nathan	3		1		1	3		1	1				10		
Sheffield	222	15	Marvin	Silas	3			1	1	1	1	1	1	1			10		
Loudon	177	4	Marvin	Sylvanus	1			1		3			1				6		
Lenox	212	9	Marvin	Ebenezer				1				1		1			3		
New Marlborough	237	18	Mason	Adam	2		2		1	2	3	1	1	1			13		
Cheshire	157	5	Mason	Alexander			1				1		1	1			4		
Sheffield	227	32	Mason	Asa		1				1		1		1			4		
Adams	135	3	Mason	Barnard			1					1					2		
Cheshire	157	7	Mason	Barnard		1		1			1		1				4		
Cheshire	153	5	Mason	Brooks		1	1	1		1				1			5		
Lanesborough	149	32	Mason	Brooks	3			1		1			1				6		
Cheshire	154	7	Mason	Daniel	2	1		1		2	1		1				8		
Cheshire	154	21	Mason	David	1	1	1	1		5			1				10		
Cheshire	155	10	Mason	Dexter	2	1	1	1				1	1				7		
Cheshire	157	30	Mason	Hezekiah	1	2	3		1	2	1	2		1			13		
Cheshire	157	50	Mason	Hezekiah	1	2	3		1	2	1	2		1			13		
Cheshire	157	8	Mason	Jesse		1	1	1			1	1		1			6		
Adams	135	34	Mason	Jonathan	2		1	1	1	4		1	1	1			12		
Cheshire	157	21	Mason	Joshua	1		2				1						4		
Cheshire	157	12	Mason	Levi		2	2	1		4	1	1		1			12		
Cheshire	153	16	Mason	Nathan	1		1	1		3	4		1				11		
Cheshire	154	6	Mason	Nathan				1						1			2		
Cheshire	157	27	Mason	Nathan			1		1	1	1		1				5		
Cheshire	157	47	Mason	Nathan			1		1	1	1		1				5		
Cheshire	157	28	Mason	Nathan J		1				1		1					3		
Cheshire	157	48	Mason	Nathan J		1				1		1					3		
Adams	136	12	Mason	Philip		1	2		1	3			1				8		
Cheshire	157	9	Mason	Reuben	1			1		2		1					5		
Sheffield	227	31	Mason	Robert	1			1				1					3		
Cheshire	154	22	Mason	Rufus	1			1		1	1		1				5		
Sheffield	227	23	Mason	Rufus		1				1	1						3		
Cheshire	155	32	Mason	Samuel	1	1				1		1					4		
Cheshire	157	4	Mason	Silas		1						1					2		
Adams	135	14	Mason	Tampson	1		2		1	2	4	1	1				12		
Sheffield	227	19	Mason	Thaddeus	3		3	1					1				8		
Cheshire	156	4	Mason	Timothy			1						1				2		
Cheshire	154	15	Mason	William	1			1				1					3		
Partridgefield	190	27	Mathews	Samuel		1					1						2		
Partridgefield	188	10	Mathews	Thomas	1			1		1			1				4		
Adams	134	5	Matteson	Joshua	4		1				1	1					7		
Savoy	139	10	Matthews	David		1			1	1		1	1				5		
Sheffield	224	22	Matthews	Jabez	1	1	2	1		1			1				7		
Sheffield	225	9	Matthews	Jabez				1						1			2		
Washington	215	10	Matthews	James	1			1		1		1	1				5		
Great Barrington	107	21	Matthews	Justice				1						1			2		
Washington	214	30	Mattoon	Philip	1			2					1	1			5		
Washington	214	31	Mattoon	Rufus		2		1		2			1				6		
New Marlborough	237	24	Maxon	Thomas			1			2		1					4		
New Marlborough	234	30	Maxon	Thompson S		1	1		1		1		1				5		
Sheffield	229	6	May	Lemuel	3			1		2			1	1			8		
West Stockbridge	249	25	Mayham	Philip			1										1		

129

TOWN	PG#	LN#	LAST NAME	FIRST NAME	FREE WHITE MALES					FREE WHITE FEMALES					TOTAL ALL OTHER	TOTAL SLAVES	TOTALS	DISTRICT/ TOWNSHIP	NOTES
					under 10	10 to 16	16 to 26	26 to 45	45 and over	under 10	10 to 16	16 to 26	26 to 45	45 and over					
Pittsfield	199	18	Maynard	Eli	1			1		2		1					5		
Dalton	192	42	Maynard	Ezra	1			1				1					3		
Pittsfield	199	4	Maynard	Jotham	3			1		2		1	1				8		
Sandisfield	170	10	McCartey	John	1			1		4			1				7		
Cheshire	154	16	McCluth	Solomon	3			1		3	1		1				9		
Pittsfield	199	20	McCoy	Paul	3	1		1		1	1			1			8		
Becket	267	36	McCullen	David	1		1			1		1					4		
Adams	136	31	McFarland	Daniel	3	2	1	2		3	1	2	1		1		16		
Cheshire	157	23	McGloth	Laurence					1				1	1			3		
Cheshire	157	43	McGloth	Laurence					1				1	1			3		
Cheshire	157	25	McGloth	Lewis	2			1		2	1		1				7		
Cheshire	157	45	McGloth	Lewis	2			1		2	1		1				7		
Washington	214	2	McKnight	James	2	1	2	1		1	1		1				9		
Washington	214	3	McKnight	John	3	2	1		1	3		1		1			12		
Washington	214	1	McKnight	Robert	2			1		2			1	1			7		
Williamstown	130	31	McMaster	Robert		1	2		1			2		1			7		
Stockbridge	256	12	McMullen	John	1	2		1		3			1				8		
Sheffield	226	8	McNiel	Wm			1						1				2		
Williamstown	125	10	Meacham	James		1		2	1	1	1	2	1	1			10		
Pittsfield	199	7	Mead	Ephraim	2		2	1				2		1			8		
Mount Washington	232	4	Mead	Jesse	3	1	2		1	1	1		1				10		
Lanesborough	151	39	Mead	Stephen	3		1	1		1	3		1	1			11		
Pittsfield	199	2	Mead	Stephen				1						1			2		
Pittsfield	199	10	Mead	Stephen Junr	1	1		1		1			1				5		
Lanesborough	150	16	Mead	Zadock	1		1						1				3		
Pittsfield	199	17	Mellen	William	1		2	1		3	1	1	1				10		
West Stockbridge	249	29	Menter	Elijah			1	2				1	1				5		
Washington	215	3	Merifield	John	1			1					1				3		
Richmond	208	11	Meriman	Abraham	1	1	1		1				1	1			6		
Mount Washington	232	17	Merit	Cornbury	1	1		1		2	1	1	1				8		
New Marlborough	235	19	Merriam	Miriam			1	2					1	1			5		
Washington	213	9	Merrick	Gideon	1	2			1		1	1	1				7		
Becket	268	1	Merrifield	Richard		1				1		1					3		
Becket	268	3	Merrifield	Thomas	2	1	1		1	3		1		1			10		
Lee	262	35	Merrill	Abijah	1	2			1			2		1			7		
Pittsfield	199	13	Merrill	Daniel	1		1	1		3	1		1	1			9		
Pittsfield	199	14	Merrill	Ezekiel	1		1						1				3		
Windsor	165	2	Merrill	Gad	4	1							1				7		
Pittsfield	199	15	Merrill	Hosea	3	2		1		2	2		1	1			12		
Alford	117	28	Merrill	Stephen		1		1		1				1			4		
Sheffield	225	24	Merrills	Seth			1										1		
Lanesborough	152	30	Merrils	Asa	2			1				1	1				5		
Richmond	208	12	Merriman	Benja				1		1		1	2	1			6		
Dalton	193	2	Merriman	Daniel		1		1				1		1			4		
Dalton	193	5	Merriman	Daniel Jr	1		1	2					1				5		
Dalton	193	3	Merriman	Jesse	3	1		1		1			1				7		
Dalton	193	4	Merriman	Nathl	1			1		1	1	1					5		
Bethlehem	181	8	Merrit	John	1			1		2	1		1				6		
Pittsfield	199	16	Merry	Samuel	1				1	3			1				6		
Becket	267	35	Merryfield	Oliver		1				1		1					3		
Sandisfield	177	8	Mery	Truman			1										1		
Southfield	183	4	Mesenger	Aron	1	1		1		3	2	1		1			11		
Becket	268	2	Messenger	Billy	1	3	1	1		3		1	1	1			12		
Becket	267	34	Messenger	Ebenz N	3	1		1		1	2		1				9		
Loudon	179	33	Messenger	Elijah	3	1		1		1			1				7		
Alford	116	32	Messenger	Elisha				1		2		1		1			5		
Tyringham	119	8	Messenger	George	1		1	1		2	2		1				8		
Tyringham	119	12	Messenger	George Jun	1		1			1		1					4		
Becket	267	32	Messenger	Hiram		1		1			1	1	1				5		
Becket	267	33	Messenger	John		1			1	3		1	1				7		
Washington	216	19	Messenger	Nathan	1	1	3	1			2	1					9		
Partridgefield	188	9	Messenger	Nathll	1		1				1						3		
Lenox	210	33	Metcalf	Alton	1			1		2			1				5		
Stockbridge	256	10	Mighlls	Elijah	2		1	1		1			1	1			7		
Stockbridge	256	13	Mighlls	Lucretia									1				1		
Loudon	178	21	Miles	Elijah	2			1				1					4		
West Stockbridge	249	28	Miles	Jonathan	3			1		1							6		
Alford	117	34	Milk	Elkhanah			1					1					2		
Alford	116	38	Milk	Job		1			1					1			3		
Alford	117	4	Milk	Jonathan		2	3		1				1	1			8		
Washington	216	1	Millakin	William		1		1		2	1		2				7		
Pittsfield	199	8	Millard	Jason	3	1		1		2			1				8		
Alford	117	55	Millard	Joshua Junr	1		1	1		1	1		1				6		
Egremont	118	23	Millard	Josiah		1						1					2		
Pittsfield	199	12	Millard	Matthew		2	1		1	1	1	1		2			9		
Becket	268	4	Millard	Oliver	2	1		1					1				5		
Becket	268	5	Millard	Orram		1				1		1					3		
Egremont	118	4	Millard	Peter	1			1					1				4		
Washington	215	38	Millekin	Alexander	3			1		1			1	2			9		

130

TOWN	PG#	LN#	HEADS OF HOUSEHOLD		FREE WHITE MALES					FREE WHITE FEMALES					TOTAL ALL OTHER	TOTAL SLAVES	TOTALS	DISTRICT/ TOWNSHIP	NOTES
			LAST NAME	FIRST NAME	under 10	10 to 16	16 to 26	26 to 45	45 and over	under 10	10 to 16	16 to 26	26 to 45	45 and over					
Bethlehem	173	13	Miller	Abner		1	1		1	1	2			1			7		
Williamstown	128	25	Miller	Benjamin	1			1		1	1		1				5		
Partridgefield	188	12	Miller	David			1		1	1	1		2		1		7		
Washington	216	20	Miller	Isaac			2	1					1				4		
Stockbridge	256	11	Miller	Jonathan	3	2	1	1		1		1	1				10		
Washington	215	16	Miller	Lewis	1			1		2			1				5		
Tyringham	119	7	Miller	Newbury					1		1			1			3		
Adams	136	13	Miller	Samuel	1			1		1	1		1				5		
Savoy	140	15	Miller	Samuel	1	1	2		1	1	2		2				10		
Bethlehem	173	9	Miller	Seth			1			3			1				5		
Pittsfield	199	19	Miller	Timothy	2	1			1		1	1	1				7		
Tyringham	111	16	Milliman	Abiram	2			1		4		1					8		
Tyringham	111	15	Milliman	Ezekiel	1		1	1				1					4		
Tyringham	112	10	Milliman	Theodoria		1				1			1				3		
Tyringham	111	2	Millman	Briant	1		1		1			2		1			6		
Hancock	158	7	Mills	Daniel	1			1		1			1				4		
Becket	267	31	Mills	Ezekiel			3						1				4		
Bethlehem	181	7	Mills	Ezekiel A	1		1	1		1			1				5		
Williamstown	131	1	Mills	Samuel	3	1	1		1		1	3	1				11		
Sheffield	231	5	Mimson	Daniel	1			1		3		1					6		
Partridgefield	188	3	Miner	Christopher	2			1	1	2		1	1	1			9		
Windsor	166	2	Miner	Ephraim	1	1	1		1		1	1		1			7		
Partridgefield	188	11	Miner	Isaac	2	1			1	2	1		1				8		
Partridgefield	188	2	Miner	Joshua	1		1					1					3		
Alford	116	21	Miner	Rufus	2	1		1		3	1		1				9		
Partridgefield	188	8	Miner	Treat	2			1		1		1					5		
West Stockbridge	249	24	Minilier	Barnabas		1			1				1				3		
West Stockbridge	249	22	Minilier	John		1			1				1				3		
Cheshire	157	26	Miranville	Robert	2			1					1				4		
Cheshire	157	46	Miranville	Robert	2			1					1				4		
Great Barrington	106	25	Mires	John					1					1	7		9		
Adams	137	40	Mixton	Gideon			1			1		1	1				4		
Sandisfield	174	32	Moar	John	1	1		1		4			1				8		
West Stockbridge	249	23	Moffatt	Lemuel		1	1		1		1		1				5		
New Ashford	162	15	Moger	Reuben	2			1				1	1				5		
Lee	262	32	Monson	Freeman		4	1			4			1				11		
Pittsfield	199	5	Montague	Seth	2	1		1			2		1				7		
Tyringham	111	22	Moon	Abram	1	3			1			1					6		
Williamstown	126	29	Moon	Benjamin	3	1		1			1		1				7		
Pittsfield	199	3	Moon	Seth		1	1					1	1				4		
Becket	268	7	Moore	Asher		1											1		
Egremont	119	5	Moore	Henry	1		1					1	1				4		
Pittsfield	199	21	Moore	Mattew B.	1			1		1			1				4		
Washington	216	7	Moore	William					1			1	1				3		
Lanesborough	148	23	More	Ishmael											5		5		
New Marlborough	237	5	More	William		1			1	1	1		2				6		
Washington	213	14	Morehouse	John	1			1		5	2		1				10		
Washington	213	18	Morehouse	Thomas	1	1	2	1			1	2	1				9		
New Ashford	163	39	Morell	Hugh			2	1					1				4		
Lee	262	33	Morey	Edy	2			1		1			1				5		
Hancock	161	25	Morey	Gideon	1			1		4	3	1	1				11		
Tyringham	111	28	Morey	Jesse			2	1					1				4		
Windsor	164	11	Morey	Nathaniel		1		1			2	1	1				6		
Sandisfield	172	7	Mowry	Stephen		1		1		3	1	1					7		
Williamstown	127	24	Morgan	Nathaniel	2			1		2	1		1				7		
Stockbridge	256	8	Morgan	Sylvia									1				1		
Bethlehem	181	41	Morley	Abner	2		1	1		2			1	1			8		
Bethlehem	173	2	Morley	Derick		1	1	1		2	1		1				7		
Bethlehem	173	4	Morley	Israel				1									1		
Partridgefield	188	13	Morly	David	1	1		1		2	1		1				7		
Lenox	210	34	Morrel	John	4	1	1		1	1			1	1			10		
Stockbridge	256	9	Morrison	John					1				2				3		
Sandisfield	173	3	Morse	Asahel	3			1					1				5		
Windsor	165	13	Morse	Enos	2		1	1		2	2		1				9		
Williamstown	127	32	Morse	James		1	2		1	1	1	3		1			10		
Sheffield	222	1	Morse	Lemuel	1	2			1	2		2	1				9		
Tyringham	114	2	Morse	Moses		1		1		3	1		1	1			8		
Tyringham	110	23	Morse	Peter			1		1				1				3		
Great Barrington	107	8	Morse	Seth		2	1	1		2		2	1				9		
Windsor	168	6	Morse	Daniel			3		1		1	1	1	1	1		9		
Washington	215	27	Morss	John			3		1	1	2	3		1			11		
Washington	215	6	Morss	John Jun			1			2			1				4		
Pittsfield	199	9	Moseley	Chester	1			1		2			1	1			6		
Pittsfield	199	11	Moseley	Josiah	3	2	1	1	1			2		1			11		
Sheffield	227	12	Moss	Darby									2				2		
Richmond	205	24	Moten	Jeremiah	1	1		1		1	1		1	1			7		
Pittsfield	199	6	Mott	Lyman									1				2		
New Marlborough	237	25	Mudge	Jervis	3	2	1	1		2			1	1			11		
New Ashford	163	19	Mudge	Stephen	1			1	1	3	3		1				10		
West Stockbridge	249	26	Munn	John	1	1		1	1	3	1		1				9		

TOWN	PG#	LN#	LAST NAME	FIRST NAME	FREE WHITE MALES					FREE WHITE FEMALES					TOTAL ALL OTHER	TOTAL SLAVES	TOTALS	DISTRICT/ TOWNSHIP	NOTES
					under 10	10 to 16	16 to 26	26 to 45	45 and over	under 10	10 to 16	16 to 26	26 to 45	45 and over					
West Stockbridge	249	27	Munn	John Junr	1			1				1					3		
Great Barrington	108	20	Murray	Jack													4		
Great Barrington	107	16	Murry	Conn	3			1		1	2		1				8		
Lenox	210	35	Murwin	Moses					1	2	1	1		1			6		
Cheshire	154	38	Nap	Jonathan	1		2	1		3		1	1	1			10		
Great Barrington	105	47	Nash	Abigail			1	1		2	1	1	2				8		
Stockbridge	256	19	Nash	Anna									1				1		
Lee	263	1	Nash	James			1										1		
Windsor	166	26	Nash	John			1			1			1				3		
Egremont	118	2	Nash	Jonathan	2			1		2			1				6		
Williamstown	131	15	Nash	Shubael	3	1	1	1		2	1	2	1				12		
Stockbridge	256	14	Nash	Stephen	2		2	1			1	1	1		2		12		
Sheffield	223	12	Negro	Isaac											5		5		
Sheffield	223	11	Negro	Peter											4		4		
Zoar	143	11	Negus	Samuel	1	1	3		1		1			1			8		
Zoar	143	9	Nelson	Daniel	3			1	1	1	3	1		1			11		
Sandisfield	170	9	Nelson	James	1			1	1	1		1	1				7		
Savoy	141	1	Nelson	James		1		1				1					4		
Stockbridge	256	15	Nelson	Moses	1			1					1				3		
Stockbridge	256	17	Nelson	Oliver	2			1		2			1				6		
Stockbridge	256	16	Nelson	William	1		1	1				1		1			5		
Adams	137	6	Nesbett	Hannah			2	1	1		1	2					8		
Adams	136	42	Nesbett	Robert	2			1		2			2				7		
Becket	268	12	Nesbitt	Robert	2	1		1		3	2		1				10		
Williamstown	128	28	Newbree	Elias		1		1		1	2	1		2			8		
Pittsfield	199	23	Newell	Aaron	2		1					1					4		
Lanesborough	152	13	Newell	Ebenezer	1		2	1		1	1		1				7		
Adams	137	26	Newell	Elisha	2		1			2			1				6		
Dalton	193	6	Newell	Ephraim	1	2		1		1			1				6		
West Stockbridge	249	31	Newell	Hart		1					1						2		
West Stockbridge	250	1	Newell	John		1		1			2		1				5		
West Stockbridge	250	2	Newell	John Jr		1		1		3	2	1	1				9		
Lenox	210	37	Newell	Josiah		2		1		1			1				5		
West Stockbridge	249	32	Newell	Sary						1		1	1				3		
Tyringham	119	20	Newman	Samuel	1	1		1		1		1	1				6		
Tyringham	119	21	Newman	Seth	3		1					1					5		
Stockbridge	258	26	Newport	Betty											4		4		
Lanesborough	152	26	Newton	Gershom			1		5			1			1		8		
Williamstown	126	24	Newton	Isaac	1		1			1			1				4		
New Ashford	162	9	Newton	Jason				1		1			1				3		
Sheffield	230	26	Newton	John	2			1		1	1		1				6		
Lanesborough	152	28	Newton	Philo	4	1		1					1		2		9		
Sheffield	230	31	Newton	Theodore		1				1			1				3		
Richmond	207	32	Nicholes	John Jun		1		1		4	3	1	1				11		
Williamstown	129	12	Nicholl	Josiah	2	1		1		1		1	1				7		
Dalton	193	9	Nichols	Amos	2	1		1		2			1				7		
Lanesborough	149	3	Nichols	David	1	1		1		2			1				6		
Sheffield	228	6	Nichols	James	2			1		2			1				6		
Becket	268	8	Nichols	John		2	2	1		3			1	1			10		
Great Barrington	109	1	Nichols	John				1		1			1	1			4		
Becket	268	9	Nichols	John Jr			1			1			1				3		
Hancock	161	1	Nichols	Jonathan	2			1		2	1		1				7		
Sheffield	228	13	Nichols	Jonathan	2			1		1	1		1				6		
Stockbridge	256	18	Nichols	Joseph				1					1				2		
Dalton	193	7	Nichols	Lemuel	1	1	1			2	1		1				7		
Becket	268	11	Nichols	Rachel	2							1					3		
Sheffield	228	7	Nichols	Samll	2			1					1				4		
Becket	268	10	Nichols	Stephen	1			1		2			1				5		
Partridgefield	188	14	Nicholson	Nathan	2			1		2			1				6		
Sandisfield	174	17	Nickerson	Jesse			1			1			1				3		
Richmond	206	38	Nickols	John				1					1	1			3		
Great Barrington	107	28	Nie	Davis	1		1						1				3		
Hancock	160	20	Niles	John		1		1		3	1		1				7		
Pittsfield	199	22	Noble	Aaron		1	1						1				3		
Great Barrington	108	14	Noble	David		1	2							1			4		
Pittsfield	199	24	Noble	David	1			3		1	1						6		
Williamstown	132	10	Noble	David		1		2		2	1	1					7		
Williamstown	132	22	Noble	Deodaties	1	1		1		1			1				5		
Sheffield	231	2	Noble	Eli		1	1			1	1						4		
Sheffield	228	30	Noble	Ezekiel P	2	1		1		1	1						6		
Sheffield	226	19	Noble	Hezekiah	1	2		1			1	1		2			8		
Sheffield	222	35	Noble	Jeremiah		1	1						1				3		
Sheffield	231	1	Noble	Matthew				1		2	1		1				5		
Sheffield	223	24	Noble	Nathll	1	1		1					1	1			5		
Sheffield	223	22	Noble	Nathll Jun	3			1		2			1				7		
Sheffield	223	23	Noble	Oliver			1			1			1				3		
Dalton	193	8	Noble	Royal			1			3			1				5		
Sheffield	223	25	Noble	Silas			1			1			1				3		
Lanesborough	149	27	Noble	Timothy			1	2		1	1		2				7		
New Marlborough	232	28	Noble	William	2												4		

TOWN	PG#	LN#	HEADS OF HOUSEHOLD		FREE WHITE MALES					FREE WHITE FEMALES					TOTAL ALL OTHER	TOTAL SLAVES	TOTALS	DISTRICT/ TOWNSHIP	NOTES
			LAST NAME	FIRST NAME	under 10	10 to 16	16 to 26	26 to 45	45 and over	under 10	10 to 16	16 to 26	26 to 45	45 and over					
Lanesborough	149	31	Noble	Winthrop			1					1		1			3		
Sheffield	229	2	Noble	Zecharh		1			1			1		1			4		
Washington	216	18	Noble	Zenas	1		2		1			3		1			8		
Pittsfield	199	26	Nogard	Isaac	1			1		1			1				4		
Great Barrington	108	5	Nokes	Isaac	1		1		1	2		1		1			7		
Windsor	166	10	Norie	Samuel			1			1			1				3		
New Marlborough	237	27	Norslot	Daniel	1		1					1					3		
Great Barrington	108	42	North	Seth			1	1						1			3		
Tyringham	112	12	Northrop	Amos			1	1				1		1			4		
Tyringham	111	10	Northrop	Barzillai	3			1		1			1				6		
Lanesborough	149	33	Northrop	Joseph	1		1	1		1	1			1			6		
Tyringham	111	30	Northrup	Amose Jur	1			1		1			1				4		
Lenox	210	36	Northrup	Elijah	1	1			1				1	1			5		
Tyringham	112	13	Northrup	John	1		1						1				3		
Cheshire	158	17	Northrup	Stephen	1	1	1		1	3				1			8		
Williamstown	125	11	Northum	Timothy	2	2	1		1		1	1	1				9		
Pittsfield	199	25	Norton	Abel				1		1			1				3		
Lanesborough	152	19	Norton	Charles		1	2		1		2	1		1			8		
New Marlborough	236	14	Norton	David	3	2		1		1		3	1				11		
New Marlborough	240	14	Norton	Isaac	3	1	1	1		1	2	1	1				11		
New Marlborough	239	20	Norton	James	1			1		1			2				5		
West Stockbridge	249	30	Norton	Joel	2			1		1			1				5		
Loudon	177	9	Norton	Jonathan Jr	1	2		1		3			1				8		
Loudon	177	8	Norton	Jonathan Sr	2		1	1	1	2	1	2		1			11		
New Marlborough	237	11	Norton	Phinehas			1	1		1	2		1				6		
New Marlborough	237	33	Norton	Samuel				1		2	1	1			1		6		
New Marlborough	239	2	Norton	Samuel	1	3	1		1		1	1		1			9		
New Marlborough	236	12	Norton	Seth	1		1		1	2			1	1			7		
Great Barrington	108	30	Notewire	George	2	2			1	3			1				9		
Lee	262	38	Nye	John	1	2			2	2		1	1	1			10		
Lee	262	36	Nye	Lewis Jun		1		1				1		1			4		
Lee	262	37	Nye	Seth	1		1	1		1	1	1					7		
Great Barrington	107	30	O'Brian	John			1	1				3		1			6		
Hancock	162	17	Olden	Gideon	1		3			1		1					6		
Great Barrington	105	22	Olds	Aaron	2	1		1		2	1		1				8		
Partridgefield	188	15	Olds	Daniel	2	2	1	1	1	1		1	1				10		
Egremont	120	4	Olds	Ebenezer			1	1		1		1	1				5		
Egremont	118	7	Olds	Isaac	1			1		1		1					4		
Washington	215	5	Olds	Isaac				1		1			1				3		
Egremont	118	5	Olds	Seth	1		1					1					3		
Alford	117	17	Olen	Leman	1		1						1				3		
Alford	117	18	Olen	Seth		2			1	1				1			5		
Great Barrington	107	33	Olmstead	Nathl	2			1	1			1	1				6		
Great Barrington	107	29	Olmstead	Nehemiah			1			2			1				4		
Stockbridge	256	20	Olmstead	Samuel	3			1		1	1		1				7		
Great Barrington	107	32	Orcott	Peter	1	1		1		2	1	1	2				9		
Great Barrington	109	33	Orcutt	Moses	1				1			1		1			4		
Becket	268	13	Ormsby	Eliajah	2	1	1		1	1		1	1				8		
Great Barrington	104	17	Ornsby	Levi	3			1					1				5		
Tyringham	114	28	Orton	Amariah	2	1		1		3			1				8		
Tyringham	114	26	Orton	Darius	2			1		3			1				7		
Lee	263	2	Orton	Roger	4	1	1	1		1		2	1				11		
Hancock	159	14	Osborn	Hezekiah			1	1						1			3		
Hancock	159	16	Osborn	James	1	1	1	1		4	1	1	1				11		
Lanesborough	151	19	Osborn	John	2	1		1		1	2		1				8		
Pittsfield	199	28	Osborn	John	1		1			1			1				4		
Lenox	210	38	Osborn	Josiah	1		4		1			1		1			8		
Pittsfield	199	27	Osborn	Richard				1		1	1	1		1			4		
Mount Washington	232	18	Osbourne	Isaac				1						1			2		
Mount Washington	232	19	Osbourne	Isaac Junr		1				1		1					3		
Mount Washington	232	2	Osbourne	Joseph				1		1		1					3		
Loudon	178	25	Owen	Elihah Jun	1	1		1		1			1				5		
Loudon	178	24	Owen	Elijah Sen		1	2	1	1					1			6		
Loudon	178	28	Owen	Erastus				1		1		1					3		
Sheffield	224	21	Owen	Minor		1		1		1	1		1				5		
New Ashford	163	18	Owens	Rhoda	2								1				3		
Bethlehem	182	12	Owles	Sarah	1	1					1		1				4		
Windsor	167	4	Packard	Zebulon	1			1					1				3		
Savoy	140	24	Paddleford	Zachariah		1	4		1	1			1	1			9		
Stockbridge	256	33	Paddock	Joseph				1		3			1				5		
Adams	134	23	Page	William		1	1	1		1	1		1				6		
Sandisfield	176	12	Paine	Joseph			2	1		1		1	1	1			7		
Williamstown	132	25	Paine	Lebbens	3			1		1			1				6		
Sandisfield	175	38	Paine	Nathan			1										1		
Cheshire	154	39	Paine	William	1		2	1		1		2	1				8		
Adams	134	10	Pall	James	3	2	1		1	1	1	1		1			11		
Great Barrington	107	36	Palmer	Annie		1		1					1				3		
Hancock	160	11	Palmer	Asahel	1	1	3		1	2	1		1				10		
Alford	117	32	Palmer	Israel				1		2				1			4		

133

TOWN	PG#	LN#	LAST NAME	FIRST NAME	under 10	10 to 16	16 to 26	26 to 45	45 and over	under 10	10 to 16	16 to 26	26 to 45	45 and over	TOTAL ALL OTHER	TOTAL SLAVES	TOTALS	DISTRICT/ TOWNSHIP	NOTES
			HEADS OF HOUSEHOLD		FREE WHITE MALES					FREE WHITE FEMALES									
Pittsfield	199	30	Palmer	Lydia	1					2			1				4		
Great Barrington	109	30	Palmer	Nathan			1		1	1				1			4		
Mount Washington	232	29	Palmer	Sarah						3				1			4		
Sandisfield	176	35	Palmer	Stephen	2			1		1			1	1			6		
Loudon	178	36	Parish	Benjamin	2			1					1	1			5		
Alford	116	14	Park	Amaziah		1		1					1	1			4		
Alford	116	13	Park	Amaziah Junr				1		2			1				4		
Tyringham	110	8	Park	Joshua	1		1	1		1			1	1			6		
Tyringham	112	20	Park	Matthias	1	1		1		1	1	1	1				7		
Tyringham	112	9	Park	Nathan			1	1		2			1				5		
Tyringham	112	16	Park	Nehemiah	1	2			1	1	1	1		1			8		
Partridgefield	188	19	Parker	Abel		1			1	1	1			1			5		
Partridgefield	188	17	Parker	Abel Junr			1	1					1				3		
Stockbridge	256	28	Parker	Abraham	1	2		1		1	1		1				7		
Stockbridge	257	1	Parker	Benjamin	1				1	1				1			4		
Richmond	205	1	Parker	Deborah				1		1	1		1				4		
Adams	136	5	Parker	Elihu	2		2	1		1	1	1					8		
Lee	263	5	Parker	George	1	1			1	2	1	1		1			8		
Tyringham	119	4	Parker	John	1		1						1				3		
Lenox	211	38	Parker	Jonathan					1	1	1			1			4		
Pittsfield	199	33	Parker	Linas	4	1	1	1		2			1				10		
Lenox	210	41	Parker	Marcy	2					1			1				4		
Adams	137	35	Parker	Oliver			1		1				1	1			4		
Lenox	211	1	Parker	Titus	1				1				1	1			4		
Lenox	210	40	Parker	Titus Jun	1				1	1				1			4		
Lee	263	3	Parker		3		1	1		2			1				8		First name blank
Dalton	193	10	Parks	Abijah		1	1	1	1	1	1		1				7		
Partridgefield	188	29	Parks	Asa	2		2		1	3	1	2	1				12		
Sheffield	224	29	Parks	John	2		1	1		1			1				6		
Pittsfield	199	31	Parmele	Asa						3			1	1			5		
West Stockbridge	250	4	Parmele	Charles	2	1	1		1	1			1	1			8		
Sheffield	221	10	Parmele	Eli	1			1		1				1			4		
Great Barrington	107	23	Parmele	Joel		1		1				1	1				4		
West Stockbridge	250	7	Parmele	Joel			1										1		
Sheffield	226	27	Parmeter	Daniel	1		2	1	1	1				1			7		
Sheffield	228	32	Parson	Batholomew			1			3	1			1			6		
Alford	117	38	Parsons	Amos	1		1			1				1			4		
Sandisfield	174	29	Parsons	Ashbel			1			3			1				5		
Sandisfield	173	35	Parsons	Benjamin	2	1	1		1	1		1	1	1			9		
Adams	138	15	Parsons	Charles	3	1			1	1				1			7		
Alford	116	1	Parsons	David	3			1		1			1				6		
Sandisfield	173	1	Parsons	Eli	1	1	1		1	2	1	1	1				9		
Sandisfield	173	36	Parsons	Elihu	1		1						1				3		
Sandisfield	170	18	Parsons	Enos				1									1		
Windsor	165	12	Parsons	Gideon	2			1		1			1				5		
Alford	116	4	Parsons	Isaac	1			1		1			1				4		
Alford	117	54	Parsons	Isaac		1		1		1			1				4		
Sandisfield	175	15	Parsons	John Jr	3	1		1		1			1				7		
Sandisfield	175	22	Parsons	John Sen		1	1		1			1	1	1			6		
Alford	116	2	Parsons	Joseph	3	2			1	1			1	1			9		
Great Barrington	107	38	Parsons	Oliver			1						1				2		
Sandisfield	175	24	Parsons	Timothy	3	1		1		1			1				7		
Sandisfield	176	40	Parsons	Timothy 2nd			1										1		
Alford	117	39	Parsons	William			1						1				2		
Dalton	193	11	Partridge	John		2		1		1	2	1		1			8		
Stockbridge	256	22	Partridge	Oliver			1										1		
Stockbridge	256	30	Partridge	Samuel		1		1		2			1				5		
Pittsfield	199	32	Partridge	William	1	2		1		4			1				9		
Tyringham	110	4	Patten	Nathal	1	1		1		3	1		1				8		
Mount Washington	231	6	Patterson	Charles		1	2	1		2	2			3			11		
Great Barrington	109	29	Patterson	David		1				1		1					3		
Becket	268	20	Patterson	Eb	2			1		1	3		1				8		
Mount Washington	232	37	Patterson	John			1				1	1					3		
Richmond	205	12	Patterson	Joseph		1			1	1		2	1	1			7		
Mount Washington	232	11	Patterson	Levi	1			1		2			1				5		
Stockbridge	256	24	Patton	Jonathan	1		1	1		1	1						5		
Sheffield	226	36	Paxton	John	2		1			1	1	1		1			8		
Pittsfield	202	34	Payn	Abel											4		4		
Partridgefield	188	16	Payn	Allen	2			1		1			1	1			6		
Partridgefield	188	31	Payn	Ebenezer	4	3	1						1				9		
Partridgefield	188	32	Payn	Stephen			1			1			1				3		
Windsor	166	34	Payson	Joseph	1	2		1						1			5		
Lee	263	10	Pearce	Isaac			1										1		
Bethlehem	181	10	Pearl	Richard		1	3		1				1	1			7		
Partridgefield	188	34	Pearse	William		1	1		1	2	1	1		1			8		
Sheffield	231	6	Peas	Allen				1		2	1		1				5		
Bethlehem	173	16	Pease	Elam	1		1			3			1				6		
Sandisfield	173	26	Pease	Elisha	1		1					1					3		
Sandisfield	174	1	Pease	Henry	3			1		2			1				7		
Sandisfield	175	4	Pease	Henry C.			1		1			1	2	1			6		

TOWN	PG#	LN#	LAST NAME	FIRST NAME	M under 10	M 10 to 16	M 16 to 26	M 26 to 45	M 45 and over	F under 10	F 10 to 16	F 16 to 26	F 26 to 45	F 45 and over	TOTAL ALL OTHER	TOTAL SLAVES	TOTALS	DISTRICT/ TOWNSHIP	NOTES
Partridgefield	188	20	Pease	James			3		1	1	1	1	1				8		
Sandisfield	176	28	Pease	Noadiah	1		1		1					2			5		
Stockbridge	256	23	Pease	Phineas	4	1	2	1		1	3	1	1				14		
Dalton	193	12	Pease	William			1						1				2		
Dalton	193	13	Peck	Benjamin	1	2				2			1				6		
Adams	137	34	Peck	Charles				1		2		1					4		
New Marlborough	239	26	Peck	Eleazer		1	2		1		1	1		1			7		
Lenox	210	39	Peck	Elisha	1	2	1		1	1		1	1				8		
Stockbridge	256	31	Peck	Elisha	2			1					1				4		
Dalton	193	15	Peck	Israel	1	2			1	4	1		1				10		
Sheffield	229	11	Peck	James	1				1		1			1			4		
Tyringham	112	39	Peck	Miller	1	1			1	1			1				5		
Stockbridge	256	25	Peck	Salmon	1			1		1			1				4		
Stockbridge	256	26	Peck	Selah	2	1		1		1			1				6		
New Marlborough	238	21	Peck	Zebulon				1					1				2		
Mount Washington	232	12	Peek	Nathan	2	1	2		1			1		1			8		
Mount Washington	232	13	Peek	Nathan Junr		1						1					2		
Sheffield	222	28	Peet	Arnold	1		1						1	1			4		
Lee	263	17	Peet	Elijah	2	1		1		1		1	1				7		
Partridgefield	188	26	Peirce	Benja		1		1				1	1				4		
Partridgefield	188	23	Peirce	Ebenezer	2	1	1		1		1	2	1	2			11		
Partridgefield	188	35	Peirce	George	1		1	1		1			1				5		
Partridgefield	188	24	Peirce	John	1			1				1					4		
Pittsfield	199	35	Peirce	Jonathan	2	1			1	1	1	1	1				8		
Partridgefield	188	25	Peirce	Levi	1	1	3		1		1		1	1			9		
Richmond	205	6	Peirson	Henry	1			1		2			1		2		7		
Richmond	208	26	Peirson	Nathan		2	4	1	2	2	1	2	2				16		
Richmond	207	17	Peirson	Nathan Jnr			2						1				3		
Richmond	207	21	Peirson	Zachariah	3	1	1	1	2			1	2	1			12		
Sheffield	222	29	Pell	Tamer										1			1		
Loudon	178	4	Pelton	Ephraim	1			1		3			1	1			7		
Loudon	178	17	Pelton	Samuel		1		1		2	1		1				6		
Loudon	178	14	Pelton	Stephen	1			1		2	1		2				7		
Lee	263	15	Penayer	James	1		1		1			1		1			5		
Hancock	158	8	Penfield	Isaac				1				1	1				3		
Adams	138	24	Penniman	Christopher	2		1	1			1		1				6		
Stockbridge	256	21	Pepoon	Daniel	3	1	1	5		2	1	1	1		1		16		
Stockbridge	256	32	Pepoon	Silas Jr		1	1	1	1		1		1	2			8		
Lenox	211	2	Percival	Elisha	1		1		1	1	2	1	1				8		
Becket	268	14	Perkins	Ephraim		2	3		1		1	1	1				9		
Lanesborough	151	30	Perkins	John	4			1					1				6		
Lanesborough	152	23	Perkins	Joseph	3	1		1		2			1				8		
Savoy	140	23	Perkins	William			1						1				2		
Williamstown	130	17	Perkins		2	1		1			1	1		1			7		First name blank
Adams	136	35	Perrey	Burden		1						1					2		
Williamstown	126	30	Perrey	Reuben				1				1					2		
Lee	263	9	Perrin	Edward	2			1		2	2		1				9		
Lee	263	18	Perritt	Mary						1	1		1				3		
Lee	263	4	Perry	Abraham	2	1		1		1	1		1				7		
Richmond	208	21	Perry	David	1	2	4		1	2	1	2		1			14		
Egremont	120	41	Perry	John		1	1	2	1	1			2				8		
Partridgefield	188	21	Perry	John		1	1	1		4	2	1	1				11		
Partridgefield	188	22	Perry	Joseph	5	1		1					1				8		
Loudon	178	10	Perry	Joseph W.	1		2					1					4		
Hancock	161	12	Perry	Josiah		1		1		2		1					5		
Stockbridge	256	29	Perry	Peter	2	1	2		1	1	1	1		1			10		
Lee	263	11	Perry	William		1			1		3	1	1				7		
Savoy	140	39	Person	Jesse		1	1	1					1				4		
Adams	137	31	Peters	Eleazer	2			1		1	1		1				6		
Adams	137	41	Peters	James	3	2		1		1			1				8		
Lenox	212	19	Peters	Robert											4		4		
Stockbridge	258	27	Peters	Thomas											3		3		
Adams	135	8	Peters	William	2	1	1		2	1	2	1	1	1	2		14		
Loudon	179	22	Pettebone	David				1		2	2		1				6		
Lanesborough	149	25	Pettibone	Amos	2			1		2	1		1				7		
Lanesborough	150	29	Pettibone	Elisha			1			3		1	1				6		
Lanesborough	149	22	Pettibone	Jonathan	1			1				1		1			4		
Lanesborough	149	23	Pettibone	Philo	2		1	1		3		1	1				9		
Lanesborough	150	30	Pettibone	Roger	3	2		1		1	1	1	1				10		
Adams	138	7	Pettis	Peleg	1		1		1		1	2		1			7		
Great Barrington	104	22	Phelps	Aaron	2			1					1				4		
Pittsfield	199	36	Phelps	Benjamin	1	1	1		1	4		1		1			12		
Williamstown	130	22	Phelps	Daniel	1		1						1				3		
Lanesborough	151	38	Phelps	Elijah	2			1		4	1		1				9		
New Marlborough	236	31	Phelps	Eliphalet	3	1		1		2	1		1				9		
Stockbridge	256	27	Phelps	Ely		1			1			1		2			5		
Washington	214	17	Phelps	George	5				1	2			1		4		14		
Loudon	178	30	Phelps	Isaac		1	2	1		1	1	1	1				8		
Becket	268	19	Phelps	Jared	2	2		1	1	2	1		1	1			11		
Great Barrington	106	15	Phelps	Josiah				1					1				2		

TOWN	PG#	LN#	LAST NAME	FIRST NAME	FREE WHITE MALES under 10	10 to 16	16 to 26	26 to 45	45 and over	FREE WHITE FEMALES under 10	10 to 16	16 to 26	26 to 45	45 and over	TOTAL ALL OTHER	TOTAL SLAVES	TOTALS	DISTRICT/ TOWNSHIP	NOTES
Sandisfield	176	25	Phelps	Levi C.			1				1			1			3		
Pittsfield	199	38	Phelps	Luther			1			1		1		1			4		
Bethlehem	180	11	Phelps	Nathan	2		1			2	1		1				7		
Cheshire	158	2	Philips	Abiner 2d	1		1					1					3		
Adams	137	12	Philips	Daniel		1	1	1		2			1				6		
Washington	213	23	Philips	Peltiah			1			2	3		1				7		
Williamstown	126	16	Philips	William	1		1			1		1					4		
Williamstown	131	16	Philips	Zebulon	2		1	1		1			1				6		
New Marlborough	232	31	Philips	Samll Jn			1			1		1					3		
New Marlborough	235	29	Philips	Samuel	2	1	1		1	2		1	1				9		
Cheshire	157	19	Phillips	Abizer	1		1		1			1		1			5		
Windsor	164	12	Phillips	Asa	5	2			1	1		2		1			12		
Adams	138	10	Phillips	Hannah									2				2		
Windsor	167	24	Phillips	Joshua			1		1	1	1		1				5		
Egremont	120	1	Phillips	Lacheus	1			1		1		1					4		
Adams	138	9	Phillips	Rufus	1	1	1		1	1	2	1	1	1			10		
Great Barrington	109	42	Phillips	Seth	1		1	1				1	1				5		
Partridgefield	188	27	Phillips	Smith	1	1			1	3		1					8		
Tyringham	114	7	Pickett	Eli			1			2			1				4		
Alford	117	19	Pickett	James		1		1					1				3		
Sandisfield	171	12	Pickett	John	2		1		2	2	2		1				10		
Sheffield	229	26	Pierammi	Caesar											2		2		
Loudon	179	36	Pierce	Adam	1	1		1				1					5		
Egremont	120	27	Pierce	Amasa			1				1						2		
Hancock	160	14	Pierce	Caleb	4	2		1		2	1		1				11		
Savoy	140	42	Pierce	Constant	3			1		2			1				7		
Windsor	165	33	Pierce	Eben	1			1		1			1				4		
Hancock	160	33	Pierce	Ebenezer				1					1				2		
Hancock	159	35	Pierce	Ephraim	1			1		1			1				4		
Adams	133	7	Pierce	James	1		2		1			1		1			6		
Savoy	140	20	Pierce	John	1				1	4	1		1				8		
Tyringham	112	6	Pierce	John	2			1		2			1				6		
Mount Washington	232	8	Pierce	Jonathan		1		1					1				3		
Tyringham	112	7	Pierce	Langarthe	2	1		1		2	1		1				8		
Tyringham	112	5	Pierce	Lawrence		1		1		1			1				4		
Mount Washington	232	34	Pierce	Orange	1			1		2	1						5		
Zoar	143	14	Pierce	Samuel	1		2		1	1	2	1	1				9		
Hancock	160	34	Pierce	Sanford	1			1		1			1				4		
Pittsfield	199	37	Pierson	David			1		1		1			1	1		5		
Dalton	193	18	Pike	Barnabas	2	1		1		1	1	1		1			8		
New Marlborough	237	12	Pike	Ozias	4	1		1		1	2		1				10		
Becket	268	22	Pinney	Aaron			1						1				2		
Becket	268	23	Pinney	Benja			1			1							2		
Becket	268	21	Pinney	Silas			1										1		
West Stockbridge	250	3	Piper	Ebenz M.			1			1			1				3		
Dalton	193	14	Pitts	Samuel	1					1	1		1				4		
Great Barrington	106	8	Pixley	Alexander	1			1		2			1				5		
Great Barrington	106	9	Pixley	Daniel			1			1			1				3		
Great Barrington	105	42	Pixley	Hall	1	1	1		1				2	1			7		
Great Barrington	105	41	Pixley	Hall Junr			1			2			1				4		
Great Barrington	106	23	Pixley	Jonathan	2		2		1	1				1	1		10		
Richmond	207	31	Pixley	Moses	1		1		1	1			1				6		
Sheffield	227	36	Pixley	Nathll	1				1				1	1			4		
Great Barrington	106	13	Pixley	Olive									1				1		
Great Barrington	106	7	Pixley	Silas			1			1	1	1					4		
Tyringham	119	14	Pixley	Squire	1	2		1			1		1				6		
Great Barrington	106	6	Pixley	William				1		2				1			4		
Lanesborough	151	5	Platt	Abiel		2	1	1				2		1			7		
Tyringham	115	27	Platt	Ebenezer			1			1			1				3		
Pittsfield	199	41	Platt	Joseph			1		1	1			1	1			5		
Adams	134	30	Plorich	David Junr	2			1	1	1	2		1	1			9		
Richmond	206	10	Plumb	Ebenezer			1	1		1			1				4		
Stockbridge	256	34	Plumb	Ebenezer		1	2		1	1			1				6		
Pittsfield	199	39	Plummer	Edward	1			1		1	1	1					5		
Richmond	208	2	Plummer	Francis	1	1	1		1			3		1	1		9		
Lee	263	14	Polly	Eleazer			1						1				2		
Partridgefield	188	28	Pomeroy	Daniel	1	1	1		1	2			1				7		
West Stockbridge	250	5	Pomeroy	Grove	2	1		1		2	1		1				8		
Pittsfield	199	34	Pomeroy	Lemuel		1	4	1				1	1		1		9		
New Ashford	163	38	Pomeroy	Medad	3	2		1			1		1	1			9		
New Marlborough	239	3	Pomeroy	Phinehas	1		1	1	1	2		2	1				9		
Pittsfield	199	40	Pomeroy	William	2		1						1				4		
Windsor	165	38	Pool	Ahirah		1	3		1	1	2	2	1				11		
Washington	213	7	Pool	Oliver	1			1		1			1				4		
Partridgefield	188	18	Poole	John	1	1		1		2	2		1				8		
Alford	117	40	Pope	Ebenezer		1	1			1	1						4		
Sheffield	222	10	Pope	Rhoda	2					1		1					4		
Dalton	193	16	Porter	Abraham	2	1	2		1	1	2		1				10		
Sheffield	228	23	Porter	Amos		1			1		1		1				4		

TOWN	PG#	LN#	LAST NAME	FIRST NAME	FREE WHITE MALES					FREE WHITE FEMALES					TOTAL ALL OTHER	TOTAL SLAVES	TOTALS	DISTRICT/ TOWNSHIP	NOTES
					under 10	10 to 16	16 to 26	26 to 45	45 and over	under 10	10 to 16	16 to 26	26 to 45	45 and over					
Williamstown	130	4	Porter	Daniel			3						1				4		
Lee	263	8	Porter	David		2		1		2			1				6		
Lee	263	7	Porter	Ebenezer				1									1		
Washington	213	8	Porter	Ebenz	2		2	1		2			1				8		
Great Barrington	105	30	Porter	Joshua	1	2		1			2	1	1				8		
Zoar	143	13	Porter	Miles	1	1	2	1	1	3	1	1	1	1			14		
Great Barrington	109	26	Porter	Nathaniel		1		1				2					4		
Sheffield	228	24	Porter	Oliver		1							1				3		
Lee	263	6	Porter	Samuel			1		1	1	2	2		1			8		
Tyringham	112	35	Porter	Samuel			1						1				2		
Williamstown	130	21	Porter	Samuel		1	1		1	2	2		1				8		
Sheffield	223	8	Post	Gideon				1	1				1	1			4		
Partridgefield	188	33	Post	Ichabod	1			1		2			1				5		
Clarkesburg	141	7	Potter	Abel			1			1			1				3		
Cheshire	154	35	Potter	Asahel	1	1		2		2			2				8		
Lanesborough	152	9	Potter	Jesse			1						1				2		
Great Barrington	107	45	Potter	Job	1	2	2		1	1	1	5	1				14		
Lanesborough	152	8	Potter	Peleg	1	1	1		1		2	2		1			9		
Adams	136	17	Potter	Simeon			1					1	1				3		
Hancock	160	13	Potter	William			1		5				1				7		
New Marlborough	238	15	Pottiss	Joseph	1	1		1					1				4		
Pittsfield	199	29	Powars	Ephraim	1			1		1	1		1				5		
Lanesborough	149	35	Powell	David			2	1		1		1					5		
Great Barrington	108	34	Powell	Elizabeth		1			2	2	1		1				7		
Lanesborough	150	20	Powell	Ephraim	1		3	1			3						8		
Lanesborough	152	32	Powell	John	3	2	1		1	2	1		1	1			12		
Lanesborough	149	34	Powell	Mary						2		1					3		
Lanesborough	148	27	Powell	Miles	2	1	1		1	1	1	1		1			9		
Lanesborough	150	3	Powell	Robert	2			1	1	2		2	1				9		
Lanesborough	151	6	Powell	Samuel	1	1		1		1			1				5		
Lanesborough	151	4	Powell	Solomon	1			1		2		1	1				6		
New Marlborough	234	32	Powell	Stephen	1		1	1					1				4		
Lanesborough	150	18	Powell	Thomas	2			1		1			1				5		
Lanesborough	151	7	Powell	William	2			1		1			2				6		
Lee	263	13	Powers	John				1					1				2		
Dalton	193	19	Powers	William	3			1		2			1				7		
Sandisfield	174	14	Pratt	Aaron	1			1		4			1				7		
Sandisfield	174	13	Pratt	Barnabas & Son			1	1			1		1				4		
Williamstown	127	7	Pratt	Ebenezer	2		1		3			1					7		
Adams	135	31	Pratt	Ebenz		2		1			2		1				6		
New Ashford	163	35	Pratt	Elias	2		1		3		1	1					8		
Tyringham	115	34	Pratt	Elnathan	1	1		1		1		1					5		
Williamstown	126	18	Pratt	Isaac			1					1					2		
Becket	268	15	Pratt	Jacob	1	2	1		1	1		2		1			9		
Clarkesburg	142	5	Pratt	Joel & Ebenezer		2											2		
Lanesborough	151	1	Pratt	John		2	2		1			2		1			8		
Cheshire	154	36	Pratt	Jonathan		1	1		1	1			1				5		
Williamstown	128	5	Pratt	Noah			1					1					2		
Cheshire	157	18	Pratt	Paul		1			1	1	1		1				5		
Partridgefield	188	30	Prentiss	Thomas		1		1	2		2		1				7		
Egremont	120	9	Preston	Ira	2		1		3			1					7		
Great Barrington	104	18	Preston	Isaac	2		1				1	1					5		
New Marlborough	239	17	Price	Ruid	5		1						1	1			8		
Cheshire	154	32	Price	William	1		1		2	2	1						7		
Great Barrington	109	39	Prichard	Benjamin	2	2			1	3	1		1				10		
Windsor	164	4	Prince	Alpheus	1	1		1	1	1		1					6		
Sheffield	222	31	Prince	Cyrus Negro											3		3		
Windsor	164	3	Prince	David Jun	2		1		1			1					5		
Lanesborough	153	3	Prince	Phebe											5		5		
Windsor	164	6	Prince	Samuel	1		1	1	3			1					7		
Windsor	164	5	Prince	William	1							1					3		
Williamstown	129	2	Prindle	Solomon			1	1		1			1		1		5		
New Ashford	163	6	Prouce	Samuel	1	2		1		1				2			7		
Lee	263	12	Prout	William		1		1					1				3		
Williamstown	125	19	Prowty	Francis				1				1					2		
Stockbridge	258	28	Purden	Anthony											2		2		
Williamstown	129	23	Purrington	Sylvanus		1		1		2	1	1	1				7		
Becket	268	16	Putnam	David		1			3		1						5		
Becket	268	18	Putnam	Joel		1			1		1						3		
Dalton	193	17	Putnam	John		1		1	3			1					6		
West Stockbridge	250	6	Putnam	Jona	1		1		1		1	1					5		
Becket	268	17	Putnam	Nathan			1	1	2	1	1	1					7		
Williamstown	129	26	Putnam	Perley	1	1	2	2	1	1	1	1					10		
Lee	263	16	Putnam	Rebekah	1					1	1						3		
Great Barrington	104	3	Pynchon	Theophilus	1		1				1						3		
Great Barrington	104	1	Pynchon	Walter	1	1	1										3		
Lenox	211	3	Quincy	Samuel	2		1			1	1						5		
Sheffield	226	12	Rainsford	Archa	1	1			1		1						4		
Sheffield	226	11	Rainsford	Solomon	1			1		2	1						5		
Sheffield	228	18	Rainsford	Thomas		3			1	2		1		1			8		

TOWN	PG#	LN#	LAST NAME	FIRST NAME	FREE WHITE MALES					FREE WHITE FEMALES					TOTAL ALL OTHER	TOTAL SLAVES	TOTALS	DISTRICT/ TOWNSHIP	NOTES
					under 10	10 to 16	16 to 26	26 to 45	45 and over	under 10	10 to 16	16 to 26	26 to 45	45 and over					
Lee	263	23	Ramsdale	John	1	1	1		1		1	1		1			7		
Lenox	211	4	Randel	Jesse	1		2			2			1				6		
Pittsfield	200	12	Rando	John G			1			4		1					6		
Egremont	119	23	Randolph	Benjamin			2	1				1		1			5		
Egremont	119	19	Ransford	Solomon	1			1					1				3		
Great Barrington	105	3	Ransom	Elias	1	1	1	1		1	1		1				7		
Egremont	119	8	Rase	Abraham	2		2	1		1							6		
Egremont	118	19	Rase	Darius	1	1		1		1		1					5		
Egremont	118	25	Rase	Isaac	1	2		1		2	2	1		1			10		
Egremont	120	2	Rase	Phillip	2	2	2	1		1	1						10		
Lenox	211	5	Rash	Jacob	3	1		1		1	1		1	1			9		
Richmond	207	3	Rathbon	Daniel		1	1	1			1		1				5		
Tyringham	111	36	Rathbon	Mary								1	1				2		
Tyringham	111	37	Rathbon	Percy	2	1		1		2		1	1				8		
Pittsfield	200	11	Rathbun	Benjamin				1		5	2		1	1			10		
Tyringham	111	21	Rathbun	Jona	3	1		1		2	1	1					9		
Great Barrington	110	10	Rathbun	Nathanl			1					1	1				3		
West Stockbridge	250	12	Rathbun	Philander	2		2	1		2	1		1				9		
Pittsfield	200	10	Rathbun	Reuben	1		1					1					3		
Great Barrington	110	12	Rathbun	Samuel	1	2	1	1			3	1					9		
Lee	263	22	Rathburn	John			1					1					2		
Sheffield	226	20	Rawley	Hiel	4	1	1	1		2	1		1				11		
New Marlborough	235	4	Rawson	Joel	2		1			1		1					5		
West Stockbridge	250	15	Rawson	Jonathan	1	1	2		2	5		1	2	1			15		
New Marlborough	235	3	Rawson	Paul									1				1		
Great Barrington	108	43	Ray	James	1	2	1	1	1	1	4			1			12		
Great Barrington	108	40	Ray	William	2	1	2		1	2	1	1	1				12		
Partridgefield	188	43	Raymond	Amos	1	1	1	1		1	2			1			8		
Sheffield	221	14	Raymond	Dan			2		1		1	2	1				7		
Richmond	208	32	Raymond	Joseph		1		1	1	1	1		1				6		
Richmond	208	38	Raymond	Paul	1	1		1			3		1				7		
Williamstown	131	35	Reab	George	2		1	1		1		1			1		7		
Cheshire	155	24	Read	Benjamin	1			2		1	3		1				8		
Tyringham	113	3	Read	Benjamin		1		1					1				3		
Windsor	164	16	Read	Jeremiah	1			1		2	1	1	1				7		
Tyringham	115	42	Read	Nathal		1		1		3	2		1	1			9		
Windsor	166	11	Read	Nathan	1		2	1		1	1		1				7		
Windsor	165	5	Read	Simeon	3			1					2				6		
Windsor	164	15	Read	William	1	1		1		3	1		1				8		
Pittsfield	200	17	Reddington	Daniel	3		1			2		1					7		
Lanesborough	150	31	Redeway	Joel	1		1	1		2	3	1		1			10		
Lanesborough	148	26	Redeway	Martha	1	1							2				4		
Richmond	206	25	Redfield	Beriah	1		1	1		2	2	3					10		
Richmond	206	24	Redfield	Edmund			1						1				2		
Richmond	208	45	Redington	Eliphalet	2		1	1		1		3		1			9		
Richmond	207	6	Redington	Nathaniel	2	1		1		2	2		1				9		
Williamstown	126	4	Reed	Benjamin			1	1				2		1			6		
Cheshire	156	7	Reed	Daniel	1	1	1	1		1							6		
New Ashford	163	33	Reed	Jesse	3	2		1		1	1		1	1			10		
Mount Washington	231	3	Reed	Joseph			1			2			1				4		
Lanesborough	151	22	Reed	Thomas	2	1		1		2			1				7		
West Stockbridge	250	20	Reed	Thomas	1		2	1	1	1	1						9		
Mount Washington	231	2	Reed	Wm		1	2	1		1		1					6		
Mount Washington	231	4	Reed	Wm Jun	1		1					1					3		
Partridgefield	188	37	Reefs	Ebenezer	3		1			1	1	1	2	1			10		
West Stockbridge	250	17	Rees	Isaac	1		1			1		1					4		
West Stockbridge	250	16	Rees	John		2	2	1				1	1				7		
Stockbridge	257	3	Reeves	John	1		1					1					3		
Lee	263	21	Remel	John			1			2		1					4		
Great Barrington	109	38	Remele	Jacob	3		2		1	1	2	1		1			11		
Great Barrington	106	14	Remele	William		1	1	1			3		1				7		
Cheshire	156	3	Remington	John	2	1		1		1	1		1				7		
Pittsfield	200	5	Remington	John		1	1	1				1		1			5		
Pittsfield	200	6	Remington	John			1			4		1					7		
Hancock	161	39	Remmington	Allen	2	1		1	1	3	2	1	1	1			13		
Sandisfield	172	5	Rew	Eliathath		1		1					1				3		
Tyringham	113	36	Rewey	Ebenezer	1	1	1			2	2		1	1			9		
Tyringham	113	16	Rewey	John		1		1					1				3		
Tyringham	114	15	Rewey	John		1		1					1				3		
Tyringham	114	17	Rewey	Thomas		2		1		2			1				6		
Hancock	162	15	Reynolds	James		1	2	1			1	1		2			8		
Tyringham	116	5	Rhoads	William		1	1	1		3	1			1			8		
Becket	268	2	Rhodes	Cynthia								2		1			3		
New Marlborough	233	25	Rhodes	David	1		1		1	2	1	1					7		
Great Barrington	109	47	Rhodes	John	1	1	1		1	1	2			2			9		
Stockbridge	257	2	Rice	Abraham	2	1		1		3	2		1				10		
Lanesborough	149	16	Rice	Adonijah		1	2		1		2	3	1				10		
Lanesborough	149	17	Rice	Asahel	2			1			1		1				5		
Bethlehem	172	2	Rice	Chester	1			1		1							4		

TOWN	PG#	LN#	LAST NAME	FIRST NAME	FREE WHITE MALES					FREE WHITE FEMALES					TOTAL ALL OTHER	TOTAL SLAVES	TOTALS	DISTRICT/ TOWNSHIP	NOTES
					under 10	10 to 16	16 to 26	26 to 45	45 and over	under 10	10 to 16	16 to 26	26 to 45	45 and over					
Bethlehem	172	4	Rice	Elizabeth Wid			1			3	1		1				6		
Bethlehem	182	5	Rice	Francis			1						1				2		
Lanesborough	152	10	Rice	Jehiel	1	2	1	1		2			1				8		
Bethlehem	173	17	Rice	Jerusha										1			1		
Great Barrington	110	8	Rice	Manly		1				1	1	4	1				8		
Stockbridge	257	5	Rice	Moses				1		1			1				3		
West Stockbridge	250	19	Rice	Moses			1		1				1				3		
West Stockbridge	250	22	Rice	Phineas	1	2				2	1		1				8		
Tyringham	110	10	Rice	Stephen	2	1			1	1	1		1				7		
Bethlehem	172	3	Rice	Watson	1		1			1		1					4		
New Ashford	162	13	Rice	William	2	1		1		1	1		1				7		
Tyringham	111	14	Ricer	Amos	1	3	2		1	1		2	1	1			12		
Williamstown	130	13	Rich	Elijah	1		1	1		1	1	2	1	1			9		
Williamstown	130	30	Rich	Moses	2			1	1	2			1	1			8		
Williamstown	130	16	Rich	Philip	1			1					1				3		
Partridgefield	188	36	Richards	William		2	1		1	2	1	1	2				10		
Cheshire	156	38	Richardson	Jonathan	1		2		1		1			2			7		
Partridgefield	188	42	Richmond	Abner	1			1		2		1					5		
Partridgefield	188	41	Richmond	Elihu	1		1	1	1	2			1	1			8		
Washington	213	1	Richmond	Elkanah		1		1		4			1				7		
Washington	213	2	Richmond	Gideon		2	1		1					1			5		
Pittsfield	200	25	Richmond	Jemima	1					2	1		1				5		
Cheshire	157	6	Richmond	Selah	1							1	1	1			4		
Partridgefield	188	44	Richmond	Zebulon	1	1	1	1		2	1	1	1				9		
Stockbridge	257	4	Rick	Joseph			1	1		1	1		1				5		
Great Barrington	104	11	Riley	Samuel	1	1		1		1	1		1				6		
Windsor	166	1	Ripley	Joseph	2	2		1		1	1		1	1			9		
Pittsfield	200	19	Ripley	Perez			1		1		1			1			4		
Sheffield	227	27	Roach	William					1	2	1	1		1			6		
Great Barrington	108	16	Robberts	John			1		1	2							4		
Partridgefield	188	39	Robbins	Ebenezer				1		3		1					5		
Windsor	168	25	Robbins	Eli	1			1		1			1				4		
Windsor	165	24	Robbins	Elias	1				1	1				1			4		
Pittsfield	200	9	Robbins	Elizabeth	2		3	1		2				2			10		
Pittsfield	200	3	Robbins	Experience	1	1								1			3		
Sandisfield	176	26	Robbins	Joshua	1		1						1				3		
West Stockbridge	250	14	Robbins	Lemll			1	1						1			3		
Pittsfield	200	16	Robbins	Lucas	1		1						1				3		
Pittsfield	200	2	Robbins	Marcus			1			3			1		2		7		
Clarkesburg	141	9	Robbins	Peter	3	1		1					1				6		
Pittsfield	200	13	Robbins	Silvester		1		1		4			1				7		
Sandisfield	176	21	Robbins	Solomon	5		1	1				1	1				9		
West Stockbridge	250	13	Robbins	Thos B	1			1		2	2		1				7		
Pittsfield	200	14	Robbins	William		1		1					1				3		
Williamstown	128	38	Robbins	William		1				1		1					3		
Great Barrington	107	44	Robbinson	Andrew		1	1	1		1			1				5		
Dalton	193	20	Roberts	Aaron	1			1		1			1				4		
Pittsfield	200	28	Roberts	Abner			1			1			1				3		
Lee	263	20	Roberts	Amos	2	1		1		1		1	1				7		
Williamstown	127	3	Roberts	Asa	1	1	1	1					2	1			7		
Dalton	193	21	Roberts	Edward		1			1	2	2	1	1				8		
Dalton	193	22	Roberts	Edward Jr		1	1						1				3		
Williamstown	133	1	Roberts	Isaac	5	1		1		1			1	1			10		
Sandisfield	175	21	Roberts	Joseph	2		1			1			1				5		
Williamstown	130	29	Roberts	Warren	2	1	1	1	1	3	2	2		1			14		
Sandisfield	175	14	Roberts	William & Son	2		1	1	1	1		1		1			8		
Windsor	168	4	Robinson	Denison		2			1	1		2	1				7		
Williamstown	127	35	Robinson	Edmund	1			1					1				3		
Richmond	208	40	Robinson	Edward	5	2		1		1	1		3				13		
Adams	139	2	Robinson	Geo.		1							1				2		
Great Barrington	106	26	Robinson	James											2		2		
West Stockbridge	250	8	Robinson	Joseph		1											1		
Adams	135	21	Robinson	Josiah D.	1		1	1					1				4		
Lee	263	19	Robinson	Levi		1		1		3	1	1	1				8		
West Stockbridge	250	11	Robinson	Noah	1			1		1			1				4		
Lanesborough	149	26	Robinson	Peter		1				1		1					3		
Partridgefield	188	38	Rockwell	Amasa	3	1		1		2		1					8		
Pittsfield	199	43	Rockwell	Elijah			1		1		1			1			4		
Bethlehem	182	8	Rockwell	Ephraim	1	2	1		1	2			1	1			9		
Lanesborough	148	20	Rockwell	Josiah	3	1	1	1		2			1				9		
Partridgefield	188	40	Rockwood	Daniel	2			1		2			1				6		
Tyringham	115	4	Rockwood	Reuben	3	1	1	1		1			1				8		
Williamstown	131	17	Roe	Elisha	1		1			1	1		1				5		
Williamstown	127	12	Roe	Thomas	1		1	1	1			1	1	1			7		
Great Barrington	106	2	Rogers	Benjamin		1	2						1				4		
Hancock	160	25	Rogers	Clark					1				1	1			3		
Pittsfield	200	26	Rogers	Ezra				1					1				2		
Hancock	160	29	Rogers	Gideon	3			1		1			1	1			7		
New Marlborough	232	33	Rogers	Jonathan	2	2		1		2			1				8		

TOWN	PG#	LN#	HEADS OF HOUSEHOLD		FREE WHITE MALES					FREE WHITE FEMALES					TOTAL ALL OTHER	TOTAL SLAVES	TOTALS	DISTRICT/ TOWNSHIP	NOTES
			LAST NAME	FIRST NAME	under 10	10 to 16	16 to 26	26 to 45	45 and over	under 10	10 to 16	16 to 26	26 to 45	45 and over					
Dalton	193	23	Rogers	William	1	1		1		1			1				5		
Sheffield	222	32	Rogers	William											5		5		
Tyringham	115	38	Role	Gideon	2			1		1		1					5		
Sheffield	229	32	Romney	Abijah		1	1		1	1		2		1			7		
Pittsfield	200	8	Root	Aaron	1	1		1		1		1	1				6		
Sheffield	222	8	Root	Aaron	1	1	2	1	1	1		2	1	1			11		
Pittsfield	200	23	Root	Abner			1				1		1		1		4		
Pittsfield	200	4	Root	Azariah	3			1		1	1		1				7		
Sheffield	222	5	Root	Azariah	2	2	9	1				1	2				17		
West Stockbridge	250	9	Root	Chauncey	1			2					1				4		
Pittsfield	200	22	Root	Daniel			2			1		1					4		
Great Barrington	108	26	Root	David	1			1	1	2	1		1				7		
Pittsfield	200	20	Root	Eli		1			1	1		1		1			5		
Pittsfield	200	24	Root	Ezekiel	1	2	1	1	1			1		1	1		9		
West Stockbridge	250	18	Root	Isaac	2	2	1	1		2	2	1	1				12		
Great Barrington	108	28	Root	Israel			1		1				1				3		
Egremont	120	26	Root	James				1					1				2		
Great Barrington	106	10	Root	James	1	1			1	1		1		1			6		
Washington	214	39	Root	Jeremiah	2		1	1		2	1		1				8		
Great Barrington	108	12	Root	John		1		1	1			1	1				5		
Pittsfield	199	42	Root	John			2		1	1	1	1					6		
Loudon	178	31	Root	Joseph	2		4	2	1			1		1	1		12		
Great Barrington	108	2	Root	Joshua	3			1		2			1				7		
Pittsfield	200	15	Root	Josiah				1		5	1		2				9		
Pittsfield	200	1	Root	Oliver	1	1	3		1		1	1		1			9		
Lenox	211	6	Root	Reuben	1	2	2		1			1		1			8		
Pittsfield	200	21	Root	Rossel	3	2		1					1				7		
Pittsfield	200	7	Root	Samuel	3			1		2	1		1				8		
Cheshire	157	31	Root	Selah	2		1			1		1					5		
Cheshire	157	51	Root	Selah	2		1			1		1					5		
Sheffield	225	5	Root	Thaddeus	3			1		1	1	1					7		
Pittsfield	200	18	Root	William	2	1	1					1					5		
Pittsfield	200	27	Root	Zenas	1			1					1				3		
Egremont	119	6	Rorepaugh	Thomas	2	1	1		1	1	1		1				8		
Great Barrington	108	21	Ross	James													4		
Clarkesburg	142	1	Ross	John	1			1		1		1					4		
Tyringham	114	43	Ross	Peleg	1	1	1	1	1	1	1	1	1				9		
Great Barrington	110	4	Ross	Thomas			1		1				1				3		
Great Barrington	109	46	Ross	William	3	1		1					1				6		
Richmond	205	5	Rosseter	Abraham	1	1		1		2		1	1				7		
Richmond	207	25	Rosseter	Benjamin		1	1	2		1		2					7		
Richmond	208	4	Rosseter	David		1	2		1		1			1			6		
Richmond	205	4	Rosseter	Nathan				1				2		1			4		
Williamstown	131	30	Rosseter	Nathan	1	2	1	2			2		1		1		10		
Richmond	205	7	Rosseter	Noah	3	1		1			1		1				7		
Cheshire	157	38	Rounds	Jabez	2		1			3		1					7		
Cheshire	157	58	Rounds	Jabez	2		1			3		1					7		
Hancock	161	32	Rounds	Joseph	2		1			1	2	1					7		
West Stockbridge	250	10	Rowell	Jacob	3			1		1		1					6		
Williamstown	129	10	Rowland	Nehma		1			1			1		1			4		
Richmond	205	18	Rowley	Erastus			2			1		1					4		
West Stockbridge	250	21	Rowley	John				1									1		
Richmond	205	14	Rowley	Reuben	3			1				1					5		
Richmond	205	17	Rowley	Richmond	3	2		1		2		1					9		
Richmond	205	8	Rowley	Thomas	1			1					1				3		
Alford	116	19	Rowse	David				1				1	1				3		
Sheffield	223	28	Royce	Abner		1	2		2			1		2			8		
Sheffield	224	15	Royce	Ezra	2			1		1		1					5		
Sheffield	223	29	Royce	Isaac	1		1						1				3		
New Marlborough	237	22	Royce	John	2			1					1				4		
Sheffield	224	37	Rubelow	Thomas		1			1				1				3		
Lanesborough	153	1	Rublee	William	3		1	1		1		1	1				8		
Becket	268	24	Rudd	Elisha & Jesse			1	1		4		1	1	1			9		
Becket	268	25	Rudd	James	2	2	1		1	1	1		1				9		
New Marlborough	234	1	Rugg	Seth	1		1	1				1					4		
Adams	135	5	Runnells	Peter	3			2	1	1	2		1	1			11		
Cheshire	156	27	Rush	Samuel	1			1		1	1		1				5		
Windsor	167	2	Russel	Asa	2			1		1			1				5		
Tyringham	110	5	Russell	Jacob	1			1				1					3		
Tyringham	112	44	Russell	James	3	1		1		1			1				7		
Tyringham	110	3	Russell	John				1					1				2		
Egremont	120	25	Rynders	Evert	1	3			1	1		1					7		
Alford	117	52	S*ipton	Jeremiah			1	1		1			2				5		
Williamstown	130	37	Sabin	Charles		1	1	1		3		1	1	1			9		
Williamstown	133	4	Sabin	Erastus	1			1		1			1				4		
Williamstown	132	21	Sabin	Jesse			1	1				1					3		
Williamstown	131	2	Sabin	Timothy	3	1		1		3			1				9		
Williamstown	131	7	Sabin	Widow			1				1	1		1			4		
West Stockbridge	251	9	Sacket	Jesse			1										1		

TOWN	PG#	LN#	LAST NAME	FIRST NAME	FREE WHITE MALES					FREE WHITE FEMALES					TOTAL ALL OTHER	TOTAL SLAVES	TOTALS	DISTRICT/ TOWNSHIP	NOTES
					under 10	10 to 16	16 to 26	26 to 45	45 and over	under 10	10 to 16	16 to 26	26 to 45	45 and over					
Pittsfield	201	13	Sackett	Daniel					1	1				1			3		
Pittsfield	201	7	Sackett	Erastus			1	1		4	2	1	1				10		
Pittsfield	201	14	Sackett	Lemuel	3	1		2		2			1				9		
Pittsfield	201	2	Sackett	Richard						2		1	1				4		
Pittsfield	200	40	Sackett	Solomon	1			1		1		1	2	1			7		
Southfield	183	5	Sackett	Solomon	1	1			1		1	3	1				8		
Partridgefield	189	1	Sackett	Walter			2					1					3		
Great Barrington	105	11	Sacklin	James											2		2		
Sandisfield	173	20	Sage	Abel	3	1	1	1	1	1		1	1				10		
Great Barrington	105	6	Sage	Elisha	3		3		1	2	1	1		1			12		
Sandisfield	176	14	Sage	Jedediah	2	1	1	1		1	1		1	1			9		
Sandisfield	174	24	Sage	Samuel Jr	3	1				2	1		1				9		
Sandisfield	174	25	Sage	Samuel Sen				1						1			2		
Sandisfield	176	10	Sage	Stephen	2	1	3		1	2	2			1			12		
Great Barrington	105	29	Sanford	David	3	2	1	1		1		1	1				10		
Windsor	167	13	Sanger	Jonathan	2	1		1		2	1	1	1				9		
Lee	263	33	Santer	Danl											2		2		
Lee	264	2	Sargeant	Erastus			1										1		
Williamstown	132	16	Satterlee	Samuel			1			1	1	2					5		
Washington	216	3	Savery	Hiram	2		1						1				4		
Adams	139	1	Sawter	William	1		1			2		1					5		
Windsor	165	30	Sawyer	Cornelius	3		1		1	1	1	1	1	1			10		
Pittsfield	200	42	Saxton	Jesse					1	2	1		1				5		
Richmond	207	35	Saxton	Michal	1			1				1					3		
Adams	135	42	Sayles	Oziel		1	3		1			1		1			7		
Sheffield	227	18	Schalenger	Gideon	2	2	1		1	1		1		1			9		
Richmond	208	27	Scott	Abijah			2						1				3		
Loudon	178	27	Scott	David	2			1		2	1		1				7		
Becket	268	35	Scott	John	2	1		1		1			1				6		
Richmond	205	2	Scott	Nathan		1		1			2	1	2				7		
Richmond	209	7	Scott	Samuel	1	1			1	2		1	1				7		
Cheshire	155	40	Scott	Silvanus	1	2			1		1	3		1			9		
Richmond	206	5	Scott	Thomas				1					1	1			3		
Partridgefield	189	3	Scovel	Jonas	1	1	1		1		1	1		2			8		
Partridgefield	189	4	Scovel	Jonas Junr	1		1					1					3		
Egremont	120	37	Scribner	Nathan	1	1	1		1	2	1		1	1			9		
Washington	215	15	Seagers	John	2	2	1			3	2		1				12		
Lenox	211	10	Sears	Calvin			1			1		1	1				4		
Southfield	182	10	Sears	Daniel	1	1		1		1			1				5		
Lenox	211	7	Sears	David		1	1		1				1				4		
Lenox	211	17	Sears	Isaac	1			1		1							3		
Washington	213	24	Sears	Luther	1		2			1		2					6		
Sandisfield	174	9	Sears	Paul Jr	1			1		2			1				5		
Sandisfield	174	8	Sears	Paul Sen & Son			1		1			2	1				5		
Lenox	211	8	Sears	Philip	1	1		1		1			1				5		
Sheffield	229	21	Sears	Rebecca										2			2		
Sheffield	229	20	Sears	Thomas	2	1		1		3	1		1				9		
Stockbridge	257	9	Sedgewick	Theod	1	3	1	2	1	1		1	1	1	1		13		
Lenox	211	11	Sedgwick	Asher		1		1		2	2		1	1			8		
Sandisfield	172	6	Sedgwick	Chancey	1			1		1		1					4		
Sheffield	226	24	Seeley	Seth	1			1		1	1	1	1				6		
Great Barrington	106	29	Seely	Abrm	1	2		1		2			1				7		
Great Barrington	106	30	Seely	Isaac	2	1	1	1		2	1		1				9		
Becket	269	9	Seely	John	2	1		1		2	1	1		1			9		
Great Barrington	106	43	Seely	John			3		1	1		2		1			8		
Stockbridge	257	11	Seely	Jonas	3	1		1		2	1		1				9		
Stockbridge	257	12	Seely	Joseph		2		1		3			1				7		
Williamstown	127	42	Seelye	Ephraim	1	1	2		1	2	2	1		1			11		
Williamstown	128	3	Seelye	Reuben		1	1		1	1				1			5		
Windsor	165	29	Seen	Charles		1						2					3		
Becket	268	28	Segar	Charles	3			1		1	1						6		
Sheffield	230	34	Segur	Ezekiel	1				1	2	1		1				6		
Washington	214	32	Sela	James				1					1				2		
Pittsfield	200	43	Selwey	Thomas	1	1	1	1	1	3	2	1	1				12		
Stockbridge	257	17	Sergeant	Erastus	1	1	3		2		1	4		1	1		14		
Great Barrington	107	25	Seripture	Simeon			1			1			1	1			4		
Sandisfield	173	32	Servent	James					1		1	1	1				4		
New Marlborough	239	35	Seymour	Jacob	2	1	1	1			1	1					7		
Lee	264	3	Seymour	John	2	1		1		1			1				6		
Sheffield	221	11	Seymour	Josiah		1		1		2		1					5		
Lanesborough	148	25	Seymour	Levi				1		1		1					3		
Stockbridge	257	7	Seymour	Natha	2		1				1		1				7		
Hancock	158	14	Shapley	David		1	1	1	1				1	1			6		
New Marlborough	237	23	Sharon	Salmon			1					1					2		
Stockbridge	258	31	Sharp	Peter											1		1		
New Ashford	163	36	Shattuck	Timothy		1	1		1					1			4		
West Stockbridge	251	8	Shaver	Abram											4		4		
New Marlborough	233	9	Shaw	Ammi	2			1		3			1				7		
Becket	269	13	Shaw	Duncan	4		1						1				6		
Bethlehem	180	14	Shaw	Joshua	2			1		2			1				6		

141

TOWN	PG#	LN#	LAST NAME	FIRST NAME	FREE WHITE MALES under 10	10 to 16	16 to 26	26 to 45	45 and over	FREE WHITE FEMALES under 10	10 to 16	16 to 26	26 to 45	45 and over	TOTAL ALL OTHER	TOTAL SLAVES	TOTALS	DISTRICT/ TOWNSHIP	NOTES
New Marlborough	234	18	Shaw	Mylo	2	1		1	1	3			1				9		
Pittsfield	200	33	Shaw	Nathan	3		1	1		2			1				8		
Stockbridge	257	21	Shaw	Prudence	1								1				2		
New Marlborough	233	32	Shead	Samuel	3			2		1	1		1				8		
Pittsfield	201	3	Shearer	Joseph			1	1		1	1		1		2		7		
Adams	136	25	Shearman	Daniel	2	2	1		1		1	1	1				9		
Savoy	140	5	Shearman	Jacob	2		2		1	1			1				7		
Savoy	140	21	Shearman	James	1		1					1					3		
Savoy	140	7	Shearman	Seth	1			1		2			1				5		
Williamstown	132	15	Shearman	Wm. B.	1		1	1		5	1		2				11		
Sheffield	226	31	Shears	Amos	1		1					1					3		
Sheffield	226	28	Shears	Jeremiah	1			1		1			1				4		
Sheffield	226	30	Shears	Samll	1		1						1				3		
Sheffield	223	27	Shears	Zechariah	1	2			1		1	1	1				7		
Sandisfield	176	1	Shelby	Ephraim	2		3		2	1	1		1				10		
Adams	137	13	Sheldon	Anthony	2	1		1		1	2	1					8		
New Marlborough	234	23	Sheldon	Asa	2		1		2	3	1	1	1				11		
Sheffield	223	21	Sheldon	Benjamin	2			1	1	3	1	2					10		
Sheffield	221	3	Sheldon	Dick											3		3		
New Marlborough	232	8	Sheldon	Eben	2	1		1		1			1				6		
New Marlborough	236	9	Sheldon	Eleazer	3	2	1		1	2	1		2				12		
New Marlborough	235	1	Sheldon	Elijah		1	2		1			1	1	2			8		
New Marlborough	236	10	Sheldon	Elisha	2	1	2			1	1		1				8		
Lee	263	31	Sheldon	Ephraim		1			1	1	1	1		1			6		
Adams	137	20	Sheldon	John	2		1		1	1	2		1				8		
Cheshire	156	32	Sheldon	John				1				1	1				3		
Adams	137	19	Sheldon	John Junr		1				1		1					3		
Clarkesburg	142	4	Sheldon	Nathan	1		1						1				3		
Williamstown	132	8	Sheldon	Rema	1	1	1			1		1	1		1		7		
New Marlborough	234	25	Sheldon	Samll				1					1				2		
New Marlborough	234	24	Sheldon	Samuel			1	1		1		2	1	1			7		
New Marlborough	236	15	Sheldon	Seth			2		1		1		1				5		
Sheffield	224	25	Sheldon	Whiting	2			1		1	1		1				6		
Cheshire	157	15	Shelly	John			1			1		1					3		
Sandisfield	171	17	Shelpon	Ceaser											2		2		
Pittsfield	201	1	Shepard	Jerre	2			1		2			1				6		
Sandisfield	176	6	Shepard	Jonathan	3	1		1			1		1				7		
Lenox	211	9	Shepard	Samuel	1	1		1		1	1		1				6		
Bethlehem	181	17	Sheperd	Nathaniel	2			1					1				4		
New Marlborough	237	6	Shepherd	Daniel		2	2	1		2		1		1			9		
New Marlborough	239	8	Shepherd	Isaac			1			1		1					3		
New Marlborough	236	23	Shepherd	Nathll			3		1	1	1	3		1			10		
New Marlborough	237	30	Shepherd	Samll			1			1		1					3		
New Marlborough	237	7	Shepherd	Solomon			1		1			1		1			4		
New Marlborough	237	9	Shepherd	Thomas	2	1	3		1	1				1			9		
Lanesborough	152	4	Sherlock	Ichabod				2		1	2		1				6		
Hancock	160	17	Sherman	Edmond	1			1		2	3	1	1				9		
Williamstown	125	20	Sherman	Elihu	1	1	1					1		1			6		
Sandisfield	174	10	Sherman	James	3			1		2			1				7		
Lanesborough	151	25	Sherman	Job	3	1		1		4			1				10		
Lanesborough	151	27	Sherman	Joel				1					1				2		
Adams	133	18	Sherman	Kelley	1		1	1		1	1	1	1				7		
Lanesborough	151	26	Sherman	Timothy	2	2		1			2	1	1				9		
Richmond	207	20	Sherril	Henry	2	2	1		1	2	1		1				10		
Richmond	206	6	Sherril	Samuel	2		1		1	2	1	1	1	1			10		
New Ashford	162	4	Sherwood	Benjamin		1	2	1		1	3		1				9		
Williamstown	131	23	Sherwood	Isaac				1		1		1	1				4		
Williamstown	131	4	Sherwood	Jona	1	1		1		3	2	1	1				10		
Williamstown	130	40	Sherwood	Samuel			1					1		1			3		
Williamstown	131	22	Sherwood	Stephen	3	2		1				1	1				8		
West Stockbridge	250	27	Sherwood	Timothy				1		1		1		1			4		
Sheffield	223	17	Shilhousen	Conrad	1			1					1				3		
Clarkesburg	141	4	Shipley	Silas	2			1		3	3		1				11		
Adams	134	6	Shippey	Henry		1	1	1	1	1			2	1			8		
Adams	137	15	Shippey	Joseph	1	1		1					1				4		
Adams	133	21	Shippey	Timothy			1			1		1		1			4		
Lanesborough	151	9	Short	Daniel	1			1		3			1				6		
Adams	135	13	Shreve	Caleb		1		2	1		1	2	1				9		
Partridgefield	189	8	Siblee	Benja	2			1					1				4		
Partridgefield	189	18	Siblee	Elisha	1		1						1				3		
Adams	137	37	Sibley	Benjm	1		2	3	1	1			1				9		
Washington	215	18	Sibley	Ezra	3			1			2		1				7		
Great Barrington	105	27	Sibley	Stephen	4	1	1	1		1	1		1				10		
Tyringham	113	5	Sigler	George	3			1		1			1				6		
Lenox	211	40	Sikes	Elijah			1			2			1				4		
Washington	213	27	Sikes	Stephen	1	2	1		1	2		3		1			11		
Cheshire	157	17	Simmons	Aaron	1			1	1	1		1		1			6		
Cheshire	158	4	Simmons	Thomas	1	1	1			1	2	1	1				9		
Cheshire	158	3	Simmons	Thomas Jr	2			1					1				4		

TOWN	PG#	LN#	LAST NAME	FIRST NAME	FREE WHITE MALES					FREE WHITE FEMALES					TOTAL ALL OTHER	TOTAL SLAVES	TOTALS	DISTRICT/ TOWNSHIP	NOTES
					under 10	10 to 16	16 to 26	26 to 45	45 and over	under 10	10 to 16	16 to 26	26 to 45	45 and over					
Sheffield	230	3	Simmons	William				1				1					2		
Williamstown	128	9	Simonds	Benjamin				1					1				2		
Williamstown	130	20	Simonds	Enoch											5		5		
Lanesborough	152	27	Simonds	James	2			1		2			1				6		
Southfield	182	6	Simons	Eli			1		1			2	1	1			6		
Stockbridge	257	6	Simons	Pearly			1			1			1				3		
Becket	269	14	Simpson	Jonathan					1				1				2		
Lanesborough	152	29	Skeels	David	1			1		2			1				5		
Windsor	164	14	Skiner	Samuel			1	1			1			1			4		
Williamstown	128	10	Skinner	Benjamin	2	2	2	1	1	1	1	1		1			12		
Williamstown	129	35	Skinner	Tompson J.	1	1	2	2	1	1		2		1			11		
Cheshire	154	4	Slade	William				1		2		2	1				6		
New Ashford	163	8	Slade	William	3		1	1		1			1				7		
Sandisfield	177	7	Slate	Solomon			1										1		
Tyringham	110	11	Slater	Giles	2	2	1		1		1	2	1	3			13		
Sheffield	230	7	Slater	John	2	1		1		1		1	1				7		
New Marlborough	236	4	Slater	Samuel					1					1			2		
West Stockbridge	251	7	Slaughter	Elijah	1	1	1			2		1					6		
West Stockbridge	250	29	Slaughter	Ephraim	2		1		1	3	2	1					10		
Becket	269	8	Slaughter	Patrick	2		1		1	1	2		1				8		
Washington	215	11	Sloan	Norman	2	1	2	1		3	1		1				11		
Williamstown	132	4	Sloan	Samuel	3	3	1	1		1	1		1				11		
Adams	133	13	Slocum	Amasa	1			1					1				3		
Adams	133	8	Slocum	Benjamin	1	2	1		1	3		1		1			10		
Sandisfield	177	1	Slocum	Charles			1					1					2		
Adams	137	39	Slocum	Ebenezer	3	3	1		1	2		3		1			14		
Bethlehem	181	31	Slocum	Edward	5				1		1		1				8		
Richmond	206	30	Slosson	Daniel					1				1				2		
Hancock	158	3	Slosson	Eliphalet			2	8				2	8				20		
Richmond	206	32	Slosson	Joseph			1						1				2		
Richmond	206	31	Slosson	Nathaniel	3		1						1				5		
Adams	134	22	Slye	William	2			1	1	1		1	1	1			8		
Williamstown	127	27	Smedley	Levi & Elijah	3		3	2		6	1	1	3				19		
West Stockbridge	250	26	Smith	Abijah	1				1	3				1			6		
Dalton	193	26	Smith	Abner	1			1		1			1				4		
Sandisfield	174	35	Smith	Amasa	2	2	1		1	1	1	1		1			10		
Dalton	193	25	Smith	Amos		3		1		1		1	1				7		
Great Barrington	109	37	Smith	Amos		1			1				1				3		
Southfield	182	9	Smith	Amos	2	3			1	3		1	1	1			12		
West Stockbridge	250	30	Smith	Asa			1					1					2		
Lanesborough	148	2	Smith	Asahel	1	1	2	1		2		1	2				10		
Sandisfield	175	32	Smith	Asahel			1										1		
Southfield	183	10	Smith	Austin	1			1				1					3		
Lee	264	1	Smith	Benja		1	1		1	1	1	1		1			7		
Adams	136	38	Smith	Benjamin	4		1	1				1	1				8		
New Marlborough	239	1	Smith	Benjamin	2		1	1		2	1	1	1	1			10		
Sandisfield	174	22	Smith	Benjamin	2	1			1	1	1		1	1			8		
Pittsfield	200	32	Smith	Betty							1		1				2		
Bethlehem	180	17	Smith	Daniel	1	1			1	1	1			1			8		
Cheshire	155	19	Smith	Daniel	3	1	1	1			1						7		
Hancock	160	38	Smith	Daniel	3			1		2	1		1				8		
Tyringham	113	15	Smith	Daniel	1		1						1				3		
Williamstown	127	38	Smith	Daniel	2	1	1	1	1	2	0		1				11		
Sheffield	224	14	Smith	David	1			1		3	1	1	1				8		
Egremont	118	1	Smith	Ebenezer	1			1		1			1				4		
New Marlborough	238	31	Smith	Ebenezer		1			1		1	3		1			7		
Partridgefield	189	9	Smith	Ebenezer					1			1		1			3		
Sandisfield	174	33	Smith	Eleazer & Benjm	1			1	1	1			1	1			7		
Bethlehem	181	16	Smith	Elijah		2	1				1	1	1				7		
New Marlborough	237	21	Smith	Elijah	1	1		1		2		2	1	1			9		
Sheffield	222	21	Smith	Elijah	2			1					1				4		
West Stockbridge	250	25	Smith	Eliph		1	3		1	2		1		1			7		
Bethlehem	173	22	Smith	Elisha	1	1	2		1	1		2		1			9		
New Marlborough	240	31	Smith	Elisha	2			1		1			1				5		
Sheffield	222	20	Smith	Elisha		1	1	1					1				4		
Sandisfield	171	1	Smith	Elizabeth									1				1		
Sandisfield	174	34	Smith	Elizabeth & Persla									2				2		
Stockbridge	257	15	Smith	Enos		1	1		1	1	1	1					6		
Sandisfield	176	17	Smith	Freelove Wido		1	3				3	2		1			10		
Sandisfield	176	24	Smith	Freeman			4					1					5		
Lanesborough	148	13	Smith	George		1			1	2	1		1				6		
Partridgefield	189	16	Smith	George	4	1		1		2			1				9		
Washington	215	33	Smith	George	1		2			1		1					5		
Dalton	193	24	Smith	George H	4			1			3		1				9		
Stockbridge	257	13	Smith	Gideon		1			1			1		1	2		6		
Stockbridge	257	14	Smith	Gideon	2		1	1									4		
New Marlborough	240	23	Smith	Gilbert			1			1		1					3		
Lenox	212	10	Smith	Heman			1		1	3			1				6		
Stockbridge	257	18	Smith	Heman Jr			1					1		1			3		

TOWN	PG#	LN#	LAST NAME	FIRST NAME	FREE WHITE MALES under 10	10 to 16	16 to 26	26 to 45	45 and over	FREE WHITE FEMALES under 10	10 to 16	16 to 26	26 to 45	45 and over	TOTAL ALL OTHER	TOTAL SLAVES	TOTALS	DISTRICT/ TOWNSHIP	NOTES
Southfield	183	1	Smith	Henry	2	1		1		1			1				6		
Partridgefield	189	15	Smith	Hugh	3	1	1	1			1		1				8		
Lanesborough	152	14	Smith	Isaac			1		1			1		1			4		
Lanesborough	152	21	Smith	Isaac		1		1			1		1				4		
Partridgefield	189	14	Smith	Isaac			1		1		2	1	1				6		
Southfield	183	7	Smith	Isaiah	1			1		4			1				7		
Alford	117	37	Smith	Jabez	3		1			2		1					7		
Sandisfield	170	16	Smith	Jabez		1	1				1	1		1			5		
Lanesborough	148	18	Smith	Jacob		1	1	1				1					4		
Becket	268	31	Smith	James	4			1		4			1				10		
Williamstown	130	1	Smith	Jeremiah	1		1	1		1			1		1		6		
Great Barrington	108	45	Smith	Jesse		2		1		4	1		1				9		
Lenox	212	4	Smith	Jesse	2	1		1		2	1	2	1				10		
Bethlehem	181	43	Smith	Joel	2			1		3			1				7		
New Marlborough	240	32	Smith	Joel	2			1	1				1	1			6		
Hancock	159	12	Smith	John	3			1		1	1		1				7		
Lanesborough	152	11	Smith	John	1			1		1			1				4		
Partridgefield	189	13	Smith	John	1	1		1		3		1	1	1			9		
Pittsfield	201	4	Smith	John		2			1	3			1				7		
Williamstown	127	16	Smith	John	3	3		1		2		1	1				11		
Lanesborough	148	1	Smith	Jonathan			2		1	1			1				5		
New Marlborough	235	23	Smith	Jonathan		1	2	1		1		1	1				7		
Sandisfield	174	2	Smith	Jonathan 2nd	1	1		1		4	1		1				9		
Sandisfield	176	23	Smith	Jonathan 2nd		1	1		1			2	1	1			7		
Hancock	158	18	Smith	Joseph			3	1	4		5	2	8				23		
Southfield	183	11	Smith	Joseph	1	2	2	1		1	1		1				9		
Dalton	193	27	Smith	Joshua	1		1	1		1		2					6		
New Marlborough	237	8	Smith	Joshua	2			1				1					4		
Bethlehem	181	6	Smith	Justus	3			1					1				5		
Sandisfield	176	18	Smith	Keisben	1	1	2		1		1	1		1			8		
Adams	137	1	Smith	Laban	1		2	1		2	2		1				9		
Sandisfield	175	27	Smith	Lemuel	1	1	1		1	1	1	1	2				9		
Sandisfield	173	24	Smith	Levi 1st	4			1			1		1	1			8		
Sandisfield	174	12	Smith	Levi 2nd	1			1		3		1	1	1			8		
Sandisfield	172	14	Smith	Lot		1	2	1		1		1	1				7		
Bethlehem	180	18	Smith	Lucias	2			1		1		1					5		
Southfield	182	13	Smith	Matthew				1					1				2		
Mount Washington	232	32	Smith	Merit				1					1				2		
Alford	117	26	Smith	Morris	2			1		1			1				5		
Williamstown	127	17	Smith	Nathan	1		1	1		1			1	1			6		
Williamstown	129	34	Smith	Nathan	1			1		2		1		1			6		
New Marlborough	238	29	Smith	Obadiah	1			1		2			1				5		
New Marlborough	233	13	Smith	Oreon			1	1						1			3		
Sandisfield	173	38	Smith	Perigran	2			1		4	3		1				11		
Sheffield	225	7	Smith	Phinehas				1						1			2		
Adams	138	16	Smith	Reuben	3			1					1				5		
Sandisfield	175	10	Smith	Reuben 2nd	1			1		3			1				6		
Richmond	207	30	Smith	Richard	1			1		1			1				4		
Stockbridge	257	8	Smith	Russel		1		1			1		1				4		
New Marlborough	233	16	Smith	Samll	1	1	1		1			1	1				6		
Bethlehem	181	25	Smith	Samuel	2			1		1			1				5		
Great Barrington	108	44	Smith	Samuel		1	1	1				1		1			5		
Mount Washington	232	33	Smith	Samuel		1		1		1			1				4		
Pittsfield	200	34	Smith	Samuel						1		1					2		
Tyringham	113	13	Smith	Samuel		1		1		1	1		1				4		
Sheffield	222	18	Smith	Sarah									1				1		
Stockbridge	257	22	Smith	Sarah									1		1		2		
Hancock	161	29	Smith	Shubel	2	2	2	1		1	1	1	1				11		
Southfield	183	9	Smith	Silas		1	1		1		1	2	2	1			9		
Adams	138	23	Smith	Solomon			1			2			1				4		
Sandisfield	176	11	Smith	Solomon & Son	1	1			1		2	2		1			8		
Sandisfield	176	13	Smith	Solomon Jr	1		1						1				3		
Adams	135	7	Smith	Stephen	1	1	1		1	1	1	2	1				9		
New Marlborough	235	24	Smith	Stephen		1		2					1				4		
Sandisfield	176	16	Smith	Stephen			1	1					1				3		
Williamstown	129	39	Smith	Stephen		1	1	1					1	1			5		
New Marlborough	239	10	Smith	Thomas	1			1		4			1				7		
Windsor	167	15	Smith	Thomas	1			1					1	1			4		
Sandisfield	175	26	Smith	Uriel	1		1	1				1		1			5		
Hancock	161	27	Smith	William	1	1	1		1	1	1	2		1			9		
Pittsfield	201	8	Smith	William			1			1			1				3		
Tyringham	113	14	Smith	William			1						1				2		
Washington	215	29	Smith	William	2			1		1		1	1				6		
Washington	216	16	Smith	William			1	1					1	1			4		
Williamstown	125	5	Smith	William		1	2	1		2	1	1	1				9		
Windsor	166	14	Smith	William		1			1	2	1	1		1			7		
Lenox	212	15	Smith	Zenar			2										2		
Becket	269	11	Snow	Amaziah	4			1		1			1				7		
Becket	268	36	Snow	Asa	2	2			1	1			1	1			8		

144

TOWN	PG#	LN#	LAST NAME	FIRST NAME	FREE WHITE MALES					FREE WHITE FEMALES					TOTAL ALL OTHER	TOTAL SLAVES	TOTALS	DISTRICT/ TOWNSHIP	NOTES
					under 10	10 to 16	16 to 26	26 to 45	45 and over	under 10	10 to 16	16 to 26	26 to 45	45 and over					
Becket	269	16	Snow	Edmund			1					1					2		
Becket	269	15	Snow	Eli				1		2				1			4		
Pittsfield	201	11	Snow	Ezra	2		2		1		1	1	1				8		
Sandisfield	175	35	Snow	Freeman	1	1	1		1	1		2		1			8		
Windsor	166	30	Snow	Jacob	1	1		1		2	2		1				8		
Becket	268	34	Snow	James		2	3		1	2	1		1				10		
Sandisfield	174	31	Snow	James		1			1	1	1	3		1			8		
Pittsfield	200	41	Snow	John	3			1		1	1		1				7		
Williamstown	125	2	Snow	John		1	1		1			1		1			5		
Becket	268	33	Snow	Levi	1			1		1	2		1				6		
Becket	268	37	Snow	Nathan	1	1		1		1	2		1				7		
Becket	268	29	Snow	Oliver	1		2		1	2	1	3	1				11		
Becket	268	30	Snow	Oliver Jr		1						1					2		
Partridgefield	189	6	Snow	Orin	2		1						1				4		
Sandisfield	170	12	Snow	Reliance								1					1		
Loudon	178	34	Snow	Selah			1					1					2		
Bethlehem	181	3	Snow	Solomon	2		1					1					4		
Sandisfield	174	30	Snow	Sparrow	1	1	1		1	2	1	1		1			9		
Becket	268	27	Snow	Sylvanus					1			1		1			3		
Becket	268	32	Snow	Timothy		2			1			1		1			5		
Williamstown	130	8	Solomon	Albert		3		1		1		1		1			7		
Stockbridge	257	24	Solomon	Ephraim	2	1	1		1	1	1		3				10		
Sandisfield	174	3	Solomon	Jacob & Elmer			1	1						1			3		
Lanesborough	148	30	Soot	Amos			1			1		1					3		
Sandisfield	172	15	Soper	Hezekiah	2			1		2			1				6		
Sandisfield	172	16	Soper	Levi			2		1					1			4		
Adams	136	24	Southwick	Asa	2			1		1			1				5		
Lanesborough	149	24	Southwick	Warren			1			4			1	1			7		
Hancock	160	2	Southworth	George	2		1	1		3		1	1				9		
Dalton	193	28	Soutworth	Thomas		1	1			1		1					4		
Dalton	193	29	Spafard	Amos	1		1	1		3			1				7		
Windsor	165	3	Spalding	Jabez			1			3	2		1				7		
Sheffield	224	13	Sparks	Asa	1	2	1		1	2	1	1		1			10		
Sheffield	224	9	Sparks	Lemuel	3		1			1			1				6		
Sheffield	226	4	Sparks	William	3			1		1			1				6		
New Marlborough	241	2	Spaulding	Aaron			1	1					1	2			5		
Sheffield	229	9	Spaulding	Aaron	1	1		1					1				4		
New Marlborough	233	18	Spaulding	Benjamin	2	1		1		2			1	1			8		
New Marlborough	239	34	Spaulding	Daniel	1	2	1	1		1		1	2	1			10		
New Marlborough	232	26	Spaulding	Moses				1						1			2		
Sheffield	229	24	Spaulding	Phinehas		3	1	1		4	3	1	1				14		
Sheffield	230	10	Spaulding	Theophilus	1		1		1				1	1			5		
New Marlborough	232	1	Spaulding	Uriah	3	1	1		1			1	1				8		
Sheffield	230	9	Spaulding	Zachhah		1			1				1				3		
Sheffield	229	25	Spaulding	Zebulon	1				1				1	1			4		
Bethlehem	181	26	Spear	John	3			1			1		1				6		
Loudon	177	16	Spelman	Levi	2	1		1		1			1				6		
Sandisfield	174	37	Spelman	Nathan Jr			1			2		1					4		
Sandisfield	174	36	Spelman	Nathan Sen		1			1	1		2		1			6		
West Stockbridge	251	6	Spencer	Amasa	1	1	2		1				1				6		
West Stockbridge	251	1	Spencer	Daniel	4	1	1	1		2			1				10		
Great Barrington	105	19	Spencer	Eliphalet	1	2	1	1		1	1	1		1			9		
West Stockbridge	250	24	Spencer	James	2			1		2			1	1			7		
Williamstown	126	12	Spencer	Jesse		1	1	1		1			1				5		
Great Barrington	107	42	Spencer	John		1		1					1				3		
Williamstown	129	33	Spencer	John	1			1		1	1		1				5		
Savoy	140	34	Spencer	Rhoda		1	1		1	1		1					5		
Alford	116	11	Sperrey	Enoch	2		1	1		1	2	1	1				9		
Bethlehem	182	2	Sperry	Elijah	2	1		1		2			1				7		
New Ashford	162	7	Spink	Shibnah	3	3	1	1		1	1		1				11		
New Ashford	163	24	Spink	Shibnah				1						1			2		
Hancock	158	16	Spires	John			3	4	5				4	3	14		33		
Sheffield	226	25	Spoor	Dirch		1	1		1		1	2		1			7		
Sheffield	226	26	Spoor	Isaac		2	1	1		1		1	1	1			8		
Adams	133	20	Sprague	Amasa		1	1	1		1				1			5		
Great Barrington	107	7	Sprague	Barnabas	2	2			1	2		1	1				9		
Alford	117	20	Sprague	Benjamin	2	2	1	1	1	2				1			11		
Dalton	193	30	Sprague	Calvin				1						1			2		
Washington	216	22	Sprague	Dyer			2	1		3	2		1				9		
New Marlborough	232	9	Sprague	James	1		1	1					1				4		
Lanesborough	151	23	Sprague	Peter	2			1		3	1		1				8		
Pittsfield	200	35	Sprague	Samuel			1			3			1				5		
Sheffield	229	5	Sprague	Seth	4			1		1			1				7		
Bethlehem	182	9	Spring	Amos	2		2		1	1	2	1		1			10		
Tyringham	115	20	Spring	Amos	1	3		1		1	2		1				9		
Washington	215	20	Spring	Ciril	1		1						1				3		
Tyringham	110	19	Spring	Ebenz	2	1				1	2	2		1			10		
Sandisfield	172	10	Spring	Henry Junr		1		1	1	5	1		1	1			11		
Washington	215	19	Spring	Silvester	2			1		2			1				6		

145

TOWN	PG#	LN#	LAST NAME	FIRST NAME	FREE WHITE MALES under 10	10 to 16	16 to 26	26 to 45	45 and over	FREE WHITE FEMALES under 10	10 to 16	16 to 26	26 to 45	45 and over	TOTAL ALL OTHER	TOTAL SLAVES	TOTALS	DISTRICT/ TOWNSHIP	NOTES
Lanesborough	152	17	Squire	Amos	1			1		2			1				5		
Lanesborough	150	9	Squire	Andrew	4	1		1		1	1		2				10		
Lanesborough	152	16	Squire	Andrew	1		1	1	1	1	1		1	1			8		
Lanesborough	150	10	Squire	Bostwick	2			1				1	1				5		
Lee	263	28	Squire	Ebenz			1		2			1		1			5		
Washington	214	29	Squires	Elijah				1		4			1				6		
Stockbridge	257	10	Squires	Jonan			2		1		2	2		2			9		
Washington	214	35	Squires	Josiah	2			1		2			1				6		
Bethlehem	173	1	Stafford	David	1		1			1			1				4		
Cheshire	155	5	Stafford	Richard	1	2		1	1	1			1	1			8		
Adams	137	42	Stafford	Samuel	1		1	1		1	1	1	1				7		
Hancock	161	14	Stafford	Thomas	1	2		1		4	2		1				11		
Williamstown	130	11	Standish	Asa	1	1	1	1		3	1		1	1			10		
Partridgefield	189	7	Standish	Jonas	1			1		3			1				6		
Partridgefield	189	19	Standish	Jonas Jr	1		1			1		1					4		
Williamstown	130	36	Standish	Moses			1			2		1					4		
Lenox	211	14	Standly	Amos		1	1		1		1			1			5		
Pittsfield	200	31	Stanford	Oliver	1				2	3	1		1				8		
Tyringham	111	19	Stanley	Abisha	2			1	4	2	2	2		5			18		
Great Barrington	106	3	Stanly	George	1			2	1	1		3	1				9		
Sheffield	230	13	Stannard	Jehiel	3			1		1	2		1		1		9		
Hancock	158	6	Stanton	Augustus		1		1		2	2		1				9		
Washington	213	33	Stanton	Latham	2	2	1	1	1	2	1	1	2	1			14		
Hancock	158	10	Stanton	Oliver				1		4		1					6		
Pittsfield	200	39	Stanton	Robert	2			1		2			1	1			7		
Lee	263	30	Stanton	Rufus	2		1		1	1		1		1			7		
Adams	136	22	Staples	David	2		2		1	2	1		1				9		
Cheshire	155	9	Staples	Jacob	1		1					2					4		
Adams	135	11	Staples	Samuel				1					1				2		
Adams	139	10	Staples		1	1			1	2			1				6		First name blank
Lanesborough	149	14	Star	Samuel	1		1	1		1		1					5		
Williamstown	128	11	Starke	Abraham	2		1	1	1			1	1				7		
Hancock	160	5	Starkwather	Lemuel			2					1					3		
Williamstown	131	38	Starkweather	William	2			1	1	3		1	1	1	1		11		
Partridgefield	189	5	Starr	Richard		1	1		2	1	2	2		1			10		
Tyringham	111	17	Steadman	Thomas	2	1		1		1			1				6		
Tyringham	112	8	Steadman	William	1			1		1			1				4		
Tyringham	110	17	Steadman	William				1		1		1					3		
Washington	214	16	Steal	Pitts	1			2					1	1			5		
Partridgefield	189	20	Stearns	Asa				1		3		1					5		
Lenox	211	16	Stearns	Daniel	3			1		2	2		1				9		
Lanesborough	152	15	Stearns	Ebenezer	2	1	1		1	3	2	1		1			12		
Partridgefield	189	12	Stearns	Elias	2	1	1		1	1	1		1	1			9		
Lanesborough	153	2	Stearns	Isaac		1		1				1	1				4		
Zoar	143	19	Stearns	Isaac	2	1			1	2		1		1			8		
Windsor	166	24	Stearns	Joseph	3			1		1			1				6		
Williamstown	127	39	Stearns	Reuben	2	1			1	1	1	2	2	1			11		
Williamstown	131	36	Stebbens	Lewis	2	2			1	1	1			1			8		
Partridgefield	189	2	Stebbins	Dan	1	1		1					1				4		
Tyringham	113	22	Stebbins	Darius	3	1	2	1		2	3		1				13		
Lenox	211	12	Steel	Thomas		1	1		1			1		2	1		7		
Lenox	211	13	Steel	Thomas Jun	2		1	1		1		1					6		
Lanesborough	150	23	Stephens	Samuel	2	2		1				2		1			9		
Sheffield	231	11	Stevens	Aaron			1			2			1				4		
New Marlborough	234	21	Stevens	Anna			1	1		2	2		1				7		
Lee	263	24	Stevens	Benja	2			1		1	3		1				8		
Lee	263	25	Stevens	Daniel		1	2	1					1				5		
Richmond	206	28	Stevens	David			1		1			1		1			4		
New Marlborough	233	26	Stevens	Ebenezer				1					1				2		
Sandisfield	177	9	Stevens	Edward			1										1		
Sheffield	222	17	Stevens	Elijah	2			1		2			1				6		
Hancock	159	4	Stevens	Eliphalet			1	1			2		1				5		
Richmond	206	13	Stevens	Elisha	2	1	2		1	1	3		1				11		
Mount Washington	231	7	Stevens	Ezra	1	1			1	1	2		1				7		
West Stockbridge	251	4	Stevens	Hubbel	1	2	1	1			1		1				7		
Windsor	164	9	Stevens	Isaac			1			1		1					3		
Lee	263	26	Stevens	James	3		1	1		1		1					7		
West Stockbridge	251	2	Stevens	Jared		1	2		1	1	1	2		1			9		
Hancock	159	5	Stevens	Jeremiah	2			1		3			1				7		
Pittsfield	201	10	Stevens	Joel		1	2		1			3		1			8		
Lee	263	27	Stevens	John	2	1	1		1	1	1	2	1				10		
Sandisfield	176	3	Stevens	John		1							1				3		
Washington	216	12	Stevens	John				1									1		
West Stockbridge	251	5	Stevens	John		1	1		1	1				1			5		
West Stockbridge	250	23	Stevens	John W	1			1		1		2					5		
Windsor	164	10	Stevens	Joseph	1	2		1		1				1			6		
Richmond	206	21	Stevens	Parker		1			1	1	3	1		1			8		
Stockbridge	257	16	Stevens	Paul	2	2			1	1			1	1			8		
Mount Washington	232	36	Stevens	Peter	3			1		1			1				6		
New Marlborough	237	31	Stevens	Phebe			1	1					1				3		

TOWN	PG#	LN#	HEADS OF HOUSEHOLD		FREE WHITE MALES					FREE WHITE FEMALES					TOTAL ALL OTHER	TOTAL SLAVES	TOTALS	DISTRICT/ TOWNSHIP	NOTES
			LAST NAME	FIRST NAME	under 10	10 to 16	16 to 26	26 to 45	45 and over	under 10	10 to 16	16 to 26	26 to 45	45 and over					
New Marlborough	233	14	Stevens	Richard		2	1		1		1		1				6		
New Marlborough	233	27	Stevens	Richard Jun			1			1	1	1					4		
Richmond	206	23	Stevens	Silas	1		1			2		1					5		
Pittsfield	200	38	Stevens	Simeon			1	1					1				3		
Sheffield	230	24	Stevens	Stephen	3		1	1		1	2		1				9		
Becket	269	10	Stevens	Thomas	1	1		1		1			1				5		
Sheffield	227	20	Stevens	Thomas	3		1	1		2			1				8		
Sheffield	229	31	Stevens	William	1	1	1		1		2	3	1	1	1		12		
New Marlborough	234	17	Stevens	William Pitt	1	1	3	1		2	1	2	1				12		
Partridgefield	189	17	Stevens	Wm	2	1		1		2		1	2				9		
Becket	269	12	Stewart	George					1	3	2	3		2			11		
Great Barrington	104	21	Stewart	John	3			1				1					5		
Williamstown	130	2	Stewart	Lemuel	1	2	3	1	2	1	1			1			12		
Sheffield	221	19	Stewart	Philip			1			2			1				4		
Williamstown	129	19	Stewart	Samuel	2	1		1	1	1			1				7		
Sandisfield	172	11	Stickland	Peter			2		1					1			4		
Hancock	161	37	Stiles	John	1	1						1					4		
Pittsfield	201	9	Stiles	Zebediah		1	1	2		1		2	1				8		
Sheffield	228	34	Stillman	David	1	1		1			1		1				5		
New Ashford	163	27	Stills	John		1		1			1		1				4		
Great Barrington	109	36	Stimson	Anthony			2		1			3		1			7		
Sheffield	223	15	Stocking	Moses		1		1		1	1		1				5		
Pittsfield	201	5	Stocking	Thomas	1	1	1		1	1	1			1			7		
Windsor	165	28	Stockwell	Solomon	1			1		1			1				4		
Lanesborough	152	36	Stodard	Lemuel	2			1		1			1				5		
Lanesborough	150	19	Stoddard	Nathan	3			1		1			1				6		
Lenox	211	15	Stone	Enos		1	2		1	1		1		1			7		
Lenox	212	6	Stone	Ethan		1		1			1	2					5		
West Stockbridge	251	3	Stone	Ezekiel	2	1	1		1	1	2		1				9		
Williamstown	129	28	Stone	Jed				1		1		1					3		
Lanesborough	149	38	Stone	John				1		3			1				5		
Windsor	165	11	Stone	Simon	4								1				6		
Lee	263	32	Stone	Squier	4		1	1		1	1		1				9		
Sandisfield	175	9	Storrs	Eleazer Rev.			1	1	1				1	2			6		
Hancock	158	17	Stovers	Amos			3	7	1			6	12	4			33		
Sheffield	230	21	Stowe	Comfort	2	1		1		1	1	2	1				9		
Sheffield	230	27	Stowe	William	3			1		2			1				7		
Partridgefield	189	11	Stowell	Cyrus		1		1		1	1	2	1				7		
Partridgefield	189	10	Stowell	Harvey	1		1		1			2	1	1			7		
Hancock	161	30	Straight	William	2		1		1	3		2		1			10		
Hancock	161	34	Strander	Abraham O		2		1		3	1		1				8		
Williamstown	126	1	Stratton	Ebenezer	1		3		1	1	1	1		1			9		
Sheffield	224	16	Stratton	Richard	3			1					1	1			6		
Becket	268	38	Stricton	Alpheus			1			2		1	1				5		
Richmond	206	2	Strong	Asael	1	1		1	1			1	1	1			7		
Pittsfield	200	37	Strong	Ashbel		1	1	1	1	2			1	1	2		10		
Pittsfield	200	29	Strong	Jonathan		1	1		1	1			1	1			6		
Pittsfield	200	30	Strong	Jonathan Jr		1						1					2		
Pittsfield	201	12	Strong	King		1	1		1	2	1	5		1			12		
Pittsfield	201	6	Strong	Noble	2		1						1				4		
Lanesborough	148	15	Strong	Solomon			2						1				3		
Clarksburg	142	7	Stroud	John	2		1			1		1					5		
Clarksburg	142	8	Stroud	William	1		1			1		1					4		
Mount Washington	232	5	Sturdevant	Cezar	1	1		1		1			1				5		
New Marlborough	239	12	Sturdevant	Ira	2			1		1		1					5		
New Marlborough	239	11	Sturdevant	James	2	1	1	1					1				6		
New Marlborough	239	18	Sturdevant	Levi	1			1		2			1				5		
Lee	263	29	Sturges	William	1		1	1		2		1	1				7		
Pittsfield	200	36	Sturtevant	Friend	2			1					1				4		
Cheshire	158	1	Sullivan	Daniel	3			1		2			1				7		
Clarksburg	141	15	Sumner	Abner	1			1		1		1	1				5		
Bethlehem	180	2	Sumner	Clemmons			1		1		1			1			4		
Bethlehem	181	29	Sumner	Daniel	1	1	2	1		1	2	1	1				10		
Bethlehem	180	3	Sumner	Hezekiah Jr	1	1	2	1		1	1	1	1				9		
Bethlehem	180	1	Sumner	Hezekiah Senr				1						1			2		
Lanesborough	148	19	Sunderland	James	1			1		1			1				4		
New Marlborough	232	19	Supon	Jedediah	3		1			1			1				6		
Williamstown	129	21	Sutton	Beemal	1	1		1				1	1	1			6		
Windsor	167	31	Svetland	Jonah	1	1	2	1				1	1	1			8		
Williamstown	129	27	Swan	Asa				1				1		1			3		
Hancock	162	18	Sweet	George	2	2			1	1				1			7		
Tyringham	112	47	Sweet	James	1			1		2	1	1	1				7		
Hancock	161	10	Sweet	Jeremiah		2	1		1	1	2			1			8		
Hancock	161	11	Sweet	John				1		3			1				5		
Williamstown	130	10	Sweet	John				1					1				2		
Tyringham	119	5	Swett	Abraham	2			1		1			1				5		
Sheffield	224	5	Swift	Asahel		1							1				2		
Stockbridge	257	20	Swift	James	3	1	1	1		2			1				9		
West Stockbridge	250	28	Swift	Lot	2	1	1	1		1	1		1				8		
Hancock	159	19	Swift	Nathan		2		1				1	1				5		

TOWN	PG#	LN#	LAST NAME	FIRST NAME	FREE WHITE MALES under 10	10 to 16	16 to 26	26 to 45	45 and over	FREE WHITE FEMALES under 10	10 to 16	16 to 26	26 to 45	45 and over	TOTAL ALL OTHER	TOTAL SLAVES	TOTALS	DISTRICT/TOWNSHIP	NOTES
Stockbridge	257	19	Swift	Owen	1			1		2			1				5		
Williamstown	125	14	Swift	Seth Revd	3		1	1	1	1		2	1				10		
Cheshire	157	29	Swift	Silas				1			2	3		1			7		
Cheshire	157	49	Swift	Silas				1			2	3		1			7		
Sheffield	223	13	Sylva	Zilpha Widow											5		5		
Sheffield	231	12	Tacher	Cyrus	3	1		1		2			1				8		
New Marlborough	237	17	Taft	Lovet	3	2	1	1		2		1	1	1			12		
Washington	215	8	Tagget	John	3	4	1	1				1	1				11		
Hancock	158	13	Talcott	Israel			2	1	4			4		4			15		
Hancock	158	4	Talcott	John		1	1	3	4	1	1	2	4	4			21		
Dalton	193	33	Talcott	Joseph		1	2	1		2			1				7		
Lanesborough	151	17	Talcott	Nehemiah			2	1		3		1	1				8		
Zoar	143	20	Taller		1		1			1		1	1				5		First name blank
Lanesborough	148	9	Talmage	Joseph	4	1	1		1	2	1		1				11		
Williamstown	128	16	Talmage	Joseph	2		1	2	1	1	1	1	1	1			11		
Adams	134	31	Tanner	Francis		1	1			1		1					5		
Tyringham	111	41	Tanner	William	1	1		1		2			1				6		
Pittsfield	201	22	Tayler	Nathan	2	1		1					1				5		
Pittsfield	201	16	Taylor	Abigail									1				1		
Tyringham	114	11	Taylor	Alvin				1		1			1				3		
New Marlborough	234	20	Taylor	Daniel Esq	1	1	1		1		2			1			7		
New Marlborough	236	32	Taylor	Eleazer			1		1			3		1			6		
New Marlborough	236	18	Taylor	Elias	1			1					1				3		
Great Barrington	110	2	Taylor	Elisha	2	1	2	1		3			1				10		
Tyringham	114	10	Taylor	Elisha	2	2	1		2		1		1				9		
Pittsfield	201	15	Taylor	James	3	2	1		1	1		2	1				11		
New Marlborough	236	17	Taylor	John	1			1		2		1					5		
Stockbridge	257	23	Taylor	John				1					1				2		
Stockbridge	257	28	Taylor	John 2d				1		1							2		
Lenox	211	19	Taylor	Jonathan	2	2			1	2	1	2	1				11		
New Marlborough	233	22	Taylor	Micah	1	1	1		1	1	1	1					8		
Richmond	207	29	Taylor	Silas	1		2						1				4		
Sheffield	227	37	Taylor	Stephen	1		1						1				3		
West Stockbridge	251	12	Taylor	Teahan	2	2		1		1			1				7		
Adams	134	26	Taylor	Thomas	2	2		1		1	1	1	1				9		
Pittsfield	201	17	Taylor	Thomas	1			1	1		2		1	1			6		
Lee	264	10	Taylor	William			1					1					2		
Partridgefield	189	34	Teethill	Nathan		1	1	1		3	1	1		1			10		
Zoar	143	1	Tenney	James	3	1		1		1	2		1				9		
Lanesborough	152	7	Terrey	Hiram	2			1		4	2		1				10		
Sheffield	225	1	Thacher	Pomp											6		6		
Savoy	140	40	Thatcher	Ebenzr	2	1	1		1	2	1		1				10		
Lanesborough	149	6	Thatcher	Gamaliel	1			1		1	1	1					5		
Lee	264	9	Thatcher	John	2		1	1		2			1				7		
Lee	264	12	Thatcher	Rowland		2	1	1			2	1	1				8		
Williamstown	130	27	Thayer	Baruch	2	1	1	1		2			1				9		
Alford	117	31	Thayer	Daniel	2	1		1		2			1				7		
Sheffield	221	15	Thayer	Enoch W.			2					1	1				4		
Williamstown	131	6	Thayer	Jona	1		1					1					3		
Partridgefield	189	37	Thayer	Jonathan	3	2	1		1	2	1		1				11		
Lee	264	4	Thayer	Nathan	2			1					1				4		
Windsor	165	31	Thayer	William	1	2	1		1	1			2				8		
Sheffield	225	6	Theley	Elisha				1			1		1				3		
Mount Washington	231	13	Thigbee	Ruth	1								1				2		
Lee	264	11	Thomas	Elijah	1	1	1	1		1		1	1				7		
Williamstown	126	10	Thomas	Elijah	2	1	1		1			2		1			8		
Loudon	179	27	Thomas	Samuel	1	1	1		1	2	2	1					10		
Partridgefield	189	38	Thomas	Samuel	2			1		1			1				5		
New Marlborough	232	27	Thomas	William	2			1		1	1		1				6		
Partridgefield	189	33	Thompson	Amherst	1	1			1	2	1		1				7		
Partridgefield	189	21	Thompson	Artemas			1					1					3		
Partridgefield	189	25	Thompson	Daniel			1	1	1				1				4		
Washington	215	13	Thompson	Edde	1					3	4		1				9		
Partridgefield	189	31	Thompson	Elias			2						1				3		
Partridgefield	189	30	Thompson	Elias 2d			1			1			1				3		
Tyringham	114	23	Thompson	Grace		1	1				1			1			7		
Pittsfield	201	23	Thompson	Isaac			1			2	1	1					5		
Southfield	182	19	Thompson	Isaac	1		1			3			1				6		
Tyringham	112	45	Thompson	James	1		1	1		3		1	1	2			10		
Tyringham	114	21	Thompson	Jared	3			1				1					5		
Adams	136	41	Thompson	Joseph	2			1		1			1				5		
New Ashford	162	10	Thompson	Joseph	2		1		1	1			1				6		
Partridgefield	189	32	Thompson	Levi	1		1			2		1					5		
Hancock	158	9	Thompson	Lodowick	2			1					1				4		
Partridgefield	189	27	Thompson	Nathan	1	2	2		1		1	1	1	1			10		
Partridgefield	189	26	Thompson	Peter	1		2		1			2	1	1			8		
Pittsfield	201	26	Thompson	Samuel			1					1					2		
Tyringham	114	22	Thompson	Samuel			1			4			1				6		
Partridgefield	189	28	Thompson	Simeon	2		1	1		2			1				7		
Lenox	211	18	Thompson	Thaddeus	1	2	2		1	1		1	1				9		

TOWN	PG#	LN#	LAST NAME	FIRST NAME	FREE WHITE MALES under 10	10 to 16	16 to 26	26 to 45	45 and over	FREE WHITE FEMALES under 10	10 to 16	16 to 26	26 to 45	45 and over	TOTAL ALL OTHER	TOTAL SLAVES	TOTALS	DISTRICT/ TOWNSHIP	NOTES
Lanesborough	150	17	Thompson	Thomas	1				1	3	2		1				8		
Sheffield	229	22	Thompson	Timothy	1			1		1			1				4		
Partridgefield	189	29	Thompson	William	1			1		1			1				4		
Southfield	182	5	Thorp	Aron	2			1		3			1	1			8		
Southfield	182	20	Thorp	Peter					1					1			2		
Cheshire	156	31	Thrasher	Charles					1					1			2		
Adams	135	6	Tibbets	Caleb	1	1	1		1	1	2		1				8		
Lanesborough	148	14	Tiffany	Eleazer		1		1				1	1				4		
Sandisfield	170	2	Tilden	Thomas		1	1		1	1		1		1			6		
Lee	264	13	Tilley	Samll				1					1				2		
Lanesborough	152	18	Tillotson	Bejamin	1	1		1		1			1	1			6		
Tyringham	113	2	Tillotson	Samuel	4			1		1			1				7		
Partridgefield	189	36	Tinney	Isaac				1			1		1				3		
Partridgefield	189	35	Tinney	Oliver	2	1		1		3	1		1				9		
Becket	269	17	Titus	David	1		1					1		1			4		
West Stockbridge	251	10	Tobey	Abram	2			1		2			1				6		
Becket	269	18	Tobey	Martha											3		3		
Lee	264	6	Tobey	Nathanl			1		1	1	1	1		1			6		
Lee	264	7	Tobey	Stephen		2	1		1	2	1						7		
Stockbridge	257	25	Tolman	Ebenzr	1	2			1				4	1			9		
Egremont	120	5	Toms	Robert	3		1	1		3		1	1				10		
Great Barrington	109	44	Tooley	Isaac				1			2		2				5		
Pittsfield	201	25	Torrey	David		1		1	1	1			1	1			5		
Adams	138	30	Torrey	John	1		1			1		1					4		
Williamstown	130	12	Torrey	John		2		1		1	1	1		1			7		
Williamstown	129	11	Torrey	John Junr		1				1		1					3		
Partridgefield	189	22	Torrey	Nathan		1	1	1	1			1		1			6		
Pittsfield	201	24	Torrey	Nathaniel	2			1		3			1				7		
Williamstown	130	14	Torrey	William	2		1	1	1				1	1			7		
Williamstown	132	12	Town	David D.		2		1		1	1			1			6		
Zoar	143	6	Towne	Eli		1		1		2	1		1				6		
Hancock	162	7	Townier	Martin	2	1	2	1		3	2	1	1				13		
Hancock	162	9	Townier	Martin Jun	1		1		1			1		1			5		
Hancock	162	6	Townier	Nathan	3	2		1		1	1		1	1			10		
Williamstown	125	6	Townor	William	4			1		3	2	1					11		
Tyringham	113	25	Townsend	Jonan	4			1					1				6		
Tyringham	113	45	Townsend	Rufus	1			1		1			1				4		
Tyringham	113	8	Towsend	Lemuel				1				1					2		
Tyringham	113	7	Towsend	Samuel	1			1				1		1			4		
New Marlborough	233	15	Tracey	David	4		1		1			1	1				8		
Richmond	209	2	Tracey	Simeon	2			1	1	2		1	1	1			9		
Pittsfield	201	21	Tracy	Elam				1					1				2		
Richmond	205	19	Tracy	Erastus	3	1		1		1			1				7		
Pittsfield	201	19	Tracy	Ezra			2		1					1			4		
Partridgefield	189	24	Tracy	James	1			1		2			1				5		
Partridgefield	189	23	Tracy	Nathll		2	2		1			1		1			7		
Dalton	193	31	Tracy	Sarah			1				2			1			4		
Pittsfield	201	20	Tracy	Seth	2	1	1	1		1	2	1	1				10		
Cheshire	154	11	Tracy	Solomon	1			1			1	1	1				5		
Stockbridge	257	27	Trask	Jesse	4	2	1				1		1				10		
Williamstown	129	5	Treadwell	Ager			1	1		4	2	1					9		
Pittsfield	201	18	Treat	Ebenezer				1		2			1				4		
Alford	116	22	Tremain	Justis	3			1		2	1		1				8		
Alford	117	43	Tremain	Nathaniel	4	2	1		1	2	1	1	1				13		
Sheffield	230	22	Trescott	Ebenezer	2				1	1	1		1				6		
Sheffield	230	23	Trescott	Samll	3	2	1	1		2	1	1	1				12		
Great Barrington	107	3	Trowbridge	Tabitha										1			1		
Hancock	160	8	Tubs	Seth				1						1			2		
Windsor	165	19	Tucker	Ephraim	2			1		1			1				5		
Great Barrington	105	10	Tucker	John	2			1		1			1	1			6		
Stockbridge	257	26	Tucker	John		1		1	1								3		
Tyringham	112	32	Tucker	John	2			1		2	1		1				7		
Great Barrington	110	1	Tucker	Newman	2			1		1			1				5		
Williamstown	132	26	Tucker	Seth				1		2	1	1					5		
Great Barrington	105	2	Tucker	Silas				1		2		1	1				5		
Dalton	193	32	Tufts	Peter		1	1	1				1		1			5		
Mount Washington	231	1	Tullar	John Jun	1	1		1		2		1					6		
New Marlborough	238	12	Turner	Anna							1		1				2		
Great Barrington	105	39	Turner	Elijah	3	1		1		2			1				8		
New Marlborough	238	16	Turner	Isaac	1			1		1		1					4		
Great Barrington	106	34	Turner	Jabez	2	2	2	1			1		1				9		
Lanesborough	151	3	Turner	Peregreen	4	1		1			1		1				8		
West Stockbridge	251	11	Turner	Peter	3	2	1		1	2	1	2	1	1			14		
New Marlborough	238	11	Turner	Samll				1		1				1			3		
Southfield	182	7	Turner	Thomas	1			1		2			1				5		
Williamstown	131	32	Turner	Zebedee	2	1	2	1			1	1		1			9		
Lanesborough	150	28	Turrell	John		2	1	1		1	1		2				8		
Lanesborough	149	29	Turrell	Samuel		1			1	1		1		1			5		
Lanesborough	150	22	Turrell	Trueman		3	1	1		2		1	1				9		
Sheffield	223	32	Tuttle	Huldah	1					1	1		1				4		

TOWN	PG#	LN#	LAST NAME	FIRST NAME	M under 10	M 10 to 16	M 16 to 26	M 26 to 45	M 45 and over	F under 10	F 10 to 16	F 16 to 26	F 26 to 45	F 45 and over	TOTAL ALL OTHER	TOTAL SLAVES	TOTALS	DISTRICT/TOWNSHIP	NOTES
Alford	116	20	Tuttle	Isaac	1			1		2			1				5		
Lee	264	8	Tuttle	James	1				1	1	1			1			5		
Tyringham	111	47	Tuttle	Jonathan	2			1		1		1	1				6		
Lanesborough	149	9	Tuttle	Sarah	2							1		1			3		
Great Barrington	107	6	Tuttle	Simon			1						1				2		
Great Barrington	106	39	Tyler	Amasa	1			1	1	1			1				5		
New Ashford	162	3	Tyler	Barchal			1				2	1	1				5		
Lenox	211	21	Tyler	John	2	1		1		3			1				8		
Lee	264	5	Tyler	Ruth				1						2			3		
New Ashford	162	1	Tyler	Samuel			1		1	3	3		1				9		
Williamstown	128	24	Tyler	Samuel	1	1	1		1	1	2			2			9		
Alford	116	27	Tyler	Solomon	1	1			1	1	1	1		1			6		
Adams	135	41	Tyler	Thomas	2			1		1			1				5		
Windsor	168	1	Tyler	William	3			1		2	1		1				8		
Lanesborough	150	32	Umberfield	Samuel			1			1		1					3		
Great Barrington	109	5	Umphrey	Hugh	1	1	3		1	2			1				9		
Lanesborough	151	10	Umphry	Chauncy	1		1			1		1					4		
New Marlborough	233	12	Underwood	Alpheus		2		1		1			1				5		
New Marlborough	232	3	Underwood	Edmond	3		1			2			1				7		
Sandisfield	175	11	Underwood	Roswell		1						1	1				3		
Bethlehem	181	13	Underwood	Samuel	2		1					1					4		
Sandisfield	176	12	Underwood	Silas	2		1			1			1				5		
Sandisfield	171	15	Underwood	Simon	1	2		1		3		1	3				11		
Tyringham	114	5	Upham	Moses				1		1		1					3		
Tyringham	114	4	Upham	Nathan	1	2		1		4			1				9		
Adams	136	26	Upton	Isaac	1			1		2	2		1				7		
Adams	136	27	Upton	Isaac Junr			1					1					2		
Adams	135	1	Upton	John			1		1			1	1				5		
Washington	213	19	Utley	Ebenz		1	1			1			1				4		
Lee	264	15	Vallett	Jeremiah				1					1				2		
Stockbridge	257	29	Vallett	Jeremiah Jr	1	1		1				1					4		
Great Barrington	106	28	Van Deusen	Abrahm 2d	1			2		1			1				5		
Great Barrington	106	21	Van Deusen	Abram		2		1		2			1	1			7		
Great Barrington	106	22	Van Deusen	Conrad		1	2	2	1		1	2		1			10		
Great Barrington	106	18	Van Deusen	Isaac	1			1	2	2			2		3		11		
Great Barrington	104	15	Van Deusen	Isaac Jr	1	2	1		1	1		1	1				8		
Great Barrington	106	27	Van Deusen	Jacob		1			1	2			1	1	2		8		
Great Barrington	106	19	Van Deusen	John			1	1	1			1					4		
Great Barrington	107	41	Van Deusen	John Jr	1	1		1		1			1				5		
Great Barrington	109	9	Van Deusen	Mathew		1						1					2		
Sheffield	230	17	Van Loven	Zacchariah		2		1		2			1				6		
Williamstown	131	5	Vanderworker	James	2			1		1	1						5		
Pittsfield	201	27	Vanschaach	Henry	1	1		1			1		1	1	3		8		
Stockbridge	257	30	Vaughan	John	2	1		1		1	2	1	1				9		
Hancock	159	39	Vaughn	David	1			2		1			1				5		
Hancock	159	40	Vaughn	David Jun	2	1		1		2	2		1				9		
Hancock	160	4	Vaughn	Jabez	2			1		3	1		1				8		
Williamstown	131	29	Vaughn	John		1							1				2		
Williamstown	131	13	Vaughn	Joseph				1		1	2						4		
Pittsfield	202	35	Venduzer	Jacob											2		2		
Cheshire	155	34	Vickery	William			1			3			1				5		
Becket	269	19	Victs	Henry			1						1				2		
Becket	269	20	Victs	Henry Junr			1			2		1	1				5		
Windsor	166	25	Vining	Israel	2	1		1		1	1		1				7		
Williamstown	129	14	Vinson	Pardon	2	2		1		1			1				7		
New Ashford	163	23	Virgison	Daniel			1			3	1	1					6		
Adams	138	39	Vizee	John	1	1	2	1	1	1		1		1			9		
Sheffield	227	3	Vosburgh	Eliakim	3	1		1		1		1	1				8		
Sheffield	226	16	Vosburgh	Henry			1			2	1		1				5		
Sheffield	226	10	Vosburgh	Isaac	2	1	1	1		1	2	1	1				10		
Sheffield	227	10	Vosburgh	Isaac			1			1			1				4		
Sheffield	227	8	Vosburgh	Martin	3	1		1		2	1		1				9		
Pittsfield	202	8	Waddams	Caleb	2			1		2	3	1		1			10		
Lanesborough	149	28	Wade	Silvanus	3			1		2			1				7		
Tyringham	113	4	Wadsworth	Asa	2			1	1	1			1	2			8		
Tyringham	115	6	Wadsworth	Barnabas			1						1				2		
Becket	269	23	Wadsworth	Benja		1		1		1	1	1					5		
Becket	269	24	Wadsworth	Benja Jr	2	1						1					4		
Tyringham	114	33	Wadsworth	Ezekiel	3	1		1		1	1		1				8		
Becket	269	2	Wadsworth	Jabez	1	2		1		1			1				6		
Becket	269	22	Wadsworth	Jonathan		1	1	1					1				4		
Great Barrington	108	27	Wadsworth	Reuben	2			1		1	1		1				6		
Becket	269	3	Wadsworth	Seth	4		1	1		1			2	1			10		
Becket	269	1	Wadsworth	Stephen		1	1		1	1		1	1				6		
Great Barrington	104	23	Wainwright	David	1	1	1	1	1	3	2	2	1				14		
Dalton	193	40	Wakefield	Nathn		1				1	1		1				5		
Becket	269	21	Walden	Eben				1					1				2		
Pittsfield	202	1	Waldron	Michael	2			1					1				4		
Dalton	193	39	Waldron	Taber	3	1		1		1		1	1				7		
Dalton	193	34	Walds	Galvin	2		1	1	1	4	2		1		1		13		

TOWN	PG#	LN#	LAST NAME	FIRST NAME	FREE WHITE MALES under 10	10 to 16	16 to 26	26 to 45	45 and over	FREE WHITE FEMALES under 10	10 to 16	16 to 26	26 to 45	45 and over	TOTAL ALL OTHER	TOTAL SLAVES	TOTALS	DISTRICT/ TOWNSHIP	NOTES
Becket	269	6	Walker	Amasa	2			1		3				1			7		
Adams	133	9	Walker	Charles		1	1		1	1		1	1	1			7		
New Marlborough	236	1	Walker	David		1	1	1				1	1	1			6		
Becket	269	5	Walker	Ebenezer	2			1		2	2		1				8		
Lenox	212	11	Walker	Edward					1		1		1	1			4		
Lanesborough	152	24	Walker	Elias	1	1			1	1	2	2		1			9		
Savoy	139	20	Walker	Ethel	3			1				2					6		
Cheshire	157	22	Walker	Hezekiah	1		1			1		1					4		
Cheshire	157	42	Walker	Hezekiah	1		1			1		1					4		
Sandisfield	170	13	Walker	Isaac	2	1		1		3	1		1	1			10		
Tyringham	115	16	Walker	Isaac	1		1	1	1		1	1	1				7		
Great Barrington	104	20	Walker	Jacob											2		2		
Becket	269	7	Walker	James	1	1		1		3	1		1				8		
Williamstown	131	28	Walker	James		1		1		1	1		1				5		
Lanesborough	149	19	Walker	Mary								1					1		
Windsor	165	20	Walker	Robert	1	1	2		1	5	2	1	1				14		
Dalton	193	35	Walker	Walter	2	2		1		1			1				7		
Savoy	140	2	Walker	Wilkes	1			1		1			1				4		
Lenox	211	33	Walker	William		1	2		1		1	1	2		1		9		
Windsor	165	18	Wallace	John	1			1					1	1			4		
Adams	137	30	Walling	David		1			1	1	1		1				5		
Great Barrington	104	12	Walling	Margaret	2					1	2						5		
Stockbridge	258	14	Wallis	James	1				1	1			1				4		
Adams	136	34	Walmarth	Shubael		1		1				2		2			6		
New Marlborough	239	13	Walter	Heman	5		1	1					1				8		
Pittsfield	202	22	Walton	Silas	2			1		1	1		1	1			7		
Lee	264	26	Wansey	Henry	2	2	1	1		3	1	1	1				12		
New Marlborough	238	26	Ward	Calvin			1			4			1				6		
Sandisfield	171	11	Ward	Daniel					1		3			1	1		6		
New Marlborough	237	19	Ward	Edmund	1			1		1			1				4		
New Marlborough	237	13	Ward	Elihu	1			1		2	1		1	1			7		
Bethlehem	182	20	Ward	Elisha	1		1					1					3		
Pittsfield	201	37	Ward	Isaac	2	1		1		1	1	1	1				8		
Pittsfield	201	39	Ward	Jacob				1		1	1		1				4		
Mount Washington	231	9	Ward	James	1	1	1	1		1			1				6		
New Marlborough	237	32	Ward	Jedediah		4	1		1		1	1	1				9		
Pittsfield	202	16	Ward	John	1	1	1		1	2	1	1		1			9		
Sandisfield	171	5	Ward	John	1			1		1			1	1			5		
Pittsfield	201	38	Ward	Josiah	1	1	1	1		2		1	1				8		
Stockbridge	258	4	Ward	Nicholas	2			1					1				4		
New Marlborough	238	3	Ward	Obadiah Esq	2		1	1	1		1	1	2				9		
New Marlborough	238	13	Ward	Ralph	1	1	1			1		1		1			6		
Bethlehem	181	11	Ward	Seth	2			1		2			1				6		
Bethlehem	182	18	Ward	Thomas		1	1		1	1		1	1				6		
Williamstown	129	13	Wareing	Betsey Mrs.						1	1		1				3		
Sheffield	228	4	Warn	Jacob		1	2		1	1	1		1				7		
Sheffield	229	13	Warn	Samll	2	1	2		1	1							7		
Sheffield	229	14	Warn	William	3	2			1	3			1				10		
Lee	264	22	Warner	Aaron	1	1	1		1		1		1				6		
Bethlehem	172	13	Warner	Consider	2	1		1		2	1		1	1			9		
Loudon	179	35	Warner	Daniel					1			1		1			3		
Stockbridge	258	5	Warner	Daniel	1			1				1					3		
Pittsfield	202	4	Warner	Ebenezer	1	1	1	2		2			3				10		
New Marlborough	234	8	Warner	Jason	3			1					1				5		
Dalton	193	36	Warner	Nathan	3	2			1	1	1	1	1				10		
New Marlborough	234	9	Warner	Samll					1				1				2		
Sandisfield	173	25	Warner	Timothy	2			1		2			1				6		
Tyringham	113	30	Warren	Benjamin				1			3		1				5		
Tyringham	113	29	Warren	Benjamin Jr		1		1		2	1						5		
Lanesborough	150	27	Warren	Daniel			1			1	1		1				4		
Tyringham	114	8	Warren	Elijah	3			1		2			1				7		
Washington	214	6	Warren	Ezra					1	4	1		1				7		
Windsor	164	8	Warren	Ezra	1	1	2		1	2		1	1				9		
Washington	214	7	Warren	Ezra Jun	3		1	1		1			1				7		
Cheshire	158	16	Warren	Jonas	4	2		1		1	1		1				10		
Tyringham	113	43	Warren	Joshua			1	1						1			3		
Lanesborough	148	24	Warren	Levi	5			1		1	1		1				9		
Lanesborough	150	25	Warren	Samuel		1		1		1				1			4		
Lanesborough	150	26	Warren	Seth				1		1		1		1			4		
Lenox	212	12	Warren	Stephen	2	2		1	1	1			1	1			9		
West Stockbridge	251	17	Warren						1								1		First name blank
Partridgefield	190	13	Washburn	Abraham				2	1				1				4		
Lenox	211	23	Washburn	Jacob	2	3		1		3			1				10		
Hancock	161	16	Washburn	Samuel	2	2	2		1		1	1		1			10		
Loudon	177	3	Waterhouse	Thomas	2	3		1		1	2		1				10		
Windsor	166	36	Waterman	Calvin	2			1		1			2				6		
Dalton	193	37	Waterman	Glading	2	2	1	1		2	1	1	2	1			13		
Windsor	166	23	Waterman	James	2		1	1		1			1	1			7		
Cheshire	156	13	Waterman	John	3	1	2		2		2	2	1		1		14		
Savoy	140	4	Waterman	Oliver	2	1		1		2	1	1					8		

151

TOWN	PG#	LN#	LAST NAME	FIRST NAME	FW Males under 10	10 to 16	16 to 26	26 to 45	45 and over	FW Females under 10	10 to 16	16 to 26	26 to 45	45 and over	TOTAL ALL OTHER	TOTAL SLAVES	TOTALS	DISTRICT/TOWNSHIP	NOTES
Adams	137	4	Waterman	R*d				1		2		1					4		
Pittsfield	202	5	Waters	Josiah					1				1				2		
Pittsfield	202	3	Waters	Philemon	2		1			1			1				5		
Partridgefield	190	20	Watkins	Amasa	3		1						1				5		
Partridgefield	189	41	Watkins	Andrew	1		1			3			1				6		
Partridgefield	190	9	Watkins	Elisha	3		1					1	1				6		
Partridgefield	189	42	Watkins	Gilbert	2	1	1			2		1	1				8		
Partridgefield	189	43	Watkins	James			1		1		1	1		1			5		
Partridgefield	190	2	Watkins	Jason	3		1			3			1				8		
Partridgefield	189	40	Watkins	John		2	2		1			3		1			9		
Partridgefield	190	1	Watkins	Oliver	1							1	1				3		
Partridgefield	190	22	Watkins	Rufus	1		1						1				3		
Partridgefield	190	10	Watkins	Saml Jr			1			1			1				3		
Partridgefield	190	8	Watkins	Samuel		1	2		1			2		1			7		
Partridgefield	190	25	Watkins	Simpson	1	1	1	1				2					6		
Partridgefield	190	7	Watkins	Zech Junr	1		1		1			2		1			6		
Washington	214	9	Watson	Hazard		1		1		1			2				5		
Partridgefield	190	18	Watson	John	2		1			2	1		1				7		
Sheffield	230	4	Watson	John	1				1		1			1			4		
Williamstown	126	35	Watson	Lois Mrs		1				1				1			3		
Great Barrington	107	27	Watson	Robert	2			2		1		1	1				7		
New Ashford	163	28	Way	Azariah	4	1	1						2				8		
Lenox	212	20	Way	Moses	1			1		1		1	1				5		
Lenox	211	27	Way	Timothy	1		2		1	1	2	3		1			11		
Windsor	166	12	Weaver	Joseph	1		1			2			1				5		
Bethlehem	181	34	Webb	Benoni	1		1						1				3		
Bethlehem	182	6	Webb	Daniel		1	1			1			1	1			5		
Egremont	120	38	Webb	James	2	1				2			1				6		
Egremont	120	35	Webb	John	2		1	1		1	2	1	1				9		
Bethlehem	182	3	Webb	Jonah			1			1		1					3		
Egremont	118	14	Webb	Josiah	1		1			1			1				5		
Dalton	193	42	Webb	Lebbeus	2		1			1			1				5		
Dalton	193	41	Webb	Naphtali		1			1	1	1	1	1				6		
Washington	214	23	Webb	Nathan		1	1		1			1	1		2		7		
Washington	214	22	Webb	Nathan Jun	1	1	1			1	1		1				6		
Bethlehem	181	44	Webb	Reuben	1		1						1				3		
Bethlehem	182	1	Webb	Samuel	1		1						1				3		
Egremont	120	42	Webb	Thomas			1	1				2	1	1			6		
Dalton	193	38	Webb	Zebulon			1			1			1				3		
New Ashford	163	1	Webber	Benjamin	3		2			1		1	1				8		
Sandisfield	176	2	Webster	Abner	1		2	1					1				5		
Cheshire	155	33	Webster	Adonijah											6		6		
Lanesborough	150	35	Webster	Clark	2		1						1				4		
Tyringham	111	32	Webster	Daniel	4		1			1	1		1				8		
Alford	116	10	Webster	David			1			2		1					4		
Bethlehem	181	21	Webster	David	1		1			1			1				4		
Sandisfield	176	5	Webster	Ebenezer	1		1						1				3		
Stockbridge	258	19	Webster	Elihu		1						1					2		
Sandisfield	175	37	Webster	Jacob	4	1			1		1			1			8		
Bethlehem	182	15	Webster	John	1		1			4			1				7		
Great Barrington	110	3	Webster	John	1		1			2	2		1				7		
Loudon	178	22	Webster	John	2		1					1	1	1			6		
Tyringham	111	48	Webster	John	3	2	1	1		1			1				9		
Tyringham	112	33	Webster	John	2	2	1			1			1				7		
Southfield	183	8	Webster	Jonathan	3	1	1			2	1		1				9		
West Stockbridge	251	13	Webster	Jonathan		1	1	1					1				4		
Loudon	178	20	Webster	Seth			1			1	1						3		
Bethlehem	181	12	Webster	Simeon	1		1			3	1		1				7		
Tyringham	112	2	Webster	Stephen	2	2	1			1	1		1				8		
Lee	264	33	Wedger	Abel	2		1						1				4		
Lanesborough	148	8	Weed	Jonathan	3	1	1			1		1	1				9		
Williamstown	128	29	Welch	Elijah	3	1				1			1				6		
Sheffield	230	35	Welch	Vine	3		1						1				5		
Pittsfield	202	10	Weller	Daniel		1	2		1		1			1			6		
Pittsfield	202	11	Weller	Daniel Jr	2		1	1	2	3	1	1	1				12		
Pittsfield	202	12	Weller	Enoch	3		1	1		2			1				8		
Pittsfield	202	13	Weller	Justus	2	2			1	2	2	2	1				12		
Lenox	211	26	Weller	Paul	1		1			3			1				6		
Pittsfield	201	41	Weller	William	1		1					1	1		2		6		
Williamstown	125	8	Welles	Simon	1	1	1	1		1				1			6		
Adams	138	27	Wells	Amos	1		1	1		2		1	1		1		8		
Tyringham	114	45	Wells	Benjm D			1	1		3			1				6		
Cheshire	155	28	Wells	Charles	2	1		1		1		1	1				7		
Cheshire	156	21	Wells	Elisha	1		1	1		4	1	1	1				10		
Williamstown	127	21	Wells	Enos	1		1	1		1			1				5		
Cheshire	155	29	Wells	John	1	1	1	1	1	2		4	1	1			13		
Adams	137	9	Wells	Peter	2			1		1			1				5		
Adams	137	17	Wells	Rufus	2		1	1		1							5		
Adams	137	8	Wells	Samuel		1	1	1	1	1	2	1	1	2			11		
Williamstown	127	19	Wells	Seth			1	1		3			1				6		

152

TOWN	PG#	LN#	LAST NAME	FIRST NAME	FREE WHITE MALES under 10	10 to 16	16 to 26	26 to 45	45 and over	FREE WHITE FEMALES under 10	10 to 16	16 to 26	26 to 45	45 and over	TOTAL ALL OTHER	TOTAL SLAVES	TOTALS	DISTRICT/TOWNSHIP	NOTES
Lenox	211	34	Wells	Stephen		1	2		1	1	1			1			7		
Cheshire	154	29	Wells	Thomas	1			1		2			1				5		
Lenox	212	5	Wells	William				1						1			2		
Williamstown	127	18	Wells	William	1			1	1			2		1			6		
Lanesborough	148	7	Wells	John			1					1					2		
Lanesborough	148	6	Wells	Melankton W.	2		1	1		1		1	1				7		
Dalton	194	5	Wentworth	Daniel	2	1	1	1		2	1	1	1				10		
Sandisfield	173	8	Wentworth	Joseph	1	2			2	2	1		1				9		
Windsor	165	17	Wentworth	Sylvanus	1		1		1	1		2		1			7		
Cheshire	154	28	Wescott	Moses	2		1	1		1	1		1				7		
Savoy	140	32	Wescott	Stutely	1	1		1		1	1		1				6		
Washington	216	21	West	Abel	4	1	1	2		1			2				11		
Richmond	206	36	West	Abner			1		1		3	1	1				7		
Richmond	206	42	West	Abner Junr			1				1						2		
Lenox	211	24	West	Daniel	3	1			1	1	1			1			8		
Lee	264	28	West	Ebenz	3	1	2	1		1	2		1				11		
Lee	264	20	West	Elijah	2	1	3		1	2	1		1				11		
Pittsfield	202	15	West	Frederick	2			1				1					4		
Sheffield	224	2	West	Josiah		1	1	1	1		2	1		1			8		
Lee	264	34	West	Levi	1			1		2		1	1				6		
Pittsfield	202	18	West	Mason				1		2			1				4		
Lee	264	29	West	Oliver		1	3		1				1	1			7		
Pittsfield	202	14	West	Samuel		1		1				2					4		
Stockbridge	257	31	West	Stephen		1			1			1		1	1		5		
Pittsfield	202	6	West	Ichabod				1				1					2		
Windsor	167	26	Westcot	Rufus	2			1		3			1				7		
Windsor	167	28	Westcot	Shukely				1			1	1		1			4		
Cheshire	157	41	Westcott	Dickins	2		1	1		1			1	1			7		
Cheshire	157	61	Westcott	Dukins	2		1	1		1			1	1			7		
Cheshire	154	2	Westcott	Reuben	2			1		1			1				6		
Cheshire	154	1	Westcott	Stephen		1		1		3	1		1				7		
Pittsfield	201	35	Weston	Jonathan	3	1			1	1	2	1					9		
Sheffield	230	6	Westover	Job	1	1	2		1		1	1	1				8		
Egremont	120	13	Westover	Jonah	2	1		1	1	1	1		2				10		
Sheffield	226	3	Westover	Oliver				1		2			1				4		
Pittsfield	201	43	Wetherel	Edward	2			1		2			1				6		
Tyringham	111	24	Whaly	John P.	2	2	1		1	3			2				11		
Hancock	162	13	Wheaton	Lucus	1			1		1		1					4		
New Marlborough	234	10	Wheeler	Benjamin	3	3	1	1					1	1			10		
Stockbridge	258	20	Wheeler	Charles			1										1		
Lanesborough	148	16	Wheeler	David				1				1		1			3		
Partridgefield	190	17	Wheeler	Ephraim	1			1		1			1				4		
Lanesborough	149	2	Wheeler	Gideon	1		1		1	1	2			1	1		8		
Zoar	143	10	Wheeler	James 1st	1	1			1	1	1	1	1	1			8		
New Marlborough	238	27	Wheeler	James T	2		1	1		1	2		1				9		
Zoar	143	15	Wheeler	John	3	1	1	1	1	1		2	1	1			12		
Lanesborough	148	21	Wheeler	Jonathan		2	1		1		1			1			6		
Great Barrington	109	32	Wheeler	Joshua	1			1		1			1				4		
Great Barrington	108	24	Wheeler	Payton R.	1		1					2					4		
Lanesborough	148	17	Wheeler	Samuel			1	1				1		1			4		
Lanesborough	150	6	Wheeler	Simeon				1						1			2		
Lanesborough	150	7	Wheeler	Simeon Jr	1		1	1		2			2				7		
Great Barrington	105	4	Wheeler	Truman	1		2		1	1	2	1					8		
Lanesborough	148	22	Wheeler	William	1			1		1		1					4		
New Marlborough	235	28	Wheeler	Zenas	2	2	1	1				1	1				8		
Tyringham	113	31	Wheelock	Amariah	1			1		3	2		1				8		
Partridgefield	190	11	Wheelock	Ralph	2	1	1	1		1	1		1				8		
Tyringham	113	6	Wheelock	Samuel		1	1		2		1	1	2	1			9		
Williamstown	127	10	Wheelock		5			1			3	3	1				13		First name blank
Stockbridge	258	11	Whelpley	Samuel				1					1				2		
Stockbridge	258	12	Whelpley	Thomas	3	1		1		2	1		1				9		
Lenox	211	25	Whelply	William		1	1		1	1	1	1					6		
Partridgefield	190	23	Whiling	Charles			1			1	1	1					4		
Partridgefield	190	24	Whiling	Ebenezer			1			1			1				3		
Williamstown	129	8	Whippey	John				1					1				2		
Adams	138	32	Whipple	Nathan	1			1		4	1		1				8		
Cheshire	153	4	Whipple	Samuel	1			2		2			1				6		
Dalton	194	6	Whipple	Samuel	3			1		2		1					7		
Cheshire	153	1	Whipple	Stephen	1	1	1		1					1			5		
Windsor	167	27	Whitaker	Abel		1			1	3	2		1				8		
Adams	138	18	Whitaker	Ezra	2			1	1	2	3		1				10		
Cheshire	155	4	Whitaker	William	2		1		1		1	1		1			7		
Windsor	167	3	Whitaker	William	1		1						1				3		
Williamstown	126	8	White	Aaron	2			1		1		1	1				6		
Pittsfield	201	32	White	Abigail		1	3		1			1	3				10		
Windsor	166	9	White	Danford	1			1		2			1				5		
Windsor	167	29	White	Daniel		2		1		1	1	1	1				7		
Windsor	165	7	White	Elijah	2			1		1			1				5		
Williamstown	129	15	White	John	2	2	1	1		2	1	1	1				11		
Richmond	208	23	White	Reuben	3			1			1		1				6		

TOWN	PG#	LN#	LAST NAME	FIRST NAME	FREE WHITE MALES					FREE WHITE FEMALES					TOTAL ALL OTHER	TOTAL SLAVES	TOTALS	DISTRICT/ TOWNSHIP	NOTES
					under 10	10 to 16	16 to 26	26 to 45	45 and over	under 10	10 to 16	16 to 26	26 to 45	45 and over					
Sandisfield	177	2	White	Rev Levi			1					1			1		3		
Becket	269	4	White	Vasal	3		1			2		1	4				11		
Adams	134	36	White	Jason	3	1	1			1		2	1				9		
Lenox	211	39	White	John			1			1		1					3		
Lenox	212	13	White	Solomon	3	1	1	1				1					7		
Adams	136	16	White	William		1		1				1	1				4		
Lee	264	31	Whiten	Joseph	1		1	1		3	1	1					8		
Great Barrington	104	5	Whiting	Abrah A.	1		1	1		2		1					6		
Lenox	211	31	Whiting	Gamaliel B.	2		1	2		1	1	1		1			9		
Great Barrington	104	9	Whiting	John			1				3		1				5		
New Marlborough	238	23	Whiting	Josian	1	1	1		1	1		1		1			7		
Great Barrington	104	13	Whiting	Mason			1				2						3		
Williamstown	129	32	Whiting	Nathan	2		1		1	1	1						6		
Great Barrington	104	7	Whiting	Samuel		1	2			2		2					7		
Great Barrington	104	6	Whiting	William		1	1	1		1		1					5		
Lenox	211	32	Whiting	William	1		2		1	2	2	2	2	1			13		
Lenox	211	29	Whitlock	John				1	1				1				3		
Adams	134	9	Whitman	Caleb	3		1					1					5		
Windsor	166	22	Whitman	Ebenezer	1	1	1	1			1	2					7		
Windsor	166	32	Whitman	Isaiah	1		1			2	1	1					6		
Windsor	166	7	Whitman	Jeptha	4		1	1		1	1	1					9		
Hancock	162	16	Whitman	John			1										1		
Williamstown	132	3	Whitman	John P.			2				1	1					4		
Partridgefield	190	3	Whitmore	John				1			1	1	1				4		
Partridgefield	190	21	Whitmore	Oliver	1		1			1		1					4		
Pittsfield	201	28	Whitney	Abijah			1			2		1					4		
Pittsfield	201	29	Whitney	Asa	1	1	4	1			1	2		1			11		
Stockbridge	258	8	Whitney	Elisha	3	2		1		2	2	1	1				12		
Loudon	177	19	Whitney	Hezekiah	2		1	1		3		1					8		
Partridgefield	190	5	Whitney	Jabez	2	2			1	2	1	1		1			10		
Partridgefield	190	4	Whitney	John			1		2	1				2			6		
Loudon	178	19	Whitney	Jonas	3			1					1				5		
Pittsfield	201	30	Whitney	Joshua			2		1	1	1	1		1			7		
Pittsfield	201	31	Whitney	Joshua Jr			1			1		1					3		
Pittsfield	201	42	Whitney	Noah	2		2	4				2					10		
Adams	135	2	Whitney	Richard			1			2		1		1			5		
Stockbridge	258	16	Whitney	Silas Jr	2		2	1		3	1	2	1				12		
Lanesborough	148	5	Whitney	Timothy	3			1		1		1	1				7		
Loudon	177	18	Whitney	Timothy Esq				1					1				2		
Lee	264	21	Whitney	William		1	1		1	2	1	2	1	3			12		
Lee	264	32	Whiton	James			1										1		
Stockbridge	258	10	Whiton	John	1	1	1	1		2	1	1	1				9		
Stockbridge	258	13	Whittley	Elphalet	2	2	3		1	1		2		1			12		
Great Barrington	108	41	Wickwire	Jonas	1	1			1		2	1		1			7		
Great Barrington	107	15	Wier	Francis	1	5	3		1	2	2		1				15		
Savoy	140	22	Wilbour	William	2	1			1					1			5		
Adams	133	15	Wilbur	Benjmain	4	1				1		1	1	1			10		
Adams	134	18	Wilbur	Gid	1	2		1		2	1		1				8		
Adams	134	14	Wilbur	Jeremiah		2	1	1		4	2	3	1				14		
Adams	133	19	Wilbur	Stephen		1	1	1			2			1			6		
New Marlborough	235	30	Wilcocks	Zaccheus				1						1			2		
Sandisfield	175	19	Wilcox	Abel Jr	1			1		2		1					5		
Sandisfield	175	18	Wilcox	Abel Sen			1	1		1		1	1	1			6		
New Marlborough	239	28	Wilcox	Ezekiel				1						1			2		
Sandisfield	174	39	Wilcox	George	2	1		1		1			1				6		
Williamstown	126	17	Wilcox	Heman		1	1			1		1					4		
Clarkesburg	142	11	Wilcox	James	1			1		1	1	1	1	1			8		
Sandisfield	170	11	Wilcox	Joel			4		1	2	2			1			10		
Sandisfield	177	11	Wilcox	John			1										1		
New Marlborough	239	7	Wilcox	Oliver	5	1		1					1				8		
Sandisfield	176	39	Wilcox	Rhoda								1					1		
Partridgefield	189	39	Wilcox	Samuel			1				2		1				4		
Lanesborough	149	12	Wilcox	Stephen			1	1		1		1					4		
New Marlborough	237	10	Wilcox	Thomas	2	1	2		1	1		3	1				11		
Lanesborough	148	29	Wildman	Nirum	1			1		1		1					4		
Dalton	193	43	Wiley	John				1						1			2		
Hancock	159	34	Wiley	Robert	1	2	1		1	2	1			1			9		
Dalton	193	44	Wiley	Samuel	3			1		1	1	1					7		
Great Barrington	106	41	Willard	Daniel		1		1						1			3		
Lenox	211	30	Willard	Ebenezer	3	1		1			1	1	1				8		
Egremont	119	25	Willard	Elijah		2	2	1		2	2						9		
Stockbridge	257	33	Willard	Enoch	1		1	1					1	1			5		
Lenox	211	28	Willard	John	1		1	1		2		1					7		
Zoar	143	16	Willard	Julias	2			1		1	1						5		
Lee	264	24	Willcox	Daniel	1			1		1			1				4		
Lee	264	35	Willcox	Edward	3	1		1		1	1		1				8		
Alford	117	9	Willcox	Israel			1		1	1							3		
Tyringham	111	29	Willcox	Matthew	2	1						1					5		
Lee	264	23	Willcox	Peter		1			1			2		1			5		

154

TOWN	PG#	LN#	LAST NAME	FIRST NAME	FREE WHITE MALES under 10	10 to 16	16 to 26	26 to 45	45 and over	FREE WHITE FEMALES under 10	10 to 16	16 to 26	26 to 45	45 and over	TOTAL ALL OTHER	TOTAL SLAVES	TOTALS	DISTRICT/ TOWNSHIP	NOTES
Alford	117	7	Willcox	Ruben	3	1		1		1			2				8		
Alford	116	34	Willcox	Rufus	1			1		1	2		1				6		
Stockbridge	258	3	Willcox	Seth	3			1		1			1				6		
Stockbridge	258	15	Willcox	Solomon	3			1		1		1	1				7		
Alford	117	8	Willcox	Sylvanus	1				1		1	2		1			6		
Adams	139	4	Willey	John	3			1		3	1		1				9		
Washington	214	21	Williams	Abraham	1		1	1		1	1		1				6		
Stockbridge	258	7	Williams	Abram	2			1		2			1	1			7		
Pittsfield	201	33	Williams	Absolem		1	1		1		1	1	1	1			7		
Stockbridge	258	2	Williams	Asa	1		2	1		1	1		1				7		
Stockbridge	258	6	Williams	Azariah					1		1		2	1			5		
Pittsfield	195	5	Williams	Bancroft	2	1				1			1				6		
Alford	117	21	Williams	Cornelius	1	2	3	1	1	3			1	1			13		
Lenox	212	7	Williams	Daniel	1			1		2			1				5		
Pittsfield	201	40	Williams	Daniel				1		2			1				4		
Stockbridge	258	1	Williams	Daniel		1		1	1			1		1			5		
Richmond	208	33	Williams	David				1		1		1	1				4		
Washington	213	26	Williams	Elezer	1	2		1		2	1		1				8		
West Stockbridge	251	26	Williams	Elijah		1		1		1	1		1	1			6		
West Stockbridge	251	14	Williams	Elisha		1				1		1					3		
Williamstown	126	9	Williams	Elisha		1		1				1		1			4		
Lee	264	17	Williams	Ephraim			1						1				2		
Lanesborough	148	36	Williams	Eunice	3		1			2			1				7		
Lanesborough	148	37	Williams	Hoddan	1		1	1		1	1		1		1		7		
Cheshire	157	35	Williams	Isaac	1			1		1		1					4		
Cheshire	157	55	Williams	Isaac	1			1		1		1					4		
Washington	213	29	Williams	Isaac			2		1	1	1	1		1			7		
Washington	213	31	Williams	Jacob	2			1				1					4		
New Ashford	163	2	Williams	James	1			1		2			1				5		
Lanesborough	149	11	Williams	Jedediah		1	1	1		1		1					5		
Richmond	208	34	Williams	John	4			1	1				2	1	1		10		
Washington	213	32	Williams	John	1			1		2		1					5		
Pittsfield	201	34	Williams	John C			1	1		1	3		1	1	1		9		
Savoy	140	25	Williams	Joseph	1			1		1		2	1		1		7		
Washington	216	9	Williams	Larkin	4			1			1	1					7		
Sandisfield	174	41	Williams	Louis Wido			4			1			1	1			7		
Cheshire	157	24	Williams	Nathaniel	2			1		1			1				5		
Cheshire	157	44	Williams	Nathaniel	2			1		1			1				5		
Richmond	206	7	Williams	Nehemiah		1		1		1			1				4		
Sandisfield	171	4	Williams	Oliver	1	1		1		1	1		1				6		
Pittsfield	202	17	Williams	Oswald		1	2		1	1	2		1				8		
Williamstown	128	37	Williams	Robert	1	1	1	1		2	1		1				8		
Stockbridge	258	9	Williams	Stephen		3	1		1	1		2		1			9		
Williamstown	128	22	Williams	Stephen		1		1		3			1				6		
Dalton	194	2	Williams	William		1	2		1	1	1	1	1	1			9		
Pittsfield	201	36	Williams	Willm P	2			1		2	1		1				7		
Williamstown	128	20	Williams	Zabin		1				1		1					3		
Sheffield	224	19	Willougbee	Salmon		1		1		2	1		1				6		
Lee	264	27	Willoughby	Josiah				1		3			1				5		
Pittsfield	202	36	Wills	Sampson											9		9		
West Stockbridge	251	22	Willson	Fairing	1	1	1	1		2			1				7		
Tyringham	115	23	Willson	James	1			1		3			1				6		
Tyringham	111	3	Willson	Joseph			1	1	1			1		1			5		
Tyringham	115	36	Willson	Joseph			2		1			1		1			5		
West Stockbridge	251	23	Willson	Nathan	1	1	1		1		1	1		1			7		
West Stockbridge	251	24	Willson	Shubal	2	1		1		3	1		1				9		
Great Barrington	107	20	Willson	Solomon	1		1			1			1				4		
Williamstown	126	19	Wilmarth	Shubael	2		1	1		2		2	1				9		
Lanesborough	151	14	Wilson	Abner	1	2	1		1	1	1		1				8		
Lanesborough	151	29	Wilson	Josiah	1		1		1		1		1				5		
Sandisfield	170	15	Wilson	Justin	2			1		4		1	1				9		
Cheshire	156	25	Wilson	Thomas	2			1				1					4		
Great Barrington	106	44	Wilty	John				1									1		
Mount Washington	232	7	Winans	Isaac		2	2		1	1	2		1				9		
Egremont	118	21	Winchel	Absalom	2			1		2		1					6		
Egremont	120	31	Winchel	Amos	3			1		1	1	2	1				9		
Egremont	118	18	Winchel	Andrew				1		2		1					4		
Tyringham	119	1	Winchel	Ephm 1st		1		1		2		1					5		
Mount Washington	232	10	Winchel	Ephraim				1		1		1					3		
Egremont	118	20	Winchel	Ephraim Jr			2	1			1		1	1			6		
Tyringham	119	16	Winchel	Jacob	1	1		1					1				4		
Sheffield	229	8	Winchel	Josiah				1									1		
Egremont	120	24	Winchel	Martin	2			1		3	2		1				9		
Great Barrington	107	26	Winchester	Stephen		1				1		1					3		
Lee	264	25	Winegar	Elizabeth			3				1	1	1	1			7		
Lee	264	30	Winegar	Jacob	1			1		1			1				4		
Lee	264	18	Winegar	Samll	1			1		1			1				4		
Washington	214	27	Wing	Elijah		1	1				1			1			4		
Partridgefield	190	16	Wing	Elisha	2	1		1		2	2	1	1				10		
Dalton	194	1	Wing	James	2	1		1		2	1		1				8		

155

TOWN	PG#	LN#	LAST NAME	FIRST NAME	FREE WHITE MALES					FREE WHITE FEMALES					TOTAL ALL OTHER	TOTAL SLAVES	TOTALS	DISTRICT/ TOWNSHIP	NOTES
					under 10	10 to 16	16 to 26	26 to 45	45 and over	under 10	10 to 16	16 to 26	26 to 45	45 and over					
Adams	138	38	Wing	Roger		1	1	1		1	1		1				6		
Partridgefield	190	15	Wing	Seth			1		1		2		1	1			6		
Richmond	208	25	Winston	Daniel				1		2			1				4		
Loudon	178	13	Winter	Alpheus	1			1	1			1	1	1			6		
West Stockbridge	251	25	Winter	John	1			1		4			1				7		
Tyringham	115	2	Wintworth	John	1			1		1			1				4		
Sheffield	224	11	Witbeck	Ephraim				1					1				2		
West Stockbridge	251	15	Witherell	Seth				1				1					2		
West Stockbridge	251	20	Witmark	Susanna	1	1	1			1	1		1				6		
Washington	214	38	Witter	Amos	2		1	1		3	1	1	1				10		
Partridgefield	190	6	Witter	Ebenezer		1			1				1				3		
Partridgefield	190	12	Witter	Joseph Junr	2	1	1	1	1	1	2		2				11		
Partridgefield	190	14	Witter	Sephimus	1	1		1		1		1					5		
Washington	216	10	Wolcot	William				1	1	2		1					5		
Sandisfield	173	29	Wolcott	Abiather			1			2		1					4		
Sandisfield	175	7	Wolcott	Joseph & Son		1	1	1	1	1	1	1		1			8		
Sandisfield	173	28	Wolcott	Samuel Jun				1			1	1	1				4		
Williamstown	128	13	Wolcott	Solomon		2		1				3		1			7		
Williamstown	131	31	Wolcott	Solomon Jr	1	1	1	1			1		1				6		
Sandisfield	173	27	Wolcott	William		1	1					1					3		
Loudon	179	28	Wolf	Ezekiel D.	1	2		1		3	1		1				9		
Loudon	179	23	Wolf	James D.	1	2		1		2			1				7		
Loudon	179	30	Wolf	Matthew D				1					1				2		
Tyringham	111	38	Wolf	Peter D.	2		3	1		1			1				8		
Partridgefield	190	19	Wood	Amariah		2		2		3			2				9		
Richmond	207	23	Wood	Comfort		1		1	1			1		1			5		
Cheshire	158	14	Wood	Daniel	2	2	1	1			2	4		1			13		
Cheshire	153	11	Wood	Edward		2	3	1		1		1	1				10		
Hancock	159	9	Wood	Elisha	1			1		1			1				4		
Richmond	207	36	Wood	Gideon		2		1		3	1	1		1			9		
Bethlehem	181	9	Wood	Hiram	4	2		1					1				8		
Egremont	119	21	Wood	Jeptha	1			1		3	1		1				7		
Dalton	194	3	Wood	Joseph			2	1					2		2		7		
Dalton	194	4	Wood	Joseph Junr	2		1	1		1			1				6		
Washington	213	15	Wood	Mary	1					1	1		1	1			5		
Cheshire	158	11	Wood	Nathan	1		2	1	1	4	3		2				14		
Cheshire	153	11	Wood	Simeon				1		1			3				5		
West Stockbridge	251	21	Wood	William	1			1						1			3		
Lanesborough	152	2	Wood	Titus	4	1	1	1		3	1	1					12		
Windsor	165	27	Woodard	Seth	1	1		1		2	1	1					7		
Stockbridge	257	32	Woodbridge	Joseph			2	1				1	1		2		7		
Williamstown	131	27	Woodcock	Bartholomew		1	1	1	1	1		1	1				7		
Mount Washington	232	1	Woodin	John			1						1	1			3		
Mount Washington	232	24	Woodin	Solomon	1	2		1		4			1	1			10		
West Stockbridge	251	19	Woodruff	Amos	1		2	1		4	1		1				10		
West Stockbridge	251	18	Woodruff	Asaph	3			1		1	1		1				7		
Sandisfield	171	10	Woodruff	Isaiah	2			1				1					4		
Lee	264	19	Woodruff	James	1				1	2			1				5		
New Marlborough	237	29	Woodruff	Lambert Jr	1	2	1	1		2			1				8		
Stockbridge	258	18	Woodruff	Noadiah	2			1		1	1						5		
Sandisfield	171	9	Woodruff	Roswell	1		1	1		1		1					5		
West Stockbridge	251	16	Woodruffe	Elisha	3	1	1		1	1	3	3		1			14		
Lanesborough	151	12	Woodson	John	2			1		2			1				6		
Williamstown	130	28	Woodwork	Nehemiah		1	1	1				1		2			6		
Great Barrington	105	23	Woodworth	Dudley	1	3	1					1	1				7		
Loudon	179	14	Woodworth	Jonathan	4			1		2			1				8		
Great Barrington	105	37	Woodworth	Stephen	2			1				1	2				6		
Sheffield	226	23	Woodworth	William	2			1						1			4		
Tyringham	119	10	Woolcot	John				1		1			1				3		
Stockbridge	258	17	Woolford	James		1				1			1				3		
Cheshire	155	38	Worden	Peter					1		1			1			3		
Cheshire	155	39	Worden	Peter Jun	2	2	1	1	1	2	1		1				12		
Lee	264	16	Wormer	Jeremiah		2		1			1		1				5		
Great Barrington	105	45	Worthy	Benjamin	1	1		1		1				1			5		
Williamstown	126	37	Wright	Aaron	1	1		1		2	2	1	1				9		
Windsor	164	1	Wright	Arahel	2	3	1	1		2	1	1	1				12		
New Marlborough	236	8	Wright	Caleb				1					1				2		
New Marlborough	235	9	Wright	Calvin	1	1		1		1			1				5		
Sandisfield	175	25	Wright	Charles		2		1		1	1	1	1				7		
Lanesborough	152	35	Wright	Eli				1		1	1		1				4		
Lenox	212	14	Wright	Gad	1		1			1			1				4		
Sandisfield	176	33	Wright	Gideon						1		1	1	1			4		
Sheffield	229	3	Wright	James		1							1				2		
Sheffield	229	4	Wright	James Jun			1			1	1		1				4		
Pittsfield	202	21	Wright	John															
Pittsfield	202	20	Wright	Jonathan	1		1			3			1				6		Enumeration blank
Pittsfield	202	19	Wright	Joseph															Enumeration blank
Lanesborough	148	3	Wright	Josiah			1	1		1	1		1				5		
Pittsfield	202	7	Wright	Josiah					1		1		1	1			4		
Williamstown	128	12	Wright	Josiah	1			1	1	2		1	1	1			8		

TOWN	PG#	LN#	LAST NAME	FIRST NAME	FREE WHITE MALES					FREE WHITE FEMALES					TOTAL ALL OTHER	TOTAL SLAVES	TOTALS	DISTRICT/ TOWNSHIP	NOTES
					under 10	10 to 16	16 to 26	26 to 45	45 and over	under 10	10 to 16	16 to 26	26 to 45	45 and over					
Williamstown	128	1	Wright	Miles			1	1	1			1		1			5		
Williamstown	127	33	Wright	Nabby	3					1			2				7		
Sandisfield	175	23	Wright	Noah			1		1		1		1	1			5		
Dalton	194	7	Wright	Samuel	2		1	1		1			1	1			7		
Lenox	211	22	Wright	Samuel	2	1	2		1	3	1		1	1			12		
Williamstown	126	6	Wright	Solomon	2	1	1		1	1	1	1	1				9		
Williamstown	129	36	Wright	Timothy	2		1					1					4		
Pittsfield	202	9	Wright	Titus			2		1					2			5		
Cheshire	155	22	Wyman	Frederick	1			1				1					3		
Pittsfield	202	2	Wyman	S. Johnson	1	1		1		3	1		1				8		
Lee	264	37	Yale	John				1									1		
Lee	264	36	Yale	Josiah	1	2			1	2		3	1				10		
Lenox	211	36	Yale	Justus	2	1	1		1			1	1				7		
Lenox	211	35	Yale	Thomas	1	2	2	1		2	2	1	1				12		
Partridgefield	190	26	Yeamans	Moses	1		1					1					3		
Williamstown	127	4	Young	Andrew	1				1	1	3	2	1				9		
New Ashford	162	12	Young	George	2			1			1		1				5		
Williamstown	131	9	Young	Moses	2	1	2	1	2		1	2		2			13		
Williamstown	131	25	Young	William	1	1		1	1	1		1	1				7		
Great Barrington	106	45	Younglove	Daniel	1	1		1		2			1				6		
Great Barrington	107	1	Younglove	John	2			1				3		1			7		
Great Barrington	108	9	Younglove	Jonathan	1			1					1				3		
Great Barrington	108	8	Younglove	Oliver	1			1					2	1			5		
Lanesborough	149	10	Youngs	John				1					1				2		
Lanesborough	149	30	Youngs	John S.	1		1		1	1	1		1				6		
West Stockbridge	251	27	Youngs	Nathan		2		1		3			1				7		
Stockbridge	258	23		Bett											2		2		Last name blank
Hancock	161	35		Cato (negro)									1		1		2		
New Marlborough	239	22		Jacob Negro											4		4		
Stockbridge	258	29		Lemon											6		6		Last name blank
Stockbridge	258	22		Rose											2		2		Last name blank
Sheffield	229	33		Simon Negro											2		2		
Stockbridge	258	30		Tummons											1		1		Last name blank

NOTES

www.ingramcontent.com/pod-product-compliance
Lightning Source LLC
Chambersburg PA
CBHW080251290526
45790CB00005B/1771